BLACK'S NEW TESTAMENT COMMENTARIES

GENERAL EDITOR: MORNA D. HOOKER

THE REVELATION OF SAINT JOHN

BLACK'S NEW TESTAMENT COMMENTARIES

GENERAL EDITOR: MORNA D. HOOKER

THE
REVELATION
OF SAINT JOHN

IAN BOXALL

 HENDRICKSON
PUBLISHERS

 continuum
LONDON • NEW YORK

BLACK'S NEW TESTAMENT COMMENTARY
THE REVELATION OF SAINT JOHN

First published 2006, A & C Black (Publishers) Limited, London
© 2006 Ian Boxall

Published in the USA by
Hendrickson Publishers, Inc.
P.O. Box 3473
Peabody, MA 01961-3473

www.hendrickson.com

Hendrickson Publishers ISBN-13: 978-1-56563-202-8 (hardcover)
Hendrickson Publishers ISBN-10: 1-56563-202-8 (hardcover)

Library of Congress Cataloging-in-Publication Data

Boxall, Ian.
    The Revelation of Saint John / Ian Boxall.
        p. cm.—(Black's New Testament commentaries ; 18)
    Includes bibliographical references and index.
    ISBN-13: 978-1-56563-202-8 (alk. paper)
    ISBN-10: 1-56563-202-8 (alk. paper)
    1. Bible. N.T. Revelation—Commentaries. I. Title. II. Series.
    BS2825.53.B69 2006
    228'.077—dc22
                     2006003669

Published in the UK by
Continuum
The Tower Building
11 York Road
London, SEI 7NX

www.continuumbooks.com

British Library Cataloguing-in-Publication Data

A catalogue record for this book is available from the British Library.

Continuum ISBN HB 0-8264-7135-8
Continuum ISBN PB 0-8264-7136-6

Typeset by YHT Ltd, London

The mosaic fretwork on the cover comes from the Galla Placidia Mausoleum in Ravenna and is used courtesy of ITALCARDS, Bologna, Italy.

For William
συγκοινωνὸς ἐν Ἰησοῦ

CONTENTS

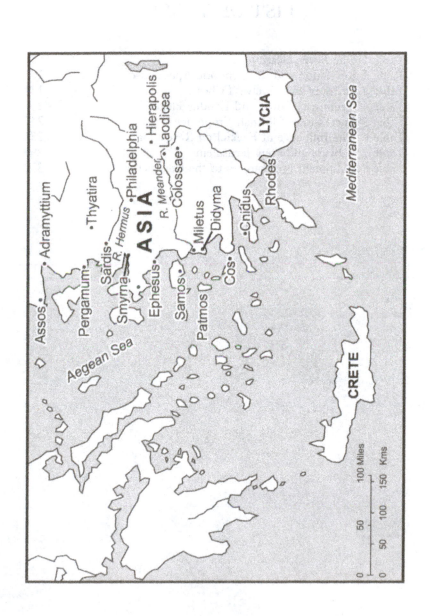

LIST OF TABLES

ABBREVIATIONS

GENERAL ABBREVIATIONS

AB	Anchor Bible
ABRL	Anchor Bible Reference Library
ACNT	Augsburg Commentary on the New Testament
AUSS	*Andrews University Seminary Studies*
AV	Authorised Version
BECNT	Baker Exegetical Commentary on the New Testament
BETL	Bibliotheca ephemeridum theologicarum lovaniensum
BGBE	Beiträge zur Geschichte der biblischen Exegese
Bib	*Biblica*
BLS	Bible and Liberation Series
BNTC	Black's New Testament Commentaries
BR	*Biblical Research*
CBR	*Currents in Biblical Research*
CFS	Cistercian Fathers Series
CT	Cahiers théologiques
EC	Epworth Commentaries
EUS	European University Studies
ExpTim	*Expository Times*
GBS	Grove Biblical Series
GNS	Good News Studies
HTS	Harvard Theological Studies
Int	*Interpretation*
JBL	*Journal of Biblical Literature*
JSJS	Journal for the Study of Judaism Supplements
JSNT	*Journal for the Study of the New Testament*
JSNTS	Journal for the Study of the New Testament, Supplement Series
JSOT	*Journal for the Study of the Old Testament*
JTS	*Journal of Theological Studies*
LQHR	*The London Quarterly and Holborn Review*
LSB	La Sainte Bible
LXX	Septuagint
MNTC	Moffatt New Testament Commentary
MT	Masoretic Text
NAB	New American Bible

NCB   New Century Bible
NCBC   New Cambridge Bible Commentary
NICNT   New International Commentary on the New
           Testament
NIGTC   New International Greek Testament Commentary
NIV   New International Version
NJB   New Jerusalem Bible
NRSV   New Revised Standard Version
NTG   New Testament Guides
NTIC   The New Testament in Context
NTS   *New Testament Studies*
NTT   New Testament Theology
PBR   *The Patristic and Byzantine Review*
PC   Proclamation Commentaries
RB   *Revue biblique*
RP   *Revue de philologie*
SABH   Studies in American Biblical Hermeneutics
SBL   Society of Biblical Literature
SC   Sources chrétiennes
SLBA   Schweich Lectures in Biblical Archaeology
SMBC   Smyth and Helwys Bible Commentary
SNTSMS   Society for New Testament Studies Monograph Series
SP   Sacra Pagina
UBS   United Bible Societies
WUNT   Wissenschaftliche Untersuchungen zum Neuen
           Testament

BOOKS OF THE OLD TESTAMENT

Gen.	Genesis	Isa.	Isaiah
Exod.	Exodus	Jer.	Jeremiah
Lev.	Leviticus	Lam.	Lamentations
Num.	Numbers	Ezek.	Ezekiel
Deut.	Deuteronomy	Dan.	Daniel
Josh.	Joshua	Hos.	Hosea
Judg.	Judges	Joel	
1–2 Sam.	1–2 Samuel	Amos	
1–2 Kgs	1–2 Kings	Obad.	Obadiah
1–2 Chron.	1–2 Chronicles	Jon.	Jonah
Neh.	Nehemiah	Mic.	Micah
Job		Hab.	Habakkuk
Ps. (Pss)	Psalms	Zeph.	Zephaniah
Prov.	Proverbs	Hag.	Haggai
Sg Sgs	Song of Songs	Zech.	Zechariah
		Mal.	Malachi

APOCRYPHAL/DEUTEROCANONICAL BOOKS

Tob.	Tobit
Jdt.	Judith
Wis.	Wisdom of Solomon
Sir.	Sirach (Ecclesiasticus)
1–4 Macc.	1–4 Maccabees

NEW TESTAMENT

Mt.	Matthew	Col.	Colossians
Mk	Mark	1–2 Thess.	1–2 Thessalonians
Lk.	Luke	1–2 Tim.	1–2 Timothy
Jn	John	Heb.	Hebrews
Acts	Acts of the Apostles	Jas	James
Rom.	Romans	1–2 Pet.	1–2 Peter
1–2 Cor.	1–2 Corinthians	1–3 Jn	1–3 John
Gal.	Galatians	Jude	
Eph.	Ephesians	Rev.	Revelation
Phil.	Philippians		

OLD TESTAMENT PSEUDEPIGRAPHA

Apoc. Abr.	*Apocalypse of Abraham*
Apoc. Adam	*Apocalypse of Adam*
Asc. Isa.	*Ascension of Isaiah*
2 Bar.	*2 (Syriac) Baruch*
3 Bar.	*3 (Greek) Baruch*
1 En.	*1 (Ethiopic) Enoch*
2 En.	*2 (Slavonic) Enoch*
3 En.	*3 (Hebrew) Enoch*
Ep. Arist.	*Epistle of Aristeas*
4 Ez.	*4 Ezra (2 Esdras 3—14)*
5 Ez.	*5 Ezra (2 Esdras 1—2)*
Jos. Asen.	*Joseph and Aseneth*
Jub.	*Book of Jubilees*
Pss Sol.	*Psalms of Solomon*
Sib. Or.	*Sibylline Oracles*
T. Abr.	*Testament of Abraham*
T. Adam	*Testament of Adam*
T. Mos.	*Testament of Moses*

Testaments of the Twelve Patriarchs

T. Ben.	*Testament of Benjamin*
T. Dan	*Testament of Dan*
T. Jud.	*Testament of Judah*
T. Jos.	*Testament of Joseph*
T. Levi	*Testament of Levi*
T. Naph.	*Testament of Naphtali*

OTHER JEWISH WRITINGS
Dead Sea Scrolls

1QH	Qumran Hymn Scroll
1QM	Qumran War Scroll
1QpHab	Qumran Pesher on Habakkuk
1QS	Qumran Community Rule
11QT	Qumran Temple Scroll
4Q246	'Son of God' fragment
4Q280	A Liturgy of Blessing and Cursing
4Q400–07	Songs for the Holocaust of the Sabbath
4Q504	Words of the Heavenly Lights
4QFlor	Florilegium or Midrash on the Last Days (4Q174)
4QpIsa	Qumran Pesher on Isaiah
4QTest	Testimonia (4Q175)
CD	Damascus Document from the Cairo Genizah

Philo Judaeus

Leg. Alleg.	*Legum allegoriae*
Legat.	*De legatione ad Gaium*

Titus Flavianus Josephus

Ant.	*Antiquitates Judaicae* (Jewish Antiquities)
B. J.	*De Bello Judaico* (On the Jewish War)
C. Ap.	*Contra Apionem* (Against Apion)

RABBINIC WRITINGS

b. Bat.	Babylonian Talmud, tractate *baba Bathra*
b. Sanh.	Babylonian Talmud, tractate *Sanhedrin*
Hekh. Rabb.	*Hekhaloth Rabbati*
m. Meg.	Mishnah, tractate *Megillah*
m. Sukk.	Mishnah, tractate *Sukkah*
m. Tam.	Mishnah, tractate *Tamid*
m. Yom.	Mishnah, tractate *Yoma*

EARLY CHRISTIAN WRITINGS

Act. Jn	*Acts of John*
Apoc. Elij.	*Apocalypse of Elijah*
2 Apoc. Jn	*Second Apocalypse of John*
Apoc. Paul	*Apocalypse of Paul*
Apoc. Pet.	*Apocalypse of Peter*
Aug. Civ. Dei	Augustine, *De Civitate Dei*
1 Clem.	*1 Clement*
Clem. Alex. Quis	Clement of Alexandria, *Quis Dives*
Did.	*Didache*
Ep. Barn.	*Epistle of Barnabas*

Eus. *H. E.*	Eusebius, *Historia Ecclesiastica*
Gos. Pet.	*Gospel of Peter*
Gos. Thom.	*Gospel of Thomas*
Ign. *Eph.*	Ignatius of Antioch, *Letter to the Ephesians*
Ign. *Philad.*	Ignatius of Antioch, *Letter to the Philadelphians*
Ign. *Rom.*	Ignatius of Antioch, *Letter to the Romans*
Iren. *Adv. Haer.*	Irenaeus, *Adversus Haereses*
Jerome, *De Vir. Ill.*	Jerome, *De Viribus Illustribus*
Jerome, *Ep.*	Jerome, *Epistulae*
Justin, *Apol.*	Justin Martyr, *Apology*
Justin, *Trypho*	Justin Martyr, *Dialogue with Trypho*
Mart. Pol.	*Martyrdom of Polycarp*
Mur. Can.	*Muratorian Canon*
Origen, *in Matt.*	Origen, *Commentary on Matthew*
Pol. *Phil.*	Polycarp, *Letter to the Philippians*
Tert. *De Anima*	Tertullian, *De Anima*
Tert. *De Resurr.*	Tertullian, *De Resurrectione Carnis*
Tert. *Praesc. Haer.*	Tertullian, *De Praescriptione Haereticorum*
Tert. *Scorp.*	Tertullian, *Scorpiace*
Vict. *Apoc.*	Victorinus of Pettau, *In Apocalypsin*

OTHER ANCIENT WRITINGS

Dio Cassius	Dio Cassius, *Roman History*
Galen, *De San. Tuen.*	Galen, *De Sanitate Tuenda*
Horace, *Carm. Saec.*	Horace, *Carmen Saeculare*
Lucian, *Alex.*	Lucian, *Alexander the False Prophet*
Ovid, *Met.*	Ovid, *Metamorphoses*
Ovid, *Trist.*	Ovid, *Tristia*
Pliny, *N. H.*	Pliny the Elder, *Natural History*
Plut. *Crass.*	Plutarch, *Crassus*
Propertius	Propertius, *Elegies*
Strabo	Strabo, *The Geography*
Suet. *Dom.*	Suetonius, *Lives of the Caesars: Domitian*
Suet. *Nero*	Suetonius, *Lives of the Caesars: Nero*
Suet. *Vesp.*	Suetonius, *Lives of the Caesars: Vespasian*
Tacitus, *Ann.*	Tacitus, *Annals of Imperial Rome*
Tacitus, *Hist.*	Tacitus, *The Histories*
Tibullus, *Eleg.*	Tibullus, *Elegies*
Virg. *Aen.*	Virgil, *Aeneid*
Virg. *Georg.*	Virgil, *Georgics*

PREFACE

In these early years of a new millennium, the Revelation to John is once again firmly on the religious and political agenda. While in the popular imagination this book continues to be viewed as a guide to the end of the world, scholarly study generally moves in rather different directions. This commentary aims to explore some of these different – though not necessarily mutually exclusive – scholarly directions (historical, theological and literary), and their implications for the interpretation of Revelation. It represents the fruit of my ongoing fascination for, and my grappling with, John's visionary book since my time as a graduate student in the early 1990s.

Many readers will know the fine predecessor to this volume by the great G. B. Caird. George Caird's Black's Commentary was and remains a masterpiece of clarity and accessibility which has earned deserved praise. It is, therefore, not without considerable trepidation that I offer a replacement here, fully aware that Caird ranks among the giants on whose shoulders I stand. Revelation studies, however, have moved on since Caird wrote, and this commentary is the fruit of engagement with subsequent developments. Several of these are worth highlighting here.

First, there is now a greater scholarly willingness to consider actual visionary experience as underlying Jewish and Christian apocalypses, John's Apocalypse included. This in turn affects the way in which Revelation is categorised, and the weight the interpreter gives to authorial intention. Second, more detailed attention has been given in recent scholarship to the structure of the work and other literary features, building upon the conviction expressed by Caird that Revelation is an essential unity rather than a hotchpotch of earlier apocalyptic fragments. Third, in the last decade or so, attention has shifted to Revelation's rich and varied reception history, reminding us that there is far more to this book than evidence for the realities of Christian existence under first-century imperial Rome. While my commentary is not primarily a commentary on reception history, elements from that wider history of reception and influence emerge from time to time within its pages. Finally, I have come increasingly to the view that attention to the author's location – Patmos – is as important for grasping the function of the book and the visionary imagination which produced it as the traditional focus on the historical and social context of 'the seven congregations of Asia'. I have included a section on the Patmos context in the Introduction, and discuss its implications at various points throughout the commentary.

Contemporary students are now well served by major English commentaries on the Apocalypse, to supplement the well-known work of R. H. Charles (1920): in particular, the three-volume encyclopaedic commentary of Aune (1997, 1998a, 1998b), that of Beale (1999), and now the fine volume by Smalley (2005). While the character of this commentary series calls for a less detailed and less comprehensive approach, I have benefited considerably from these more substantial works. However, much of recent significance for the interpreter of Revelation is to be found in the wealth of monographs and articles which have appeared since the publication of George Caird's book: these are referred to in the Bibliography to this volume, and throughout the commentary itself. Particular mention should be made of the important work on Revelation's reception history, notably Wainwright (1993), Rowland (1998) and Kovacs and Rowland (2004).

Besides those authors whose writings have influenced me, I must also express my debt and gratitude to particular individuals without whom this commentary would not have seen the light of day. First of all, I am grateful to Morna Hooker, general editor of this series, for her confidence and generosity in entrusting this volume to a relative newcomer. Her wise advice, and helpful and judicious comments on the manuscript, have ensured that this commentary is a better one than it might have been. I am grateful also to Robin Baird-Smith and his staff at Continuum for guiding me expertly through the various stages towards publication: particular thanks are due to Ben Hayes, Anya Wilson and their copy-editor T. W. Bartel.

Staff and students of St Stephen's House have helped and encouraged me in ways which they may not have realised, and I have appreciated the stimulus and friendship of the Revelation Seminar at the British New Testament Conference, ably chaired by Steve Moyise. Other friends and colleagues in the scholarly community have continued to stimulate my thinking and encourage me in my writing: among them John Ashton, Mark Goodacre, Robert Morgan, David Moss and Barbara Shellard deserve particular mention. Above all, a special debt is owed to Christopher Rowland, whose enthusiasm for the Apocalypse was the original spark which fired my ongoing fascination. I have learned more from him about this book than from anyone else.

Finally, I am indebted to friends and family, especially to William Whittaker, who first persuaded me to start writing, and who has been a constant source of encouragement and support throughout the whole process: this commentary is dedicated to him in grateful thanks.

Ian Boxall
Oxford
Advent Sunday 2005

INTRODUCTION

The Character of the Book

The Revelation to John (or, according to its Greek title, the Apocalypse) is unique among the writings of the New Testament. Although recent scholarship has increasingly recognised the indebtedness of the earliest Christians, and even Jesus himself, to the apocalyptic mindset, Revelation plainly requires different interpretative skills than a Gospel or a Pauline letter. The Apocalypse's visionary, symbolic nature, with its cycles of cataclysm, angelic hosts, grotesque monsters and often puzzling numerology, presents the early Christian message in a quite distinctive discourse. Moreover, attempts to define the literary form of the book are often frustrated by its hybrid nature. Although the opening words describe it as an 'apocalypse' or 'revelation of Jesus Christ' (ἀποκάλυψις: 1:1), the author nevertheless presents his book as a 'prophecy' (προφητεία: 1:3; 22:7, 10, 18, 19). Furthermore, epistolary features reveal Revelation as a circular letter destined for 'the seven congregations of Asia' (1:4–6; 22:21). All these elements need to be taken seriously.

This complexity has led some to deny that Revelation belongs to the literary genre of 'apocalypse' (e.g. Roloff 1993). Certain features of this genre, such as pseudonymity (see below, pp. 5–7) are absent. Moreover, the detailed interpretation of symbolic visions, so important for apocalypses such as Daniel and *4 Ezra*, is not a major feature of the Apocalypse of John (the exceptions include 1:20; 7:14–17; 13:18; 17:9–18). This is not an insurmountable difficulty, however. Diversity is a feature of the apocalypse genre: the famous SBL definition distinguishes between the 'historical' apocalypses with their temporal focus and the more spatial apocalypses describing 'otherworldly journeys' (J. J. Collins 1979: 9).

Indeed, the Apocalypse of John fits the formal SBL definition well, as well as exhibiting other characteristics often associated with the genre. It claims to reveal or unveil heavenly mysteries, set within a narrative framework. This revelation is mediated by a number of 'otherworldly beings': the exalted 'someone like a son of man' (1:9—3:22), a heavenly elder (e.g. 7:13), interpreting angels (e.g. 17:1; 21:9). The book promises privileged access to a supernatural world, in which the true source of authority is unveiled in the heavenly throne-room, and a slaughtered Lamb is proclaimed as victor in the decisive battle for the heart of the world (4:1—5:14). Moreover, although Revelation along with other apocalypses is concerned with a wide range of heavenly secrets (Stone 1976; Rowland 1982), it does have a particular focus on eschatology, that is the unfolding process which will culminate in the end of this age and the dawning of a new heaven and new earth (especially 19:11—22:11). Finally, Revelation shares with the apocalyptic tradition a dualistic perspective on the world. Not only does it distinguish between heavenly and earthly realms; it also describes a cosmic battle between the forces of God and the Lamb on the one hand, and those of Satan and his assistants on the other (although, as the commentary will reveal, this 'dualistic' description is much more subtle than at first appears).

The apocalyptic character of this book is a particular difficulty for many contemporary interpreters, who are less familiar than their forebears with features of the apocalyptic tradition. The division of the cosmos into heaven, earth and the underworld, or the belief that it is populated by diverse spiritual beings, both angelic and demonic, is foreign to the mindset of many. The ability to engage with the grammar of symbolic vision and numerology does not come naturally. In our global village, however, this difficulty can be overstated: interpreters from collectivist societies, or from cultures in which the spirit-world is omnipresent, may have an innate sympathy with the worldview that apocalypses espouse (for insight into this, see Rhoads 2005).

Nevertheless, 'apocalypse' is insufficient in itself for understanding the Apocalypse. Its other literary features must also be borne in mind. Its prophetic character is explicitly stated by the seer, who presents himself on a par with his brother prophets of the past (e.g. 1:3; 22:7, 9, 18–19; see D. Hill 1972). He acts as prophetic mouthpiece for the oracles of the exalted Christ to the churches addressed (2:1—3:22). He is bidden to eat a scroll containing divine words and to prophesy as a result, echoing the prophetic call of at least one of his predecessors (10:8–11; cf. Ezek. 2:8—3:11). His book contains regular prophetic exhortations to the faithful, as well as warnings about impenitence and compromise, and hints that repentance remains a possibility even for the ungodly (e.g. 2:5, 7; 8:13; 9:21; 11:13; 13:9–10; 14:12; 16:15). The lament over Babylon at Revelation 18 is effectively a prophetic doom song. The 'I, John' of 1:9 and 22:8 echoes the prophetic 'I' of Ezek. 1:1 and Dan. 10:2.

However, one should perhaps beware of making too sharp a distinction between 'apocalyptic' and 'prophecy'. The combination of vision and audition that permeates John's book is reflected in a number of prophetic books in the Hebrew Bible (e.g. Isa. 1:1–2;

Obad. 1:1; Neh. 1:1; Hab. 1:1). Indeed, two visionary prophets have exerted particular influence on Revelation: Ezekiel (Ezek. 1:1–3) and the apocalyptic Daniel, the latter also regarded as a prophet in first-century Judaism (e.g. Josephus, *Ant.* 10:245–49, 267–69; Mt. 24:15). Nor is John simply in the mould of Israel's canonical prophets. He is also a representative of early Christian prophecy (Fiorenza 1980), which believed that the spirit of prophecy had been renewed in the new age inaugurated by Christ, and which manifested itself in oracles spoken in God's or Christ's name, received especially in a liturgical context (Acts 13:1–3; 1 Corinthians 14; cf. Mt. 7:15–20; *Did.* 11—13).

Finally, Revelation's apocalyptic 'word of prophecy' is presented in the form of a letter, with epistolary features at both beginning and end (1:4ff.; 22:21). This also has implications for interpretation. It means on the one hand that its named recipients, 'the seven congregations in Asia' (Roman proconsular Asia: 1:4), are the primary focus of 'what must soon come to pass' (1:1). While attention to these primary addressees and their context does not exhaust the meaning of the book, interpretations which ignore them risk misunderstanding its purpose. On the other hand, unlike most of the letters in the Pauline corpus with which it is regularly compared (Galatians and possibly 2 Corinthians being the exceptions which prove the rule: Gal. 1:1–4; 2 Cor. 1:1–2), the Apocalypse is a circular letter addressed to seven diverse Christian congregations, to be read in its entirety to each. This more general focus, together with the apocalyptic-prophetic nature of the book, suggests that precision on the historical situation of specific congregations may not always be possible. It also invites closer comparison with those other circular letters in the New Testament, especially James and 1 Peter (Jas 1:1; 1 Pet. 1:1–2).

A Visionary Text

Yet unlike the New Testament's other circular letters, Revelation contains a significant proportion of visionary material. This is accompanied by repeated claims on the part of John that these are visions he 'saw', beginning with a dramatic inaugural vision of the exalted Christ received 'on the Lord's Day' (1:9–11; cf. e.g. 4:1; 5:1; 7:9; 14:1). Commentators have often treated this aspect of the book as a literary fiction, the author using the apocalypse form as a convenient vehicle for conveying his message. Recent scholarship, however, has been more willing to consider actual visionary experience as at least one of the ingredients involved in Revelation and other apocalypses (e.g. Gruenwald 1980; Rowland 1982). This issue is a complex one, not least because of the influence of a visionary's cultural and religious background on visions received. Not only does a seer's heritage provide the language and thought-forms for subsequent attempts to articulate what was seen; it is also claimed that this heritage will have laid down foundational patterns to which visionary experience will conform (Ashton 2000: 113–16). Moreover, there is ample evidence for careful composition on the part of the author (see e.g. Bauckham 1993a), including conscious reflection upon and creative use of Old Testament texts (see e.g. Moyise 1995; Beale 1999: 76–99).

Although certainty is not possible, there are several reasons for taking seriously John's claim to visionary experience. First, the Apocalypse combines structured and stereotypical features (e.g. its series of sevens; patterns of eschatological woes also found in other apocalypses; occasional explicit interpretation of symbolic visions) with the more fluid, dream-like quality associated with the visionary. John's visions of 'someone like a son of man' (1:12–20) and the heavenly throne-chariot (*Merkavah*: 4:1–11) do not evidence straightforward literary dependence on their antecedents, such as Daniel 10 and Ezekiel 1. Rather, the author resorts to simile upon simile, as if struggling to articulate a profound visionary experience rather than exegete a previous text (similar fluidity is found in other *Merkavah* visions, e.g. *1 En.* 14; *T. Lev.* 5; *Apoc. Abr.* 18). Second, John regularly presents himself not simply as witness to his visions but as an active participant within them (e.g. 5:4; 10:10; 11:1; 17:3, 6; 21:10; cf. *1 En.* 71; *Apoc. Abr.* 10), and describes the awesome, terrifying and occasionally physically draining nature of what is seen (e.g. 1:17; cf. *1 En.* 14:13; 71:11; *4 Ez.* 6:29; 10:25, 30). Third, there are hints in his book of the careful preparation for visionary experience attested in Jewish and Christian mystical texts (e.g. prayer, 1:10; eating, 10:9; cf. Ezek. 2:8—3:3; Dan. 9:3; 10:2–3; *4 Ez.* 5:13; 6:35; 9:24–25; *2 Bar.* 5:7; 20:5, 11; 21:1; 47:2; *Apoc. Abr.* 12:1; see Boxall 2002: 30–36).

This visionary claim need not be in conflict with the fact that the Apocalypse is also a carefully crafted document, drawing heavily on Old Testament antecedents and the Jesus-tradition (note especially the parallels between Revelation 6 and Mark 13 and its Synoptic parallels), and showing evidence of conscious reflection on particular visions (though the latter is limited in scope: e.g. 1:20; 7:13–17; 17:7–18). Careful study has revealed hidden secrets embedded in the text (Bauckham 1993a: 29–37), as well as a quite sophisticated interweaving of themes and scenes. Yet there is some evidence that Jewish visionaries could also be precise exegetes (e.g. Jer. 25:11–12), although we should perhaps envisage John less as a scholar scouring textual variants at his desk than as a scholar-mystic who meditated systematically upon particular biblical books. Ezekiel's *Merkavah* vision seems to have been especially favoured by Jewish mystics for study and meditation (Rowland 1982: 214–47), and Ezekiel is a particular influence on John. Nevertheless, one implication of interpretation is that it renders the search for authorial intention more difficult. If John believes he is transmitting actual visionary experience rather than simply using the visionary mode as a vehicle for his message, then his conscious intention cannot be the determining factor at every point. Accordingly this commentary, while not ignoring historical allusions which first-century audiences are likely to have detected within the text, will not treat these as exhausting the rhetorical power and multivalent resonances of its symbolism.

Author and Date

Author

Who precisely was this John, and when was his literary work composed? The author of Revelation describes himself simply and modestly as 'John' (1:9; 22:8), God's or Christ's 'servant' (1:1), and 'brother' of fellow Christians (1:9). In a real sense, the precise identity of the author is immaterial, given that the book presents itself as the 'revelation of Jesus Christ' (1:1). John is only the messenger (Sweet 1979: 38), whose identity is not crucial to interpretation. Nevertheless, the authorship of Revelation is a question which has been debated since the early period. There are three main solutions worth considering:

(a) The author is John the apostle, son of Zebedee, so identified by early tradition (Justin, *Trypho* 81.4; a tradition earlier indeed than the identification of the apostle with the Fourth Evangelist). This also appears to be the view of the author of the *Apocryphon of John*, possibly dated in an early form to the mid-second century (Helmbold 1961; Feuillet 1965: 96). This became the dominant tradition among patristic authors.

(b) The author is another John well-known to early disciples of Jesus: John the Baptist (e.g. Ford 1975: 28–37); John Mark (e.g. Acts 12:12, 25; 15:37); the shadowy 'Presbyter John' or 'John the Elder' (Eus. *H. E.* 3.39.2–6, sometimes identified with 'the Elder' of 2 and 3 John); another, lesser-known prophet John. Ford's identification of Revelation's 'John' as John the Baptist, while highlighting the Apocalypse's profoundly Jewish character, requires a complex theory of composition which has failed to convince many. It also depends upon Revelation being an essentially non-Christian text, whereas the gospel story of the crucified and risen Christ permeates the whole. The suggestion that the author is a less well-known John should only be resorted to when better-known candidates have been ruled out, which is not the case here. Moreover, it is less likely that such an

5

author's work would have survived outside its immediate circles, still less found a place (albeit with some reservations) within the New Testament canon. The 'John Mark' theory was already raised by the third-century Dionysius of Alexandria (Eus. *H. E.* 7.25.15), only to be dismissed by him because of the lack of evidence for John Mark's presence in Asia. The most plausible of these alternatives is the one identifying our author as 'John the Elder' (Eus. *H. E.* 3.39.6; cf. Swete 1906: pp. clxx–clxxxi: while inclining to the 'traditional view', Swete sees the merits in this alternative proposal). However, Eusebius' differentiation between 'John the disciple' and 'John the Elder' may be due to a misunderstanding of Papias, on whom he is dependent (*H. E.* 3.39.4). Similarly, the two tombs of John at Ephesus (Eus. *H. E.* 3.39.6; 7.25.16) may well be memorials to the same John, rather than to two different figures (cf. Jerome, *De Vir. Ill.* 9).

(c) The book, like other apocalypses, including the early Christian *Apocalypse of Peter*, is pseudonymous (see e.g. Dunkerley 1961: 298), written in the name of the apostle John. However, pseudonymity as found in the apocalypses is generally focused on figures of the distant past (e.g. Enoch, Moses, Abraham, Daniel). Those later Christian apocalypses which do claim authorship by a renowned Christian leader are explicit in their identification: 'Apocalypse of the holy apostle Paul' (Greek version of *Apoc. Paul*); 'Apocalypse of Saint John the Theologian' (*2 Apoc. Jn*: Court 2000: 33). Similarly, other New Testament books often regarded as pseudonymous (e.g. the Pastorals, 1 and 2 Peter) imitate the authentic letters in identifying their presumed author as an 'apostle'. The lack in Revelation of any explicit claim to apostleship by, and of further definition of, this 'John' (a name common among first-century Jews) counts against pseudonymity (as it does also for the letters of James and Jude).

While certainty is not possible, the grounds for rejecting the traditional apostolic authorship of Revelation are not conclusive. At least since Dionysius' discussion in the third century, the question has been tied up with that of the authorship of the Fourth Gospel. So well established was the apostolic authorship of the Gospel of John in Dionysius' day that his conclusion that the two texts could not have sprung from the same pen necessarily led him to deny apostolic authorship to Revelation. An alternative solution, however, is possible: that Revelation rather than the Fourth Gospel is the work of John son of Zebedee. This would accord with some recent trends in Johannine scholarship, which distinguish between the Fourth Evangelist and the rather shadowy 'Beloved Disciple' on whose testimony the work is based.

There is a significant correlation between the traditional portrait of John the apostle and the 'implied author' of the Apocalypse. Both are

Jewish followers of Jesus, probably of Palestinian provenance (e.g. Mk 1:19–20; Rev. 1:1; 2:9; 3:9), for whom Greek would have been a second language (e.g. Rev. 1:4; on Revelation's rather eccentric Greek, see e.g. Charles 1920: I, pp. cxvii–clix; Maier 2002: 108–16). Both were recognised leaders within the Christian community (e.g. Mk 9:2–8 and par.; Acts 3:1–11; Gal. 2:9; Revelation 1—3), such that they could be identified simply as 'John' (e.g. Acts 3:1; Rev. 1:9; 22:8). Both came to be associated with the Roman province of Asia, including the city of Ephesus (Iren. *Adv. Haer.* 3.1.1.; Rev. 2:1—3:22). Both, moreover, could experience dissent from their position within the church (e.g. Gal. 2:9; Rev. 2:2, 6, 14–15, 20). Indeed, it would not be inappropriate for a text such as Revelation, with its fiery visions of judgement, to spring from the pen of one known to posterity as a 'son of thunder' (Mk 3:17; Lk. 9:51–56).

Two objections might be made to this tradition of apostolic authorship, however. First, John of Patmos presents himself as a prophet rather than an apostle (1:3; 10:8–11; 22:7). But scholarship should beware about hard-and-fast distinctions between 'apostles', 'prophets' and 'visionaries': the apostle Paul could refer to both his prophetic gifts and his visionary experiences (e.g. 1 Cor. 14:19; 2 Corinthians 12), and also describe himself, as does John, as a 'servant' (Rom. 1:1; Gal. 1:10; cf. Jas 1:1; 2 Pet. 1:1; Jude 1; Rev. 1:1). It is not inconceivable that one of the Twelve should emphasise his prophetic credentials in a text which claims to transmit the prophetic word of the Lord (and in imitation of the prophet-Lord whose apostle he was: e.g. Mk 6:4; Jn 4:44). The second objection relates to Revelation's description of the 'twelve apostles of the Lamb' as the foundations of the new Jerusalem: i.e. as figures of a past apostolic age (see commentary on 21:14; cf. Eph. 2:2). Yet this may not be as insurmountable as at first appears, for Revelation's new Jerusalem vision is a vision not of the past but of the eschatological future. Its description of the Twelve, moreover, is not wildly dissimilar to their designation in an earlier period as 'pillars', presumably pillars of the new temple (Gal. 2:9).

A certain agnosticism is perhaps called for as to the precise identity of this early Christian prophet-visionary John of Patmos. Nevertheless, his traditional association with John son of Zebedee and 'son of thunder' deserves serious consideration, at least as much as Eusebius' alternative solution, which identifies him with the rather shadowy 'John the Elder'.

Date
Early Christian witnesses attest a range of possible datings for the Apocalypse: to the reign of Claudius (41–54: Epiphanius), of Nero (54–68: two early Syriac versions), the later years of Domitian (81–

96: Irenaeus), and the reign of Trajan (98–117: an earlier tradition referred to by the eleventh-century writer Theophylact: Swete 1906: pp. c–ci). However, the dominant position in the patristic period follows Irenaeus in dating the book to the latter years of Domitian's reign (c. 90–96: Iren. *Adv. Haer.* 5.30.3). According to the standard reading of Irenaeus, the Apocalypse was seen – i.e. John received his visions – towards the end of Domitian's reign (an alternative reading is that *he*, i.e. John, was seen at that time: Boxall 2002: 90). Irenaeus' words would not rule out the book itself having been written later, in the reign of Nerva or even Trajan. However, most early witnesses seem to have understood Irenaeus as dating the book itself to the 90s; this remains the consensus among scholars today.

Yet this view places great weight on the external evidence of Irenaeus. Much of the internal evidence is at best ambiguous, while other evidence tips the balance in favour of an earlier dating, during or soon after the reign of Nero, who died in 68. This date was favoured by nineteenth-century scholars, such as Westcott, Lightfoot and Hort, and is undergoing something of a revival in scholarly circles (e.g. Robinson 1976: 224–26; Bell 1978/79; Rowland 1982; Smalley 1994: 40–48; Boxall 2002: 89–98; for a recent robust defence of the Domitianic dating, see Beale 1999: 4–27). Though the apostolic authorship of Revelation does not necessarily require an early dating, that would make it more plausible. Moreover, if one allows for some theological connection between Revelation and the Fourth Gospel (e.g. Smalley 1994; though see Fiorenza 1985: 85–113), then Revelation would represent an earlier example of the Johannine stream, with the Gospel and Epistles as the more mature reflections of later Johannine authors. The following internal evidence is pertinent to the discussion:

(a) *The seven congregations.* The messages to the seven congregations (Revelation 2—3) present a mixed situation in which some Christians have faced or are facing hostility or even persecution, while others are condemned for spiritual lethargy. Some claim that this favours a later dating, to allow sufficient time for such spiritual deterioration to take place (e.g. Beale 1999: 16). Moreover, the Christians of Laodicea are criticised for their wealth and self-sufficiency (3:17): given that the city had been destroyed by a violent earthquake in 60/61, this is also thought to count against a dating in the late 60s. These arguments are not conclusive, however. 'Spiritual lethargy' need not require decades to set in. Further, the criticism of the Laodiceans could have been made within a few years of the devastating earthquake, not least given their arrogant refusal of imperial aid in the rebuilding programme (Tacitus, *Ann.* 14.27.1; see Hemer 1986: 193–94; *Sib. Or.* 4.107–08, dated to c. 80 CE, already knows of the resurrection of that city).

(b) *The Temple*. The description of the measuring of the Temple and its outer courts at 11:1–2 can be interpreted to support either dating. Some commentators understand it as a description of the Jerusalem Temple, still standing. For others, it presents a post-70 reflection on the events leading up to Jerusalem's destruction, or a symbolic reinterpretation of those events to refer to the new temple of the Church. Yet even this symbolic interpretation does not require a late dating, given the early ecclesial appropriation of temple-language (e.g. 1 Cor. 3:16–17, following the precedent set at Qumran).

(c) *Rome as Babylon*. The use of the symbol of Babylon to describe imperial Rome in Revelation 17—18 is often regarded as conclusive evidence in support of a post-70, Domitianic dating. The destruction of Jerusalem by Rome in 70 CE undoubtedly prompted comparisons among Jews and Jewish Christians with the destroyer of Solomon's Temple, Babylon (e.g. 2 Kings 25; cf. 1 Pet. 5:13; *4 Ez*. 3:1; *2 Bar*. 8:3–5). However, Babylon's significance should not be reduced to its destruction of the Temple: the city is remembered elsewhere in scripture as oppressor of God's people (e.g. Isaiah 47; Daniel 5; cf. Revelation 18) and as place of exile (Ps. 137:1; cf. Rev. 1:9). It is possible that a Jewish-Christian prophet prior to 70 could have chosen to describe Rome in such terms, particularly in the turbulent times of the late 60s with the outbreak of the Jewish revolt against the empire and with the Christian memory of Nero's persecution still raw (precedents would include 1QpHab 2.10–14, *Pss Sol*. 8:15, and the book of Daniel itself: see Boxall 2002: 94–96).

(d) *The Nero myth*. Many commentators accept that Revelation contains several allusions to a potent myth which evolved in the months and years following the demise of Nero (e.g. 6:2; 13:3–4; 17:8, 11). This took a number of forms: that Nero was not really dead but would return to reclaim the throne, or that he had fled to the East to raise up an army amongst the Parthians; that he had died but would return from beyond the grave. The presence of such allusions would rule out a dating during Nero's reign itself. Indeed, they have often been treated as supporting the 90s dating, on the grounds that 'presumably it took time for the myth to arise, develop, and circulate after Nero's death in 68 A.D.' (Beale 1999: 17). This is not so obvious, however: the first Neronian pretender emerged, on the back of intense speculation and rumour, in 69 (Tacitus, *Hist*. 2.8), prior to the death of Nero's immediate successor Galba.

(e) *The heads of the monster*. Revelation 17:9b–10 identifies the seven heads of the monster as seven kings or emperors, of whom 'five have fallen, one is now reigning, and the other has not yet come'. The usual reading of this is that John is writing in the reign of the sixth king. Though often ingeniously interpreted to make Domitian the sixth king currently reigning, the most straightforward correlations of

9

the heads to Roman emperors would suggest that Revelation was written in the late 60s, the sixth emperor being Galba (68–69) or, if the three short-lived emperors of 69 are omitted, Vespasian (69–79: see commentary on 17:9–14).

In short, much of the internal evidence is ambiguous, susceptible to interpretations which support datings in the late 60s or early-to-mid-90s. Only the weight of Irenaeus' testimony tips the balance in one direction. The most straightforward reading of the 'seven heads' passage, however, would appear to support the earlier dating. A mediating alternative, posited by David Aune, is that an earlier form of John's book underwent subsequent editing towards the end of Domitian's reign (Aune 1997: pp. lvii–lxx; this requires a complex theory about composition).

The Patmos Context

Revelation 1:9 states that John 'was on the island called Patmos' when he had his visionary experience on which the Apocalypse is based. Although commentators have regularly, and rightly, attended to the context of Revelation's recipients in the Roman province of Asia, the neglected context of John remains fruitful for exploration. The precise reason for his sojourn there is stated only obliquely: literally 'on account of the word of God and the witness of Jesus' (see commentary on 1:9). But the most likely interpretation is the traditional one, that he was exiled to this small Aegean island as a result of his Christian testimony (e.g. Clem. Alex. *Quis* 42; Origen, *in Matt.* 16.6; Tert. *Praescr. Haer.* 36; *Act. Jn* 14; 88; Vict. *Apoc.* 10.11; see also Worth 1999: 93–100).

Despite the popular perception (reflected in representations of this scene by Western artists such as Bosch, Memling and Velázquez), Patmos in the first century was not a deserted cultural backwater, but a historic outpost of the mainland city of Miletos with a population large enough to support a gymnasium and various associations (Haussoullier 1902; Saffrey 1975; McCabe and Plunkett 1985). Moreover, the imaginative landscape would have been dominated by the cults of Artemis and her brother Apollo. Inscriptional evidence points to Patmos being regarded as Artemis' own island, appropriately marked by a temple, while the political dominance of Miletos may have encouraged the veneration on Patmos of Apollo (his oracle-shrine at Didyma was connected to Miletos by a Sacred Way). If local tradition is to be believed, the Temple of Artemis would have occupied the same dominant position over the island as does the Monastery of St John the Theologian today. Images from these rival cults may have penetrated the seer's visionary imagination, and surfaced in visions as diverse as the first horseman carrying a bow (the symbol of Apollo: 6:2), the plague of demonic locusts presided over by Apollyon (9:1–11), the woman clothed with the sun (12:1–2: the woman echoes both Artemis and her mother Leto), and the second monster or 'false prophet' (13:11–18: 'the Prophet' (ὁ προφήτης) being the title of Apollo's high priest in Didyma).

The broader imaginative landscape is provided by the Aegean Sea. Although Patmos is only about forty miles off the coast of Asia Minor (modern Turkey), the sense of physical separation from the mainland is palpable. The visible world is reduced to sea, small islands (some of which emerge monster-like from the water), and on the horizon the mountains of larger islands such as Samos. It may not be coincidental that, leaving aside Gospel references to the Sea of Galilee, the majority of New Testament references to 'the sea' are to be found in Revelation (26 occurrences), generally with negative connotations. The first monster is one that emerges 'out of the sea' (13:1), reflecting that Roman dominance over the waters evident to an exile on an Aegean island (cf. 18:17–19). The Day of the Lord is accompanied by the removal of every mountain and island (6:14), while the new heaven and new earth are characterised by the absence of sea (21:1). This is the perspective of the exile, consigned to a liminal place between land and sea, alienated from and urging resistance to the powers of the monster and Babylon, currently played out under the guise of imperial Rome (for contemporary readings of Revelation 'from the margins', see e.g. Boesak 1987; Richard 1995; Maier 2002; Rhoads 2005).

There is one further implication of this Patmos context. A Jewish-Christian prophet, regarding himself as exiled by an idolatrous empire for his faith, would not have been without antecedents for understanding his situation or role models for sustaining his prophetic ministry. It should not surprise us that particular influence upon John's visionary book has come from those who were considered exiled prophets of the past: Jeremiah, Daniel, and especially Ezekiel. These have, as it were, provided the raw materials and the interpretative lens for making sense of John's current situation, and for his urgent message for the churches. Indeed, in places Ezekiel's influence is so strong as to have determined even the ordering of what John describes (see e.g. Vanhoye 1962; Goulder 1981; Ruiz 1989). John has 'devoured Ezekiel's scroll' (10:8–11), consuming it and transforming it as he makes it his own.

The Setting of the Primary Addressees

Nevertheless, Revelation has also been marked by John's prophetic concern for his original addressees. These primary intended audiences are clearly stated: 'the seven congregations in Asia' (1:4). His apocalyptic-prophetic letter was first sent from Patmos to representative Christian communities dwelling in seven named cities across the water on the mainland (though the number 'seven' marks them out as representatives of a larger number of Asian churches, with whom the book may well have been shared: cf. Col. 4:16). 'Asia', as elsewhere in the New Testament, refers to the Roman province of that name located in western Asia Minor. But what was the situation of these urban Christians, and what compelled John to address his visionary message to them?

Persecution

A common answer is that they were undergoing and facing state persecution: according to most authorities who accept this view, following Irenaeus' dating and the tradition attested by Eusebius (Eus. *H. E.* 3.17–18), under the emperor Domitian. More recently scholarship has claimed that this setting is appropriate, on the grounds that apocalypses emerge out of a situation of crisis. On the surface, this does appear to be an appropriate setting for Revelation. The book is replete with visions revealing the rewards for those who remain faithful despite hostility and even death. Its visions of the souls under the altar (6:9–11) and the 144,000 clothed in white (7:9–17) have contributed much to a Christian theology of martyrdom. From earliest times (e.g. the *Letter from the Churches of Vienne and Lyons*, preserved in Eus. *H. E.* 5.1.2ff.; Tert. *Scorp.* 12), Christians facing persecution and even martyrdom have found in the Apocalypse inspiration and comfort for their situation.

But, however powerfully Revelation has spoken to subsequent generations of martyrs, there are two main reasons for questioning this as an account of the actual situation of Christians in the seven congregations: one internal, one external. The internal evidence of the messages to the seven congregations (Revelation 2—3) suggests a rather mixed picture. While actual or impending hostility is referred to for some (e.g. 2:9, 13; 3:9), others are criticised for their complacency and compromise (e.g. 2:4, 14–15, 20; 3:1–2, 16). Moreover, there is no clear indication that suffering is at the hands of Roman authorities, or involves formal legal proceedings (though that may have occurred in the case of the one named Christian martyr, Antipas of Pergamum, whose death was some time in the past: 2:13). Rather, the seven messages attribute hostility in Smyrna and possibly also Philadelphia to the instigation of 'those who say they are Jews but are not' (2:9; 3:9). This points to localised tensions in certain cities between John's supporters and other Jews (whether Christians or not: see commentary on 2:9), even if the civic authorities may have been brought in from time to time (cf. e.g. Acts 18:12–17).

Externally, in certain circles there has been a radical reassessment of the portrait of Domitian as a megalomaniac demanding worship from his subjects, and doubts have been expressed as to the extent of any persecution of Christians during his reign (e.g. Thompson 1990; though see e.g. Janzen 1994). The standard Roman portrait of Domitian is largely dependent upon historians writing in the reign of Trajan (98–117), – Pliny the Younger, Dio Chrysostom, Suetonius and Tacitus – who had a vested interest in denigrating the Flavians in favour of the Antonines. The evidence for a Domitianic persecution of Christians is slight and ambiguous (e.g. it requires the identification of the executed Flavius Clemens and his exiled wife Domitilla as Christians: see Bell 1978/79; Boxall 2002: 98–100). Indeed, the early-second-century *Ascension of Isaiah* seems to know nothing of a persecution under Domitian, despite its allusion to what occurred under Nero (*Asc. Isa.* 4:3; Knight 1999: 24). However, the internal evidence of Revelation does not suggest a situation of state persecution, while the earlier dating cuts the link with the reign of Domitian. This is not to deny that martyrdom features strongly in the visionary section of the Apocalypse: but these are more likely allusions to Nero's past action against Christians in Rome, and visionary anticipations of what Rome will be capable of in the future, than descriptions of present state persecution.

Compromise with Culture
If Revelation is not primarily written to comfort the persecuted, it nevertheless represents a rallying cry to Christians to place themselves in a position in which they might find themselves being persecuted. Warnings against assimilation to and compromise with an idolatrous and unjust culture run like threads throughout the book. The angel of the congregation in Ephesus has lost his initial love (2:4), while the lukewarm Laodiceans boast in their material wealth and self-sufficiency (3:17). Christians in both Pergamum and Thyatira are charged with following 'Balaam' and 'Jezebel' in eating idol-meat and in fornication/sexual immorality, a metaphor for idolatry (2:14, 20: this is probably also the content of the 'teaching of the Nikolaitans' at 2:6, 15). Most likely, this implies an enthusiastic participation in the lives of their respective cities, in which religion, politics and economics were intricately interwoven. The extent to which Christians could maintain membership of trade guilds (a particular issue in Thyatira), engage in commerce, and contribute to political well-being, without compromising their commitments, was a burning issue in earliest Christianity.

Other early Christians might have taken a more optimistic view of the Church's relationship to society (e.g. Romans 13; 1 Corinthians 8—10; 1 Tim. 2:1-4). Revelation's apocalyptic unveiling, however, presents a sinister picture of the dangers. The dualistic rhetoric of

Revelation draws a wedge between those who bear the name of God and the Lamb (14:1) and those marked with the branded mark of the monster (13:16–17). Economics is brought into the equation with the claim that the ability to buy and sell requires the monster's mark (13:17). Moreover, references to the worship of the monster and the dragon (13:4, 12–14) are almost certainly allusions to the imperial cult, which arose in the East and was particularly popular in the eastern provinces as a means of proving loyalty (the goddess Roma had had a temple in Smyrna as early as 195 BCE, while Pergamum and Ephesus had temples to Roma and Augustus and Roma and Julius Caesar respectively). It is probably not the case, despite repeated claims, that official encouragement of the imperial cult reached new heights under Domitian. Indeed, the claim that he demanded to be called *dominus et deus noster* ('Our Lord and God', 4:11) is not attested by sources contemporary to his reign. But participation or non-participation in the imperial cult was one of those issues confronting Christians living in the urban centres of the first-century Roman world.

Turbulent Times in the Empire
Assimilation and temptation to compromise points to a situation of relative stability and contentment for at least some Asian Christians. Rome the beneficent had brought not only peace but also economic prosperity to the provinces. The stories that Rome and her emperors told about themselves were stories of order being restored out of chaos, of a golden age of tranquillity resulting from the birth of Augustus, of a universal *Pax Romana* enveloping the earth (see especially the commentary on Revelation 12). Yet John the prophet-visionary sees a very different picture. Fed by the scriptures of Israel, inspired by the radical witness of Jesus and alerted by his visionary experience on Patmos, John sees monsters on the horizon. If the earlier dating of Revelation is preferred, John's prophetic intuition would have been especially insightful: with the death of Nero in 68, Rome was on the verge of civil war; in Palestine, the Jewish revolt against the Romans had already broken out; among the rumours circulating about Nero were hints that the Parthian enemy was in the ascendant.

Whichever dating is preferred, the alternative story told by Revelation turns the imperial story on its head. Imperial power and political rulers are revealed to be on the side of chaos, whereas order and peace are accomplished by the birth of another child, who is himself the victim of that empire. The apocalyptic story is the gospel story of the one who is victorious through allowing himself to be killed (e.g. 12:5, 10–11).

Moreover, this story is set within the context of two other ancient and interlocking stories: that of the Exodus and of the return from exile, the latter viewed by prophets such as Second Isaiah as a New Exodus. God's people are once again enslaved to Egypt, with its dragon-like Pharaoh (12:3; cf. Ezek. 29:3; 32:2); liberation is available, however, through the shedding of a Lamb's blood and by passing through the Sea (1:5; 5:6; 15:2–4). Babylon has re-emerged, and God's people are once again in exile. The apocalyptic challenge is to wake up to the reality of this situation, and dissociate oneself from Babylon, as John the Patmos exile has done. The climactic chapters of Revelation will describe in great visionary detail the characteristics of both Babylon and the new Jerusalem toward which God's people are travelling (17:1—22:5).

Theatre of Reception

The context in which this apocalyptic message is received is also important. The Apocalypse was originally intended to be read aloud to a group or groups of Christians. Reflecting ancient practices of public reading, Rev. 1:3 refers to the singular 'reader' and 'those who hear' (cf. e.g. Exod. 24:7; Neh. 8:3; 2 Macc. 2:25; Mk 13:14 and par.). This contrasts dramatically with the highly individualised, silent reading by which both scholars and many contemporary Christians approach the book. The seven congregations were not readers but audiences, and John's book has made its impact over many centuries as an aural experience. This is an important consideration in interpretation, and attempts to detect the structure of the book should appropriately attend to the impact on the ear, paying particular attention to repetitions, rhythmic patterns, assonance and alliteration in the Greek text, and natural breaks in the narrative flow.

Furthermore, there are good grounds for proposing that the book was designed for reading during Christian gatherings for worship, probably the Eucharist (Barr 1986; Garrow 1997; on reading in the early Church see Gamble 1995). Early Christian sources attest to the reading of what later became New Testament scripture within the Christian assembly (e.g. Col. 4:16; 1 Thess. 4:27; 1 Tim. 3:13; Justin, *Apol.* 1.67). Oracular prophecy, which has influenced the essentially literary prophecy of John, was normally uttered within the context of worship (e.g. 1 Cor. 14:29–33). References in the seven messages to eating from the tree of life (2:7; cf. 22:2), receiving the hidden manna (2:17), and sitting down to dine with Christ (3:20; cf. 19:9) are likely to have been heard as eucharistic allusions. The announcement of the Lamb's marriage feast (19:7, 9) represents the culmination of repeated references to the sacrificial death of that Lamb and the saving power of its blood. There is also a repeated note of 'thanksgiving' (4:9; 7:12; cf. 11:17) directed towards the one seated on the throne.

Particularly striking are the parallels with the eucharistic section of the *Didache*, notably the title of God as 'Master Almighty' (δέσποτα παντοκράτορ: *Did.* 10:3; Rev. 4:8; 6:10), the ascribing to God of 'glory' (*Did.* 9:2, 3, 4; 10:2, 4, 5; Rev. 1:6; 4:11; 5:13), and the prayer for the Lord to come (*Did.* 10:6; Rev. 22:20; cf. 1 Cor. 16:22). It is even possible that the book was so divided as to form manageable 'instalments' intended to be read during a series of successive Eucharists (see Garrow 1997).

If the eucharistic assembly was the Apocalypse's intended 'theatre of reception', then this has significant corollaries. First, Revelation would have functioned imaginatively to connect the sporadic gatherings of early Christians with the eternal worship of heaven. Christian assemblies within the seven cities of Asia are likely to have been tiny in proportion to the overall urban population: one recent estimate of the size of the first-century church in Ephesus is between fifty and a hundred within a total population of approximately two hundred thousand (Howard-Brook and Gwyther 1999: p. xxii). Revelation's visions of the heavenly liturgy, and its revelation that these small congregations are part of a huge multitude 'too large to be counted' (7:9), would have served as a powerful challenge to rival claimants to the throne, whose dominance was built into the very fabric of Asia's Roman cities.

Second, given that early Christian prophetic oracles and revelations were generally delivered within a worship context, the reading of Revelation would have served as a literary and oral compensation for the absence in the liturgical assembly of the prophet-seer John, currently consigned to exile on an island. This would have given the reader a significant role as the mouthpiece of the absent seer, and through him of Jesus Christ (1:9; 2:1—3:22; cf. the similar function of Paul's letters, e.g. 1 Cor. 5:3–5). The explicit statement that John received his inaugural vision 'on the Lord's day' matches the time of the week when, across the sea, the seven congregations would have been gathered for worship (1:10; *Did.* 14:1). Finally, the conjoining of the Apocalypse with celebration of the Eucharist gives a further dimension to the frequent and urgent references to the 'coming' of the Lord (e.g. 1:4; 2:5, 16; 3:3, 20; 22:20). In the worship accompanying the reading of this text, these Christian communities would have encountered the repeated coming of Christ to them in judgement and salvation, anticipating that final coming at his Parousia (for the influence of the Apocalypse on the Orthodox Liturgy, see Ashanin 1990).

Structure

Readers over the centuries have frequently found themselves at a loss when it comes to making sense of the book's structure. Its haphazard juxtaposition of visions have resulted in a plethora of rival, and often mutually exclusive, structural analyses. Many commentators, indeed, have concluded that the text as we have it lacks an overall pattern, and have either attempted to 'improve' on it or posited complex theories of composition. Nevertheless, there are good grounds for upholding the essential integrity of the book (Bauckham 1993a, 1–37). If this is the case, our presumption should be that there is some underlying pattern or structure (though allowing for elements of fluidity appropriate to a text which claims its origin in visionary experience). The following comments are pertinent:

(a) A prologue and epistolary introduction (1:1–8) precedes John's account of his first Patmos vision at 1:9–20, and similar epilogue material is found towards the end of chapter 22.

(b) There is a natural break at 4:1, which marks the transition from the seven messages to John's heavenly ascent and symbolic visions proper.

(c) Sequences of seven, at least four of which are explicitly marked (messages, seals, trumpets, bowls), ought to be taken seriously. Moreover, given John's capacity to provide implicit sevens embedded in the text (e.g. seven beatitudes), one should not rule out the possibility of other implicit septets.

(d) There are good grounds for making a break halfway through the book (at 12:1 or more likely 11:19). The new section, which deals with the fate of God's people in the events leading up to the last day, is often related in some way to the 'little scroll' delivered to John in chapter 10. Moreover, the second half overlaps to some degree with the first half: warnings from the seven messages about remaining faithful and resisting compromise (Revelation 2—3) are played out in visionary form in the battle between the woman and the dragon, and the appearance of the two monsters (Revelation 12—13); there is a striking similarity between the trumpet-plagues of 8:2—11:18 and the bowl-plagues of 15:5—16:21).

(e) There is evidence for significant interludes which delay the action and prepare for what is yet to come (e.g. 7:1–17; 10:1—11:14), and also evidence for overlapping, whereby different sections are bound to each other by passages which look forward and back simultaneously (e.g. 8:3–5).

(f) Recapitulation of the trumpets sequence in the bowls septet, albeit with some progression, should alert us to the possibility of similar recapitulations elsewhere, and warn against viewing Revelation as primarily chronological in sequence. Rather it may present different aspects of the same scene or theme at different times: e.g. God's people are at one time the temple of God measured for divine protection, at another the whole holy city, at another a pregnant woman, at another a mighty army (11:1–2; 12:1–2; 14:1–5; see also the succession of 'battle scenes', e.g. 12:7–12; 16:12–16; 17:13–14; 19:17–21; 20:7–10).

(g) There are strong literary parallels between the visions of Babylon (17:1—19:10) and the new Jerusalem (21:9—22.9; Giblin 1974). Both are introduced by the appearance of one of the seven bowl angels, who carries John off 'in the spirit' with a similar invitation (17:1–3; 21:9–10); both describe a woman who is also a city; both, moreover, conclude with the seer being rebuked for trying to worship the interpreting angel (19:10; 22:8–9). This could mean either that the two visions create an *inclusio* around the intervening visions (thus forming a substantial final section incorporating 17:1—22:9), or that they are parallel endings to two separate sections (15:5—19:10; 19:11—22:9 or —22:11). Garrow's instalment theory would suggest the latter, allowing for six instalments of relatively equal length.

Three further general observations are also pertinent:

(h) Revelation claims to be a text based upon visionary experience, however much subsequent reflection and ordering has taken place. If one allows for this possibility, then lack of apparent structure in places ought not to be a surprise. Visions, like dreams, are not necessarily received in chronological or even thematic sequence.

(i) Literary criticism has recently highlighted the importance of story and plot in interpreting narrative texts such as the Gospels and Revelation. Attention to Revelation's story or plot will provide clues as to whether our structural pattern is on the right lines. Moreover, repetition, and passages which might appear out of place because they delay progress, may in fact be evidence of deliberate literary artistry and dramatic tension.

(j) As stated above, the Apocalypse was intended to be read orally, probably in a liturgical setting. Its first audiences would have relied on aural indicators as they heard the book read, such as repetition, in order to make sense of the whole. Moreover, the proposal (Garrow 1997) that the book was not intended to be read in one sitting, but is structured according to six instalments, is an attractive one. The number six, rather than the complete seven, is appropriate: the book in itself is incomplete, for it offers only the promise of the End, not the End itself (Boxall 2002: 80–81).

All of these considerations have been taken into account in the body of the commentary, and in the following structural outline.

OUTLINE OF REVELATION

Prologue (1:1–8)
    Superscription (1:1–3)
    Epistolary Opening (1:4–8)

Part I The Preparation of the Church and the Opening of the Lamb's Scroll (1:9—11:18)

1   Inaugural Vision and Seven Messages (1:9—3:22)

Vision of Someone Like a Son of Man (1:9–20)
The Messages to the Angels of the Seven Congregations
    (2:1—3:22)
    To Ephesus (2:1–7)
    To Smyrna (2:8–11)
    To Pergamum (2:12–17)
    To Thyatira (2:18–29)
    To Sardis (3:1–6)
    To Philadelphia (3:7–13)
    To Laodicea (3:14–22)

2   Throne-Vision and Seven Seals (4:1—8:1)

Vision of the Heavenly Throne (4:1–11)
The Lamb and the First Scroll (5:1–14)
The Opening of the First Four Seals: The Four Horsemen
    (6:1–8)
The Opening of the Fifth Seal (6:9–11)
The Opening of the Sixth Seal (6:12–17)
Interlude 1: The Sealing and Preservation of God's People
    (7:1–17)
The Opening of the Seventh Seal (8:1)

3   Seven Trumpets (8:2—11:18)

Preparation for the Seven Trumpets (8:2–6)
The First Four Trumpets (8:7–13)
The Fifth Trumpet (9:1–12)

COMMENTARY

Prologue (1:1–8)

The words 'Apocalypse of John' by which Revelation is commonly known are not original (the book's true title is 'Apocalypse [*or* Revelation] of Jesus Christ'). They may well have been added by a scribe either to the beginning or, more likely, to the end of a scroll, or attached to it on a label, in order to identify it more easily (Aune 1997: 3–4). It was certainly known by this title from the second century onwards (e.g. Iren. *Adv. Haer.* 4.14.2; cf. *Mur. Can.* 71). As the book was increasingly copied in codex form, this title (now firmly the inscription) became more elaborate, 'Apocalypse of St John the Theologian' (or 'St John the Divine') being the most famous.

The opening verses of the book proper comprise two sections (1:1–3 and 1:4–8), which highlight different aspects of its literary genre. Nevertheless, there are good literary grounds for treating both sections together as the prologue to the work. Careful analysis points to striking literary parallels with Revelation's epilogue in chapter 22. The claim that God (or Jesus) has sent his angel to show his servants what must soon happen (1:1) is reiterated at 22:6 (cf. 22:16). The divine statement 'I am the Alpha and the O' concludes the prologue at 1:8 and is repeated towards the beginning of the epilogue at 22:13. Both sections contain a beatitude (1:3; 22:14; cf. 22:7), and a warning that the time is near (1:3; 22:10). The liturgical response 'Yes indeed! Amen!' is found at 1:7 and 22:20, in conjunction with sayings about the Lord's coming (see also 1:3 = 22:18; 1:7 = 22:12). These parallels form an overarching *inclusio* for the whole text.

Superscription (1:1–3)

(1) **A revelation from Jesus Christ, which God gave him to reveal to his servants what must soon come to pass. Jesus made it known by signs to his servant John, through his angel whom he sent to him. (2) John now bears witness to all the things he has seen: God's word, that is, the witness which Jesus Christ himself bore. (3) Happy is the one who reads aloud, and happy are the people who hear the words of this**

21

prophecy and observe what is written in it. For the crucial time is very close!

Ancient books were often prefaced by a title or superscription defining the nature of the work (e.g. Mk 1:1; Mt. 1:1), or by a fuller prologue setting out the author's intentions (e.g. Lk. 1:1–4; Josephus, *C. Ap.* 1.1). The first three verses of John's book fulfil this task. Although, as we shall see (1:4–5a; 22:21), Revelation is presented in the form of a letter, this title declares that it is primarily revelatory and prophetic in character. Indeed, many have been struck by the way in which these opening verses (in fact the whole section, 1:1–20) echo the prologues of Old Testament prophetic books. The opening chapter of Ezekiel seems to have been a particular influence: that prophet describes how he received 'visions' while in exile by the River Chebar (Ezek. 1:1; cf. Rev. 1:9–12), in which the 'word of the Lord' came to him (Ezek. 1:3; cf. Rev. 1:2); the opening vision describes Ezekiel's vision of the throne-chariot, surrounded by the four cherubim (Ezek. 1:4ff.; cf. Rev. 4:1ff.). Ezekiel will continue to exert a crucial influence throughout John's Apocalypse (Goulder 1981). However, the openings of other prophetic books may also have left their mark: some speak of the word of the Lord coming to the prophet (e.g. Jer. 1:1–4; Hos. 1:1; Hag. 1:1), others of visions received (e.g. Isa. 1:1; Obad. 1:1). Our author is clearly – and boldly! – locating his work within the same tradition of Israelite prophecy.

The fact that Revelation's title is in the third person, contrasting with the 'I, John' (or occasionally 'I, Jesus') of the rest of the book, has led to the suggestion that 1:1–3 is the work of an anonymous editor of John's visions (Malina and Pilch 2000: 29). Comparisons with the canonical prophets, however, render such an explanation superfluous: here we find the same combination of third person in the title and first person (of the prophet or the Lord) in the main body of the text. A single author, modelling his work on this prophetic tradition, could be expected to follow this pattern.

1 Yet the prophetic tradition is not the only influence on John's book. His title defines it as a **revelation**, an 'unveiling' or 'uncovering'. Whether or not the author intends to describe here the particular literary genre 'apocalypse', he certainly invites comparison with both the oral 'revelations' of early Christian liturgical assemblies (e.g. 1 Cor. 14:26) and the literary apocalypses and related literature of the Judaeo-Christian tradition. There are particular literary parallels with *1 En.* 1:1–2, *Apoc. Abr.* 1:1, the prologue to *3 Baruch*, and *Apoc. Adam* 1:1–3. John's first-century audiences are led to expect that his book will reveal heavenly mysteries normally hidden from human eyes,

forcing them to reconsider their limited perspective on the world and their place in it.

But unlike these Jewish apocalypses, which link the revelation or apocalypse with the name of the seer, John's revelation is defined specifically as **a revelation from Jesus Christ**. This claim to heavenly origin gives the book its incontestable authority. The Greek has the ambiguous 'of Jesus Christ'. This could mean that Jesus is the content of the revelation (objective genitive); i.e. this is a revelation about Jesus Christ. Yet far more will be revealed in this book than christological secrets. More likely, John is describing the process by which the revelation comes to him: it is an unveiling which Jesus Christ passes on to him (subjective genitive). This is supported by the statement that **God gave** it to Jesus. God is the ultimate origin of what this book describes; the one who reveals it, and therefore reveals God, is Jesus Christ (cf. Jn 1:18).

The claim that this revelation is primarily that of Jesus has led some commentators to relate it to the so-called 'Little Apocalypse' of the Synoptic Gospels (Mark 13 and par.), in which the departing Jesus speaks of the events of the end (e.g. Sweet 1979: 19–21). Certainly there are interesting parallels between the Synoptic passage and John's revelations (not least in the visions of Revelation 6). We should perhaps not be surprised if the teaching of Jesus, as well as Israel's scriptures, has left its mark on the work of a Christian visionary such as John. Nevertheless, verse 9 will make clear that this book emerges primarily out of John's post-Easter visionary experience on Patmos. However much John's apocalyptic imagination has been fired by the sayings of his Lord and the writings of the prophets, the primary context for the visions described in this book is his Patmos experience.

Nevertheless, if we take seriously that this is **a revelation from Jesus Christ**, the quest for John's intention and purpose (while not unimportant) becomes less central. John claims to be transmitting visions and auditions received from the heavenly realm, rather than articulating his own message. Even though his personality and cultural heritage will have shaped his written text, and there are rare points at which explicit interpretations are offered (e.g. 1:20; 7:14; 17:8–10), Revelation may not reflect authorial intention to the same degree as a Pauline letter or even a Gospel. Hence even the identity of the author can fade into the background, so as not to detract from the heavenly message he mediates.

The intended recipients of this message are **his** (probably God's) **servants**. Though John can speak elsewhere specifically of 'his servants the prophets' (10:7; possibly 11:18; cf. Amos 3:7), its use here seems to have a wider application to all those who acknowledge the lordship of God, i.e. all faithful followers of the Lamb (see also 2:20;

7:3; 19:2, 5; 22:3, 6). The revelation to be disclosed is for the churches, not simply an educated or 'wise' elite within them (compare *4 Ez.* 14:46). Its content is **what must soon come to pass**. While many over the centuries have plundered the pages of Revelation for eschatological schemes and timetables related to their own time, the primary focus is on John's own generation. Whatever capacity it has to inspire subsequent generations, the Apocalypse must have had a particular message to those first-century congregations who originally heard it.

But what precisely will be revealed over the next twenty-two chapters? The phrase **what must soon come to pass** may hold the key. It echoes a similar one in the book of Daniel (Dan. 2:28), which ranks alongside Ezekiel as one of John's major influences. Certain Jewish visionary writings suggest that Jewish mystics meditated upon particular biblical texts as preparation for visionary experience. It is not impossible that Ezekiel and Daniel were used by John in this particular way (Ezekiel's vision of the throne-chariot seems to have been particularly favoured). Certainly the John who has the Old Testament scriptures pulsating through his veins seems to hold these two books at the forefront of his visionary imagination. In Dan. 2:36b–45, Daniel interprets a disturbing dream which has been troubling the Babylonian King Nebuchadnezzar, concerning what must come to pass 'at the end of days' (2:28). The composite statue which the king sees in his dream is interpreted as a succession of four great kingdoms, beginning with Nebuchadnezzar's own (i.e. the Babylonian, Median, Persian and Greek). Just as the terrifying statue is destroyed, so will this succession of pagan empires give way to another kingdom established by God, which will never be destroyed (Dan. 2:44).

Jewish Christians among Revelation's first hearers would no doubt detect the allusion. It signals the transition from the kingdoms of this world to the kingdom of God. But what for Daniel was to be kept for the distant future 'at the end of days', for John's audiences was to take place **soon**. The urgency of John's words may well have contrasted with the expectations of many of his Christian contemporaries, for whom an impending crisis in the political realm may have been far from their minds (see comment on Revelation 2—3).

Having established Revelation's divine authority as from God through Jesus, a further chain of communication is set up. Jesus has **made it known to John**, not directly but **through his angel whom he sent to him**. Interpreting angels play a key role in the apocalypses, and John's is no exception. The mighty angel of Rev. 10:1 may be particularly in view here, though the seer will encounter others along the way (e.g. 7:2; 14:6; 17:1; 21:9). The sequence Jesus–angel–John will apparently be broken, at least temporarily, when 'someone like a son of man', almost certainly the exalted Christ, reveals himself directly to John at 1:13. Nevertheless, the order of delegation (God–Jesus Christ–his (Jesus') angel–John) may provide a clue to the structure of the book as a whole. In the heavenly vision of Revelation 4—5, the one on the throne will hand over a sealed scroll to the Lamb; this will be followed in chapter 10 by a mighty angel delivering a little scroll (the same scroll, it will be argued) to John, enabling him to prophesy God's word. The manner in which Jesus transmits the revelation is also significant for interpreters. Jesus **made it known by signs**: although the verb σημαίνω can be simply translated 'indicate' or 'make known', it is related to the word for 'sign' (σημεῖον). The choice of this verb should alert the reader to be attentive to the symbolic nature of the visions as they unfold (Beale 1999: 52).

John is at the end of this revelatory chain, and indeed is referred to as **his** (probably Jesus') **servant**. On the surface at least, this has the effect of distancing John the seer from the aforementioned heavenly beings; he is on same level as the other servants to whom his book is addressed. Yet perhaps we should not be too swift to draw this conclusion. The rhetoric of this passage actually has the effect of exalting John's status as a privileged communicator of heavenly secrets to whom his Christian hearers should attend. The term 'servant' was one claimed by Israel's prophets to describe their privileged role (e.g. Isa. 49:5; Jon. 1:9 LXX), and was also used of privileged individuals such as Moses (e.g. Mal. 4:4), David (e.g. Ezek. 37:24) and Zerubbabel (e.g. Hag. 2:23). Moreover, John is not on equal terms with the recipients of Revelation, for they are one stage further down the chain of communication. He has established his position as the mediator of an authoritative revelation, which will countenance no disagreement or opposition (see Carey 1999).

Whatever the nature of John's visionary experience, he has reflected 2 upon it and **now bears witness to all the things he has seen**. Though the verb **bears witness** is literally in the Greek past (aorist) tense, it is probably an epistolary aorist appropriately translated as present (Aune 1997: 6): John bears witness in the present as he writes or dictates his Apocalypse, though it will be a past event by the time his book reaches its recipients. Revelation is John's written testimony to **all the things he has seen**. Some, particularly those who hold to apostolic authorship, see this as a reference to John's record of Jesus' earthly ministry. While we should not rule this out completely, he is primarily referring to the visions described in this book (note the repeated phrase 'and I saw'). Bearing witness is a crucial activity in the Apocalypse, and links it to the Fourth Gospel. Jesus is the first to do so (τὴν μαρτυρίαν Ἰησοῦ Χριστοῦ understood as a subjective genitive, **the witness which Jesus Christ himself bore**: e.g. Sweet 1981; contrast Vassiliadis 1985), in his life and particularly in his death (1 Tim. 6:13). His followers continue to bear witness to God's truth, just as Jesus did, even if that leads to hostility and even death (e.g. 6:9; 11:7; 12:11; 19:10). Though this verse is not easy to translate, the witness which Jesus Christ himself bore and **God's word** are probably two ways of speaking of the same reality. The word of God is particularly his secret purposes as revealed in the prophets (e.g. Amos 3:7). But those secret purposes have now been made clear in Jesus Christ, in the witness of his life, teaching, and especially his death and resurrection. John's vision of the risen Lord, and the revelations mediated through Christ's angel, have opened his eyes to this. Not for nothing has Revelation been called the climax of prophecy (Bauckham 1993a).

3 But John's testimony to all this is not to remain silent in a book. It is to come alive in Christian congregations through oral performance. Revelation distinguishes between **the one who reads aloud**, the lector, and **the people who hear**, the audience. Partly, this reflects the social reality of the early Christians, many of whom would have been illiterate. But there are clues throughout the Apocalypse that a liturgical – even eucharistic – context is the implied arena for the public reading of this text (e.g. 1:10; 2:7, 17; 19:7, 9; 22:17, 20; cf. 1 Cor. 16:22; *Didache* 9—10; Barr 1986; Garrow 1997). This would not be surprising in a Judaeo-Christian environment (Neh. 8:2; Lk. 4:16; Acts 13:15; Col. 4:16; 1 Thess. 5:27; 1 Tim. 4:13; see Tert. *De Anima* 9). Hearing the text in a liturgical setting, attending to its narrative plot, its sequences of sevens, its recurring themes and repetitions, early Christian congregations would have entered imaginatively into the world of the text. Their worship – perhaps as vulnerable minorities in the back streets of great Roman cities – would have been caught up into the worship of the heavenly temple, presenting them with an alternative vision to challenge the visions presented by city and empire. Perhaps this aspect of Revelation is the most challenging for twenty-first-century readers, whose imaginative muscles have become rather flabby, and whose capacity for attentive listening is severely reduced.

The role of lector would have been important for another reason. In the ancient world, the art of reading demanded careful preparation. Ancient Greek manuscripts lacked punctuation, and even divisions between individual words. Thus **the one who reads aloud** would not have taken the initial task lightly, and no doubt would have continued to study the text carefully in preparation for subsequent readings. Indeed, the reader may have been called upon to explain and clarify disputed points in the text (the phrase 'let the reader understand' at Mk 13:14 may point to a similar role).

Yet **the people who hear** are no less important. Other apocalypses reserve access to revealed secrets to 'the wise' or literate elites (e.g. Dan. 12:3–4; *4 Ez.* 14:46). This may have functioned as a literary device to explain how revelations, apparently made known to seers such as Abraham, Daniel or Ezra many centuries before, had only recently been published. The early Christian belief that the last days were upon us, however, removed the need for such a device. This urgent message is not for the scribal class alone, but is to be shared with all God's people.

Both the reader and the audience are declared **happy**, provided they **hear** and **observe** the words. This is the first of seven beatitudes scattered throughout the book (see also 14:13; 16:15; 19:9; 20:6; 22:7; 22:14), which speak in their different ways of the salvation promised to those who remain faithful (see Table 1). Their increasing frequency towards the end of the book may be related to the narrative tension as the eschatological events reach their climax. What they are to observe are **the words of this prophecy** (which suggests that the author does not expect his book to be read once and then shelved). This apocalyptic unveiling of what must soon take place is to be regarded as the prophetic word (a challenge to biblical scholars who are perhaps too eager to separate 'prophetic' and 'apocalyptic' traditions). We have already seen how this whole section imitates the form and style of Old Testament prophetic writings, and this will continue throughout the book. Revelation sets itself up unselfconsciously as a prophetic message, and implicitly, it sets up John as a prophet.

As if to heighten the need for faithful response, this section concludes with the warning: **For the crucial time is very close!** The καιρός refers to an appointed or opportune time (e.g. Gen. 18:14; Exod. 23:15; Hab. 2:3), and often describes the eschatological time when God will act decisively (e.g. Jer. 50:27; Dan. 7:22; 11:27; Mt. 13:30; Mk 1:15; Lk. 12:56; 19:44). John's hearers would be in no doubt of the imminence of the crisis prophesied by Daniel.

Epistolary Opening   (1:4–8)

(4) From John, to the seven congregations in Asia.

Grace and well-being to you from he who is, and who was, and who is coming, and from the seven spirits before his throne,

(5) and from Jesus Christ, the trustworthy witness, the first to be born from the dead, and the ruler of earth's kings.

To the one who loves us and has set us free from our sins by

Table 1: The Seven Beatitudes

1:3   Happy is the one who reads aloud, and happy are the people who hear the words of this prophecy and observe what is written in it.

14:13   Happy are the dead who die in the Lord from now on.

16:15   Happy is the one who stays awake and protects his clothes, so that he does not go around naked and people see his shame.

19:9   Happy are those who have received an invitation to the Lamb's wedding banquet.

20:6   Happy and holy is the one who has a share in the first resurrection.

22:7   Happy is the one who observes the words of the prophecy contained in this scroll.

22:14   Happy are those who wash their robes clean, so as to have access to the tree of life, and to enter through the gates into the city.

his blood – (6) he has made us sharers in his royal rule, and priests to minister to his God and Father – to Jesus be glory and power for ever and ever.
    Amen!
    (7) Look! He is coming with the clouds,
    and every eye shall see him,
    even those who pierced him.
    All earth's peoples shall lament over him.
    Yes indeed! Amen!
    (8) 'I am the Alpha and the O,' says the Lord God, who is and who was and who is coming, the Almighty.

4–5a   The opening three verses have asserted the Apocalypse's divine origin, in a manner which evokes both the literary apocalypses and the writings of the canonical prophets. Now the author (or narrator) comes to the fore, as the characteristic form of a letter is utilised. Graeco-Roman letter openings typically comprised three elements: (i) the name of the sender; (ii) a reference to the recipients; (iii) a greeting. Revelation 1:4–5a contains all three elements, the third expanded in a distinctive way to highlight both the Christian and the apocalyptic nature of this letter.

    This use of the letter form has a threefold effect. First, it makes explicit who are the primary recipients of Revelation, **the seven** congregations in Asia, addressing its visionary message to them in a specific way. Parallels are often sought with the letters of Paul, which often directly confront difficult situations in particular Christian communities. However, one should not neglect other New Testament paradigms: Paul's letters are for the most part directed to Christians in one particular city (Galatians and possibly 2 Corinthians are the exceptions which prove the rule). Revelation, however, is here presented as a circular letter, inviting comparison also with James and 1 Peter. All seven congregations will receive the book in its entirety.

Second, the undisputed authority of the heavenly revelation is transferred to the author of the letter, John. The fact that he names himself so simply, mentioning no additional title or office (contrast e.g. Rom. 1:1; Gal. 1:1–4; Jas 1:1; 2 Pet. 1:1), suggests that he is already a familiar figure of some authority within the Asian churches (though not without some prophetic rivals: 2:20). Nevertheless, the claim to be communicating a message of divine rather than human origin has the rhetorical result of enhancing whatever residual authority John possesses, and effectively silencing any rival voices. Many commentators in recent centuries have questioned this claim.

There is a third, related consequence of the use of the letter form: via the mouthpiece of the reader, standing in the midst of the liturgical assembly, it has the effect of making John's absent persona present among them. A similar technique can be found at 1 Cor. 5:3–5, where Paul's presence 'in spirit' despite his physical absence enables the community to deal with a potentially destructive situation. In the liturgical performance of this apocalyptic letter, the sea separating the seer of Patmos from the seven congregations is temporarily traversed, enabling his voice to be heard with challenging and terrifying immediacy.

The recipients are described as the seven congregations in Asia. While the word ἐκκλησία was commonly used to describe a variety of assemblies gathered for political or religious purposes, it is clear from Revelation 2—3 that seven Christian congregations are meant ('the congregation of God/YHWH' as a description of God's people Israel is an Old Testament antecedent: e.g. Deut. 23:2; Neh. 13:1; Mic. 2:5). Asia throughout the New Testament refers to the Roman province of that name, comprising the regions of Mysia, Lydia, Caria, Ionia and parts of Phrygia, in what is now western Turkey (Acts 2:9; 6:9; 16:6; 19:10, 22, 26, 27; 20:16, 18; 21:27; 24:19; 27:2; Rom. 16:5; 1 Cor. 16:19; 2 Cor. 1:8; 2 Tim. 1:15; 1 Pet. 1:1). John never uses the singular ἐκκλησία to denote the universal Church (cf. Mt. 16:18; Eph. 1:22; 3:21; 5:22–32; Col. 1:24; possibly 1 Cor. 12:28; Gal. 1:13), but only the individual congregations (e.g. 2:1; 3:22; 22:16; cf. Acts 11:26; 1 Cor. 1:2). Nevertheless, while the number

seven refers to real first-century churches, the symbolic use of numbers throughout the Apocalypse may point to a wider significance. Seven is the number of completion or perfection, and is a key organising number in Revelation, both implicitly (seven beatitudes) and explicitly (seven messages, seals, trumpets and bowls). Hence the seven congregations are probably meant to be representative of the whole Asian church. As George Caird noted, there would have been more than seven churches in Asia in the second half of the first century, certainly Alexandrian Troas (Acts 20:5–12), Colossae (Col. 1:2) and Hierapolis (Col. 4:13), the latter two close to Laodicea in the Lycus Valley. Caird adds as almost certain Magnesia-on-the-Meander and Tralles, both well established by Ignatius' time (though this may depend on a late dating of Revelation: Caird 1966: 15). It is only a small step from this to the patristic claim that the seven churches of Asia stand for the Church Universal. This may have implications for our interpretation of chapters 2—3.

John's greeting wishes **grace and well-being** on the recipients. Grace (Greek χάρις) is a theologised form of the more usual and similar-sounding Greek χαίρειν ('greetings'; cf. Jas 1:1). It proclaims the 'giftedness' of the salvation offered to God's people. **Well-being** or 'peace' denotes the Hebrew greeting *Shalom* (e.g. Num. 6:26; Judg. 6:23; 1 Chron. 12:19), which also evokes the state of God's eschatological people (e.g. Rom. 5:1). It is often claimed that John's greeting formula betrays the influence of Paul, and this is not improbable, even allowing for an early dating for Revelation, given the activity of the apostle to the Gentiles in the province of Asia during the 50s. **Grace and well-being** is Paul's typical form of greeting in his letters (e.g. Rom. 1:7; 1 Cor. 1:3; Phil. 1:2). Nevertheless, two words of caution are called for. First, although Paul uses this formula, we cannot be sure that it originates within Pauline circles rather than being more widely used in early Christian tradition. The phrase is also found at 1 Pet. 1:2 and 2 Pet. 1:2, while 2 John has the threefold 'grace, mercy and well-being' (2 Jn 3). Second, Revelation's triadic formula to describe the divine source of the blessing differs significantly from Paul's usual 'God our Father and the Lord Jesus Christ'.

The first-named in John's triadic formula, itself a triad, is the **he who is, and who was, and who is coming**. The author's ungrammatical style breaks through at this point, denoted in this translation by the equally ungrammatical English **from he who is** (rather than 'from him ...'). Commentators disagree as to the reason for what Dionysius of Alexandria called John's 'barbarisms' (Eus. *H. E.* 7.25). Is it because he is primarily a Semitic-speaker, unsure of himself in the Greek language (though he correctly uses the genitive after ἀπὸ in the succeeding phrase about the seven spirits)? Or is he wanting consciously to evoke the style of the Hebrew scriptures, as part of his strategy of presenting his own work as the continuation of the prophetic tradition? Particularly attractive is the suggestion that he is deliberately barbarising the language as part of his protest against the dominant culture of Rome (e.g. A. Y. Collins 1984: 47; Maier 2002: 108–22). In this case, he would be subverting rival claims to authority and divinity, by presenting Israel's God as the ultimate subject, who can be confined by no-one's grammatical rules.

The divine name **who is, and who was, and who is coming** is repeated at 1:8; 4:8; 11:17 and 16:5, the latter two cases without the third, future element. It echoes the revelation of the divine name at Exod. 3:14, and subsequent Jewish reflection upon it (e.g. Targum Pseudo-Jonathan on Exod. 3:14 and Deut. 32:39; *Sib. Or.* 3.16) which understands it in terms of God's present, past and future existence. The God who now exists is also the one who was in the beginning, and will continue to be into eternity. Nevertheless, John parts company with earlier Jewish exegetes by replacing the expected 'who will be' with the rather more dynamic 'who is coming' (significantly a present participle). Israel's God, the God of Jesus Christ, is known in his relationship to God's world, as the one who is coming in salvation and judgement (Bauckham 1993b: 28–30).

Along with God, there are **the seven spirits before his throne**. God's heavenly throne or *Merkavah*, which was the goal of mystical ascent, is implied here. Opinion is divided as to the identity of these spirits. Traditionally, they have been understood to represent the Holy Spirit in its sevenfold manifestation (Isa. 11:1–2; e.g. Caird 1966: 15), seven having already been introduced as the number of perfection. The 'trinitarian' structure of the greeting is thought to suggest this. Moreover, John evokes a vision of Zechariah, in which the prophet sees seven lamps which are identified as the 'eyes of the Lord, which range through the whole earth' (Zech. 4:10). The key to Zechariah's vision seems to be verse 6, where the Lord's word is: 'Not by might, nor by power, but by my Spirit, says the Lord of hosts' (Zech. 4:6). In other words, the **seven spirits** signify the completeness of God's Spirit, the source of true power for the churches in contrast to rival powers in the world, for whom might is right (cf. 5:6). This would be in contrast to singular references to 'the Spirit', which focus on one particular activity of the Spirit of God, as inspirer of the prophets (Bauckham 1993b: 115; but see Barr 1998: 32).

However, this solution may too readily assume a developed trinitarianism in a text so influenced by Jewish apocalyptic tradition. The alternative solution has much to commend it: the **seven spirits** are the seven principal angels who 'stand ready and enter before the glory of the Lord' (Tob. 12:15; cf. *1 En.* 20), and who will reappear at 8:2

(where ἐνώπιον τοῦ θεοῦ is synonymous with this verse's ἐνώπιον τοῦ θρόνου αὐτοῦ). John, after all, can speak unambiguously of 'the Spirit' in the singular (e.g. 1:10; 2:7; 14:13), without specifically denoting it as 'the Spirit of prophecy'. Furthermore, the plural 'spirits' is sometimes used of angels (e.g. 1QS 3:17–26; Heb. 1:7, citing Ps. 104:4; possibly 1 Pet. 3:19). Moreover, at 3:1 we hear that the heavenly Christ 'possesses' the seven spirits and the seven stars, which seems to favour their angelic identity. This identification would enhance the role of the archangels as mediators of heavenly blessings. They act on behalf of God in ensuring **grace and well-being** for his people.

The third element of John's formula, **Jesus Christ** or Messiah, is also mentioned as a source of blessing, thus setting him on the heavenly side above human recipients of grace and well-being. His credentials for holding such a position are given: he is **the trustworthy** (or 'faithful') **witness** and **the first to be born from the dead**. Given the use of the Greek word μάρτυς (= 'witness') elsewhere in Revelation, the first phrase refers to his testimony to the point of death. Like the Fourth Gospel, Revelation declares that there is a trial taking place in the cosmos, and witnesses have been called to speak the truth. Jesus is the pre-eminent example, for his fidelity to his witness led to his death; others, however, are invited to imitate him (e.g. Antipas at Pergamum, 2:13). The second phrase, **first to be born from the dead**, proclaims how God overturned the apparent shame of the cross by raising Jesus from death and proving his testimony to have been truthful (cf. Rom. 8:29; Col. 1:18). Some might detect an ironic reversal of the fate of the Egyptian 'first-born', who were also destined for death (e.g. Exod. 11:5; 12:12; Num. 3:13; Ps. 134:8; 135:10 LXX; Heb. 11:28). By virtue of his resurrection and exaltation, Jesus is now **the ruler of earth's kings** (Psalm 89, read as a prophecy of the Davidic Messiah, lies in the background here). The earth's kings will appear as a group throughout the book (6:15; 17:2, 18; 18:3, 9; 19:19), usually in opposition to God's rule, though not always (see 21:24), a sign that the emphasis upon judgement and destruction of God's enemies is not God's final word. This transferral of the language of royalty and power to one who has been slain represents something of a signature tune for the Apocalypse. It calls for a radical reassessment of the nature of power and where it is to be located.

5b–8   In Paul's letters, the epistolary introduction is generally followed by a thanksgiving for the recipients or a doxology, and John provides the latter here. Yet many have been struck by its profoundly liturgical ring. It is as if John's audiences are invited to burst into song as they make his vision their own, perhaps joining in the responses of a liturgical dialogue with the lector (Vanni 1991). In support of this, one should note the sudden change to the first person plural in verse 5b (following the better reading), and the repeated 'Amen!' The dialogue would then function something like this:

Reader:	verses 4–5a
Congregation:	verses 5b–6, concluding with 'Amen!'
Reader:	verse 7
Congregation:	'Yes indeed! Amen!'
Reader:	verse 8

Elements of these verses may have been derived from existing liturgical tradition, and therefore congregations could have joined in on a first hearing (accounting for the jarring transition at the beginning of verse 6). If so, John would not be alone among New Testament writers: others are also believed to have cited extant hymns and creeds familiar to their addressees (e.g. Rom. 1:3–4; 3:24–25; Phil. 2:6–11; Col. 1:15–20; Jn 1:1–18). Or perhaps this dialogue aspect may only have been picked up on subsequent readings of the Apocalypse. Either way, this section has the effect of drawing the hearers more closely into the 'point of view' of the text.

Christ is designated as **the one who loves us**. It is important to hold onto this, for the violent apocalyptic imagery in the rest of Revelation means that this aspect of the gospel is sometimes lost sight of. According to the majority reading, he **has set us free** (λύσαντι; a minority of later readings have 'washed' (λούσαντι), which is probably due to scribal error) **from our sins by his blood**. This evokes the story of the Exodus, that great 'setting free' of God's people which became a key paradigm for the Christian liberation in Christ. Sin here is understood not primarily as human wrongdoing, but as a power which enslaves (cf. Rom. 3:9; 5:12–14; 6:5–11). The story of the new Exodus, already present in exilic prophets such as Second Isaiah, will be one of those key plots in the rest of the book, which will describe in visionary form how the Lamb leads his people from slavery to freedom, from Babylon to new Jerusalem. The means of achieving this is not – as in the first Exodus – the slaughter of the Egyptian first-born, but by Christ's own death, **by his blood**. Though John does not spell out the mechanism by which this occurs, the reference to blood suggests sacrifice.

Echoes of the Exodus story continue with echoes of Exod. 19:6, where God promises to make the Israelite refugees a priestly kingdom and a holy nation. In the Apocalypse, that promise is broadened to include those of every nation who hear and keep the words of this prophecy (e.g. 7:9; cf. 14:6). Already **he has made us sharers in his royal rule, and priests to minister to his God and Father.**

The first phrase, 'sharers in his royal rule' or 'kingdom', evokes the proclamation of Jesus during his earthly ministry that God was beginning to act to overcome all that stood in the way of his reigning as King. In the present, and not just at the end, Christians share with Jesus in his royal status. With such a claim comes an implicit challenge to rival claims to ultimate power and authority in the political realm, which is as pertinent to the contemporary reader as it would have been to the first hearers of Revelation in their imperial context. They are also 'priests to minister to his God and Father'. Priesthood, so often restricted to a privileged elite (and at least in Judaism restricted to males), is here democratised. It would involve the offering of fitting worship and sacrifice to God (the latter is particularly the prerogative of the martyrs). But it probably also gives Christians a mediatory role vis-à-vis the world. The gift of such a vocation appropriately leads into a doxology, the first of several which will proclaim Jesus' exalted role: he, like his Father, possesses **glory** (a standard word for the divine Presence or *kavod*: e.g. Exod. 16:10; 24:16; Ezek. 3:23; Jn 1:14; 2:11) **and power for ever and ever.**

The section continues (verse 7) with an oracle proclaiming Christ's vindication when he comes again, apparently drawing upon Dan. 7:13 and Zech. 12:10–14 (also combined at Mt. 24:30). Whereas now Christ's possession of glory and power is veiled – and uncovered only in an apocalypse such as John's – it will one day become universally clear. The reference to him **coming with the clouds** (significantly a present rather than future tense) evokes the scene of judgement of Daniel 7, where 'someone like a son of man' comes to the Ancient of Days to receive dominion, glory and kingship (Dan. 7:13–14). Early Christians had long understood this to speak of Christ's Parousia (e.g. 1 Thess. 4:17; Mt. 24:30; 25:31). But John emphasises the response of **every eye** to that revelation, and especially **those who pierced him**, both the leaders of his own people and especially the authorities of the great empire, Rome. Here we have another indication of Revelation's links with the Johannine tradition, for both Rev. 1:7 and Jn 19:37 seem to follow a version of Zech. 12:10 which speaks of 'him', rather than the MT and LXX's 'me', as the pierced or insulted one.

But why will Christ's enemies lament? The phrase (which follows the MT rather than the LXX) is often translated as 'on account of him' **all earth's peoples shall lament,** that is, they are lamenting for themselves out of fear of the impending judgement. But exactly the same Greek construction is used at 18:9, which can only refer to the kings of the earth mourning over Babylon (Thompson 2000). The same degree of pathos is surely implied here. That is echoed by the Zechariah passage, which envisages the inhabitants of Jerusalem mourning as over an only child. At Christ's coming, all earth's people (and not simply the people of Jerusalem, though they are included among 'those who pierced him') will experience grief for the one who was pierced and died. Of course, the corollary of this may be their own sense of remorse and even repentance, offering a hopeful thread which will recur from time to time as the tapestry of Revelation unfolds.

Finally, as if to confirm what has already been said, the voice of the reader becomes the vehicle for the voice of God. This is the first of four 'I AM sayings' (another Johannine trait) in Revelation, two of which are spoken by God (here and 21:6), and two by Jesus, highlighting his exalted status (1:18; 22:16; cf. 2:23). The triadic formula already used to describe YHWH, **who is and who was and who is coming**, is combined with two others. **The Alpha and the O** (paralleling the first and last letters of the Hebrew alphabet, *aleph* and *taw*) reflects the kind of speculation about divine names found in both Jewish and pagan sources (Bauckham 1993b: 25–28; Aune 1987: 489–91). It is just one indication that the author of Revelation swims within a broad stream of mystical tradition, many of whose details are now lost to us. Here it conveys God's role as the one from whom creation emerges and the goal towards which the cosmos is moving (see also Isa. 44:6; 48:12). The second title, **the Almighty**, translates the Hebrew Bible's *YHWH sebaoth* or 'Lord of hosts'. Given the key role of the heavenly host in the visions John describes, it is not surprising that this title vies with 'the one seated on the throne' as his preferred title for God (see also 4:8; 11:17; 15:3; 16:7, 14; 19:6, 15; 21:22). The divine intervention at this point functions to reassure the audience: despite appearances to the contrary, it is God the Almighty who remains in control of the universe and the course of history.

Part I The Preparation of the Church and the Opening of the Lamb's Scroll (1:9—11:18)

1 INAUGURAL VISION AND SEVEN MESSAGES (1:9—3:22)

Vision of Someone Like a Son of Man (1:9–20)

(9) I, John, your brother, who share with you in the tribulation and the royal rule and perseverance in Jesus, was on the island called Patmos as a result of proclaiming God's word, that is, the witness which Jesus bore. (10) I fell into a spiritual trance on the Lord's Day, and I heard behind me a loud voice like a trumpet-blast, (11) saying, 'Write down what you see in a scroll and send it to the seven congregations, to Ephesus, Smyrna and Pergamum, to Thyatira and Sardis, to Philadelphia and Laodicea.'

(12) I turned round to see the voice that was speaking with me. When I turned, I saw seven gold menorahs, (13) and in the middle of the menorahs someone like a son of man, dressed in a long robe, with a gold belt wrapped around his breast. (14) His head and his hair were shining white, like wool which is white as snow, his eyes were like a fiery flame, (15) and his feet were like polished bronze that had been refined in a furnace. His voice was like the sound made by many waters. (16) He held in his right hand seven stars, and out of his mouth there came a sharp, double-edged sword. His face was like the sun when it is shining with its full force. (17) When I saw him, I collapsed at his feet as if dead.

But he laid his right hand on me and said, 'Stop being afraid! I am the First and the Last, (18) the Living One. I was dead, but look! I am alive for ever and ever, and I hold the keys to Death and to Hades. (19) Therefore write down what you see, both what is now happening and what is to happen after this. (20) This is the secret of the seven stars which you saw in my right hand and of the seven gold menorahs: the

**seven stars are the angels of the seven congregations, and the
seven menorahs are the seven congregations.'**

One of the features of apocalypses is that they present the heavenly
revelation within a narrative framework (J. J. Collins 1979). That
framework begins here, with a brief autobiographical account from
the narrator, introducing the first of his apocalyptic visions, which
itself leads into a sequence of seven messages. Thus begins the first
visionary section of the Apocalypse, taking us to the end of chapter 3.
But we are surely to regard this autobiographical statement as pre-
facing the rest of the book also. However much visionary experience
and exegetical reflection underlies the work in its final form, John
locates what he describes on a particular island and on a particular
day, to be sent by divine commission to the seven congregations.

9 The visionary, **John,** presents himself in such a way as to evoke a
sense of solidarity with his hearers (though see commentary on 1:4).
Whatever office he may have held within the Church, it suits his
literary strategy at this point to stress only what they share, or what
he would like them to. As a fellow-Christian, he can call himself their
brother, sharing with them in 'the royal rule' (1:6). Moreover, what
they share in common, they share **in Jesus:** this phrase, reminiscent
of the Pauline 'in Christ' (e.g. Rom. 6:23; 8:1; 12:5; indeed, one
variant reading of Rev. 1:9 has ἐν Χριστῷ), highlights their solidarity with one another in Jesus and their close relationship with him.
   But there is a more challenging side to their Christian identity.
Although any hostility towards Christians in John's time seems to
have been localised and sporadic rather than official and sustained,
John is deliberately intensifying the rhetoric of crisis. Whatever their
actual social situation (and the evidence is rather mixed), the vision
he wishes to confront them with is one of hostility, of danger, of a
battle which needs to be engaged for the soul of the world. Thus he
speaks also of their sharing in **tribulation** (θλῖψις), like the Jesus
whom they follow and in whom they share solidarity one with
another. The tradition about Domitian has often led to this word
being translated as 'persecution', but that need not be at issue here.
The word can describe physical afflictions and hardships (e.g. Acts
20:23; Jas 1:27), though in the New Testament it often refers to the
particular tribulation of the end-times (e.g. Mt. 24:21, 29; Rom.
8:35). John's choice of words challenges his hearers to re-evaluate
their lives in the light of the eschatological tradition: what appears to
them to be the hardships of mundane life may actually be signs of the
eschatological crisis, the 'great tribulation' which will shock God's
people out of their complacency (cf. 7:14). In such a critical context,

perseverance is called for: not passive endurance but an active willingness to see the battle through to its bitter end.

John is on **the island called Patmos** when he has his vision. Patmos, now one of the Dodecanese in the eastern Aegean, functioned in the Hellenistic period as one of a series of fortress islands for the mainland city of Miletos, protecting it from attack from the sea (Saffrey 1975). This meant that in the first century it was far from being a cultural backwater, with a Milesian population large enough to justify a gymnasium and a thriving cult of both Artemis and Apollo (Miletos being connected to the famous shrine of Apollo at Didyma). John is somewhat ambiguous as to the nature of his presence on the island, except that it is connected in some way with **God's word, that is, the witness which Jesus bore**. The preposition he uses (διά + accusative) could just denote the purpose of his sojourn on Patmos: i.e. he came there 'for the sake of' proclaiming God's word. That would not be impossible, given that there was a population on the island (though one might suspect a larger mission territory would have been more promising!).

However, the construction is used elsewhere in Revelation to describe the result rather than purpose of an action (2:3; 4:11; 6:9; 7:15; 12:11; 13:14; 18:10; 20:4). But even this retains some ambiguity. Was it the word of God which impelled him to come to the island, perhaps in search of retreat? Did he choose voluntary flight, to avoid difficult circumstances on the mainland? Or did he come as an exile, banished here because of his prophetic activity? Tradition favours the last, as does John's claim to be sharing in the tribulation. Patmos may not have been a Roman penal colony, as is often claimed (see Caird 1966: 21), and the later accounts of John being banished by the emperor from Rome itself are probably legendary elaborations. A more likely scenario is that John was sent to Patmos by the local Asian authorities for his troublesome prophetic activities, perhaps in Miletos itself. This means that John sees and writes from the perspective of an exile, a marginal figure removed from the communities whom he knew so well. It is perhaps no surprise that throughout Christian history, some of John's greatest advocates have been those who have also found themselves disenfranchised by the powers that be. Others are invited to a radical change of perspective, to view the world not from the centre but from the periphery.

This Patmos exile describes how he **fell into a spiritual trance** 10 (literally 'I became in spirit'), the tense of the verb suggesting a change of state. Three further times (4:2; 17:3; 21:10) John will use a similar phrase to describe possession by the Spirit akin to an altered state of consciousness. There are good biblical antecedents for his experience, not least the prophet Ezekiel (e.g. Ezek. 2:2; 3:12), as well as in the Jewish and Christian apocalypses (e.g. *Asc. Isa.* 6.8–15; cf. *Hekh. Rabb.*). Others have detected striking parallels between such an experience and shamanism in other cultures (Niditch 1980; Ashton 2000). John tells us that it happened **on the Lord's Day**: while some have argued that he is evoking the Old Testament 'Day of the Lord' as the day of judgement (e.g. Ezek. 13:5; Joel 1:15; Amos 5:20), his precise phrase most likely refers to Sunday, the day of the resurrection and increasingly the day of Christian worship (Mt. 28:1; Acts 20:7; 1 Cor. 16:2; *Did.* 14:1; the same adjective meaning 'belonging to the Lord' is used to describe the Christian Eucharist at 1 Cor. 11:20). It is possible that John had fellow-Christians with him on Patmos, and indeed later traditions mention not only his scribe Prochorus, one of the seven 'deacons', but also a growing band of Christian converts. If so, John would be like other early Christian visionaries who received their revelations during the liturgy (e.g. 1 Cor. 14:6, 30). Or he may be a solitary figure, joining himself 'in spirit' with his fellow-Christians who would have been gathered for worship across the sea. Either way, a liturgical context is evoked. The place of exile, far from the Jerusalem Temple, becomes the place of divine worship as John participates in the heavenly liturgy.

In his trance-like state, John heard behind him **a loud voice**, its volume and power likening it to **a trumpet-blast**. Auditions as well as visions are integral to apocalypses, and the expectation is that a heavenly voice or the voice of an angel is the authoritative voice to be heeded. Though it is not made explicit, verse 12 implies that the voice John hears is that of the exalted Lord, who was expected to be present with his people at the Eucharist. Indeed, there seems to be a concentric pattern to this section, highlighting the central role of what John sees at the heart of the section:

A. John falls into a trance and hears a voice telling him to write (verses 9–11)
   B. John turns to see the voice (12a)
      C. Vision of 'someone like a son of man' (12b–16)
   B′. John falls at his feet (17a)
A′. John hears the voice telling him to write (17b–20)

11 The voice commands him to **write down** what he sees **in a scroll**: this is the first of three scrolls mentioned in Revelation, the second and third being delivered to the Lamb and John respectively. There is debate as to how far the contents of the latter two scrolls are divulged in the book, and whether they are in fact one and the same. There is no doubt about this first scroll, however: it is the very scroll which the audiences of Revelation are hearing read out, for it is to be sent **to the seven congregations**. While **what you see** refers

particularly to the vision John is about to relate and the seven messages which flow from it, it also includes the visions of chapters 4—22, which are included among the contents of this scroll (see 1:4; 22:8). For the first time we are given the names of the cities in which the seven congregations are located. Their order reflects the natural route followed by the deliverer of Revelation, first sailing from Patmos to **Ephesus**, then heading north to **Smyrna** and **Pergamum**, and making a circuit of the major roads, through **Thyatira, Sardis** and **Philadelphia**, to return to Ephesus via **Laodicea** and the Lycus Valley (Ramsay 1904).

John turns to see the voice that was speaking with me. Con- 12 temporary readers will find such an expression jarring, for voices are not generally *seen*. It is a reminder of the bizarre and disturbing nature of apocalyptic vision, which communicates as much by its effect on the hearers as by its ability to be decoded. The first thing he sees are **seven gold menorahs** or lampstands (the same word is used of the golden lampstand/menorah which stood within the Tabernacle: Exod. 25:31–40; 37:17; Zech. 4:2). Like Isaiah before him, who saw a vision of the Lord while in the Temple in Jerusalem (Isaiah 6), John is caught up into a vision of the heavenly sanctuary, on which the earthly was modelled (Exod. 25:40; Heb. 8:5). But John sees seven menorahs, not one. This may have been suggested by the seven lamps which burn on the one lampstand (e.g. Num. 8:2; Zech. 4:2), yet the symbolic significance of that number must be to the fore.

John now attempts to describe the heavenly being at the centre of his 13–15 vision. Exegetes have detected obvious allusions to Daniel 7 and Ezekiel 1, with Dan. 10:5ff. being the dominant influence on John at this point. But before we envisage the seer sitting at his desk on Patmos, scouring a selection of scrolls in front of him, we should note the complex manner by which actual visionary experience is articulated. Mystics describe their visions and auditions in terms drawn from their own cultural heritage; moreover, this heritage has probably also provided patterns to which such visions will conform (Ashton 2000: 114f.). It would be surprising if John had not used the language of Old Testament predecessors to describe his visionary encounter. Yet his echoes of these passages suggests something more complex than straightforward literary borrowing, as does the repeated use of similes, as if he is struggling to express what is ultimately inexpressible.

The figure that he sees is **someone like a son of man**, the precise phrase used at Dan. 7:13 to describe a heavenly figure who is probably the angelic representative of God's people (angels regularly appearing in human form in the apocalypses). John avoids the titular

41

use of the phrase 'the Son of Man' (with the definite article), more common in the Gospels (also *1 En.* 46:3), as if he wishes to stress the angelomorphic nature of this vision. But the description of the figure's hair, **shining white, like wool,** and his eyes **like a fiery flame,** echoes Daniel's description of the hair and throne of the Ancient of Days (Dan. 7:9; the LXX of Dan. 7:13 has the son of man figure coming not 'to' but 'as the Ancient of Days', which may have influenced John's visionary apprehension). This is no mere angel, for he bears some of the traits of God himself, the white-haired Alpha. Moreover, it is the 'man clothed in linen' of Dan. 10:5–9 whom most Jewish Christians would recall on hearing John's description. Similarities between the two include their clothing (though the LXX of Dan. 10:5 omits the **gold belt**), their eyes, and their feet (Daniel: arms and legs) **like polished bronze.** Though often taken to be the archangel Gabriel, this figure seems rather to be an angelic manifestation of the 'Glory of the Lord', the glorious figure of Ezek. 1:26–28 which in certain strands of Jewish tradition seems to have become separated from the divine throne (e.g. *Apoc. Abr.* 11; *Jos. Asen.* 14: Rowland 1980). Finally, Ezekiel's description of the sound made by the cherubim's wings, or the 'glory of the God of Israel', supplies the description of this heavenly figure's voice, **like the sound made by many waters** (Ezek. 1:24; 43:2).

But in all this vision of glory, John can detect the unmistakable features of Jesus Christ. This is a reminder that, from an early stage, Jewish Christians found merely human categories inadequate for saying what they wanted to say about the exalted Jesus, and began to plunder traditions more readily associated with the heavenly realm. Their experience of the risen Lord in worship may have been a particular catalyst for exploring the more mystical elements of Jewish tradition (Hurtado 2003). John's evoking of traditions about exalted angels, and even of God, should not surprise us.

The juxtaposition of the seven menorahs, evoking Temple worship, and the description of Christ's clothing strongly suggests that John sees the son of man figure as High Priest in the heavenly sanctuary. His **long robe** (ποδήρη) and **gold belt wrapped around his breast** echo descriptions of the high-priestly vestments (Josephus, *Ant.* 3.153–55, 159; cf. Exod. 28:4; Lev. 16:4; Wis. 18:24). We know from Hebrews that the understanding of Christ as High Priest in the heavenly sanctuary was able to emerge within New Testament Christianity; Revelation 1 suggests that Hebrews might not be as unique in its christology as is sometimes assumed. If all believers now participate in the priesthood (1:6), and angels fulfil liturgical roles in the worship of heaven (e.g. 8:3–5), a unique role nevertheless remains for Christ. His presence now in the midst of the seven menorahs, that is **the seven congregations** (v. 20), may evoke the high-priestly role of mediator and intercessor (e.g. Heb. 7:25).

But there are two features of this vision which cannot be traced to the 16
main Old Testament antecedents of Daniel 7, 10 and Ezekiel 1. First, the 'someone like a son of man' holds **in his right hand seven stars**, which are interpreted at verse 20 as angels. The Jewish trad-ition had already likened angels to the stars (e.g. Dan. 12:3), perhaps in part a recognition of their controlling influence on human lives. But early Christians claimed that the exalted Christ had been raised far above 'all rule and authority and power and dominion' (Eph. 1:21). He is the one who controls even the stars, thus breaking the shackles of fatalistic worldviews (Barr 1998: 47). Second, he has a **sharp, double-edged sword** coming **out of his mouth**. This prepares us for the great battle which is about to be played out on the pages of Revelation, and warns us that this will be no ordinary battle. For the sword is the only weapon which the Lamb's forces will employ. It is the word of God, cutting more keenly than any double-edged sword (Heb. 4:12), which emerges from the Messiah's mouth (cf. Isa. 11:4; *Pss Sol.* 17:23–25; *4 Ez.* 13:8–11). Faithful testimony to the truth, even if that should lead to death, is the way of Jesus Christ and of those called to imitate him.

Visionary texts regularly describe the terrifying effects of such 17–18
encounters on the recipients (e.g. Ezek. 1:28; Dan. 10:15). So awe-some is John's vision that he falls **at his feet as if dead**. Many artists have attempted to present the awesome majesty of this scene, recognising that words alone cannot convey what the seer wishes to express. Yet there is a reassuring aspect to the action and words of this son of man figure: **But he laid his right hand on me and said, 'Stop being afraid!'** Similar words are used by the Synoptic Jesus to reassure his disciples after they witness another visionary event, the Transfiguration (Mt. 17:7). What is lacking is any remonstration of John for what could be understood as a posture of worship (see also 5:8, 13; contrast 19:10 and 22:8–9, where John is rebuked by an angel). The Jesus who died is appropriately to be worshipped as more than an angel (see also Mt. 28:17; Lk. 24:52).

Here we have the first explicit reference to Christ's resurrection. Echoing the 'Alpha and O' saying of God at 1:8, Jesus declares that **I am the First and the Last** (already implied in the whiteness of his hair, which is that of the Ancient of Days). Aspects of divinity have now been transferred to the Human One who died but now is **the Living One**, who is **alive for ever and ever**. As the Apocalypse unfolds, we shall be constantly reminded of the great irony that one who was crucified by agents of the apparently invincible empire is himself truly invincible. There may even be a sideswipe at prevalent pagan myths, in the declaration that Christ, not any rival deity such as Hekate, holds **the keys to Death and to Hades** (Aune 1997: 104).

19–20   The mysterious man clothed in linen that Daniel saw was sent to help him understand 'what will happen to your people at the end of days' (Dan. 10:14). Now that the end of days has arrived, the exalted Christ comes to John to show him **both what is now happening and what is to happen after this.** This showing (as 1:1 has led us to expect) will take place in the symbolic visions of this book (**what you see**, another epistolary aorist). Those who read Revelation in a futurist way understand verse 19 to refer to three chronological phases corresponding to three sections of the book: 'what you have seen' (1:12–20); 'what now is' (chapters 2—3); 'what is to come after this' (chapters 4—22). But Revelation cannot be reduced to such a tidy chronological pattern. More likely, a rather untidy mixture of past, present and future realities are implied (cf. *Ep. Barn.* 1:7). In any case, John is given a crucial role in committing these realities to writing, so that they may benefit the seven congregations. This command to **write down what you see** may indicate that the current vision functions as some kind of commissioning for John the prophet (though there will be another in chapter 10).

Finally, the **secret** or 'mystery' (a popular apocalyptic word: e.g. Dan. 2:18, 19, 27, 30, 47) of the **seven stars** and **seven gold menorahs** is uncovered. Such is the complexity of apocalyptic imagery that the interpreting angel often has a crucial role in making clear what particular details mean (this is especially the case in Daniel and *4 Ezra*). This is one of the rare occasions, however, where John passes on specific explanations. This relative lack of explicit interpretation gives John's visions a fluidity and multivalency which discourages the kind of detailed decoding to which interpreters often succumb. But the interpretations at this point tie this vision more firmly to the seven messages which are immediately to follow. Walking in the midst of the **seven gold menorahs**, the risen Christ is never very far from **the seven congregations**, witnessing their tribulations and their complacency. In an apocalypse such as this with its regular reference to angels in heaven, **the angels of the seven congregations** are surely not merely human leaders, whether monarchical bishops or prophets (for a survey of the options, see Aune 1997: 108–12). Most likely Revelation evokes the Israelite belief that each nation or people had its corresponding heavenly guardian. These angels are the angelic representatives of the seven congregations, who are ultimately answerable for the failures of their earthly charges.

The Messages to the Angels of the Seven Congregations (2:1—3:22)

John, or his scribe, now begins to transcribe seven messages, as they emerge from the lips of the exalted Christ. 'Someone like a son of man' is the speaker, and the seer of Patmos presents himself simply as the prophetic vehicle of the divine word to the churches. Although the contents of Revelation 2—3 are often described as 'the letters to the seven churches' (and 2 Bar. 78–87 shows that letters are not out of place in apocalypses), what we find here is rather more akin to public proclamations or prophetic oracles (Aune 1990). Those who knew the Greek Old Testament would recognise the introductory formula τάδε λέγει as a rather archaic, biblical-sounding phrase, the 'Thus says the Lord' of Israel's prophets. Israelite prophetic oracles were sometimes conveyed in letter form (e.g. Elijah's letter at 2 Chron. 21:12–15; letter of Jeremiah to the exiles, Jeremiah 29), and the prophet John resorts to this to compensate for his physical absence from the seven congregations. Christian converts from a pagan background might also recall Greek oracles such as 'Thus says Zeus'; others would hear the solemn introductions to Persian royal decrees (e.g. 2 Chron. 36:23) or Roman imperial edicts. The voice of the Lord, who is the true King, thunders once again, albeit speaking with the accent of Jesus Christ (the recurring 'Let the one with an ear listen . . .' is but one of those points at which the exalted Lord of Revelation speaks with the voice of the Jesus of the Gospels, e.g. Mt. 13:9; Mk 4:23; Lk. 14:35).

Nor should it be overlooked that these are not primarily divine messages to the seven congregations (despite 1:11), but rather to their angels, as befits an apocalypse. The churches are no mere sociological phenomena, but spiritual realities, which have their guardian or representative on the heavenly plane (for the close relationship between angelic and earthly individuals and institutions, see Deut. 32:8 LXX; Dan. 10:13, 20; 12:1; Acts 12:15; Jub. 35:17; Jos. Asen. 14; and possibly 1 Cor. 2:6, 8). Despite appearances to the contrary, the apocalyptic tradition does not sharply distinguish heaven from earth, but claims there is an intimate connection between the two (hence the seven messages can occasionally lapse from the second person singular into the plural, e.g. 2:10, 24). Characters and events seen in heaven reveal what is the case, and what will be, in the world below. Yet there is a certain irony in the fact that John, a human being, now has a role of mediator of heavenly mysteries to angels, in contrast to the chain of communication of 1:1 (but akin to a figure like Enoch: e.g. 1 Enoch 13). Or perhaps this is appropriate, for John is a witness to the revelation of Jesus Christ, that into which angels longed to look (1 Pet. 1:12).

All seven messages follow a similar format (Aune 1990):

(i) 'To the angel of the congregation in X, write';
(ii) a *praescriptio* consisting of the prophetic 'Thus says' formula, and a christological title linking each message to the preceding vision of 'someone like a son of man';
(iii) a *narratio* consisting of a description of each community, its past and present, introduced by the verb 'I know';
(iv) the *dispositio*, which forms the heart of the message, often including a command to 'remember' and 'repent';
(v) the recurring phrase 'Let the one with an ear listen...';
(vi) a promise to the victor. (The order of (v) and (vi) is reversed in the final four messages.)

Within this structure, however, there is a good deal of variety, particularly in the *narratio* and *dispositio*. For all their stereotypical form, and their 'public' nature, the seven messages reflect in part the particular challenges and idiosyncrasies of specific congregations (or of their angels). Many commentators, indeed, have stressed the function of Revelation 2—3 in grounding the symbolic visions of chapters 4—22 in the cut and thrust of first-century Asian Christian life. This is surely a crucial aspect of interpretation, and the work of Sir William Ramsay and Colin Hemer has highlighted the extent of local allusions to the cities of Asia (Ramsay 1904; Hemer 1986). These messages provide clues as to the social situation of the churches, their trials and their compromises, external pressures and internal rivalries. What the heavenly 'someone like a son of man' shines his spotlight on are not perfect churches of some ideal apostolic age, but real, vulnerable, and at times tarnished communities.

Yet historical reconstruction is not the only function of the commentator, and over-emphasis on the first-century situation (many details of which are now lost to us) may cause us to neglect other aspects of the text's meaning. Even in the first century, the specific messages would have been regarded as having a wider application to all seven congregations (and others in the province also, symbolically included in the sevenfold church). All seven messages would have been read out to all the churches, with the recurring refrain to 'listen to what the Spirit is saying to the congregations'. Moreover, the 'public' nature of the oracle/proclamation form also suggests a wider address. This has led many in the history of interpretation to attend to the challenge of the seven messages to the whole Church in every age. Over these two chapters, with their juxtaposition of comfort and challenge, rebuke and encouragement, one can find every state of the Church and every conceivable type of Christian addressed (Kovacs and Rowland 2004: 54–58).

To Ephesus (2:1–7)

(1) 'Write this to the angel of the congregation in Ephesus:
"Thus says the one who holds the seven stars in his right hand, who walks in the middle of the seven gold menorahs:
(2) I know your deeds, your hard work and your perseverance. I know that you cannot tolerate evildoers, and that you have tested those who call themselves 'apostles' but are not, and have found them to be liars. (3) I know too that you have perseverance and have tolerated much as a result of my name, and have not grown weary. (4) But I have this against you: you have let go of the love you had at first.
(5) So remember from where you have fallen; repent and act as you did before. Otherwise, if you do not repent, I shall come to you and remove your menorah from its place. (6) However, you have this in your favour: you hate the deeds of the Nikolaitans, just as I do.
(7) Let the one with an ear listen to what the Spirit is saying to the congregations. I will allow the one who conquers to eat fruit from the tree of life, which is in God's paradise."

The first message that John is commanded to **write** is addressed to **the angel of the congregation** in the great city of **Ephesus**. Ephesus would have been the first of the seven congregations reached by a traveller arriving from Patmos by sea. The city known to John, situated in the valley between the two hills Panayir Dağ and Bülbül Dağ, retained its importance as a seaport and commercial centre, despite the silting up of its harbours. This, along with ease of access by land routes, accounts for its cosmopolitan feel, the presence of oriental cults including Judaism, and its important role as centre of Christianity in the province. Ephesus had long been renowned for its Temple of Artemis Ephesia, considered one of the seven wonders of the ancient world (e.g. Acts 19:27). But imperial Rome had also left its mark in striking terms on the city, from its state *agora* with a temple to the goddess Roma and Divus Julius, through its statue-lined streets of gleaming marble, to the impressive theatre capable of seating 25,000.

Christ addresses himself to the angel of the Ephesian congregation as **the one who holds the seven stars in his right hand, who walks in the middle of the seven gold menorahs**. The christological titles at the beginning of each of the seven messages are drawn either from John's terrifying vision of 'someone like a son of man', or from the concluding visions of Revelation 19—22. This heightens for the audience the imaginative effect of the inaugural vision (whose kaleidoscopic images are allowed to do their work one by one), as well as tying these messages into the book as a whole. The liturgical context in which Revelation would have been read is important here: far from the great Ephesian temples to Artemis or Serapis, perhaps in back-street houses or hired halls, tiny groups of Christians are invited to enter imaginatively into a rival temple, whose high priest walks in the middle of the seven menorahs. Rather as God walked in Eden in the cool of the evening (Gen. 3:8), this is a potentially reassuring image for Christians who find themselves in the minority, or facing a dominant culture which is perceived as threatening. They are part of the true sanctuary where the great High Priest ministers, and participate in that heavenly liturgy in their own liturgical assemblies. So too, the Ephesian angel is reminded that he and his heavenly colleagues are held secure as **the seven stars** in Christ's **right hand**. Yet, as vision after vision in this book will make clear, how divine action is perceived depends upon where one stands. The holding of seven stars/angels is not simply a sign of security, but also of control by the one who is now higher than the angels and victorious over all rival powers (e.g. Eph. 1:21; Heb. 1:4; 2:9). Similarly, the presence of Christ with his people may be experienced either as salvation or as judgement.

2–3   The *narratio* of the Ephesian message is initially promising. The angel is praised for **your deeds, your hard work and your perseverance**. It begins, as in all seven messages, with the phrase **I know**, for the omniscient Lord has his finger on the pulse of the whole Church. The word **deeds** is not meant to suggest some kind of 'works-righteousness', an idea which is probably far less Jewish than Christian exegetes have often wanted to claim (see Sanders 1977). Indeed, both Jewish and Christian texts envisage that it will be in accordance with one's works, as a loving response to the divine call, that one will ultimately be judged (e.g. Rev. 20:12). The vocation of Christians in continuing the faithful witness of Jesus is here stressed: the Ephesian angel, and those whom he represents, are praised for their **hard work** and **perseverance**. Revelation continually uses the language of struggle and faithful endurance, even when the battle is far from evident to those hearing its message.

Yet there is no indication in this message that hostility is external. Rather the angel of the Ephesian congregation is praised for testing and finding wanting **those who call themselves 'apostles'**. How an angel might express disapproval of Christians in his charge is not made clear (though Paul may be concerned with just such angelic disapproval, of liturgical misdemeanours in this case, at 1 Cor. 11:10). The language of 'so-called apostles' suggests internal dissensions within the Christian community, akin to battles that Paul had with those he considered 'false apostles' in Corinth (2 Cor. 11:13). Indeed, given that John's later vision of the new Jerusalem bears the names of only 'twelve apostles of the Lamb' (21:14), some regard this verse as a sideswipe at Paul's claims to apostleship in the city in the previous generation (cf. 1 Cor. 9:1). The precise situation is now lost to us, however, since Revelation resorts to the kind of stereotypical language regularly found in Jewish and Christian writings to describe religious enemies, whose own voice is rarely heard (e.g. 2 Pet. 2:1–3; Jude 8). Though the phrase **evildoers** suggests that the issue has more to do with ethics than doctrine, even this may be stock language.

Such disagreements between different Christian groups in Ephesus are perhaps unsurprising. New Testament references to Ephesus remind us that various trajectories of early Christians could come together in one location. Paul and his circle (Acts 18:19–21; 19:1—20:1; 1 Cor. 16:8–9; Eph. 1:1; 1 Tim. 1:3), Apollos (Acts 18:24–26), John (e.g. Iren. *Adv. Haer.* 3.1.1; 3.2.4; Eus. *H. E.* 3.31.3; 3.39.1–7) and the disciples of the Baptist (Acts 19:1–7) are all associated with this city. This should warn against the scholarly tendency to imagine the early communities as self-contained congregations of Pauline, Petrine and Johannine believers. Nevertheless, in a city of the size of Ephesus (estimated as a quarter of a million in the first century) it would be possible for a number of house- and even synagogue-churches to emerge. Tensions between these, and even within these, are to be expected. How one deals with such tensions depends in part upon how firm one believes the boundaries separating church from world should be. John's apocalyptic vision of impending crisis calls for strong boundaries which cannot countenance internal dissension, or much haziness in the distinction between 'insiders' and 'outsiders' (see e.g. Thompson 1990). Other voices within the New Testament canon advocate a rather different approach (e.g. 1 Corinthians 8—10; 1 Timothy 1—2).

The angel is also praised for **perseverance** and because he has **tolerated much as a result of my name**. This need not refer to organised persecution, but to more general hostility and difficulties facing a distinctive, countercultural group within a city like Ephesus. Alternatively, it could be related to the internal ecclesial dissensions. Whatever may have been the case, Revelation again uses the language of the eschatological woes to heighten the sense of crisis and – through their angel – to encourage the members of the Church, or that Ephesian congregation faithful to John, to hold fast.

All is not well, however. The angel has **let go of the love you had 4–5 at first**. To ask whether this is love for God or love for human beings is probably a false dichotomy: the two are intimately related. Nevertheless, this failure of Ephesus' angel (and Christians associated with him) is probably especially manifested in lack of love towards other Christians. Love growing cold is one of the expected features of the end-times (Mt. 24:12), another indication of Revelation's rhetoric of eschatological crisis. *Didache* 16:3 interprets this saying of Jesus as love turning to hate. Passion for truth, especially religious truth, can so easily degenerate into an unloving witch-hunt against those with whom one disagrees. Hatred of deeds is one thing (see v. 6), hatred of brothers and sisters something else entirely (1 Jn 2:11; 3:15).

This rebuke links the 'what is the case' of the *narratio* to the 'this is what you must do' of the *dispositio* which begins at verse 5: **So remember from where you have fallen; repent and act as you did before.** The Ephesian angel is jolted out of his complacency by being described as a **fallen** angel. That he is not in the same league as Satan and his angels (Rev. 12:9), however, is made clear by his ability to **repent and act as you did before.** This call to repentance or change of mind will also be made to the angels at Pergamum, Sardis and Laodicea (2:16; 3:3, 19; the angel in Sardis is also urged to 'remember'), and to the followers of 'Jezebel' at Thyatira (2:22). The angel of the congregation in Ephesus is not irredeemably fallen. Nor are those humans he represents. Repentance will be a recurring theme throughout the Apocalypse. Not only will it be offered to the churches; one of the purposes of the heavenly plagues will be to lead those who worship the monster to repentance (e.g. 9:20; 16:9). The alternative is that Christ will **come to you and remove your menorah from its place.** The coming of Christ, whether on the last day or in the Eucharist, can be experienced as either salvation (as at 3:11) or judgement (here and at 2:16). This warning is generally taken as a threat to the Ephesian congregation that it will lose its status as the pre-eminent church in the province, or even its very status as a church, unless it repents. Yet these words are addressed not to the congregation/menorah itself, but to the angel who has charge of that menorah. It is just possible that it is the angel's position as heavenly representative of that church which is under threat: the menorah is not being well tended, and it is in danger of being removed into the care of another.

6 The demanding call to repentance is mitigated somewhat by what the angel has **in your favour**: sharing the son of man figure's hatred of **the deeds of the Nikolaitans** (though not the Nikolaitans themselves). Though this echoes what is said about the 'false apostles' in verse 2, we should not automatically assume that the two groups are identical. No further details are given here of the Nikolaitans, who seem not to have made inroads into the Ephesian congregation. We

shall have a clearer (though still rather opaque) picture of them in the message to Pergamum, and possibly also in the message to Thyatira (see below on 2:14–15, 20). Later patristic descriptions which claim that this group was named after Nicolaus of Antioch, one of the seven deacons of Acts 6, and associated with Gnosticism (e.g. Iren. *Adv. Haer.* 1.26.3; Tert. *Praesc. Haer.* 33; Eus. *H. E.* 3.29.1), may be of little help in shedding light on the actual historical situation.

The message concludes, as will all seven, with two stereotypical 7 sayings. Both indicate how a message to the angels can turn almost imperceptibly into one for the Christians in their charge. The first, **Let the one with an ear listen to what the Spirit is saying to the congregations**, echoes a Synoptic saying of Jesus (also *Gos. Thom.* 8, 21, 24, 63, 65, 96), and is a reminder that what is said to one congregation is for the benefit of all the congregations. Here, as in the Synoptic parables discourses (e.g. Mk 4:9, 23), the call to listen points to a particular kind of discernment, a hint that heavenly secrets are being offered to those with ears attuned. That the Spirit is mentioned as speaking may strike one as odd, given that the exalted Christ has been the subject so far. We need not conclude that for John, Christ and the Spirit are identical (that would make nonsense of a saying such as 22:17). Rather the saying emphasises the role of the Spirit of prophecy throughout the Apocalypse in mediating the message of the risen Lord.

The second saying consists of a promise to **the one who conquers**, linking individual Christians with the victorious Christ. The language of victory, frequent in the Johannine tradition (e.g. 1 Jn 2:13; 4:4; 5:4; Rev. 11:7; 17:14), reminds us that in the apocalyptic language of this book there is a battle being fought, albeit one whose outcome has already been established. In each of the seven messages, what is promised points us forward to the visions of salvation with which Revelation ends. Here the conqueror is promised **fruit from the tree of life, which is in God's paradise**. Jewish hopes for God's future sometimes spoke in terms of a restoration of what had been lost, 'Paradise regained' (e.g. *1 En.* 25:4–6; *3 En.* 23:18; *T. Levi* 18:10–11). The tree of life (Gen. 2:9; 3:22) will appear again in the new Jerusalem (22:2), producing fruit for the healing of the nations. Eating at the messianic banquet, of which the Eucharist is a current foretaste, will be an integral part of the new age.

But there is probably also a local reference, which first-century Ephesian Christians would detect. The Artemisium of Ephesus contained a tree-shrine which functioned as a place of asylum, enclosed within a boundary wall. 'Paradise' is derived from a Persian word meaning 'enclosure', 'garden' or royal park. What the victorious among God's people are offered is a far greater sanctuary than the temple 'paradise' of Ephesian Artemis. Indeed, there may even be a hint here of how the battle has been won, for the tree of life would evoke in the Christian mind the cross of Christ, the means by which victory is assured (e.g. Acts 5:30; 10:39; Gal. 3:13; 1 Pet. 2:24).

To Smyrna (2:8–11)

(8) 'Write this to the angel of the congregation in Smyrna:
"Thus says the First and the Last, who was dead but came back to life:

(9) I know your tribulation and your poverty (though in reality you are rich), and the slander you receive from those who call themselves 'Jews' and are not but are a synagogue of Satan.

(10) Do not be afraid of anything you are going to suffer. Look! The devil is going to put some of you in prison so that you may be tested, and you will endure tribulation for ten days. Be faithful, even if that leads to death, and I will give you the wreath of life.

(11) Let the one with an ear listen to what the Spirit is saying to the congregations.
The one who conquers will not be harmed by the second death." '

The second message is delivered to **the angel of the congregation in Smyrna** (present-day Izmir), a port city with a population in Roman times of 100,000 located an estimated thirty-five miles north of Ephesus. Built in an impressive setting at the foot of Mount Pagros, it was called by Strabo 'the most beautiful city of all' (Strabo 14.1.37). Smyrna had had a temple to the goddess Roma since 195 BCE (the first in Asia Minor), and a temple to Tiberius had been added in 26 CE. The city also had a sizeable Jewish population. The New Testament is silent as to the origins of the church there. According to Smyrna's bishop Polycarp (d. 155), the Smyrneans had not yet come to know Christ when Paul wrote to the Philippians (Pol. *Phil.* 11:3). Nevertheless, a tradition preserved in Pionius' *Life of Polycarp* 2 claims that Paul visited the city having arrived in Asia from Galatia, i.e. during his second missionary journey (Acts 18:23; 19:1; Acts 19:26 speaks of Paul's activity 'in almost the whole of Asia').

8 Again the exalted Christ introduces himself by titles drawn from the opening vision (1:17–18). The divine oracle **Thus says** comes from **the First and the Last, who was dead but came back to life**. The first part of this title, 'the First and the Last', evokes Christ's

eternal status, as the one present at creation and the goal of the historical process. Many detect in the phrase 'who was dead but came back to life' an allusion to the city's history, for Smyrna too had 'come back to life' when it rose from the ruins *c.* 300 BCE after its destruction some three centuries previously. Yet that is not the primary focus of the message. The story which will unfold throughout the Apocalypse is of a victory won not by killing but by allowing oneself to be killed. The death and resurrection of the Lamb (parodied by beastly imitators, e.g. 13:3, 11) offers the paradigm for true Christian witness. Indeed, even the city's name (Greek for 'myrrh') provides a symbolic connection with the Christ who was anointed with myrrh after his death (Jn 19:39; cf. Mt. 2:11), but rose from the grave.

Whereas the *narratio* in most of the other letters begins with 'I know 9 your works' (either positively or negatively), the knowledge which Christ has of the Smyrnean angel is of **your tribulation and your poverty**. That actual hardship and material poverty is in view is implied by the reference to **slander**, and the antithesis **though in reality you are rich**. This is a clear example of apocalyptic unveiling: what in the world's eyes looks like poverty is revealed as true riches, a theme also unveiled in the Beatitudes (Mt. 5:3; cf. Lk. 12:21; 2 Cor. 6:10; 8:9; Eph. 3:8, 16). A similar idea may be expressed at Jas 2:5, which speaks of God having chosen the poor in the world to be 'rich in faith'. Similarly, the word **tribulation** interprets their local sufferings as part of those crucial tribulations of the end-times (e.g. Mt. 24:21), understood as in some way hastening the End (cf. Rev. 6:9-11). In contrast to the complacency and compromises of their wealthier brothers and sisters in other cities, the poor Smyrnean Christians have not lost their sense of dependence upon God, a characteristic manifest in their heavenly personification, the angel. This may point to the small size and socio-economic makeup of the congregation in Smyrna, or equally their withdrawal from the public life of their city, with its consequent financial implications.

However many they are, they have been subject to **slander** from **those who call themselves 'Jews'**. Again, the apocalyptic mentality comes into play as these 'Jews' are unveiled as in reality **a synagogue of Satan** (and again, the stereotypical language makes precision about their identity impossible). Many would see this as an attack on hostile members of the non-Christian Jewish synagogue, who have rejected rival claims of Christians to be 'true Jews', possibly expelling them from the synagogue community (a similar situation is envisaged at Jn 9:22) and reporting them to local magistrates. Cut loose from the Jewish community, Christians would have lost the privileges accorded to Judaism as a *religio licita* and been more vulnerable to prosecution for refusal to worship the local gods, whose goodwill was necessary for the maintenance of public order, or to participate in the imperial cult (a sign of disloyalty). This is a plausible hypothesis: the language of slander could well allude to delation to the civic authorities, and the references to **Satan** ('the accuser') and **the devil** (a word meaning 'calumniator', 'seducer' or 'accuser'), as well as the warning of imprisonment in verse 10, also point to legal proceedings against Christians.

But that is not the only reading of the evidence. Given the role of the Smyrnean Jewish community in the arrest and martyrdom of Polycarp, commentators have perhaps been too ready to read an identical situation into Revelation. Yet all we can be sure of is that the rival group accused of 'slandering' the Christians of Smyrna claim the title of 'Jew' for themselves. A second possibility is that they are Jewish Christians, perhaps of a rival 'synagogue' or 'congregation' in this sprawling city, who are understood to be too closely accommodated to the 'satanic' culture of the province and the empire. Later on, we shall discover how the dragon **Satan** is the power behind the imperial monster (13:1–2), and therefore that all those seduced by what it has to offer have unwittingly sold their souls to Satan. Paul, in a previous generation, could use equally harsh polemic against Jewish-Christian Judaisers, effectively undermining their claims to the title 'Jew' (e.g. Phil. 3:2). The Fourth Gospel testifies not only to the 'family squabbles' between expelled Christian Jews and their non-messianic counterparts; the charge that 'you are from your father the devil' is specifically aimed at 'the Jews who had believed in' Jesus (Jn 8:31, 44). Alternatively the rival group could be Christians from a Gentile background who had Judaised in order to escape hostility from the authorities (Wilson 1992: 613–15, who sees avoidance of persecution as the particular issue; Michaels 1997: 74). Gentile-Christian Judaisers would fit in a very literal sense the charge of being people **who call themselves 'Jews' and are not**. However, it is less clear whether a group of Gentiles by themselves would be appropriately described as a 'synagogue'. Of the three possibilities, the first and second options are more persuasive. Sadly, however, John's allusive references do not allow us to identify the 'opponents' definitively.

One kind of slander is often reciprocated by another, hence these slanderers are called **a synagogue of Satan**. This sort of name-calling has a powerful place in religious and political rhetoric, and is regularly found in the biblical tradition. Biblical writers suffered fewer scruples than some of their modern critics about negative stereotyping of those with whom they disagreed (though see the possible critique of this at Jas 3:9). However, the contemporary interpreter cannot be deaf to the sometimes malevolent 'history of effects' of passages such as this. A number of considerations need to be taken into account here. First, one should remember that such intemperate language reflects the heat of debate, mediated to us through John's visionary perspective. Moreover, in its first-century setting addressed to Smyrna, it articulates the perspective of the threatened minority. Such sayings, however, contain the potential for great harm when that minority subsequently becomes the powerful majority, and real synagogue communities occupy the position of the underdog. Second, it is surely significant that the speaker in this case is not John, or any other Christian leader, but the exalted Christ himself. This is the heavenly voice, which challenges all hearers to consider their own position and adjust their perspective accordingly. When his earthly followers take it on themselves to demonise others, however, they are all the more susceptible to arrogance and self-deception. Finally, whatever anti-Semitic effects this verse subsequently engendered, the use of the word 'Jew' here is almost certainly wholly positive (unlike its usage in the Fourth Gospel). God's people are recognised as such in that they are legitimate heirs to the traditions of Israel, like the seer himself. Those who are too closely associated, wittingly or otherwise, with the satanic empire forfeit the right to the name of Jew.

Recognising your dependence upon God, and witnessing to that fact, 10 may well lead you into suffering. Indeed, it is part of the expected eschatological scenario that God's people would be a particular focus of the devil's activity, and for Christians this was given added poignancy in the light of the actual sufferings of Christ (e.g. Col. 1:24). In its Matthean version, the Lord's Prayer teaches Christ's disciples to pray that they may be rescued from the Evil One in the time of trial (Mt. 6:13). The vocabulary of being **tested** and enduring **tribulation** evokes this role of believers in the last days (a role already taken up by John on Patmos, 1:9). So the angel is told **not** to **be afraid of anything you are going to suffer**. This is one of the rare occasions in the seven messages that actual or impending hostility is mentioned: the paucity of such references counts against readings of Revelation as a response to fierce state persecution. Nor is it explicitly stated that the impending suffering is directly due to the slander of the 'so-called Jews' (though this is often assumed, particularly in the light of the Polycarp story).

If there is uncertainty about the instigators, the precise action is clear: **The devil**, presumably acting through civic authorities, **is going to put some of you in prison**. The subtle shift from the second person singular to the plural at this point is yet another indication of the close relationship between the heavenly angel and his earthly counterparts in the Church. The warning of prison is a serious one, for prisons in the ancient world were not primarily long-stay institutions, but places where prisoners were detained to await trial, which often meant awaiting death (e.g. Phil. 1:3–26; 2 Tim. 4:6–8). The purpose of this is **that you may be tested**, a phrase evoking Satan's testing of Jesus in the wilderness prior to his public ministry (Mk 1:13), as well as the 'time of trial' of the Lord's Prayer (Mt. 6:13). As if to provide some reassurance in the dark days ahead, the angel is told that the **tribulation** will only last **for ten days**. In the numerological symbolism of this book, ten days denotes a limited period: the phrase evokes the testing of Daniel and his Judaean companions at the hands of the Babylonians (Dan. 1:12, 14; cf. *Jub.* 19:8; *T. Jos.* 2:7). Ultimately, however, it will be the devil who finds himself thrown into prison (20:1–3).

Nevertheless, we should not underestimate the seriousness of the battle: **Be faithful, even if that leads to death**. Faithful witness to the point of shedding one's blood will be a recurring theme in the visions that follow. That does not mean that Revelation expects all Christians to become martyrs. But its uncompromising call is for all Christians to reconsider their commitment vis-à-vis their surrounding culture, and place themselves in a situation where they might well find themselves being opposed and even persecuted. The Christians of Smyrna, like those in Philadelphia (3:7–13), score high on the scale of faithful witness: the angels of these cities are the only two of the seven who are not warned either to 'remember' or 'repent'. Many Christian brethren in the other cities will be found severely wanting.

Fidelity even to death will result in **the wreath of life** (cf. Jas 1:12). The wreath (Greek στέφανος) or garland was used in the ancient world in a range of contexts, signifying such ideas as honour, victory, joy and peace. The wreath is worn elsewhere in Revelation by the twenty-four elders (4:4, 10), the woman clothed with the sun (12:1) and 'someone like a son of man' (14:14). Victory seems to be the dominant theme, as also in the two negative references: a gold wreath is worn by the rider on the white horse who comes out to conquer (6:2), and the demonic locusts wear what look like wreaths of gold (9:7, possibly a demonic parody). So here too, the paradoxical gospel victory through dying will be rewarded by the victor's **wreath of life**. John's first audience may well also have detected a local allusion to the wreath or garland of leaves awarded to victorious athletes, for Smyrna was well known for its games (Swete 1906: 32).

11 The recurring call to **listen to what the Spirit is saying to the congregations** is repeated here, as if to remind us that the summons to faithful witness even to death is meant to be the witness of the whole Church. Then comes the promise: **The one who conquers**

will not be harmed by the second death. It was the early Christian conviction that by his resurrection Christ had conquered the power even of death itself (e.g. 1 Cor. 15:26), and John has already encountered him as the one who holds the keys of Death and Hades (1:18). Followers of Christ may not be promised here rescue from physical death; indeed, they are positively encouraged to court it. But the second death will not harm them. The phrase appears again in chapter 20 to describe the ultimate fate of those on the side of Satan and the monster, being thrown into 'the lake of fire' (20:14; 21:8). Those beheaded for the testimony of Jesus will be immune from the power of this second death (20:4–6). A significant parallel in the Targum on Jer. 51:39, 57 seems to interpret this death as annihilation: 'they shall die the second death and shall not live in the world to come' (Harrington 1993: 60), though at least on the surface Rev. 20:10 seems to count against this. But the fate of others is not at issue here: what is crucial is the promise to those facing the current, impending crisis. However satanic the circumstances may seem, believers are to remain confident in the outcome and firm in their faithful witness, for the devil has been definitively defeated.

To Pergamum   (2:12–17)

(12) 'Write this to the angel of the congregation in Pergamum: "Thus says the one who has the sharp, double-edged sword:

(13) I know where you are living, where Satan's throne is situated. Yet you are holding on to my name, and you did not deny your faith in me even in the time [of] Antipas my trustworthy witness, who was put to death among you, where Satan lives. (14) But I have a few things against you. You have some people there who hold to the teaching of Balaam. He taught Balak to set a trap for the children of Israel, leading them to eat meat that had been sacrificed to idols and thus to be unfaithful. (15) In the same way you too have people who hold to the teaching of the Nikolaitans.

(16) So repent. Otherwise, I shall come to you soon and wage war with these people with the sword of my mouth.

(17) Let the one with an ear listen to what the Spirit is saying to the congregations.

I will give the one who conquers some of the hidden manna, and also a white stone, with a new name written on it which no-one knows except the one who receives it." '

Continuing about forty miles north from Smyrna, one reaches the impressive city of **Pergamum**, dominated by its acropolis rising to a height of 900 feet above the Caicus Plain. A conservative estimate puts the population of Roman Pergamum at 120,000 (Aune 1997: 181). Visitors today can still see the base of the Great Altar of Zeus Soter (the altar itself is in the Pergamum Museum in Berlin), the theatre built precariously on the slope, and an early second-century Temple of Trajan. Literary evidence reveals that a temple to Dea Roma and the emperor Augustus had been dedicated in Pergamum in 29 BCE, thus making it an early centre of the imperial cult. In the plain below was located the shrine of the healing god Asklepius, whose cult had been introduced to the city in the fourth century BCE (though the shrine became most extensive in the second century CE). Scholars continue to debate whether the city was still the capital of the Roman province, or had ceded that privilege to Ephesus (for this debate, see Hemer 1986: 82–84). Its role as a centre of the imperial cult, however, is not in doubt.

12 The exalted Christ introduces himself as **the one who has the sharp, double-edged sword** (1:16). Though there may well be a local allusion here, perhaps to the proconsular *ius gladii* or *imperium* (Hemer 1986: 71), the primary reference is to the all-powerful divine word, which issues forth from the mouth of the Messiah (19:15, 21; cf. Isa. 11:4; 49:2; Heb. 4:12; *4 Ez.* 13:10). In the battle in which the Pergamene angel and his human charges are involved, there will be no weapons allowed except the word of faithful witness, the truth which will reveal the lie for what it is (12:11; cf. Jn 18:37–38). Any Roman judgement issued by magistrates or proconsul in Pergamum is insignificant beside the judgement brought to bear by Jesus' witness, and that of his followers.

13 The *narratio* begins with words of encouragement to the **angel** of the Pergamene congregation: **I know where you are living** (rather than the usual 'your works'), **where Satan's throne is situated**. Many commentators accept that **Satan's throne** alludes to a particular feature of the city. The main possibilities are: (a) the Altar of Zeus Soter, or the wider complex including the temples to Zeus and Athena (on the latter, see A. Y. Collins 1998); (b) the Temple to Augustus, symbol of the imperial cult; (c) the healing shrine of Asklepius, one of whose symbols was the serpent Propylon (cf. Rev. 12:9); (d) the whole acropolis, as the seat of Roman power. Not all of these are mutually exclusive (as noted by Caird 1966: 37). That an aspect of Roman rule is implied here is supported by 13:2, which states that the dragon (Satan) gives its 'throne' to the monster from the sea (from where John stands, that monster bears the features of imperial Rome and its emperors). But this surely points to the more significant meaning of this statement: there is a rival throne to the true throne of God, which has been set up on the earth, not only in

Pergamum but wherever opposition to God's kingdom manifests itself. In chapter 4 the true 'throne' or source of authority and justice will be unveiled in heaven, in the light of which all rival claimants to the throne will be unmasked as beastly and satanic.

The angel of the church receives praise for **holding on to my name**, which is reiterated by the phrase **you did not deny your faith in me** (the Greek literally reads 'you did not deny my faith', μου being an objective genitive). Many have linked these words to legal proceedings in which Christians were forced to curse Christ publicly, drawing upon the later correspondence between Pliny the Younger, governor of Bithynia, and the emperor Trajan. But formal proceedings need not be in view. More significantly, this testing time for the angel and the Pergamene church was some time ago: **even in the time [of] Antipas my trustworthy witness, who was put to death among you, where Satan lives**. Variant readings of this verse are clearly scribal attempts to deal with another example of John's idiosyncratic Greek syntax, for the harder reading has **Antipas my trustworthy witness** in the nominative case, rather than the genitive **of Antipas**. The name is a form of Antipatros, which although a Greek name could be used of Jews (Aune 1997: 184). Unfortunately we know nothing more about this Antipas (though see the imaginative fictional correspondence in Longenecker 2003). That only he is mentioned as being **put to death** counts against there having been a systematic persecution of Christians in Pergamum (he may have been no more than the victim of a lynch mob, rather like the protomartyr Stephen, Acts 7:54—8:1). In any case, this was not a recent occurrence. His description as **my trustworthy witness**, however, raises his isolated death to a new significance in the cosmic battle against Satan, setting it alongside the death of that great trustworthy witness, Jesus Christ (1:5). Indeed, his identification as 'witness' probably moves us one stage closer to the early Christian usage of μάρτυς for 'martyr' (cf. *Mart. Pol.* 14:2).

Nevertheless, despite the widespread praise of this angel, Christ has a **14–15** **few things against you** (cf. 2:4). There are some in the congregation **who hold to the teaching of Balaam**. The trustworthy witness has been tarnished. Again we find the stereotypical language of religious polemic. Balaam is not the actual name of a particular individual in Pergamum, but functions as a nickname either for one specific leader or for a group. Most likely the teaching of Balaam and **the teaching of the Nikolaitans** are one and the same (see Charles 1920: I, 52–53 for a possible etymological link). The movement which had been stalled in Ephesus had made severe inroads into the church in Pergamum. Balaam was an ambiguous figure in the Jewish tradition (Boxall 1998), who blessed Israel with a messianic prophecy

(Num. 24:15–19; cf. Mt. 2:1–12), but was also held responsible for the apostasy of the Israelites at Shittim/Peor (Num. 31:16; cf. 25:1–9). Revelation evokes that more negative tradition: **He taught Balak to set a trap for the children of Israel.** With this name-calling, the present situation in Pergamum is transformed into a replay of the ancient biblical story. Pergamum's present-day 'Balaams', the Nikolaitans, are teaching Christians **to eat meat that has been sacrificed to idols and thus to be unfaithful.** The first phrase refers to an issue of great debate among urban Christians, as evidenced by Paul's rather nuanced response (1 Corinthians 8—10). Revelation's more critical words may have been troubling to Christians of a Pauline persuasion. The second phrase (πορνεῦσαι, literally 'commit sexual immorality' or 'practise fornication') is taken here in the metaphorical sense it often has in the LXX, as a metaphor for Israel's infidelity through worshipping other gods (e.g. Hos. 3:3; Ezek. 6:9). In the apocalyptic worldview of this book, no alternative can be allowed to the worship of the true God: even something as apparently innocuous as eating meat could set one on the slippery slope towards idolatry.

16 As in Ephesus, so in Pergamum the angel is urged to **repent**, though here the sin is undue tolerance as opposed to the Ephesian intolerance. Whereas elsewhere in Revelation the coming of the Lord is a cause for urgent and joyous expectation (e.g. 22:17, 20), and Jewish sages discussed whether the coming of the Messiah was dependent upon the repentance of all Israel (Rowland 1998: 579), here it is something which repentance can avert: **Otherwise I shall come to you soon and wage war with these people with the sword of my mouth.** The battle alluded to already, in which Christ's sword is the most destructive weapon, is not simply one between Church and world. Part of the Apocalypse's shocking message is that even those within the churches might find themselves on the wrong side of the battle-lines through cowardice and compromise.

17 But the promise to **the one who conquers** reveals that faithful witness remains a real possibility. The specific gifts mentioned remain rather obscure. The **hidden manna** may refer to a Jewish tradition that the heavenly manna would be given once again in the last days (e.g. *2 Bar.* 29:8; *Sib. Or.* 7:149). A eucharistic reference is not impossible here, given the symbolism of the true manna in John 6: this would make the promise not simply a distant hope, but one in which the victor can participate in the present. The **white stone** may refer to a vote of acquittal (black stones being used for votes of condemnation: e.g. Ovid, *Met.* 15.41–42), declaration that its possessor was among the victors. Alternatively, it could be a ticket of

admission to a public occasion, in this case the Lamb's feast, of which the Eucharist is a foretaste, or a magical amulet to protect its owner from harm (for detailed discussion, see Hemer 1986: 96–104). **White** functions elsewhere in Revelation as the colour of heaven (1:14; 14:14; 20:11) and of victory (3:4–5, 18; 6:2, 11; 7:9, 13; 19:14). The **new name** may refer to a new personal name given to the victor, as in Isa. 62:2. However, given the references to 'my new name' at 3:12 (cf. 19:12; 22:4), it is most likely a reference to the name given to Christ, made known to **the one who receives it** via the same route by which Christ himself received it, that is through suffering (Phil. 2:8–9). A sharp contrast is made with those who have the mark or name of the monster (13:17; 14:11).

To Thyatira   (2:18–29)

(18) 'Write this to the angel of the congregation in Thyatira:
"Thus says the Son of God, whose eyes are like a fiery flame and whose feet are like polished bronze:
(19) I know your deeds, your love and faithfulness, your service and perseverance. I know that you are doing better now than formerly. (20) But I have this against you: you tolerate that woman 'Jezebel', the one who calls herself a prophetess, but teaches my servants to be unfaithful by eating meat that has been sacrificed to idols, and so is leading them astray. (21) I have given her time to repent. But she refuses to repent of her infidelity.
(22) Look! I shall throw her onto a couch, and bring those who have committed adultery with her great tribulation, unless they repent of what she has done. (23) And I will put her children to death. Then all the congregations will know that it is I who search minds and hearts, and will repay each of you according to what you have done. (24) But I say to the rest of you people in Thyatira, who do not follow this teaching, who do not know 'the deep things of Satan' (as they call them): I impose on you no other burden, (25) but that you hold fast to what you already have until I come.
(26) The one who conquers and keeps working for me until the end, I will give authority over the nations. (27) Such a one will shepherd them with an iron sceptre, as earthenware vessels are broken in pieces. (28) And I will give that one the Morning Star, as I have received it from my Father.
(29) Let the one with an ear listen to what the Spirit is saying to the congregations."'

The message to **the angel of the congregation in Thyatira** is the longest of the seven, and occupies the central place in chapters 2–3 (marked also by the new positioning of the 'Let the one with an ear ...' phrase at the end of the letter). This has led some (e.g. Duff 2001) to argue that its subject matter, and particularly John's clash with 'Jezebel', is the key to understanding the whole Apocalypse. While the issues it raises are crucial, and anticipate that fundamental vision of Babylon the Great in chapter 17, the purpose of Revelation cannot be reduced to an internal struggle for the leadership of the Asian churches:

From the perspective of Roman Asia, the choice of **Thyatira** as the fourth congregation is a somewhat surprising one. Though our knowledge of early Christian foundations in Asia is rather sketchy, there may well have been more impressive contenders for inclusion among the 'seven congregations of Asia'. Magnesia-on-the-Meander, for example, which certainly had a well-established church by Ignatius' time, was also located on the circular route which the Apocalypse presumes (situated between Laodicea and Ephesus). There is surely something significant in Revelation's addressing not simply the 'high flyers' among Asian cities, but also those which, from the empire's perspective, appear more modest.

One reaches **Thyatira** by following the main road south-east from Pergamum for about thirty-five miles. Founded originally as a Seleucid colony in a strategic but vulnerable location, it had functioned for much of its life as a military garrison. Inscriptional evidence from the Roman period suggests it was an up-and-coming commercial centre with an unusually large number of trade-guilds and other voluntary associations or *collegia*. Among the guilds, which seem to have been under the patronage of Apollo Tyrimnaeus, were those for wool- and linen-workers, potters, bronze- or coppersmiths, and dyers. This provides an interesting link with Lydia, Paul's convert in Philippi, who was a trader in purple goods from Thyatira (Acts 16:14; her purple dye was probably derived from the local 'madder-root' rather than the more expensive murex shellfish).

18 This is the only time in Revelation that the familiar christological title **Son of God** appears (though see 21:7). In a Jewish context (which dominates in this most Jewish of texts), the word 'son' is used of those who have a close relationship with God and function on his behalf: angels (e.g. Gen. 6:2; Job 1:6), Israel as God's people (e.g. Hos. 11:1), a righteous Israelite (e.g. Wis. 2:13–18), the king as representative of the people (e.g. Pss 2:7; 89:27), and therefore probably the kingly Messiah (on the much debated 4Q246, see J. J. Collins 1995: 154–72). Further allusions to Psalm 2 throughout this message (e.g. 2:26–27 = Ps. 2:8–9) emphasise the royal, messianic aspect. But Revelation seems to share that more exalted view of the

Son of God (or simply 'the Son') found in the Fourth Gospel. This is
reiterated by the two elements derived from the inaugural vision. The
description of his **eyes** as **like a fiery flame** evokes both the heavenly being of Daniel 10 and the throne of the Ancient of Days at
Dan. 7:9 (see above on 1:13–15). The **feet ... like polished bronze**
(χαλκολίβανος is unknown outside Revelation; on its derivation,
see Hemer 1986: 111–17) would probably remind the first hearers not
only of Daniel's vision but also one of Thyatira's cult statues, either
of Apollo Tyrimnaeus or Helios. By speaking thus to an angel (a 'son
of God'), the risen Christ proclaims his exalted status even above the
angelic world; to the citizens of Thyatira, he is their true patron,
beside whom rival 'patrons of the guild' such as Apollo Tyrimnaeus
are idolatrous impostors.

The **angel** at Thyatira receives extensive praise in the *narratio*, for 19
your love and faithfulness, your service and perseverance. In
his perseverance he is likened not only to the Ephesian angel (2:2),
but also to John himself (1:9), which evokes the kind of active
resistance required of all faithful witnesses (indeed, the angel's
faithfulness is also approved). Unlike the angel of Ephesus, however,
love remains a defining feature, as does service (διακονία), the
quality of ministry exemplified by the Lord himself. Indeed, if
anything the angel's rating, and that of his congregation, is on the
rise: **I know that you are doing better now than formerly**.
Those who emphasise the author's literary strategy would see this as
an attempt to win over waverers in Thyatira who might be less
inclined to accept the seer's authority. The rehearsing of an audience's strengths and gifts is a sure way to get them on side. This is all
the more important as preparation for what follows.

The heavenly voice now articulates the angel's one major failure: **you** 20–21
tolerate that woman 'Jezebel'. A number of manuscripts have the
variant reading 'your woman' or 'your wife', perhaps a scribal
accommodation to the Old Testament story, thus criticising the angel
for acting like another Ahab (Swete 1906: 72; others find in this
variant support for the interpretation of the seven angels as bishops of
the churches). Here we have another example of Revelation's name-
calling, this time directed at a leader within the Thyatiran church,
the one who calls herself a prophetess. Jezebel is almost certainly
not her real name: rather, her role and her teaching are being
shockingly recast in the light of the biblical story of Queen Jezebel,
pagan consort of King Ahab of Israel, whose great adversary was the
prophet Elijah (1 Kgs 16ff.). Whether the Thyatiran prophetess was
of Gentile origin, she too is certainly castigated here for polluting the

purity of the people of God, perhaps through blurring the boundaries which demarcated the Church from those outside.

This 'Jezebel' only 'calls herself a prophetess': the denial of her prophetic status, like that of the claims to apostleship of those in Ephesus (2:2), ought to make the audience sit up and listen, for it comes from the voice of the exalted Christ, albeit through his mouthpiece John. However, matters are more complex. Even allowing for a visionary encounter underlying such a message, the prophet or seer plays a crucial role in mediating and interpreting the divine encounter, such that he or she leaves an indelible mark (often unconsciously) on the final message or visionary description. Thus we should not be surprised if something of John's perspective and personal animosity emerges in what he describes. That the angel is said to **tolerate** her points to her widespread recognition as a prophet within Thyatira itself (a challenge to John's own prophetic credentials).

Her crime, namely that she **teaches my servants to be unfaithful by eating meat that has been sacrificed to idols**, is the same as that of the Nikolaitans/followers of 'Balaam' in Pergamum (sexual unfaithfulness understood as a metaphorical reference to idolatry). Again, the issue seems to be one of Christian practice, and the extent to which a Christian may engage with the life of the city and the empire of which it is a part. In Thyatira, with its plethora of trade-guilds and other societies, the issue of eating meat at cultic meals, perhaps in honour of the patron god, would have been a perennial one for the wealthy and those involved in commerce. 'Jezebel' may even have appealed to the Pauline tradition for a more accommodating attitude towards this issue (Boxall 2004). That her teaching **my servants to be unfaithful** is to be taken as a metaphorical reference to idolatry is strengthened by the parallel with the 'harlotries' of Queen Jezebel (referring to her worship of Baal, 2 Kgs 9:22). As a false prophet, 'Jezebel' of Thyatira is **leading them astray** (leading God's people astray is a mark of the false prophet in Deuteronomy 13), thus revealing herself, from Revelation's perspective, to be on the side of the 'false prophet' who serves Satan and the monster (cf. 12:9; 13:14).

In other messages where criticism is made, it is the angel who is called to repent. Here repentance is focused on the prophetess herself, and **her children** (verse 23). Repentance, the call and the opportunity to change one's mind, will be held out as a possibility throughout Revelation. Here, however, the opportunity has apparently been missed, for the son of man figure has **given her time to repent**. Perhaps a similar prophetic oracle has been uttered against her in Thyatira itself, maybe even through John himself on a previous visit. However, **she refuses to repent of her infidelity**. What we fail to hear is the voice of 'Jezebel' herself, and many have been critical of the prophetess' silencing here and of Revelation's stereotyping of the female generally (e.g. Pippin 1992; Thimmes 2003). She may well have responded to this prophetic critique as one prophet to another. Distinguishing between rival prophetic claims was already a burning issue in ancient Israel (e.g. Jer. 23:16–40). With the re-emergence of the Spirit of prophecy within the early Church and the regular exercise of prophecy within its liturgical assemblies (e.g. 1 Cor. 11:2–16; 14:26–33), the need to test prophetic utterances became all the more important (Mt. 7:15–20; 1 Cor. 14:37–38; 1 Jn 4:1–3; *Didache* 11—12).

As we move into the *dispositio* of the Thyatiran message (verses 22– 25), the threat of the Son of Man coming in judgement is heightened. The fate of 'Jezebel' herself is shockingly ambiguous: **Look! I shall throw her onto a couch**. The word for 'couch' (Greek κλίνη) could refer to the bed where one sleeps, either suggesting some kind of punitive illness to bring her to her senses (cf. 1 Cor. 11:30; one variant reading for κλίνη in verse 22 is ἀσθένεια, 'illness' or 'weakness'), or prolonging the sexual metaphor as the couch where the adultery took place. But here metaphor merges with reality, for the word could also refer to couches on which one reclined to eat, thus offering a critique of her participation in banquets associated with the guilds. **Those who have committed adultery with her** would then be her pagan associates (note the parallel with Babylon and 'earth's kings' at 17:2 and 18:3), who are threatened with the **great tribulation** of the last days. Like pagans elsewhere (9:20–21; 16:9, 11), however, they are provided with the opportunity to repent, oddly **of what she has done** (this harder reading is to be preferred to the alternative 'of what they have done'). ^{22–23}

Those described as **her children**, on the other hand, would be her followers within the Church. They are threatened with being put **to death**. The metaphorical language of the rest of this message surely applies to this saying too, for a God who inflicts death on his own causes much moral soul-searching. Perhaps the second death is in view here. Nevertheless, the purpose of the rhetoric is surely to shake compromising Christians out of their complacency to reconsider their position. In what is effectively a reversal of the slaughter of Egypt's first-born, those in the churches are warned that apparently bearing Christ's name does not render them immune from giving account of their lives. Christians are always under the divine scrutiny (**I who search minds and hearts**, a phrase used of Israel's God, is here found on the lips of Christ: cf. Jer. 11:20). Nor is this warning simply for all of Thyatira, but for **all the congregations**.

24–25 Recalling the initial praise to the angel, however, we learn that there are others, **the rest of you people in Thyatira, who do not follow this teaching**. We cannot tell from this which group was in the majority, though the amount of space that John devotes to this situation might suggest that his rival had the upper hand. We are given a tantalising if obscure glimpse of that teaching, the claim to **know 'the deep things of Satan'**. It is unlikely that the rival group actually used the words 'of Satan' (though this has been claimed by commentators who view them as Gnostics); rather this is John's prophetic reproof to their claims to know 'the deep things of God', probably insight into heavenly mysteries (e.g. Dan. 2:22), and even intimate knowledge of God (1 Cor. 2:10). Their interest taps into a yearning for spiritual enlightenment which can emerge in any age, not least among a certain intellectual elite. John the apocalyptic seer certainly would not dispute the possibility that divine mysteries are revealed to humans (his book claims precisely that they are). However, the revelation he presents calls for a radical stance against the kind of compromises with the 'satanic' culture that 'Jezebel' is advocating.

The faithful in Thyatira are reassured that **I impose on you no other burden, but that you hold fast to what you already have until I come**. 'No other burden' (βάρος) evokes the 'Apostolic Letter' of Acts 15 (especially Acts 15:28), which is concerned – as is the message to Thyatira – with maintaining appropriate boundaries around the people of God, given the influx of Gentiles into an originally Jewish reform movement. In particular, it addresses the question of idol-meat (Acts 15:29). What the faithful Thyatirans **already have** is impressive enough, as was spelt out in verse 19: that will suffice to see them through to the judgement.

26–27 The promise to **the one who conquers**, that is who **keeps working for me** (literally 'keeps my works') **until the end**, echoes Psalm 2, already alluded to at verse 18. Christians, following Jewish precedents (e.g. *Pss Sol.* 17:26–27), had already interpreted this as a messianic prophecy. What is surprising is that victorious Christians are promised a share in the Messiah's own tasks. They will have **authority over the nations**, though theirs is an authority very different from the world's, for it is a sharing in the Lamb's authority, achieved through sacrifice. They will also **shepherd** or 'rule' **them with an iron sceptre** (cf. 12:5): the LXX of Ps. 2:9 (ποιμᾶνεις) can have both senses. While the image of **earthenware vessels** being **broken in pieces** (cf. Jer. 18:1–11) may not be the obvious image related to the work of a shepherd, the reality is that the Lamb's role may be received as benevolent shepherding (e.g. 7:17) or as a harsh judgement (e.g. 6:16), depending on one's stance.

Finally, the victor is promised **the Morning Star**. This phrase 28 would normally be understood as a reference to Venus, a symbol of victory (Sweet 1979: 96). But in its Christian context, it may well pick up on the allusion to the prophecy of Balaam (Numbers 24) in the previous message to Pergamum, which mentions both a star and a sceptre/rod. Christ, or the messianic status which he received from his Father, is the true **Morning Star** (cf. 2 Pet. 1:19). That he has received it **from my Father** is a reminder that the Christian ability to address God as Father is a fiercely won privilege (Revelation, like the Fourth Gospel, is reluctant to refer to Christians as 'sons' of God). Christ is the one who overcomes all rival heavenly powers, even those stars which threaten to enslave human lives (cf. Ign. *Eph.* 19 for the view that the coming of the star marking Christ's birth was the overcoming of magic). This same victory over such powers is shared with those who remain faithful with him.

To Sardis   (3:1–6)

(1) 'Write this to the angel of the congregation in Sardis:
    "Thus says the one who possesses the seven spirits of God, and the seven stars: I know your deeds. You have a reputation for being alive, but in reality you are dead!
    (2) Wake up, and put some life back into what little remains, for that is dying off too. For I have found nothing in what you do which is perfect in my God's eyes. (3) Therefore remember how you first received and heard the message; obey it and repent! If you refuse to wake up, I shall come like a thief, and you will not know at what hour I am coming upon you. (4) Yet you do have a few people in Sardis who have not soiled their garments. They will walk with me dressed in shining white, for they are worthy.
    (5) The one who conquers will also be dressed in shining white garments, and I shall never remove his name from the scroll of life. I will acknowledge such a one in the presence of my Father and of his angels.
    (6) Let the one with an ear listen to what the Spirit is saying to the congregations." '

Sardis is located approximately forty miles south of Thyatira, at the crossroads of roads from Pergamum and Smyrna. Sardis had originally been the capital of the Lydian kings, eventually coming under Roman influence in 133 BCE, after control by the Persians and Seleucids. Even today, its citadel, perched on a rocky spur overlooking the Roman city in the valley below, seems impregnable. But significant defeats in its history had revealed its vulnerability. It was also severely hit by the major earthquake of 17 CE, although it seems to have recovered relatively swiftly (with imperial aid). Evidence for this impressive rebuilding can be seen in the archaeological excavations. As far as religion was concerned, the city had long had a temple to Artemis, probably identified with the ancient mother-goddess Cybele. Sardis in the first century also had a prominent Jewish community, which may well have existed for some centuries. The impressive synagogue seen among the ruins of Sardis today, although later than Revelation, gives some indication of how well integrated the Jewish community was in the life of the city. Indeed, its architectural style points to a significant degree of assimilation to the surrounding pagan culture.

1 The Sardian **angel** is addressed by 'someone like a son of man' under the title of **the one who possesses the seven spirits of God, and the seven stars**. We have already encountered the seven spirits before the heavenly throne (1:4), either representing the sevenfold Spirit of God or, more likely, the seven angels of the Presence. Thus Christ holds them in his control, and they act on his behalf in the world (see also 5:6). As he told the Ephesian angel, he also holds **the seven stars** (or seven planets), symbolizing the angels of the seven churches. For the more wayward of the angels, this warns them that even they are under the control of the one who is Lord of all creation.

The **deeds** of this particular angel offer nothing to be proud of: **You have a reputation for being alive, but in reality you are dead!** Here we have another apocalyptic unveiling of the truth about the angel and the community he represents (cf. the more positive unveiling made to Smyrna at 2:9). Appearances can be fiendishly deceptive! The reputation (literally 'name', an ironic contrast to holding to Christ's name) may be that of the community among other Christian communities, or even among their pagan and Jewish fellow-citizens. Indeed, in the apocalyptic world which Revelation evokes, it may refer to the angel's own reputation among his fellow angel-guardians. But what appears to be a thriving community from one perspective may look very different from the divine perspective. In contrast to the Living One who addresses him, the Sardian angel is not **alive** but **dead**. In all this emphasis upon death, John's original audience in Sardis may have detected an allusion to the 'necropolis' mountain to the west of the Temple of Artemis, containing a large number of striking Lydian cave-tombs.

2 In fact, however, death has not quite set in, and repentance remains a possibility. It is still possible to **put some life back into what little remains**, even though **that is dying off too**. The real problem is that the angel, and the community for the most part, have fallen

asleep. They have lost that heightened sense of being awake and watchful, and have become complacent. Perhaps, like the members of the synagogue, they are in too much danger of assimilation to the surrounding culture. The result is that nothing has been found **perfect in my God's eyes**, whether love, service, toil or faithful perseverance. The phrase 'my God' is not common in the New Testament, but in both Revelation and the Fourth Gospel it describes Christ's close relationship with the Father (four times in Rev. 3:12; Jn 20:17; cf. Mk 15:34 and par.). The divine call is for the angel to **Wake up** or 'watch' (from the Greek verb γρηγορέω, regularly used to urge watchfulness for the Lord's coming, e.g. Mt. 24:42; 25:13). Some commentators propose that John here evokes that (probably baptismal) hymn cited at Eph. 5:14 (although the vocabulary used is quite different).

A much clearer echo is with traditions about the coming Day of the 3 Lord, and especially its Christian version referring to the future return of the Son of Man. A number of parallel sayings liken the unexpectedness of that coming to **a thief** or burglar (1 Thess. 5:1–6; Mt. 24:42–44; Lk. 12:39–40; 2 Pet. 3:10), giving us a glimpse of that deep reservoir of Jesus-tradition on which early Christian writers might draw, sometimes independently. Indeed, the presence of such a saying here on the lips of the exalted Jesus, dictated by his prophetic servant John, raises the question as to the influence of early Christian prophets upon Gospel sayings of Jesus. The emphasis of this saying is certainly on the suddenness of Christ's coming, and therefore the need to be watching and ready, for **you will not know at what hour I am coming upon you**. As noted earlier, it is a good rhetorical device when attempting to persuade an audience to pursue a particular course to remind them, positively, of their previous achievements. Hence the angel is urged to **remember how you first received and heard the message**: the required readiness was once there when the gospel was first received. In these messages, however, remembering is a preparation for the call to **repent**. There may also be another aspect to the thief saying: thieves and burglars plunder people's goods if they manage to get into the house, and can do untold damage. It is far better to welcome the Lord's coming with eager readiness than to encounter him as an unwanted thief. The original Sardian audience may well have recalled how their apparently impregnable city had twice fallen to unexpected attacks, as if by thieves in the night: to Cyrus in 586 BCE and to Antiochus III in 214 BCE. The city's angel is warned not to be found sleeping again.

With another rhetorical twist, we discover that even now things are 4–6 not quite as bleak as the initial assessment of this congregation's angel suggested. The angel does have **a few people** (literally 'a few names', contrasting with the undeserved 'reputation'/'name' of the angel) **who have not soiled their garments**. Unsoiled garments suggests a pure, unsullied commitment to their Christian vocation, a refusal to be compromised by the lure of what the empire has to offer. Already such people **are worthy**: it is not just the martyrs, those who actually lay down their lives, who **will walk with me dressed in shining white**, but all those who strive to follow the Lamb. Later we shall hear that it is the blood of that Lamb which has washed them so white (7:14). However, there is no mention here of external hostility towards Christians (whether past or impending), as there is in the messages to Smyrna and Pergamum. Moreover, this is no localised promise to faithful disciples in Sardis: it is part of that growing list of promises to **the one who conquers**, white being the colour associated with victory and heaven (see commentary on 2:17). There may be a suggestion here that faithful Christians will become like the angels (e.g. 19:14; *1 En.* 62:15–16), who regularly wear dazzling white (e.g. 2 Macc. 11:8; Mt. 28:3; Jn 20:12; Acts 1:10).

The name which is unsoiled will never be removed **from the scroll of life**. Exodus refers to a book of names that the Lord has written (Exod. 32:32–33), from which those who sin against him are blotted out. This 'book of the living' or 'the righteous' (e.g. Ps. 69:28; cf. Isa. 4:3; Mal. 3:16) had an important role in the apocalyptic tradition, as the heavenly ledger according to which judgement would be made (e.g. Dan. 12:1; *Asc. Isa.* 9:19–23). For Revelation, there is nothing fatalistic about such a scroll; whether or not one's name remains in it depends upon whether one perseveres in the battle. The third promise reiterates the previous two, echoing another saying of Jesus about the final judgement, in which he will have the role of either accusing or vindicating those on trial (Mt. 10:32; Lk. 12:8). Here we have only the positive portion of that saying: **I will acknowledge such a one in the presence of my Father and of his angels.**

To Philadelphia (3:7–13)

(7) 'Write this to the angel of the congregation in Philadelphia:
    "Thus says the Holy One, the True One,
    who holds the key of David,
    opening so that no-one can close,
    and closing so that no-one can open:
    (8) I know your deeds. Look! I have opened a door before you, which no-one will be able to close. For you have little power, yet you have observed my word and have not denied my name.

(9) Look! I am going to make those of the synagogue of Satan – who call themselves 'Jews' and are not, but are liars – I shall make them come and fall down at your feet, acknowledging that I have loved you. (10) For you have observed my command of perseverance; therefore I shall protect you through the hour of testing which is coming over the whole world, to test those who make their home on the earth. (11) I am coming soon! Hold fast to what you have, that no-one may take your wreath from you.

(12) I will make the one who conquers into a pillar in the sanctuary of my God, and he will never leave it. I will also write on him the name of my God, and the name of the city of my God, the new Jerusalem which is descending out of heaven from my God, and my new name.

(13) Let the one with an ear listen to what the Spirit is saying to the congregations."'

Approximately thirty miles east of Sardis on the road into the interior lies the city of **Philadelphia**. Founded in the second century BCE and named after Attulus Philadelphus, its geographical location meant it was a perfect centre for the dissemination of Greek culture in Lydia and Phrygia. Like its neighbour Sardis, Philadelphia was badly hit by the great earthquake of 17 CE. Rebuilt with imperial assistance, the city adopted the new name of Neocaesarea. The later letter of Ignatius to the church here testifies to ongoing debates about the relationship between Christians and the Jewish community (Ign. *Philad.* 6).

Christ introduces himself to **the angel** in a poetic passage as **the** 7 **Holy One, the True** (or 'Reliable') **One**, titles used together of God at 6:10 (see Isa. 43:15; though note also the use of 'Holy One' as a messianic title at Mk 1:24 and Jn 6:69). The reference to him holding **the key of David** echoes the inaugural vision, though there Christ holds the keys of Death and Hades (1:18). The strong emphasis on David here may suggest that the question of Christ's messianic status is a particular issue in Philadelphia (see also 5:5; 22:16; cf. Rom. 1:3; Mt. 1:1–25; Lk. 1:32; Jn 7:42; 2 Tim. 2:8). In the background is Isaiah's prophecy of the replacement of Shebna by Eliakim son of Hilkiah as steward of the royal household and his being given the key of the house of David, with the power to open and shut (Isa. 22:15–25). In John's vision, the Messiah Jesus is presented to the Philadelphian angel as the one with ultimate authority over God's household, just as he also has authority over the negative powers of Death and Hades.

This vision of Christ as the key-bearer may be directly connected 8 with the vulnerable situation of the Philadelphian Christians. Only here and in the message to Smyrna do we find praise alone, with not a hint of blame. Moreover, verse 9 will offer another link with the Smyrnean situation through its reference to 'the synagogue of Satan'. The Philadelphian angel has **little power**, but has **observed my word** and **not denied my name**. From the world's perspective, therefore, the Church is weak. But true power is revealed as something very different throughout the Apocalypse: it is wielded by a Lamb which is slaughtered, and by followers who are equally prepared to lay down their lives. Because of their lack of power (which paradoxically renders them truly powerful), the great key-holder has **opened a door before you, which no-one will be able to close.** There are several suggestions as to what this opened door refers to. In Paul's letters, an 'open door' refers to a missionary possibility (1 Cor. 16:9; 2 Cor. 2:12; see Col. 4:3), and perhaps this vulnerable community was being offered a similar opportunity. This would echo Philadelphia's role as a centre for the spread of Hellenistic culture. Others suggest that the phrase was offered as a word of comfort for Christians who had found themselves expelled from the synagogue, thereby linking it closely with the reference to 'Jews' in the following verse (e.g. Harrington 1993: 70). They could then expect a reversal of their bitter rejection in the Kingdom. Yet Revelation is rather less explicit than the Fourth Gospel that synagogue expulsions have taken place. There is a third possibility, however, suggested by the apocalyptic nature of this book. At 4:1 the 'open door' will provide John with privileged access to the heavenly throne-room, and with it to heavenly mysteries otherwise hidden from him. The same privileged access is offered to the faithful Philadelphians, and indeed all who heed the words of this message, enabling them to see their own difficult situation from God's perspective, and thus make sense of it. When one is privileged to glimpse through the opened door, what originally appeared to be a defeat is transformed into a glorious vision of victory.

9–10 As in Smyrna, so in Philadelphia there are people **who call themselves 'Jews'** but belong to **the synagogue of Satan**, whether these are non-Christian Jews or rival Jewish followers of Jesus who are not part of the congregation addressed through John (see on 2:9). Unlike Smyrna, however, there is no suggestion that any kind of hostility (instigated by this group or by others) is impending. What is promised is that ultimately the angel and the vulnerable congregation he represents will be acknowledged as those whom the Messiah has **loved**, by those who currently deny the possibility. The battle for the name of Jew, and the position of legitimate heir to Israel's tradition, was a fiercely contested one in the first-century world. Ironically, this reversal of fortunes echoes those promises according to which

Gentiles would come in subjection to Israel in the last days (e.g. Isa. 45:14; 49:23; 60:13–14): **I shall make them come and fall down at your feet.** The verb translated here 'fall down' (προσκυνέω) is used elsewhere in Revelation of 'worship'; its use here is puzzling and suggests its weaker sense, for at 19:10 and 22:8–9 John will be rebuked for attempting to worship an angel.

As a result of the angel's faithfulness, and especially that **perseverance** required to see the battle through to its completion, he is promised that **I shall protect you through the hour of testing which is coming over the whole world** (on this see Brown 1966). The **hour of testing** refers to that time of tribulation which will precede Christ's coming (e.g. Mt. 6:13; Lk. 11:4; 1 Cor. 10:13), to encompass the whole world (for this reason it is unlikely to refer specifically to a persecution against the Church). Christ's promise, not only to faithful Philadelphians but to all victorious readers of this book, is to keep them safe *through* the hour of testing, not remove them from it, as the Dispensationalist doctrine of the 'pre-tribulation Rapture' maintains (cf. 7:14; for a similar use of τηρέω ἐκ see Jn 17:15). The purpose of this hour will be **to test those who make their home on the earth,** probably in the sense that such trials reveal who God's friends and enemies really are. The phrase **those who make their home on the earth** (lit. 'the inhabitants of the earth') is used throughout Revelation of those in the world who are hostile to God and the Lamb (6:10; 8:13; 11:10; 13:8, 14; 17:8), akin to the Fourth Gospel's 'the world' (e.g. Jn 1:10; 16:33). The centre of their world, which limits their sphere of vision and orders their priorities, is the realm of 'earth', which is temporarily estranged from God (in contrast to heaven, where God is acknowledged as God, and from where a true perspective on our world is possible: see on 4:1).

In a number of the seven messages, Christ's coming has had some- 11 thing of the character of a threat. In each case, whether this refers to the ultimate coming at the Parousia, or to a more specific coming, is left unclear, perhaps deliberately so. It helps maintain that sense of urgency demanded of all God's people, and parallels the various reinterpretations of Christ's advent in the Fourth Gospel (Boxall 2002: 153f.). Indeed, the probable eucharistic context in which the Apocalypse was originally read may be important here, for in such a context Christ comes to his expectant people, anticipating his final coming. As received by the Philadelphian angel, however, the words **I am coming soon!** are not a threat but a promise. Indeed, the athlete's victory **wreath** is already possessed, despite what is still to come, and cannot be taken away provided that the call to **hold fast** is heeded (in Isa. 22:21 LXX, Shebna does indeed have his wreath or crown taken away and given to Eliakim).

12 The promise to **the one who conquers** returns to the liturgical
theme of the inaugural vision, in which the heavenly High Priest
walked in the midst of the seven menorahs in his Temple. The victor
will be made **into a pillar in the sanctuary of my God**. Early
Jerusalem Christianity seems to have referred to the original apostles
as 'pillars' (στῦλοι: Gal. 2:9), indicating their crucial role in the new
living sanctuary of God, the Church. A similar, non-Christian
identification of a community of the faithful as a temple can be found
at Qumran (e.g. 1QS 9), and is reflected throughout the New Testament (e.g. 1 Cor. 3:16–17; 1 Pet. 2:5; possibly Jn 2:21). Here,
however, it points to eschatological salvation still to be achieved (of
which the heavenly sanctuary John is about to see is an assurance).
This pillar is firmly established, unlike the pillars of so many Philadelphian temples and other buildings which collapsed in the various
earthquakes and tremors that afflicted the city.

There seems to be some contradiction here with the final vision of
the new Jerusalem in Revelation 21—22, for John will see no sanctuary in that city, yet the victor is here promised that **he will never
leave it**. To regard John as contradicting himself, however, is to fail
to appreciate the kaleidoscopic nature of Revelation's apocalyptic
imagery. The city itself merges almost imperceptibly into a temple, as
the presence of God and the Lamb are revealed inside it (21:22; it is a
perfect cube, like Solomon's Holy of Holies: 21:16, cf. 1 Kgs 6:20).
Indeed, almost in the same breath there is a reference to **the city of
my God, the new Jerusalem**. Bearing names, like being branded
with a mark, is a sign of ownership or possession. At 22:4 those who
worship God and the Lamb in the new Jerusalem will have *his* name
(a singular apparently covering both) written on their foreheads. So
too here the pillar will be marked out as belonging to the true
sanctuary-city; the one it symbolises is marked out as owned by **my
God** and a citizen of **the new Jerusalem**. The present participle
descending highlights the imminence of this promised fulfilment.
Finally, the victor will have written on him **my new name**. A
change of name denotes a change of status. But that it is 'my new
name' suggests that Revelation has in mind that 'name above every
name' which early Christians claimed had been bestowed upon Jesus,
marking out his authoritative status as the one who acts on God's
behalf (Phil. 2:9; cf. e.g. Jn 5:43; 17:6). In other words, the divine
name YHWH, believed in some Jewish traditions to have been
inscribed on the high priest's headdress (e.g. Josephus, *B. J.* 5.235;
Ant. 3.178; *Ep. Arist.* 98), is inscribed by the exalted high priest
Christ on those he claims as his own. The sanctuary, and those who
belong to it, will remain safe. Names may come and go (Philadelphia
had changed its name to Neocaesarea after the earthquake of 17 CE),
but this name abides for ever.

To Laodicea   (3:14–22)

(14) 'Write this to the angel of the congregation in Laodicea:
"Thus says the Amen, the trustworthy and true witness, the
origin of God's creation:
(15) I know your deeds. You are neither cold nor hot. I wish
you were either cold or hot!
(16) But because you are tepid, and neither hot nor cold, I
will spit you out of my mouth! (17) For you say, 'I am rich! I
have made my fortune and am in need of nothing!' You do not
realise what a miserable one you are, to be pitied, poor, blind
and naked. (18) I advise you to buy from me gold refined by
fire to make you truly rich, and shining white garments to put
on, that your shameful nakedness might not be seen, and eye
ointment to anoint your eyes with, that you may really see.
(19) It is those whom I love that I rebuke and instruct.
Therefore be earnest, and repent! (20) Look! I am standing at
the door, knocking. If anyone hears my voice and opens the
door, I will come in and we will share a meal together.
(21) I will allow the one who conquers to sit with me on my
throne, just as I have conquered and have sat with my Father
on his throne.
(22) Let the one with an ear listen to what the Spirit is
saying to the congregations." '

The final congregation of the seven is located in **Laodicea**, situated
about forty miles south-east of Philadelphia. It was an impressive city
which under Roman rule had become an important banking and
commercial centre, situated in the middle of the fertile valley of the
River Lycus (hence its ancient title *Laodicea ad Lycum*), a tributary of
the Meander, and close to the cities of Colossae and Hierapolis. The
important trade route from Syria across Anatolia linked Laodicea to
the east, while roads radiating to north and west connected the city to
the congregations in the northern cities (via Hierapolis) and Ephesus
respectively. This meant that the emissary from Patmos, having
delivered the scroll containing the Apocalypse to this seventh city,
could then easily complete the circuit back to Ephesus via Tralles and
Magnesia-on-the-Meander.

The city derived its name from Laodice, wife of Antiochus II, who
rebuilt it in the mid-second century BCE. It prospered in the Roman
imperial period: excavations of the site have uncovered two theatres,
an impressive stadium, a gymnasium/bath complex and an aqueduct.
Numismatic and inscriptional evidence also attests to the number of
deities worshipped in the city, the most famous of whom was Zeus
Laodicenus. Like Sardis and Philadelphia, it was hit by the great

earthquake of 17 CE, and restored with the help of an imperial grant. Similar help was famously refused, however, when Laodicea was destroyed by another earthquake *c.* 60 CE (Tacitus, *Ann.* 14.27). References in Colossians (Colossae was about ten miles from Laodicea in the same valley) link both Laodicea and nearby Hierapolis with the Pauline mission, probably through Epaphras (Col. 4:12–13, 16).

14–15 Christ introduces himself to the Laodicean **angel** as **the Amen**, the one whose word can be trusted (in the MT of Isa. 65:16, 'God of truth' is literally 'God of Amen'), reiterated by the phrase **the trustworthy and true witness** (cf. 1:5). The further title **origin of God's creation** is close to the description of Christ as 'first-born of all creation' and 'the beginning' or 'origin' in the so-called Colossians hymn (Col. 1:15, 18). In both Colossians and Revelation we may catch a rare glimpse of the kind of early Christian confessions circulating in hymnic form in the churches of the Lycus Valley. Christ is here presented in terms hitherto used of Divine Wisdom (e.g. Prov. 8:22–23), a tradition applied by Jewish Christians to Christ as pre-existent and agent of creation (e.g. 1 Cor. 1:30; 8:6; Jn 1:1ff.).

The *narratio*, as in the message to Sardis, contains only words of criticism. Unlike in that message, however, there will be no mitigating circumstances, nothing mentioned to alleviate the negative assessment. The angel is **neither cold nor hot**, but merely **tepid**. First-century Laodicean Christians would almost certainly pick up on the local allusion, for Laodicea was almost equidistant between Hierapolis (modern Pamukkale), with its hot thermal springs, and the cold-water springs of Colossae. It was probably not the case that Laodicea's aqueduct transported the hot water from Hierapolis to the north, as it comes into the city from the south (although calcareous deposits show that it transported water from other hot springs in the area, presumably losing some of its heat in the process). But certainly one can see clearly from Laodicea the sulphurous waters cascading over Hierapolis' terraces, forming those white 'cotton castles' which give the city its modern name. This local echo counts against the angel being criticised for spiritual lukewarmness, for loss of fervour (after all, surely it is better to be tepid in one's commitment than completely cold). Rather, the tepid water of Laodicea does not produce any obvious benefit, unlike the healing properties of the hot baths at Hierapolis Spa or the refreshingly cool drinking water available to the Colossians (both of which are equally beneficial). The Laodicean angel has lost his effectiveness.

16–17 The *dispositio* of this message (verses 16–20) continues this bleak picture, and advocates its remedy. Because the angel is tepid, Christ warns him that **I will spit you out of my mouth!** There is a certain irony here in that elsewhere it is the word of God, the sharp double-edged sword, that comes out of Christ's mouth (1:16; 2:16; 19:15). The Laodicean angel and the congregation he represents have lost the capacity to proclaim that prophetic word, and therefore are in danger of losing their place. Their arrogant claim to self-sufficiency, echoing that of the city itself (which refused imperial help in rebuilding after the earthquake of 60 CE), simply compounds their predicament: **For you say, 'I am rich! I have made my fortune and am in need of nothing!'** Rather like 'Jezebel' in Thyatira, the angel of the Laodicean church is in danger of too closely identifying with the arrogant city Babylon, who boasts in similar terms at 18:7. In Revelation's apocalyptic reversal, those who have become rich by her stand under judgement (e.g. 18:3), while true riches are to be found elsewhere. Again, we may have a hint that the failure of Laodicean Christians is due to undue assimilation into the life of their economically prosperous city. But the Apocalypse unveils the angel's true state, very different from what appears to be the case: **You don't realise what a miserable one you are, to be pitied, poor, blind and naked** (cf. 17:16). Yet again, Revelation deconstructs attempts (including at times its own!) to drive a wedge between Church and world: even the churches stand under judgement, and must constantly ask themselves whether they are too heavily implicated in the seductions of the monster.

Even in this bleakest of messages, however, a way out is offered. If **18** the angel really wishes to overcome his poverty, nakedness and blindness, the risen Christ has the remedy. In verse 14 he has already spoken of himself as Wisdom personified, and here again we hear Wisdom speak, urging the angel to **buy from me** (Sir. 51:25; Isa. 55:1–2). No doubt there are allusions here which would have particularly resonated with Laodicean Christians: **gold** with the city's banking reputation; **white garments,** a contrast to the area's famous black wool; **eye ointment** with the famous Phrygian eye-salve (Galen, *De San. Tuen.* 12). But the real focus is on the superior riches offered by Christ, like the treasure hidden in a field or the pearl of great price (Mt. 13:44–46). His gold has been **refined by fire,** an image of tried-and-tested faith at 1 Pet. 1:7. The garments he offers are the white garments with which the victorious are clothed. His eye ointment is that messianic anointing which enables people to pass from darkness to light (possibly an allusion to baptism: cf. John 9). Indeed, the whole purpose of John's Apocalypse is **that you may really see**: a particular depth of apocalyptic insight which enables the privileged to draw back the curtain and view reality from a new perspective.

19–20   The harsh criticism here is not for its own sake, but a sign of Christ's love for the angel, and for the congregation he represents before the throne. **It is those whom I love that I rebuke and instruct**: all this has a remedial purpose. Wisdom speaks similarly to her child of the Lord's discipline at Prov. 3:11–12 (cf. Heb. 12:5–7). In a text containing such violent and terrifying imagery as does Revelation, it is at times hard to hold on to a vision of God's love: many may find themselves agreeing with Jung's famous description of the book as 'a veritable orgy of hatred, wrath, vindictiveness, and blind destructive fury' (Jung 1984: 125). But the love of God revealed in Christ, and throughout the New Testament, is no soft and easy emotion, but a costly and demanding love.

    The metaphor changes from the demanding tutor to that of the unexpected visitor. With this change of metaphor, one can detect a shift from a narrow focus on the Laodiceans to a wider audience, a reminder that the seven messages are drawing to a close, and are addressed through the prophetic Spirit to all the congregations. **Look! I am standing at the door, knocking.** This image has inspired artists in diverse ways throughout the centuries, though many will particularly visualise that famous depiction of the scene by Holman Hunt. It has also functioned regularly as a popular and very effective evangelistic slogan, urging the unconverted to open the door to Christ. But in John's vision, Christ stands at the door of members of the Church (however tepid they are), not of outsiders. Like the beloved Bridegroom of the Song of Songs, a book interpreted allegorically as God seeking out Israel at the Exodus (Sweet 1979: 109), Christ knocks at the door of the Bride's house (Sg Sgs 5:2 LXX; cf. Lk. 12:35–38). Others may detect echoes of the Good Shepherd who is also the Door of the sheep, each of which **hears my voice** (John 10). The promise to the one who **opens the door** from the inside is that **I will come in and we will share a meal together** (the verb δειπνέω, and the noun related to it, are used for the Lord's Supper at 1 Cor. 11:20, 25; cf. Rev. 19:9, 17). Again, we are reminded of the eucharistic context within which Christians are likely to have heard this read: a summons to wake up and be ready to eat the bread and drink the cup of the Lord worthily (1 Cor. 11:27). What each of the seven congregations are now doing, and what countless other congregations do in every time and place, is an anticipation of that final banquet when the Lamb will feast with his bride (19:7).

21–22   The final promise to **the one who conquers** offers a privilege which elsewhere the Lamb shares with the Father: **to sit with me on my throne, just as I have conquered and have sat with my Father on his throne**. There is an interesting parallel with the saying at Lk. 22:28–30, where those who have stood by Christ in his trials (in this case the Twelve) will eat and drink in his kingdom, and sit on thrones judging the twelve tribes of Israel. Whereas the Lamb will have a unique role in sharing his Father's throne (so that both are legitimately the objects of worship), the privilege of reigning in the kingdom will be shared by all Christ's faithful followers (indeed, already they share in his royal rule, 1:6).

But for them, as for Christ, the way to that throne is the way of tribulation, the way of suffering and even death. That is no less the way for John, who shares with his brothers and sisters in the tribulation (1:9). The scene is now set for him to ascend to that throne, through that open door which, as we have just learned, can be opened by the one on the inside. The churches have been assessed, their senses heightened and their awareness of Christ's imminent coming sharpened. They are now ready to attend to the story in detail. When that door is opened, though in rather more symbolic visionary terms, this story will be played out. Now more than ever is the καιρός, the crucial time to **listen to what the Spirit is saying to the congregations.**

2   THRONE-VISION AND SEVEN SEALS (4:1—8:1)

At this point, we enter a new phase in the unfolding drama, as John is caught up to heaven and granted privileged access to the heavenly throne-room. This vision (which continues into chapter 5) inaugurates the opening of the seven seals (6:1—8:1), just as the vision of the exalted Christ in chapter 1 introduced the seven messages. Thus 4:1—8:1 forms the second great cycle of sevens in Revelation. But it is no less crucial for understanding the remaining visions of the book, acting as the orienting vision for the whole of chapters 4—22. In these remaining chapters, a kaleidoscope of images and symbols will flash before the mind's eye, presenting from different perspectives the character of the battle described in the preceding seven messages. Revelation 4—5 provides as it were the appropriate perspective from which to view and make sense of what is happening on earth. Indeed, again and again we shall revisit this heavenly scene (e.g. 7:9–17; 8:1–5; 11:15–18; 15:1–8; 19:1–8), which reveals the one who is truly in control, and to whom true worship is due. Here is 'apocalyptic' in the true sense of the word: a drawing back of the curtain which normally restricts humanity's view of the heavenly realm, enabling John, and those privileged to hear his Apocalypse, to see the world in a radically new light.

Vision of the Heavenly Throne (4:1–11)

(1) After this I looked, and there in heaven was an open door. The voice which I had first heard speaking to me like a trumpet said: 'Come up here, and I will reveal to you what must happen after this.' (2) I immediately fell into a spiritual trance, and look, a throne was standing in heaven, with someone seated on it. (3) The seated figure had an appearance similar to jasper and carnelian, and around the throne was a rainbow that looked like emerald. (4) Surrounding the throne were twenty-four thrones, and seated on the thrones twenty-four elders, dressed in shining white garments, with gold wreaths on their heads. (5) Out of the throne come flashes of lightning, voices, and claps of thunder, and in front of the throne there are seven fiery lamps burning, which are the seven spirits of God. (6) In front of the throne there is also something like a sea of glass, like crystal. On the throne, that is surrounding it, are four creatures, covered with eyes in front and on the back. (7) The first creature is like a lion, the second creature like a calf, the third creature has a human-like face, and the fourth creature is like a flying eagle. (8) The four creatures, each of which has six wings, are covered with eyes all around and on the inside. Day and night they never cease singing:

'Holy, holy, holy, is the Lord God Almighty,
who was and who is, and who is coming!'

(9) Whenever the four creatures give glory and honour and thanks to the one seated on the throne, who lives for ever and ever, (10) the twenty-four elders fall down in front of the one seated on the throne and worship the one who lives for ever and ever. They throw their wreaths in front of the throne and sing:

(11) 'Worthy are you, our Lord and our God,
to receive glory, honour and power.
For you created the universe;
by your will all things existed, yes, were created.'

The precedents for what John here describes are well established. Our seer has obviously been influenced by Ezekiel's bizarre vision of God's throne-chariot or *Merkavah* (Ezekiel 1); indeed, it has already been noted how Ezekiel's book seems to have exercised a particular influence on the content and structure of John's Revelation. Elements of Revelation 4—5 also echo the earlier temple vision of Isaiah (Isaiah 6), Daniel's vision of the Ancient of Days seated on a throne (Daniel 7) and Micaiah ben–Imlah's sight of the enthroned Lord surrounded by the heavenly host (1 Kgs 22:19). But we should not be too hasty to present John primarily as a biblical exegete, imagining him sitting in a dusty Patmos study, cutting and pasting diverse biblical texts like some first-century don. Nor should we conclude that, because visions and dreams are stock features of apocalyptic writings, what he describes is little more than a fictional literary device. As noted in the Introduction, John's claim to have seen what he describes ought to be taken seriously. A number of Jewish apocalypses describe a similar experience of mystical ascent to the heavenly throne-room (e.g. *1 Enoch* 14; *Apocalypse of Abraham* 18; cf. 4Q400–07; 2 Cor. 12:1–5), and may well represent an early form of the tradition which later emerged as fully fledged *Merkavah* mysticism within Judaism (Gruenwald 1980; Rowland 1982). What is most surprising about these parallel accounts is their relative lack of verbal agreement with each other, and indeed with the foundational vision of Ezekiel 1, contrary to what one might expect were one dealing with literary borrowing. Rather, the fluidity of language, and the piling up of similes and metaphors to express what is seen, may point us in the direction of actual visionary experience on the part of their authors. The relationship between vision and tradition is a complex one (Boxall 2002: 30–36). Ezekiel 1, with its vision of God on his throne, seems to have been a favourite passage for meditation on the part of Jewish visionaries (so much so that certain rabbis considered the passage too dangerous for the uninitiated: e.g. *m. Meg.* 4.10). It should not surprise us, therefore, if it holds a crucial – though not exclusive – key to John's visionary account.

But there is another feature of the throne-vision tradition which is pertinent to understanding John's vision, and its role in the Apocalypse as a whole. It probably has its origins in ancient Near Eastern courts in which the king is envisaged as surrounded by his courtiers. Within biblical tradition, Isaiah, Micaiah and others claimed to have been admitted to the inner sanctum of the heavenly court, to listen in on a session of the divine council, where they were privileged to hear the divine plan for the world so as to be able to announce it to Israel. John too is offered access to the heavenly council as a prophet and seer: what he will see and hear there will form the content of his message to the congregations, the 'word of prophecy' which all hearers of his book are bidden to heed.

The phrase **After this I looked** indicates a change of scene, which 1 should seize the reader's attention (the same phrase is used again at 7:9; 15:5; 18:1). John sees **in heaven ... an open door**. The notion that access to heaven (as to the underworld) can be gained via a door or gate is found in both Jewish and pagan traditions (e.g. *1 En.* 14:15; *T. Levi* 5:1; Virg. *Aen.* 6), and parallels the opening of the heavens witnessed by Jesus at his baptism (Mk 1:10). Implied here is a cosmology in which a firmament covering the sky separates the heavenly realm, where God is enthroned, from the earthly. But we should not automatically assume that the ancient world was so unsophisticated as to understand this over-literally, as if God could be reached by a rocket powerful enough to penetrate the firmament. As the psalmist notes: 'If I ascend to the heavens, you are there; if I make my bed in Sheol, you are there also' (Ps. 139:8). The apocalyptic tradition may use the language of height, but depth might be a more comprehensible metaphor for our contemporaries: John's vision of heaven takes him deeper into reality, rather than removing him from it. **Heaven** is where God is acknowledged as King, and where true worship occurs. But far from being separated from this world, it is intimately connected to it, for what is seen in heaven either has been or will be played out on the earth. Indeed, later in the book we shall hear of the new Jerusalem which has been carefully prepared in heaven for its ultimate descent to earth (21:2). That is why John's access to the heavenly throne-room is so significant, for what he sees will enable the churches to make sense of their own situation and see God's hand in the ensuing crisis. The **open door** allows John his new visionary perspective. Yet though John is here presented as a privileged seer, ultimately the open door is accessible to all the faithful who embrace the tribulation by continuing the witness that Jesus bore (there is nothing to suggest, *pace* Caird 1966: 60, that this is a different 'open door' to the one offered to the Philadelphians and Laodiceans). Doors onto heaven can be opened wherever God's people are, though particularly where they are gathered for the eucharistic liturgy (3:20). Heaven is never very far away, for those with the eyes to see.

But apocalyptic unveilings require some kind of interpretation. At this point, a heavenly voice fulfils that role, **the voice which I had first heard speaking to me like a trumpet** (a reference back to 1:10). Christ, the Word of God, is the one who speaks (elsewhere the role of apocalyptic interpreter will be fulfilled by an elder or an angel). This reminds us that, though we are moving into a new phase, nevertheless this is a continuation of the revelation of Jesus Christ begun in John's initial Patmos vision. The content of the revelation will be **what must happen after this** (cf. Dan. 2:29). The same voice at 1:19 spoke of 'what is now happening' and 'what is to happen after this': given this apparent twofold division (see above on 1:19–20), the 'what is now happening' probably refers primarily to the seven messages, which have shone a torch on the seven congregations, illuminating both their faithfulness and their compromises. **What must happen after this** then speaks especially of the visions of Revelation 4–22, which will play out in visionary form the divine purposes, and the role of the Christian community in these eschatological events (the verb δεῖ, 'it is necessary', denotes the fulfilment of God's plan for his world). However, we should avoid too great a distinction between the present in Revelation 1—3 and the future in Revelation 4—22. The seven messages themselves referred to events yet to come (e.g. 2:10, 22–23; 3:9), as well as making future promises which will be encountered again in later visions. Similarly, this throne vision will use a combination of past, present and future tenses, and the same ambiguity about Revelation's timeline will continue to the end of the book. This causes difficulty for those who would treat the Apocalypse as a neat, chronological guide to the End of the World, or indeed for any interpretation which regards John's book as offering a straightforward account of the unfolding historical process.

For ancient audiences schooled in the Jewish apocalypses, or even modern readers whose imaginations have been energised by Tolkein's Middle-earth, Lewis's Narnia, or other contemporary fantasy literature, John's description of his throne-vision will be disappointing in the extreme. Jewish apocalyptic writers present in vivid detail the seers' ascent, often through more than one level of heaven, describing their physical state in the process (e.g. *1 Enoch* 14; *Apocalypse of Abraham* 18). Even Paul speaks, albeit modestly in the third person, of his being caught up 'to the third heaven ... into Paradise' (2 Cor. 12:2, 4). While at this point Revelation is influenced by the same motif of the heavenly ascent, John tells us next to nothing about his personal state or whether he actually passed through the door into heaven itself. He simply tells us that he **fell into a spiritual trance** (see 1:10), echoing the experience of Ezekiel (e.g. Ezek. 11:1, 24). Nor does he linger to describe the details of the throne-room: instead he moves straight to the **throne**, and to **someone seated on it**. Even Ezekiel 1 shows interest in the form of the throne-chariot, its wheels, and the cherubim who support it (the source for much mystical speculation in the centuries following). John, however, has little to say about the *Merkavah* itself, and delays mentioning the creatures/ cherubim until later. The throne is important primarily because this is a vision of where true power and authority lie in our universe. The world is full of rival claims on human devotion and commitment, whether political, economic or religious. Readers of Revelation in every age, and not simply in first-century Roman Asia, should be challenged by this vision to consider whether their attachment is to this ultimate throne, or to one of the many rival thrones (which amounts to Revelation's great sin of idolatry). Not for nothing has Revelation acquired a reputation throughout Christian history for being politically subversive.

The seated figure on the throne is a fundamental element of

2–3

throne-visions in the apocalypses, inspired as they are by what Ezekiel saw (Ezek. 1:26–28). Ezekiel describes 'something that seemed like a human form' seated above the throne, which he identified as 'the appearance of the likeness of the glory of the Lord' (we may already have encountered this manifestation of the divine glory, apart from the throne, in the vision of the risen Christ at 1:12–20). What is most striking about John's parallel description here, however, is its reluctance to resort to such anthropomorphic language. He uses imagery derived not from humanity, but from the mineral world: the enthroned figure **had an appearance similar to jasper and carnelian.** First-century audiences would have been jolted out of complacency by the striking contrast between John's description of the true God and the often crass anthropomorphisms associated with the gods of paganism and the deified emperors of Rome. The God worshipped by Christians is wholly other than the only-too-human representations of Zeus, Apollo and Artemis renowned throughout proconsular Asia, or the impressive marble statues of past and present emperors lining the streets of its cities.

The use of precious stones in John's description, as in Ezekiel's antecedent (Ezek. 1:27), evokes the dazzling splendour of the divine presence, a scene before which human beings can only bow down in adoration and worship. So too does the **emerald**, which is used to describe the **rainbow** encircling the throne. It may also remind us powerfully of the one who is the true source of riches. Elsewhere in Revelation jasper will describe the radiance of God's holy city and its wall (21:11, 18), while all three jewels will be found in the city's foundations (21:19, 20). In Jewish tradition, they are among the jewels on the high priest's breastplate (e.g. Exod. 28:17–20) and those adorning the king of Tyre in the garden of Eden (Ezek. 28:13). The ancient jasper (Greek ἴασπις from the Persian), unlike its modern counterpart, seems to have been translucent (Swete 1906: 67); carnelian or sardius (Greek σάρδιον) is a fiery red gem: their juxtaposition evokes both the brilliant splendour and the fiery awesomeness of the divine presence. The reference to an emerald-like rainbow in John's vision is explained by its role in Ezekiel's vision (Ezek. 1:28), again functioning to articulate the magnificence of the heavenly scene. However, sensitive readers might also detect an echo of the covenant made with Noah, the sign of which was a bow in the clouds (Gen. 9:13). If the latter echo is present, then this would serve to undermine widespread eschatological readings of Revelation which claim that God's purposes include the radical destruction of God's creation.

4 One significant addition in Revelation to the standard throne-vision of the apocalypses is the presence of the **twenty-four elders**

(Hurtado 1985), themselves seated on **twenty-four thrones** around the great throne. Their location on thrones suggests they have a share in judgement (cf. Lk. 22:30), though the overall scene is probably meant to evoke a session of the heavenly council. Their garments and headwear suggest priestly and royal functions respectively. The key issue for most commentators is the identity of these elders. There are two main lines of interpretation: (i) the elders are angels; (ii) they are exalted human beings. In favour of the first is the fact that they are **surrounding the throne** like the heavenly court (e.g. 1 Kgs 22:19; Isa. 6:1–2), that they are **dressed in shining white garments**, often the clothing of angels (e.g. 2 Macc. 11:8; Mt. 28:3; Mk 16:5; Acts 1), and that angelic beings are regularly portrayed in human form in apocalypses (e.g. Dan. 7:13; 10:5–6; *Joseph and Aseneth* 14). Further, Isa. 24:23 suggests that angels could on occasion be described as elders, and 'thrones' denotes a particular category of angel at Col. 1:16. The role of one of the elders as a kind of *angelus interpres* (5:5; 7:13–17) also strengthens the case for (i).

In favour of their identification as exalted human beings is the fact that angels are explicitly designated as such elsewhere in Revelation, and that the **shining white garments, wreaths** and **thrones** have already been promised to the victorious faithful (2:10; 3:4–5, 18, 21). This solution is found among the Apocalypse's earliest interpreters: Victorinus, for example, sees them as 'the twelve apostles and twelve patriarchs', representing the people of God of both Testaments. **Twenty-four** as a multiple of twelve may indeed lie in the background, given that John can use twelve elsewhere to denote the people of Israel, as well as the Lamb's apostles (e.g. 7:5; 12:1; 21:12, 14). Twelve itself is a number of completeness, achieved by multiplying the divine number three by the number of the universe, four. However, we cannot rule out the influence of 1 Chron. 24:1–18, which speaks of the twenty-four divisions of the sons of Aaron, thus underlining the elders' priestly role in offering worship before the throne.

Yet need these two lines of interpretation be mutually exclusive? The apocalyptic tradition taught that individuals and nations had their own angelic guardians or personifications in heaven, and we have already seen how Revelation can apply this to the seven congregations. Only a similar solution will do justice to all the evidence here. In short, the twenty-four elders are almost certainly the angelic, heavenly personifications of the people of God. Their presence here, close to the divine throne, serves as an assurance to the vulnerable but faithful among the seven congregations that the promises made them by the son of man figure will indeed come to fruition. As in heaven, so ultimately on earth.

5–6a We now come to the heart of this important first throne-vision, as Giblin's concentric structural analysis reveals (Giblin 1998: A = verses 2b–3; B = verse 4; C = verses 5–6a; B' = verses 6b–7; A' = verses 8–11). As the author of the Letter to the Hebrews reminds us, it is terrifying to fall into the hands of the living God (Heb. 10:31). Hence, as our line of vision is directed back towards the throne itself, we encounter phenomena associated with the awesome divine presence, and particularly that crucial manifestation of God on Mount Sinai: **flashes of lightning, voices, and claps of thunder** (Exod. 19:16–18; cf. Ezek. 1:13–14; *Jub.* 2:2 suggests that these phenomena are due to angelic activity). The terrifying God who brought his people from slavery to freedom at the Exodus and made a covenant with them is revealed again as the one who continues to set his people free from oppression. At strategic points throughout Revelation, similar phenomena will recur with increasing intensity, as God acts again with judgement to overcome injustice and save his people (8:5; 11:19; 16:18).

Ezekiel's surreal description of the *Merkavah* spoke of 'something that appeared like coals burning in fire, like torches moving back and forth among the creatures' (Ezek. 1:13). John too sees **fiery lamps burning**, the number **seven** (no doubt influenced by the seven lamps/eyes of the Lord of Zech. 4:2, 10) denoting the totality or completeness of God's fiery watchfulness. But in this most polyvalent of visions, they are further interpreted as **the seven spirits of God**, that is the seven angels of the Presence who attend on God and are sent out to perform his will on earth (see on 1:4; for the idea that angels are composed of fire, see *2 Bar.* 21:6; *4 Ez.* 8:21–22).

John also describes **something like a sea of glass, like crystal** before the throne. This probably reflects ancient Israelite cosmology, in which the firmament that separated heaven from earth had waters above it as well as below (Gen. 1:7; cf. Exod. 24:10; at Ezek. 1:22 this firmament or 'dome' shines like crystal). This mythological restraining of the waters of chaos seems to have found a place as the bronze sea among the furnishings of Solomon's Temple (1 Kgs 7:23), and therefore at the heart of Israel's worship (for further possible meanings, see Sweet 1979: 119). Its presence here at the heart of the heavenly temple highlights the seductive yet threatening nature of evil, which will be a major theme of the visions in chapters 12—18 (Caird 1966: 65f.; contra Michaels 1997: 92f.). To be sure, its calm, crystal-like appearance suggests it has been tamed somewhat; yet the sea or abyss remains an ongoing threat as the dwelling-place of evil and chaos (at 13:1 a monster will arise from the sea), still to be traversed and conquered by God's people of the new Exodus (15:2). At 12:7–9 we will hear of Satan's presence in heaven and expulsion from it. Only when both heaven and earth are renewed will there be no more sea (21:1), and the crystal will be transmuted into the splendour of the new Jerusalem (21:11, 18) and the unthreatening river of life (22:1). It would be tempting to remove all traces of evil from the heavenly realm, yet Judaeo-Christian monotheism ultimately rejects that dualism which would attribute the darkness to a rival god. God is not the author of evil, yet he is Lord of the world in which evil has a foothold, and the one who ultimately will bring evil to destruction.

Balancing the twenty-four elders in the concentric structure of this vision are the **four creatures**. A typical feature of the *Merkavah* tradition, they are the four terrifying cherubim whom Ezekiel saw supporting the throne-chariot (Ezek. 1:10), though bearing some of the features of Isaiah's seraphim (Isaiah 6). John's difficult Greek phrase at verse 6b (lit. 'in the middle of the throne and around the throne') probably means that the cherubim were **on the throne, that is surrounding it**: i.e. an integral part of the throne, as carved cherubim were part of the 'mercy seat' covering the ark of the covenant (Hall 1990; cf. Exod. 25:17–22; 37:6–9). We are not to think of them as actually occupying the throne, for that privilege will be accorded to the worshipped Lamb (5:6; cf. 7:17; 22:1). Like the wheels on Ezekiel's chariot, they are **covered with eyes**, suggesting their watchfulness in worshipping the one on the throne. In later Jewish tradition, Ezekiel's *ophannim* (Hebrew for 'wheels') come to refer to a category of angel (*1 En.* 71:7; *3 En.* 1:8; 2:1).

The four creatures that Ezekiel saw were composite creatures, each bearing multiple faces of human, lion, ox and eagle. They are a far cry from the chubby, childlike cherubs of baroque art, and are rather more akin to the Assyrian and Babylonian winged human-headed creatures which guarded the entrance to royal palaces and temples (*Apoc. Abr.* 18:8–10 presents them as rather threatening beings). John's vision simplifies this complex scene, attributing to each the characteristics of a different creature: the first **like a lion**, the second **like a calf**, the third with **a human-like face**, and the fourth **like a flying eagle**. In so doing, he stresses how they symbolise the totality of God's created order: wild animals, domestic creatures, humans and the birds of the air. John Sweet cites an illuminating passage from the (admittedly much later) *Midrash Shemoth R.* 23: 'Man is exalted among creatures, the eagle among birds, the ox among domestic animals, the lion among wild beasts; all of them have received dominion ... . Yet they are stationed below the chariot of the Holy One' (Sweet 1979: 120). It is as if the whole of creation (whether knowingly or not) is caught up in the worship and praise of God, through their heavenly representatives around the divine throne.

Later Christian tradition, of course, equates the four cherubim with the four Evangelists. The earliest attestation to this is in Irenaeus (*Adv. Haer.* 3.11.8): the lion = John; the calf = Luke; the human = Matthew; the eagle = Mark (in the more widespread interpretation derived from Jerome and reflected in Christian art, Mark is the lion and John the eagle). While the fourfold Gospel is hardly likely to have been in the mind of the seer when he described his vision (and still less in the case of his predecessor Ezekiel), this reading should not be so readily dismissed as pure Christian fancy. Irenaeus uses it as part of his argument that the four Gospels together present the universal gospel sufficient for the whole world (and he also draws upon arguments from the created order, such as the presence of four zones in the world, and four principal winds). It emerges as a quite natural, albeit secondary, reading of a vision in which John sees the heavenly representatives of creation in all its fullness.

8 The four creatures also bear characteristics of Isaiah's seraphim or 'burning ones', who also had **six wings** (though Revelation stresses their watchfulness – **covered with eyes** – rather than their functions of shielding the creatures from the glory of the divine Presence, protecting their modesty, and enabling them to move around the Temple: Isa. 6:2). Indeed, the Isaian parallel heightens their role of divine worship, singing or chanting the praises of God **day and night** without ceasing (for the work of worship continues even on the Sabbath). The first part of their canticle follows word for word that of the seraphim seen by Isaiah: **Holy, holy, holy, is the Lord God Almighty** (the Greek παντοκράτωρ being John's preferred translation of *sebaoth*). The God revealed in John's vision is holy, 'set apart', before whom evil and injustice must ultimately flee in fear (cf. *1 En.* 39:12; *1 Clem.* 34:6). The threefold 'holy' is paralleled by the threefold description of God met first (though in a slightly different order) at 1:4: perhaps we are meant to think of God as holy in creation (**who was**), holy in his being (**who is**), and holy in his eschatological judgements (**who is coming**).

Angelic canticles and hymns punctuate the Apocalypse at strategic points, fulfilling something of the role of the chorus in a Greek drama, which provides a running commentary on the action. Their vocabulary is so distinctive to Revelation as to suggest that they were composed for John's visionary book rather than reflecting existing hymns sung in Judaeo-Christian congregations (though we should not rule out the possibility that John is describing angelic singing heard during his visionary experience: see e.g. *Apocalypse of Abraham* 17; 1 Cor. 13:1; cf. 2 Cor. 12:4). But we should note their primary role as liturgical hymns, focusing the worshippers' minds upon the deity, proclaiming an alternative worldview which challenges the presumption and arrogance of rival claims to authority and worship. Throughout history, religious and political minorities have sustained their vision and found renewed strength through singing. The participation of vulnerable Christian congregations in the worship of heaven – not least through angelic hymns – offers them just such a vision.

The ceaseless singing of the cherubim is reciprocated by action on the   9–11
part of others in the heavenly liturgy. John's scene presents us with a series of concentric circles around the throne of the Holy One. The four creatures are closest to it (along with the seven torches/spirits). Their singing of the Trisagion is described as rendering **glory and honour and thanks** to the one on the throne (threefold attributes, as is appropriate to the divine).

The next circle is that of the elders. They take up, as if antiphonally, the song of the four creatures. But theirs is no merely cerebral activity of speaking or singing. They **fall down in front of the one seated on the throne** in a gesture of divine worship, casting their golden **wreaths** before the throne. It may be that such a ritual parodies practice in the imperial court, where senators and representatives of provincial cities presented the emperor with golden crowns on specific occasions (Aune 1983: 8–9). It is not the emperor, but the Holy One seated on the authentic throne, who deserves such honours. This vision is a salutary reminder that the rather cerebral activity which often passes for religious worship would have been unrecognisable as such in the ancient world, and certainly finds no support in the Apocalypse. Here the worship of heaven – which provides the paradigm for Christian worship – is an activity which involves the whole person, and all the human senses: speech, sight, hearing, touch and even smell (e.g. 5:8; 19:20).

The canticle of the elders focuses on the phrase **Worthy** (which is also a defining characteristic of the Lamb: 5:9, 12). God is worthy to receive the praises of creation generally, and of his faithful people specifically, precisely in his role as Creator. **The universe** is his because he created it. To him belongs the appropriate understanding and use of **power** (δύναμις, also 7:12; 11:17; 12:10; 19:1), which will be exercised inappropriately by the dragon (13:2), the monster (17:13) and Babylon (18:3), but given to the Lamb at 5:12 and shared with the faithful Philadelphians (3:8). The one on the throne, and no human rival, is worthily acclaimed as **our Lord and our God**. Even if Domitian did not claim the title *Dominus et deus noster* for himself (an assertion now disputed by some historians, e.g. Thompson 1990), or we prefer an earlier dating for Revelation, its first-century audiences might detect here a critique of trends within the imperial cult. This emphasis on God as the one who **created the universe** (reiterated at a climactic moment of eschatological judgement at 10:6) challenges those interpretations of the Apocalypse which regarding it as world-denying, envisaging the violent destruction of God's creation.

Some have noted the apparently illogical order of the last phrase of the canticle, for creation surely precedes existence. This may explain the variant reading 'by your will things were *not*, and were created' (i.e. out of a state of non-being). But we should not expect such straightforward logic in hymnic sections; indeed, this practice of inverting the logical order of events is regularly used by John (e.g. 3:17; 5:2, 5; 6:4: see Aune 1997: 312). The main point is clear: one alone is the object of worship; to be privileged to witness the heavenly liturgy is to have the veil removed from one's eyes, such that rival claimants to the throne on earth can never be viewed in the same light again.

Additional Note 1: Numbers in Revelation

Numbers have particular prominence in the Book of Revelation, and perform an important symbolic function. Certain numbers recur explicitly and implicitly throughout the book: notably three, four, seven and twelve. Multiples of these numbers also play an important role.

Three seems to have a special association with the divine. It is present implicitly in the divine name 'who was and who is and who is coming' (a tripartite formula which occurs three times in Revelation, at 1:4, 8 and 4:8; a shorter bipartite form occurs at 11:17; 16:5). Similar threefold descriptions of the divine are found in Judaism and in the wider Graeco-Roman world (see Aune 1997: 30–33). The pattern of three woes at 8:13 highlights the divine origin of these judgements upon unrepentant humanity (also 16:19). Elsewhere in Revelation, the divine is parodied by the triumvirate of the dragon, monster and false prophet, from whose mouths come three demonic frogs (e.g. 16:13; 20:10).

Four is often associated with the earthly created order, built into its very structure (e.g. Iren. *Adv. Haer.* 3.11.8: the world in which we live has four zones and four principal winds); there are also four elements from which the earth is composed, and four seasons. In Revelation, the created world is represented by the four cherubim around God's throne (e.g. 4:6, 8; 5:6, 8, 14), while the altar in the heavenly temple has four horns (9:13). The number is appropriately associated with those who execute judgements on the earth: four angels stand at the earth's corners restraining the four winds (7:1; cf. 20:8), while another four are bound at the River Euphrates (9:14–15).

Seven seems to have been regarded as a sacred number in the ancient world, and one which evoked completeness or perfection (it being the number of days in the week and of the planets, therefore built into the structure of the universe). For Jews, it reflected the pattern of creation, which culminated in God's sabbath rest on the seventh day (Gen. 1:1—2:3). Furthermore, it is the sum of three and four (associated with the divine and the universe respectively). Seven plays a key structuring role in the Apocalypse: notably in the seven messages (2:1—3:22), the seven seals (6:1—8:1; cf. 5:1, 5), the seven trumpets (8:2—11:18) and the seven bowls (15:5—16:21). Interestingly, two of these septets are divided into four and three, thus highlighting the significance of these two numbers: the four horsemen are set apart from the remaining three seals (6:1–8); the last three trumpets are associated with the three woes (8:13). Elsewhere in Revelation there are seven spirits (1:4; 3:1; 4:5; 5:6), seven angels/stars (1:16, 20; 2:1; 3:1; 4:5), seven congregations/lampstands (1:4, 11, 12, 20; 2:1), seven trumpet-angels (8:2, possibly to be identified with 'the seven spirits'), seven thunders (10:3–4), seven bowl-angels (15:1, 6–8), and seven kings (17:9–10). There are also seven unnumbered beatitudes scattered throughout the book (see Table 1). The Lamb has seven horns and seven eyes (5:6). Again, the divine is parodied by the dragon and the monster from the sea, who both have seven heads despite their demonic nature (12:3; 13:1; 17:3).

Related to seven are two additional numbers. Half of seven is *three and a half* (derived from Daniel's three and a half years of persecution: e.g. Dan. 7:25; 12:7). As half of a complete number, it represents a limited, incomplete period of persecution for God's people, in which they will be preserved from spiritual harm though not from suffering. It is found in its variants of 'a time, times and half a time' (12:14), 'forty-two months' (11:2; 13:5), and '1,260 days' (11:3; 12:6), and the two witnesses rise from the dead after three and a half days (11:9, 11). One less than seven is the number *six*. If seven denotes completeness, then the number six falls short of this as a number of incompleteness or imperfection. This may be one of the resonances of the 'number of the monster' at 13:18, which is 666 (though the four creatures have six wings: 4:8, influenced by Isa. 6:2).

Twelve is the product of three and four. Its association with the zodiac in the ancient world is significant, revealing it as a number embedded into the cosmos. Like seven, it also symbolises completeness (the twelve tribes of Israel at 7:5; the twelve stars of the woman's crown at 12:1, possibly also symbolising the zodiacal signs). Revelation's description of the new Jerusalem is shot through with the number twelve, symbolising the order and perfection of this visionary city: twelve gates made of twelve pearls, with twelve angel guards; twelve foundations; twelve names written on both its gates and foundations; twelve kinds of fruit on the tree of life (21:12, 14,

21; 22:2). Moreover, its twelve gates are divided into four sets of three (21:13). Multiples of twelve are also important. There are twelve thousand sealed from each of the tribes of Israel (7:5–8): the symbolic significance of the resulting 144,000 points to a number of inclusion, 'a huge number, which no one could count' (7:4; 14:1, 3; see commentary on 7:4–8). Similarly, order and perfection are signified by the multiples in the description of the new Jerusalem: the length, width and height of the city are 12,000 stadia, while the measurement of its wall is 144,000 cubits (21:16, 17).

Other numbers also occur in Revelation, though with less regularity. Among the most important are the following.

Two is the number of witness in the Jewish tradition, based on texts such as Deut. 19:15. Appropriately, Revelation describes the prophetic ministry of two witnesses (11:4, 10).

Five is a natural round number, being the number of fingers on the human hand, and therefore having the significance of 'a few' (Aune 1998a: 530). In Revelation, the demonic scorpions are allowed to torment people for five months, i.e. for a limited period (9:5, 10).

Ten is another round number with a sense of human completeness, and is regularly used in Jewish texts to measure time. In Revelation, the faithful in Smyrna will be tested for ten days, a limited period of time (2:10; cf. Dan. 1:12, 14). Elsewhere, the dragon and the monster have ten horns (12:3; 13:1; 17:3, 7), the horns of the latter representing ten kings (17:12, 16): this may express the human limitations of their power. Multiples of ten include one thousand, denoting a large number (e.g. 5:11; 7:5); related to a period of time, it is used of the 'millennium' or thousand-year reign of Christ (20:2).

The Lamb and the First Scroll (5:1–14)

(1) Then I saw in the right hand of the one seated on the throne a scroll covered with writing inside and on the back, sealed with seven seals. (2) And I saw a powerful angel proclaiming in a loud voice: 'Who is worthy to open the scroll by loosening its seals?' (3) But no-one could be found to open the scroll or see inside it – not in heaven nor on earth nor under the earth. (4) I broke down in tears, because no-one worthy could be found to open the scroll or see inside it. (5) But one of the elders said to me, 'Stop weeping! Look, the Lion of the tribe of Judah, the Root of David, has conquered; therefore he can open the scroll and its seven seals.' (6) Then I saw in between the throne and the four creatures, in the middle of the elders, a Lamb standing as if it had been slaughtered. It had seven horns and seven eyes, which are the seven spirits of God sent by him into all the earth. (7) The Lamb came and

took the scroll from the right hand of the one seated on the throne. (8) When it had taken the scroll, the four creatures and the twenty-four elders fell down in front of the Lamb, each with a harp and gold bowls full of incense (which are the prayers of the holy ones). (9) They sang a new song:
'Worthy are you to receive the scroll
   and open its seals.
For you were slaughtered,
and with your blood have redeemed for God
   people from every tribe and language, people and nation.
(10) You have made them sharers in our God's royal rule,
priests ministering to him,
   and they shall reign on the earth.'
(11) Then I looked, and I heard the sound of a vast quantity of angels around the throne and the creatures and the elders (ten thousand times ten thousand, yes, thousands upon thousands in number). (12) They were singing with a mighty voice:
'Worthy is the slaughtered Lamb,
   to receive power and wealth,
   wisdom and strength,
   honour and glory and praise.'
(13) Then I heard every created thing in heaven and on earth, under the earth and in the sea (that is, everything in them), saying:
'To the one seated on the throne and to the Lamb,
   be praise and honour, glory and strength, for ever and ever.'
(14) The four creatures replied: 'Amen!' And the elders fell down and worshipped.

Apart from the otherwise unattested appearance of the twenty-four elders, the first scene of John's throne-vision in chapter 4 could simply be another Jewish account of a heavenly ascent and vision of the *Merkavah*. As this vision continues here into its second stage, however, we are sharply reminded that this is a distinctly Christian text (contra Ford 1975). The introduction of a new character into the visionary drama, the Lamb, adds an unexpected twist to traditional narratives of the throne-vision (though not very surprising for Christian audiences versed in the gospel story). Chapters 4 and 5 are like two panels of a visionary diptych, which only when taken together provide the interpretative key to what will follow. Both highlight the fundamental theme of the heavenly liturgy, culminating in the singing of canticles by the heavenly choirs. It is as though only in worship is a correct orientation to be discovered: true worship is presented here not as some naïve flight from the world, but that which enables its participants to confront the realities of the world with renewed vision and insight. Van Eyck's *Adoration of the Lamb* in St Bavo's Cathedral, Ghent evokes in a particularly potent way this interpenetration of heaven and earth in the eucharistic liturgy.

1 John's **I saw** (cf. 4:1) marks a new and dramatic stage in his description of the heavenly throne-room. He now focuses in on **the right hand of the one seated on the throne**. The right hand of God in the Hebrew scriptures denotes God's power, particularly his power to save and to execute judgement, which are two sides of the same coin (e.g. Exod. 15:6; Job 40:14; Ps. 48:10; Isa. 41:10; cf. Rom. 1:16–17). Elsewhere in Revelation, those who act on his behalf, whether Christ (1:16–17) or a mighty angel (10:5–6), do so with their right hand (more sinisterly, humans are marked with the mark of the monster on their right hand, 13:16). This suggests that the **scroll** held in that hand (βιβλίον: a book in roll form, such as was used by Jews and perhaps the earliest Christians for their sacred writings) has something to do with God's plan to establish justice and salvation in his world.

But can we be any more specific about the significance of the scroll, and its contents? A range of possibilities has been suggested. For some, it is the Lamb's book of life (e.g. 3:5; 13:8; 20:12), which contains the names of the faithful. We are told that it is **covered with writing inside and on the back**, unusual given that scrolls generally contained writing on only one side. The need to use both sides of the scroll would be accounted for by the countless number of the redeemed (cf. 7:9). But this interpretation would detach the scroll from the unfolding drama of the next few chapters, which seem to be directly related to its opening.

Others, often following the variant reading 'inside and outside', regard the βιβλίον as some kind of legal document, such as a marriage contract or deed (e.g. Jer. 32:9–10), which would have been folded and sealed, with a summary of its contents on the outside (i.e. a codex rather than a scroll). In other words, this is a document which marks the marriage of the Lamb to his bride, or hands over the deeds of the Kingdom to God's people. The variant reading is likely to be secondary, however, the correction of a later scribe more used to codices than to scrolls. Some note that in Roman law a will or testament had to be witnessed and sealed in wax by seven witnesses, to ensure that the document could not be tampered with before its opening on the testator's death. This is not impossible as part of the background, for what allows the scroll to be opened is the death of the Lamb. Still others propose, with some validity, that the scroll in question represents the Old Testament scriptures, now to have their true meaning opened up for God's people by the definitive interpreter, the Messiah (for succinct discussions of the options, see Caird 1966: 70–72; Sweet 1979: 122–24; Reddish 2001: 107–08).

However, the story so far has led us to conclude that Daniel, and especially Ezekiel, have exercised a particular influence upon John's book. Their witness here will be decisive. Ezekiel sees a scroll in an outstretched hand (presumably that of the human figure on the throne), with writing on front and back, containing 'words of lamentation and mourning and woe' which he is to speak to the house of Israel (Ezek. 2:8—3:3; cf. Rev. 10:8–11). Similarly, the angelic figure of Daniel 10 recounts to the seer what is written in the book of truth, specifically 'what will happen to your people at the end of days' (Dan. 10:14, 21). These antecedents suggest that the scroll seen by John is also concerned with what is to happen in the last days, particularly to God's people, and that its contents will be revealed when the scroll is opened (in fact they do not begin to be revealed until John has devoured this same scroll and begun to prophesy at 10:10–11). This would accord with the presence of heavenly books and tablets in other apocalypses, which contain heavenly secrets pertaining to the destiny of the world (e.g. *1 En.* 81:1–3; 93:1–14; 103:1–4).

Yet it would be a mistake to suppose that the contents of the scroll concern only events still to come, in the future from John's perspective. Rather, as the rest of the chapter will make clear, the slaughter of the Lamb has already inaugurated the eschatological times. The Apocalypse shares the early Christian conviction that with the death and resurrection of Christ, the last days have arrived, such that some of the eschatological events expected by pious Jews in the future were for the early Christians present and even past. This scroll, in other words, contains God's plan to bring salvation and establish justice, a plan which has now been put into action through the crucified and risen Jesus (for the relationship between this scroll and the 'little scroll' that John will be given to eat, see on 10:2).

There is one major difference between Ezekiel's scroll and that in Revelation. Ezekiel's is open and spread out before the prophet, while the scroll John sees is **sealed with seven seals**. Seven, the number of perfection or completion, makes clear that it is well and truly sealed so as to prevent any premature opening or tampering. More negatively, the sealing means that the execution of God's redemptive plan is, at least temporarily, delayed. Some might detect echoes of Isa. 29:11, where the people's sinfulness means that the visions of God's future are hidden from the eyes of prophets and seers, like the words of a sealed document.

How will things proceed? In apocalypses, the action is moved on and mysteries explained by heavenly beings such as angels. Hence a 2–4

powerful angel appears on the scene to articulate the question which was surely on the seer's lips, if not also on the lips of every reader of Revelation: **Who is worthy to open the scroll by loosening its seals?** Who is worthy to initiate the unsealing which will not only allow the contents of the scroll to be revealed, but also enable its words to come to pass? For these are divine words, the words of the one who spoke, and it came to be (Ps. 33:9; cf. Gen. 1:3). The identity of the **powerful angel** has intrigued many commentators (a similar angel will appear with a little scroll at 10:1, and at 18:21 with a millstone symbolising fallen Babylon). Given the angelomorphic description of the son of man figure in Revelation 1, one might be tempted to identify the **powerful angel** here with Christ; yet Jesus is about to appear, though in a different guise, in a few verses. More likely he is one of the principal angels such as Michael, Metatron or Yahoel (e.g. Dan. 10:13; *3 En.* 1:4; *Apoc. Abr.* 10:3), especially exalted heavenly beings who appear in Jewish apocalypses to perform particular tasks as God's representative (the angel of Dan. 4:13 LXX may have been the immediate influence). Perhaps he is Jesus' own angel (see 1:1, and on 10:1). Yet John is not concerned to identify him further at this point: however exalted this heavenly being is, his identity is apparently insignificant beside the one who is now about to appear on the scene.

At this stage the dramatic tension mounts, as any residual hope that the scroll can be unsealed and its contents played out in the world is apparently shattered: **no-one could be found to open the scroll or see inside it.** This statement presupposes the three-tier universe of ancient Near Eastern cosmology (though not necessarily understood literally: see on 4:1): **heaven** above the firmament, **earth** below it, and the territory **under the earth**, which included Sheol or Hades, as well as the Abyss where the forces of chaos and evil lurk (9:1–2, 11; 11:7; 17:8; 20:1, 3). Nowhere in the whole of creation is there found anyone able to open the scroll. The mention of **heaven** is particularly surprising, for surely God is worthy to break the seals (see 4:11). But God holds back, for in the divine economy the outworking of our human destiny is to be effected by one of our own (Caird 1966: 73).

A number of apocalypses describe the reaction of the seer to what is seen or heard, whether that be fear, trembling and rocking, or physical collapse. Here too John is caught up emotionally in what he sees and hears, and he **broke down in tears.** Expectations have been raised, promises have been made that he will learn 'what must soon come to pass', his Christian conviction that Jesus' death and resurrection has ushered in the end-times has received apparent divine confirmation. Now that he has come so close to seeing those things, however, the scroll remains resolutely closed in the hand of the enthroned one. Readers can sense the pathos here as the seer weeps uncontrollably.

At this point **one of the** twenty-four **elders** steps in to break the 5 dramatic tension, thus acting as authoritative interpreter (a role played in other apocalypses by angels, which seems to confirm the elders' angelic identity: see on 4:4). He commands John to **stop weeping**, for a worthy candidate has indeed been found who **can open the scroll and its seven seals.** John hears the identity of the worthy figure: **the Lion of the tribe of Judah, the Root of David.** Both titles would evoke in the Judaeo-Christian mind an image of the Davidic Messiah, God's anointed king who would act on his behalf in the last days. Jacob's blessing at Gen. 49:9–10 presents Judah as 'a lion's whelp', from whom the royal sceptre shall not pass, and this gave birth to the expectation (just one messianic expectation among many) of a fearless warrior king who would defeat the enemies of God's people (e.g. *Pss Sol.* 17). Such a figure is reflected for example in Ezra's vision of a (Rome-like) Eagle defeated by a Lion, who is explicitly identified as the eschatological Messiah (*4 Ez.* 11:37; 12:31–32). The Root of David is probably an allusion to the root of David's father Jesse, and the branch which would emerge from it (Isa. 11:1, 10, interpreted messianically by at least some Jews: e.g. 4QpIsa; 4QFlor; *T. Jud.* 24:5). The earliest Christians were keen to show that Jesus came from the tribe of Judah and the royal line of David, thus fulfilling such messianic expectations (e.g. Rom. 1:3; Mt. 1:2–16; Lk. 1:27; Heb. 7:14). John the seer is no exception to this tradition.

The good news that John hears is that this Lion-Messiah **has conquered.** The language of conquering has been used in the messages to the seven congregations to describe those Christians who remain faithful in the last great battle. Used of the Messiah, it suggests that this figure has already played a decisive role in that battle, whose outcome has already been decided. The fact that he can open the scroll through loosening its seven seals (verse 2 uses the verb λυεῖν) echoes his ability to release or set free his people from their sins, liberating them in the new and greater Exodus from whatever enslaves them (the same verb was used in the preferred reading of 1:5).

But there is a sharp disjunction, never quite resolved, between what 6–7 John hears and what he finally sees (the relationship between hearing and seeing in the Apocalypse is an important though complex one). Instead of the handsome yet terrifying 'king of the forest', leaping upon his enemies with paws ready for the kill, John sees **a Lamb** (this, rather than 'someone like a son of man', will be the crucial christological title from now on, occurring 28 times (i.e. 4 × 7) in the

Apocalypse). Christian and Jewish hearers would know of the tendency in apocalypses to portray human beings as animals (e.g. *1 Enoch* 85–90), and the elder's words have made clear that the Messiah is meant. The location of the Lamb is somewhat ambiguous, for the phrase used of the four creatures (ἐν μέσῳ τοῦ θρόνου, 4:6) is used again here, though it is also 'in the middle of' the creatures. If they themselves are around and attached to the throne (see on 4:6), it could mean that the Lamb is literally 'in the middle of the throne', i.e. actually seated on it (this certainly appears to be the case at 7:17; 22:1, 3; cf. 3:21). The ambiguity may well be deliberate. Nevertheless, at this stage in the action we are probably to prefer the alternative translation: the Lamb is situated **in between the throne and the four creatures**, i.e. on the point of actually being enthroned but still approaching (we are only told that it **came and took the scroll** in verse 7). We then have a series of concentric circles in heaven, radiating out from the focus of worship: the throne (and the Lamb), the four creatures, the elders.

What are we to make of this juxtaposition of **the Lion of the tribe of Judah** and the **Lamb standing as if it had been slaughtered**? For some, the latter image has totally redefined the first, such that an image of power has been reinterpreted as a symbol of weakness. They consider the sacrificial lamb (e.g. Gen. 22:7; Exod. 29:39; Lev. 12:6; Num. 6:12), or the application of that motif to the suffering Servant of the Lord (Isa. 53:7), as the principal background here, as the language of 'slaughter' suggests (though the LXX prefers ἀμνός or πρόβατον to Revelation's ἀρνίον; the one exception is Jer. 11:19, which likens the prophet to an innocent ἀρνίον led to slaughter). Certainly when Revelation uses conquering language of Christ and his followers, the cross is never far away (e.g. 2:11; 12:11; 15:2). Here is a Messiah who conquers through allowing himself to be slain.

But perhaps we should not so swiftly overlook the more violent, powerful lion imagery, but allow Lion and Lamb to interpret one another. For however much it has been redefined, Revelation certainly views what Christ has done as powerful, and in many ways terrifying (e.g. 6:16: for a judicious discussion of some of these issues, see Moyise 2001). Nor is it clear that the Lamb is only a figure of weakness, for the emphasis on its having been **slaughtered** is juxtaposed with its **standing**, a position of strength. So too its **seven horns** suggests that this Lamb has perfect power (for the horn as a symbol of power, see e.g. 1 Sam. 2:10; Ps. 112:9; Sir. 47:5; Jer. 48:25; Dan. 7:21). Alternative backgrounds in Judaism would support this more military image. Some point to the warrior lamb or ram in the apocalyptic tradition, symbolising the Messiah or other 'saviour' figures such as Judas Maccabeus (e.g. *1 En.* 90:9; *T. Jos.* 19:8). Perhaps we should not try to discriminate too much between the various possibilities in an apocalypse which works by evoking associations rather than offering one-to-one correspondences. Indeed, the wider narrative script of Revelation may suggest an additional nuance. John has already given us clues that the Exodus story is an important motif (e.g. the most likely reading of 1:5), and this will become clearer in the visions ahead. Hence among the associations here we should almost certainly see the Passover Lamb, the lamb without blemish whose blood delivered God's people from death and heralded the liberation from slavery in Egypt (Exodus 12).

The Lamb's perfect number of **seven eyes** speaks of its perfect vision and knowledge, its ability to see as God sees. Indeed, under the influence of Zech. 4:10, they are further identified as **the seven spirits of God** (or angels of the Presence, see on 1:4) **sent by him into all the earth**. Revelation is not alone among New Testament writings in advocating the view that angels are subordinate to the exalted Christ (see e.g. Eph. 1:21; Heb. 1:4). Here even the archangels keep watch at his bidding, acting as his eyes, as hitherto they had done for the one on the throne (perhaps we can detect here a crucial stage in that transformation of an angelic being into the Spirit-Paraclete which seems to underlie the Fourth Gospel).

We now witness what is effectively the enthronement of the Lamb in 8 heaven, as it takes **the scroll**. The effect is another act of worship, closely modelled on that which occurred in chapter 4, but this time focused on **the Lamb**. This depiction of the worship of Jesus, in terms so thoroughly Jewish, reflects the early emergence of 'Christ-devotion' within the worship of the first Christian communities (Hurtado 2003). The priestly actors in this heavenly liturgy are **the four creatures** and especially **the twenty-four elders**. Each of the latter (though the ambiguous Greek might include the former) has a **harp**, an instrument used for sacred music in the Jerusalem Temple (e.g. Pss 33:2; 150:3; 1 Chron. 25:1, 6; 1 Macc. 4:54). They also have **gold bowls full of incense**, that aromatic substance widely used in both Jewish (e.g. Exod. 30:7; 2 Chron. 2:3; 2 Macc. 10:3) and pagan worship. This borrowing from Israel's cult (whether remembered from actual participation in Jerusalem Temple worship or from the tradition) reflects the firm belief that the earthly liturgy of both Tabernacle and Temple was patterned upon the true heavenly liturgy in which angels minister as priests (e.g. Exod. 25:40; Heb 8:5; 4Q400–07). John is privileged to participate, albeit as an observer, in the priestly liturgy of heaven.

The gold bowls full of incense are also **the prayers of the holy ones**. 'Holy ones' or 'saints', although originally a title of the angels (e.g. Deut. 33:2; Tob. 11:14; *1 En.* 1:9; 14:23; 39:5; 45:1), was also claimed for the people of Israel, the nation God had set apart (e.g.

Lev. 11:45; Pss 33:12; 34:9; the identity of the 'holy ones' in Dan. 7:21–22 and 8:24 is ambiguous). Therefore it was claimed by the new or renewed people of God, the Church (e.g. Acts 9:13; 1 Cor. 1:2; 6:1–2; Eph. 1:1). The ascent of human prayers to God, sometimes delivered by angels (e.g. Tob. 12:12, 15; *T. Levi* 3:5–7) and here by the elders, had already been likened in the biblical tradition to sweet-smelling incense smoke ascending to God's throne (e.g. Ps. 141:2). The mention here of the prayers of God's faithful people relates it closely to the opening of the sealed scroll which the Lamb is about to effect. The prayers of the holy ones will be referred to again as the drama develops (8:3–4; cf. 6:9–11), while seven gold bowls will contain the seven last plagues effecting God's judgement (e.g. 15:7; 16:1; 17:1). This is what God's people have been praying and longing for, and what John has been weeping for: the putting into action of God's final plan to judge injustice and wickedness, and establish God's kingdom of justice and salvation.

9–10 The recognition in heaven that the Lamb is the worthy agent through whom the divine plan can be put into operation provokes a **new song**, which according to Psalm 96 would proclaim God's salvation, and the marvellous deeds done among all peoples (Ps. 96:1–3; cf. Pss 33:3; 40:3). Just as the worship of God was accompanied by a canticle, addressing him in the second person as 'worthy to receive' (4:11), so too the Lamb is worshipped in the same way: **Worthy are you to receive the scroll and open its seals.** The reason why the Lamb can open the seals on the scroll is that it has been **slaughtered,** and by its **blood** (i.e. its death) has **redeemed** people **for God.** Just as the one on the throne was acclaimed as Creator of the universe, so the Lamb is here acclaimed as the Redeemer.

We should not downplay the violent connotations of the claims that the Lamb was **slaughtered**: the verb σφάζω is used elsewhere in Revelation of those who have been killed violently (6:4, 9; 13:3; 18:24), a reminder of the cruel death by crucifixion which Jesus himself endured. Yet the early Christians were able to make sense of such barbarity and shame by interpreting what happened to Jesus – and what would happen to his followers – in the light of what occurred in the Temple (e.g. Rom. 3:24–25; 1 Cor. 15:3). His apparently shameful death was in fact a sacrifice, the sacrifice of the Lamb whose **blood** has **redeemed for God people from every tribe and language, people and nation** (some manuscripts read 'redeemed *us* for God').

Indeed, Revelation has already hinted (e.g. 1:5–6) that a new Passover and Exodus may be taking place, and the juxtaposition of **slaughtered** and **redeemed** in relation to the Lamb supports this. Redemption is the language of the slave-market, the cost of setting a slave free, and the Exodus narrative describes the liberation of the Hebrews from slavery in Egypt, to become 'a kingdom of priests and a holy nation' (Exod. 19:6). But in the new Exodus which John will see taking place in apocalyptic vision, there are fundamental differences. First, the tyrant from whom God's people need liberating is no earthly ruler, but Satan himself. Second, the redeemed people is no longer restricted to the people of Israel, but is called **from every tribe and language, people and nation** (see the redefinition of the 'twelve tribes' in Revelation 7). Third, with the death and resurrection of the Lamb, what is promised has already come to pass, at least in part: **You have made them sharers in our God's royal rule** (contrast the activities of 'earth's kings' at 6:15; 17:2; 18:3; 19:19), **priests ministering to him**. However much the Apocalypse envisages future eschatological salvation, there is a powerful streak of 'realised eschatology' running through it. Already God's people share in the Kingdom, and share with the angels in priestly ministry, able to offer true worship to God, and to mediate on behalf of the world. This would be particularly powerful when Revelation's canticles were heard – and perhaps repeated by the congregation – in a liturgical setting: in the liturgy, the gulf between present reality and future hope is temporarily bridged. Indeed, the first part of verse 10 has suggested to some commentators that we should follow the minority reading in treating the final verb as a present tense: 'they reign on the earth' (βασιλεύουσιν, rather than the majority future βασιλεύσουσιν: e.g. Charles 1920: I, 148). While this reading is attractive, the wider context of Revelation suggests that the establishment of God's kingdom *on earth* is still a future hope, which finds its visionary fulfilment in the millennial reign of 20:4–6, and ultimately in the new Jerusalem. Thus we should prefer the majority reading **they shall reign on the earth**. For John, as for Jesus, the Church must continue to pray that the Father's Kingdom may come in its fullness, when God's will is done on earth as in heaven (Mt. 6:10).

Up to this point, John's focus has been on a relatively small band of 11–12 figures in the heavenly throne-room: the one on the throne, the Lamb, the seven spirits, the four creatures and the twenty-four elders. Now the view pans out, and John sees **around the throne and the creatures and the elders** what other visionaries have seen before him and since (e.g. Dan. 7:10; *1 En.* 14:22), the huge number of the angelic hosts. In the symbolic numerology of Revelation, John describes a countless multitude, which artists across the centuries have struggled to portray: **ten thousand times ten thousand** (the Greek μυρίας, 'ten thousand', can simply mean a large number, as in the English 'myriad'), **yes, thousands upon thousands in** number. The angelic liturgy is impressive indeed in its scale and intensity. These 'lesser angels' also sing a canticle which proclaims that the Lamb is worthy, and John notes in passing the volume of their singing. Though they use the third person rather than the second, the qualities they attribute to the Lamb – **power and wealth, wisdom and strength, honour and glory and praise** – the perfect number of seven attributes, include three already ascribed to God at 4:11. That which the Creator is worthy to receive from both angelic and human creatures is now also to be shared with his agent for the redemption of the cosmos, the slaughtered Lamb. Here we find the paradox of the cross, for in the eyes of the world that shameful death was anything but wise or honourable, and certainly the antithesis of power.

13–14   But even this is not the end of the story. When one thought the canvas could not contain any more, a massive panorama opens up to encompass yet another concentric circle around the throne, beyond the myriads of angels. As this vision reaches its climax with ear-splitting intensity, the whole of creation is caught up in the praise of God and the Lamb. **Every created thing** is involved, not only the angels **(in heaven)** but also those **on earth, under the earth and in the sea.** Animals, birds and fish join with humanity in a great act of divine worship. Even the underworld, the abode of the dead and dwelling-place of evil, is involved. Clearly this vision does not reflect present reality from John's perspective, for rebellion and injustice still exist in God's world. Rather we catch a glimpse here of what creation was intended for, and what can be in God's great plan, on earth, as it is in heaven. God and the Lamb, hitherto addressed separately, are now acclaimed together in one great concluding doxology, the objects of **praise and honour, glory and strength, for ever and ever** (the fourfold doxology reflects the number of the universe). The appropriate liturgical response – the great **Amen** – is given by **the four creatures**, perhaps on behalf of the universe whom they represent near the throne, while **the elders** fall down before the throne and the Lamb in a posture of silent and profound worship.

The Opening of the First Four Seals: The Four Horsemen (6:1–8)

(1) Then I saw the Lamb open one of the seven seals, and I heard one of the four creatures say in a voice as loud as thunder: 'Come!' (2) I looked, and there was a white horse. Its rider held a bow; he was given a wreath, and rode out as a conqueror, to conquer again.

(3) When it opened the second seal, I heard the second

creature say: 'Come!' (4) Then another horse rode out, fiery red, and its rider was permitted to remove peace from the earth, so that people slaughtered each other. He was also given a large sword.

(5) When it opened the third seal, I heard the third creature say: 'Come!' I looked, and there was a black horse, whose rider held a pair of scales in his hand.

(6) Then I heard what seemed like a voice coming from the middle of the four creatures, saying: 'A quart of wheat for a whole day's wages, and three quarts of barley for a whole day's wages! But do not harm the olive oil and the wine.'

(7) When it opened the fourth seal, I heard the fourth creature say: 'Come!' (8) I looked, and there was a sickly green horse; the name of its rider was Death, and Hades followed him. They were given power over a quarter of the earth, to kill by the sword and by famine, by pestilence and through the earth's monsters.

Like the calm before the storm, this great act of worship now issues forth in a voice **as loud as thunder,** as the Lamb begins to open the seals which will enable the scroll's contents to be read, and thereby put into effect. The throne-vision of Revelation 4—5 is intimately connected with the seals sequence of 6:1—8:1. But so too is the sequence of seven trumpets (8:2—11:18) which will be inaugurated by the opening of the seventh seal. Indeed, although there will be a gap in the narrative, the sequence of seven bowls (15:5—19:10) – which overlaps thematically with the trumpets in many ways – is also generally thought to be connected with the Lamb's action at this point. From this chapter onwards, the Lamb's role in enabling the fulfilment of God's salvific plan will be evident.

Although the current sequence includes all seven seals, the first four belong thematically together in their description of the four horsemen. Few scenes from John's book have been as influential in art, literature and wider culture as this. Perhaps its most famous representation is Albrecht Dürer's woodcut in which the four ride out together, trampling bishops, princes and merchants in their wake, an indication that power and prestige cannot render human beings immune from what John sees. The rider on the fourth horse has entered more subtly into the popular imagination in the person of the Grim Reaper. But this vision also raises a host of interpretative issues and theological conundrums. Are we witnessing the fulfilment of the scroll's contents as these horsemen emerge, or simply the prelude to their taking effect? Moreover, what is the precise connection between this sevenfold seals sequence and those of the trumpets and bowls which follow? Are the four riders demonic forces opposed to God and his people, or angelic agents performing the divine will? If the former, then what does this say about God's omnipotence? If the latter, then harsh questions are posed about God's righteousness. Particular questions are also raised about the identity of the first horseman, given the striking parallels between his description and the later description of the victorious Christ at 19:11–16.

According to the earliest surviving Latin commentary on the Apocalypse, that of Victorinus of Pettau, we are presented in the sequences of trumpets and bowls with a recapitulation of the same eschatological events rather than a chronological progression through them (Dulaey 1997: 78–89). Others have wanted to include the seals in this repetition, thus giving us three canvases portraying with increasing breadth of vision God's establishment of justice and overcoming of injustice. They note the strong structural parallels between the seals and trumpets septets: in both, the first four of the seven (6:1–8; 8:6–13) are set apart from the other three, and both have a delay between the sixth and seventh elements (7:1–17; 10:1—11:14).

Yet there are indications that this seals sequence (or at least the early part of it) presents an earlier stage in the action than what is described in the trumpets and bowls sequence. First, the scroll is tightly sealed with seven seals, so its contents can only be seen once all seven seals have been broken. Those explanations that posit a different kind of scroll which could be partially opened before all the seals were broken (e.g. Reddish 2001: 124–25) are ultimately unconvincing. While it is possible that John envisages a scroll with a summary of its contents written on the outside, at most we should expect that what John now sees is a foreshadowing or summary of the scroll's contents, not a revelation of the contents themselves (see e.g. Garrow 1997: 16–20). Second, the parallels between the trumpets and bowls (echoing the Exodus plagues on Egypt) are much stronger than those linking them to the seals, with the notable exception of the sixth seal (6:12–17). At this stage we are probably being presented with nothing new, but rather a vision of the expected 'messianic woes' frequently found in early Jewish and Christian thought, particularly in the apocalypses (e.g. *4 Ez.* 5:1–12; *2 Baruch* 25—27; *Jub.* 23:11–31). This belief held that a time of disaster, which would particularly impinge on God's people, would precede the establishment of God's reign.

John's antecedents may shed light here. Though the general theme of John's vision may have been inspired by Ezekiel's prophecy of judgement against Jerusalem (Ezek. 5:13–17), his primary Old Testament antecedent for the four horsemen is Zechariah. Zechariah 1:7–17 describes a vision of a rider accompanied by red, sorrel and white horses, interpreted as those sent by the Lord to patrol the earth, charged with punishing those nations who oppress God's people. A further vision of four chariots drawn by red, black, white and dappled grey horses (Zech. 6:1–8) identifies them as the four winds sent out by God to patrol the four quadrants of the earth. Thus what John sees would likely be understood by him and his contemporaries as a declaration that, despite appearances to the contrary, God remains in control of his world, including those forces which can appear to wreak cosmic havoc, and will ultimately act on behalf of his oppressed and persecuted people.

But commentators from earliest times have also recognised the strong parallels with the so-called Synoptic Apocalypse (Mark 13; Matthew 24; Luke 21), a reminder that ultimately this whole book is 'a revelation from Jesus Christ' (see Table 2). These are not such as to demand a literary relationship between Revelation and one or more of the Synoptic Gospels, but almost certainly point to shared knowledge of a common tradition. The whole seals sequence contains such parallels, though Revelation delays the coming of the Son of Man until chapter 19 (compare Mk 13:26–27 and par.). Particularly striking is the close relationship between the roles and identities of the four horsemen and the 'beginning of the birthpangs' described in the Synoptic discourse (especially the Lucan version, whose additional reference to 'plagues' at 21:11 correlates with John's fourth horseman). John's riders herald those things which must happen in that turbulent time of trial prior to the coming of God's Kingdom (the eschatological earthquake is delayed until the sixth seal). Although the power of John's vision lies in its ability to speak to the tragedies of human history in every age (Giblin 1994: 85; Kovacs and Rowland 2004: 80–88), this link with Jesus' teaching makes clear that these are specifically eschatological events.

Previously we have heard that only **the Lamb** is worthy to open the 1–2 scroll. The dramatic tension now rises again as, one by one, the Lamb opens **the seven seals**. This means that, whatever the nature of these four horsemen or the phenomena they signify, the Lamb as God's messianic vice-regent is ultimately in control. Though the sequences of seals, trumpets and bowls have their dark side, from the perspective of the threatened, vulnerable and persecuted this vision is one of gospel reversal. It is ultimately the one who allowed himself to be slaughtered, not the mighty empire responsible for that slaughter, who holds the fate of human history in his hands.

As each of the first four seals is broken, **one of the four creatures** utters the command to **Come!** A variant reading 'Come and see!' (here and in verses 3, 5 and 7) makes John the addressee, drawing him more directly into the action. But this can be accounted for either as a scribal error (a misreading of καὶ εἶδον at the beginning

Table 2: Revelation and the Synoptic Apocalypse

Revelation	Synoptic Apocalypse (Mk 13; Mt. 24; Lk. 21)
6:1–2: first seal (Antichrist)	Mk 13:6 and par.: those coming in Christ's name who lead many astray
6:3–4: second seal (takes peace; kills by sword)	Mk 13:7 and par.: wars and rumours of wars (Lk.: insurrections)
6:5–6: third seal (famine)	Mk 13:8 and par.: earthquakes and famine
6:7–8: fourth seal (pestilence)	Lk. 21:11: plagues (λοιμοὶ)
6:9–11: fifth seal (souls of martyrs)	Mk 13:9–13 and par.: arrest and persecution of Christ's followers (cf. Mt. 10:17–22; Lk. 12:11–12)
11:1–2: trampling of holy city	Lk. 21:20–24: Jerusalem surrounded by armies; falls by sword and taken captive among nations; Jerusalem trampled on by Gentiles until 'times of Gentiles fulfilled'
13:1–18: visions of monster from sea and monster from earth/false prophet	Mk 13:21–23 and par.: false messiahs and false prophets
6:12–17: sixth seal (darkening of sun; moon turns to blood; stars fall from heaven)	Mk 13:24–25 and par.: darkening of sun and moon; stars fall from heaven; powers of heaven shaken
8:1–2: seventh seal (silence in heaven and appearance of angels with seven trumpets)	Mk 13:26–27 and par.: coming of Son of Man; angels gather elect from four winds (Mt. 24:30–31 has angels sent with a trumpet-call)

of verse 2 as καὶ ἴδε), or more likely a correction on theological grounds, a refusal to accept that God could be ultimately responsible for the destructive activity of the horsemen. The reading followed here is the *lectio difficilior*. We are not told in which order the four creatures speak, though some commentators follow the order of Rev. 4:7 and think it appropriate that the first speaks in a manner appropriate to a lion, **in a voice as loud as thunder**. More likely the reference to **thunder** is meant to stress the authoritative nature of the voice (e.g. 4:5; 14:2), closely associated with the God of Sinai (8:5; 11:19; 16:18), though we should not forget that later Jewish tradition was aware of the terrifying, rather unruly nature of the cherubim (see on 4:6b–7).

Who does the first creature summon? The only other command to **Come!** (ἔρχου) in the Apocalypse is addressed to Christ (22:17, 20).

One early line of interpretation sees this first rider on **a white horse** and wearing a victor's **wreath** (στέφανος) as Christ, or the effects of his coming (Christ will appear on a white horse and wearing many diadems at 19:11; 'someone like a son of man' will wear a golden wreath at 14:14). Wreaths have already been promised to faithful followers of the Lamb (e.g. 2:10; 3:11; cf. 4:4, 10; 12:1); further, the verb **to conquer** will be used both of the Lamb's victory (3:21; 5:5; 17:14) and that of the martyrs (2:7, 11, 17, 26; 3:5, 12, 21; 12:11; 15:2; 21:7). Moreover, **white** elsewhere in the Apocalypse is a symbol of victory and purity, associated with God and his saints (e.g. 1:14; 2:17; 3:4, 18; 4:4; 6:11; 7:13; 19:14), pointing to the significance of colours in John's vision. For Victorinus, the sequence of seals reveals the effects of Christ's sending the Spirit and of the preaching of the gospel (Dulaey 1997: 78–81). A similar view is found in the influential Greek commentary of Andreas of Caesarea: the first horse represents the sending out of the apostles; the other horses symbolise the negative effects of the gospel on those who oppose it (Taushev and Rose 1995: 125). It is a powerful reminder that the good news brings in its wake judgement no less than salvation (cf. Rom. 1:16–31).

More likely, however, this rider on a white horse represents not Christ or his agents but false Christs, even Antichrist, a potent indication of the way in which the demonic subtly but convincingly parodies the divine. The first sign of the 'beginning of the birthpangs' noted in Mark 13 and parallels is the appearance of many proclaiming 'I am he' (Mk 13:6; Lk. 21:8; Mt. 24:5: 'I am the Christ'). This is reiterated by the warning of 'false messiahs and false prophets' at Mk 13:22 and parallels. The activity of the monster from the sea, and a second monster from the earth (also known as the 'false prophet') will play a prominent role in the second half of the Apocalypse. Moreover, the verb **to conquer** will be used of the monster's victory over the two witnesses (11:7) and over the saints (13:7a, missing in some manuscripts). The demonic locusts wear wreaths at 9:7, while both the dragon and the monster wear diadems, seven and ten respectively (12:3; 13:1; compare the 'many diadems' of Christ at 19:12). Thus even the colour of the **white horse** is a demonic parody. Revelation unveils the shocking truth that the dividing line between good and evil, truth and falsehood is at times almost imperceptible: what so often passes as morally neutral, even positively good, may well be a satanic deception.

This means that all four horsemen are to be understood as demonic rather than angelic figures, the agents of chaos and destruction who are not simply behind the human activity of warfare and disaster throughout history, but also play a key role in that time of intense tribulation prior to the End, which affects even God's people.

Nevertheless, the 'good news' of John's vision is that these rebellious forces, though their mayhem is temporarily permitted by God (note the repeated ἐδόθη, variously translated **was given** and **was permitted**: verses 2, 4, 8), are ultimately destined to lose their power. Their victory is a hollow victory, for it is founded on warfare and its consequences, a sharp contrast to the true victory of the slaughtered Lamb. Yet it is one of the paradoxes of the Christian gospel that even the forces of Satan can be used for divine purposes.

For all the stereotypical nature of John's vision, his first audiences in Roman Asia would almost certainly have detected a certain 'local colouring' which would have given Revelation's prophecy added conviction. Two sets of historical echoes have been suggested, which are not mutually exclusive. The first highlights the juxtaposition of the **horse** and the **bow**. In the first-century Roman world this would most naturally have evoked the greatest threat to Rome on the eastern borders, the Parthian Empire, noted for its mounted bowmen (there are probably also echoes of the Parthians at 9:14 and 16:12). Other Jewish authors believed the Parthians would play a role in eschatological events as Rome's enemies (*1 En.* 56:5–7; *Sib. Or.* 5:438).

Yet there may be an additional twist to the imagery. Not only had the Parthians under Vologeses inflicted a shocking defeat on the Roman army at the River Tigris in 62 CE. The demise of the great tyrant Nero in 68 was met with a flurry of speculation as to whether he had actually died, or had gone off to the east to raise an army and reclaim his throne (Tacitus, *Hist.* 1.2; 2.8f.; Suet. *Nero* 57; *Sib. Or.* 4:119–24, 137–39; 5:137–52, 361–85). The Parthians seem to have supported a succession of pretenders, the first in 69 (and others in 80 and 88–89). This would not have been lost on Roman hearers of the Apocalypse: the antichrist Nero was about to return, backed by his Parthian allies. Rome, that apparently impregnable empire, would face destruction at the hands of one of her own.

The second possible allusion detected by early Asian Christians is to the figure of Apollo. Apollo, the source of oracular prophecy, was regularly depicted as carrying a bow. This iconography was known to Jews (e.g. Philo, *Legat.* 95–96; Josephus, *C. Ap.* 2.33–34) as well as pagans. Moreover, the association of Apollo with prophecy would have been particularly familiar to Asians, for the renowned Oracle of Apollo at Didyma was located within their province (for the particular influence of Apollo on Patmos, see on 1:9). Thus the bow may be a caricature of the sword associated with Christ on his white horse (19:15), a counterfeit divine word contrasted with the true word of God. Mark 13:22 and parallels warn of false prophets no less than false messiahs: here we have a vision of the two together (Kerkeslager 1993).

Yet again, Christian audiences might also detect a sideswipe at recent imperial pretensions. Not only did certain Roman historians note Nero's similarities to Apollo as singer, lyre-player and charioteer (Suet. *Nero* 53; Tacitus, *Ann.* 14.14.1f.), but coins minted towards the end of Nero's reign exploited this further by portraying the emperor as Apollo (Kreitzer 1996: 208). John's vision would then have unveiled Nero's messianic pretensions, and the continuing hopes of his supporters, as a demonic if slightly comic parody of the true Messiah, and Nero's role as **conqueror** a pale shadow of the Lamb's true victory.

A **second creature** now takes centre stage, as the second seal is **3–4** opened. The parallel with Zechariah 6 might suggest that each creature summons its respective rider to a different quadrant or corner of the earth (see on verse 8), though the primary idea is that the whole earth and all its creatures know the consequences of these birthpangs. The second horse is **fiery red**, the colour of blood, the consequence of war and conquest, and associated elsewhere in Revelation with the dragon Satan (12:3). That the colour also evokes wealth and luxury is suggested by the use of its variants scarlet and purple to refer to Babylon (17:4; 18:12, 16) and the monster on which she sits (17:3). The Apocalypse gives a brutal reminder that the wealth of empires and the prosperity of their citizens are so often founded on the shedding of blood.

If the first rider signifies the seduction of false messiahs and false prophets, typified in John's time by the victorious claims of Rome and particular emperors, the second horseman symbolises 'wars and rumours of wars' (Mk 13:7), and particularly the unspoken result of military conquest, bloodshed. That God's people will be particular victims of such bloodshed in the last days is suggested by the fifth seal (6:9–11). Bearing witness to the truth will leave one vulnerable to attack from the 'rulers of this age' (1 Cor. 2:6–8). Indeed, many commentators have seen in the **large sword** (μάχαιρα μεγάλη) given to the rider echoes of Jesus' warning to his disciples: 'I have come to bring not peace, but a sword' (μάχαιρα, Mt. 10:34). This is possible, provided that the sword here is understood in a negative sense as the destructive response of those who oppose the gospel. The word is used elsewhere in Revelation of violent death (13:10, 14), whereas the sword of God's word associated with Christ is ῥομφαία (1:16; 2:12, 16; 19:15, 21; though cf. 6:8).

The **peace** that is removed **from the earth** is not the true peace which only God and his Messiah can offer (1:4) but the pseudo-peace offered by victorious empires which human beings are bidden to put their trust in. The consequence of this removal of such peace is that **people slaughtered each other**. Although this verb is used regularly in Revelation to speak of the death of the Christ and his followers (5:6, 9, 12; 6:9; 13:8), it is not used exclusively in this sense (see 13:3; 18:24). First-century audiences may have detected in such language echoes of recent political events. The civil war which broke out after the death of Nero in 68 (heralding the 'year of the four emperors' in 69) meant an effective end to the *Pax Romana*, the 'golden age' of peace established by Augustus. Indeed, on the earlier dating of the Apocalypse, its first recipients would still be in the throes of this political turmoil.

5–6 A further consequence of war and military conquest is famine, and this features in the Synoptic Apocalypse as another of the 'birth-pangs' of Christ's final coming (Mk 13:8 and parallels). Hence the rider summoned by **the third creature**, riding on **a black horse**, holds **a pair of scales in his hand**. A constant concern of the biblical writers is that scales should be fairly balanced to ensure that the poor and vulnerable are not exploited (e.g. Lev. 19:36; Ezek. 45:10; Amos 8:5; Hos. 12:8; Prov. 11:1; 20:23). These scales, however, herald a heavy burden upon the victims of war and disaster. Revelation's only other use of the word **black** (μέλας, 6:12) will continue this connection with disaster, as the sun becomes black as hairy sackcloth.

The arrival of this horseman is accompanied by **what seemed like a voice coming from the middle of the four creatures**. Unlike the fourfold command to **Come!** this cannot be the voice of any of these four. Rather, this is the voice of the Lamb, whom we have already been told stands in this location (4:6). Again this places the unfolding events under the ultimate control of Christ. The voice first proclaims the highly inflated prices which the famine brings: **A quart of wheat for a whole day's wages** (literally 'a denarius', a worker's average daily wage), **and three quarts of barley for a whole day's wages!** A 'quart' or 'measure' (χοῖνιξ) of wheat would have been roughly a day's ration for human need, and three quarts of barley sufficient for a horse. Aune's conservative estimate is eight times the usual price for wheat and just over five times for barley (Aune 1998a: 397). Given that the staple diet in the Roman world was grain-based, this would have had a devastating effect.

Yet at the same time as announcing the eschatological famine, the Lamb's voice ameliorates its effects: **But do not harm the olive oil and the wine**. Shortage of grain was devastating enough; the loss of vines and olive trees would have had the effect of extending the famine for years to come. Some commentators, viewing olive oil and wine as luxury items, suggest that this preservation of grapes and olives would have widened the gap between rich and poor. But this is not so obviously the case: olive oil was a basic commodity in cooking; wine was widely drunk as a safer alternative to water. Some have detected an allusion to an edict issued by Domitian between 90 and 92 which called for the cutting down of provincial vineyards (e.g. Suet. *Dom.* 7.2; 14.2), probably to encourage the production of grain. But the imperial edict had nothing to say about olive groves, nor is the Lamb's saying necessarily evidence for the Domitianic dating of the Apocalypse. More important than any specific historical reference is the general point: even in the midst of the eschatological woes, the restraining hand of God and his Messiah is at work, ameliorating their excesses.

Finally, at the instigation of **the fourth creature**, the final horseman 7–8 rides out. His horse is a **sickly green** colour. A number of English translations have the rather bland 'pale' or occasionally 'grey'. But John's visions are regularly described in technicolour, and the word χλωρός is often translated 'green' at 8:7 and 9:4: the shade of this horse is meant to evoke the deathly pallor which its rider leaves in his wake (Tyndale's preference was for 'green', in contrast to the AV's 'pale').

The rider of this fourth horse is **Death**, and he has an accomplice, **Hades**. The connection with the Synoptic Apocalypse may not be immediately obvious, except in general terms: death is the inevitable consequence of war and famine. Yet the Greek word for 'death' (θάνατος) is regularly used in the LXX to translate the Hebrew *deber*, 'plague' or 'pestilence', and hence would have had that added resonance for Greek-speaking Jews (indeed, the second use of θάνατος in this very verse probably has that meaning). Luke's version of Jesus' eschatological discourse specifically refers to pestilence as one of the birthpangs along with famine (though using a different Greek word, λοιμός: Lk. 21:11).

But if pestilence provides the link with Jesus' teaching about the birthpangs, that is not the primary focus of what John sees. **Death** and **Hades** are both personified, as terrifying forces from whom human beings flee in fear. Paul knew that the last enemy to be destroyed was Death (1 Cor. 15:26), and John has already told us that the risen Christ now holds the keys to Death and Hades (1:18), giving him authority to release those held in their realm. The personification of Death was familiar both to Greeks (in the person of Thanatos) and to Jews (probably influenced by the Canaanite god of death, Mot; see e.g. Isa. 25:8; Hos. 13:14; Hab. 2:5). In John's vision he is accompanied by Hades, who in Dürer's famous woodcut has huge jaws to devour whoever falls in his path. In Greek mythology Hades is not simply the underworld, the place of the dead, but also the god of that underworld. Greek-speaking Jews seem to have noted strong similarities between Hades and Sheol, the rather shadowy abode of the dead in the Hebrew Bible, for the Greek word is used to translate *she'ol* in the LXX (e.g. Job 14:13; Isa. 28:18; Hos. 13:14; see Bauckham 1992).

As with the third seal, here too a limit is set upon the havoc which Death and Hades can wreak. Again John stresses the divine permission which allows them, albeit temporarily, to ply their trade: **They were given** (ἐδόθη αὐτοῖς) **power over a quarter of the earth** (note the increased proportion of the earth affected by plagues as Revelation progresses: 'a third of the earth', 8:7; 'every living thing', 16:3). The specific mention of a quarter of the earth may suggest that, like Zechariah's horse-drawn chariots, each of the horsemen is sent out into a different section of the earth. But in fact they have a hand in all of the aforementioned seals, as well as what is yet to come: they are allowed **to kill by the sword and by famine, by pestilence** (θάνατος) **and through the earth's monsters** (the monsters will make their appearances in Revelation 11, 13 and 17). Yet again, Ezekiel plays a fundamental role in what John sees: his list of judgements at Ezek. 5:16–17 perfectly corresponds to what Death and Hades bring here.

The four horsemen represent a wake-up call for those who hear John's book. As we saw in the seven messages, many in the seven congregations were far from seeing their world as in crisis. Although some (perhaps a minority) were maintaining faithful witness and were prepared to shed their blood, for a good number the empire was benevolent and stable, the establisher of peace and the arbiter of justice. Meditating upon prophets such as Ezekiel and Zechariah, pondering the inherited tradition about Jesus' end-time teaching, and contemplating recent political events, John sees a vision of foreboding which threatens such complacency. All is not well with the world. The apparently impregnable empire has sown the seeds of its own destruction. Consequently, to put one's trust in any political or economic system built upon conquest or exploitation is ultimately futile. Yet even this alternative vision of a world collapsing upon itself is not the final word. In words attributed to Jesus, 'These things must take place, but the end is not yet' (Mk 13:7). For those with eyes to see, a broader horizon becomes visible. At the very point at which the Apocalypse shows the empire up for what it really is, the Lamb, the victim of this empire, appears on the scene to take control, so that out of the chaos and futility, the consequences of injustice and human hubris, a new world might be born.

The Opening of the Fifth Seal (6:9–11)

(9) When it opened the fifth seal, I saw under the altar the souls of those who had been slaughtered as a result of proclaiming God's word, that is, the witness they bore to it. (10)

They shouted in a loud voice: 'How long, O holy and true
Master, before you act justly, and vindicate us for our deaths
against those who make their home on the earth?' (11) Each of
them was given a shining white robe, and they were told to
rest for a little while longer, until the full number had been
completed of their fellow servants, their brothers and sisters,
who had to be killed like them.

In contrast to the violent scene of earthly destruction wrought by the 9
four horsemen, the opening of **the fifth seal** takes us back to heaven,
and to the heavenly liturgy which John has already seen taking place
in the previous two chapters. Although not explicitly stated, the
altar is almost certainly not the earthly altar, but the one standing in
the heavenly sanctuary, for further references to it will describe
angels ministering as priests (8:3, 5; 14:18; cf. 9:13; 16:7; the location
of the altar at 11:1 is ambiguous). The earthly sanctuary, believed to
have been modelled on a heavenly pattern revealed to Moses, had two
altars (Lev. 4:7), one for sacrificial offerings (e.g. Exod. 20:24; Lev.
1:5) and one for burning incense before the Lord (e.g. Exod. 30:1;
Lk. 1:11). In the Jerusalem Temple, the former was located outside
the shrine itself, in the Court of the Priests, whereas the latter was
within the Holy Place. In John's vision, however, we have just one
altar fulfilling both functions, suggesting that in the heavenly temple
the sacrificial offering of God's people and their prayers which rise
'like incense' are intimately connected.

At this point, the sacrificial aspect is stressed. **The souls of those
who had been slaughtered** are located **under the altar**, evoking
Lev. 4:7, where the blood of sacrificial animals is poured out on the
base of the altar of burnt offering (cf. Lev. 4:18; 8:15). In other
words, these brutally slaughtered human beings are revealed as
sacrificial victims, just as in the early Christian imagination the
shameful cross of Christ had become the supreme altar of sacrifice.
These 'souls' (Greek ψυχαὶ) are not confined to some nebulous half-
life in Sheol or Hades, but are located close to the divine throne, so
that their cries may be heard in the heavenly liturgy. Perhaps John is
articulating the Semitic concept of *nefesh* (often translated by ψυχή
in LXX) rather than a Greek anthropology: the very life-blood of
these slaughtered ones (Lev. 17:11), their personhood, is sustained by
God despite their violent deaths. Passages such as this, building on
emerging Jewish reflection upon martyrdom and the afterlife, gave
birth to an early Christian theology of an intermediate heavenly state
for the martyrs (Hill 2001: 220–21), and eventually for all the saints,
prior to the general resurrection.

But who precisely are these souls crying out for divine action? That
they have been slaughtered suggests a strong connection with the

Lamb, and their deaths are explicitly attributed to their **proclaiming God's word, that is, the witness they bore to it** (see the similar phrase used of John at 1:2, 9, and of faithful Christians at 12:17; 19:10; 20:4). Thus from early times this passage has been understood as a vision of the souls of Christian martyrs awaiting their heavenly reward (on martyrdom as sacrifice, see Phil. 2:17; 2 Tim. 4:6; Ign. *Rom.* 2:2). Some interpreters have been even more specific, viewing them as the martyrs of specific Roman persecutions, whether of Nero or the supposed persecution of Domitian. Certainly martyrdom seems at issue here. Moreover, the Synoptic Apocalypse continues from where John's vision of the four horsemen leaves off, with a warning of the persecution of God's people as part of the expected woes of the end-times (Mk 13:9–13 and par.). As noted earlier, this is a far cry from the highly influential doctrine of 'the pre-tribulation Rapture', so prevalent among Dispensationalist and other contemporary Christians, whereby the saints will be caught up to heaven to escape the time of trial coming upon the world.

But perhaps we should hesitate before identifying them too readily as exclusively Christian. First, unlike the parallel verses just mentioned, there is no explicit reference to Jesus' witness, only to **the witness they bore**. This suggests a wider group than Christian martyrs. Moreover, the language evokes the Jewish tradition of the blood of the righteous crying out for vindication, which traces its origin to the story of Abel (e.g. Gen. 4:10; 2 Macc. 8:3–4; 4 Macc. 17:22; 18:11; Mt. 23:35; *1 Enoch* 47). Elsewhere John does not always distinguish clearly between the faithful of old and new covenants. Here too, we probably have a vision of all the righteous slain from among God's people, from righteous Abel through the murdered prophets and Maccabean martyrs up to the victims of Nero's persecution in the recent past. Indeed, we should not exclude the possibility that John also sees the martyrs of the visionary future, in an apocalypse which has already warned of hostility to come (e.g. 2:10), and which seems determined to raise the stakes for those Christians who view the world in anything but terms of crisis. This would mean that the interpretations found in the *Letter from Vienne and Lyons*, or in Tertullian (e.g. Tert. *Scorp.* 12; *De Resurr.* 25), both of which understand Revelation as a text of consolation during the martyrdoms of the authors' own day, are at one with the perspective of the seer of Patmos.

10 Zechariah's vision of the horseman had prompted a question from an angelic observer as to how long the Lord would withhold mercy from Jerusalem (Zech. 1:12; cf. Ps. 79:5–10). The same **How long** issues forth here from human questioners. Their trust in a God who can and will act is conveyed by their address to the Deity as **holy and**

true Master (the two adjectives are used of Christ at 3:7). Though liberal Westerners often balk at the desire for vengeance apparently implicit in this call, how one hears this shout is utterly dependent on where one stands. From the perspective of the vulnerable, oppressed or persecuted, this is a heartfelt protest against the world's injustice, the voice of the voiceless struggling to be heard above the noise of the powerful (e.g. Boesak 1987: 68–73; Richard 1995: 70). It is a call for vindication, for that which should not be in God's world to be redressed (a similar idea is expressed at Lk. 18:1–8). Their oppressors throughout history have thought that such witnesses could be silenced by the sword, or the torture chamber, or the execution squad. But John hears that their voices cannot be silenced.

This great body of witnesses joins its voice in heaven with that of the angelic host, and with the tears of John (5:4), urging God to **act justly**, and to **vindicate us for our deaths** (literally 'our blood') **against those who make their home on the earth** (see on 3:10). Various strands within Judaism (e.g. Job; Wisdom of Solomon) had long challenged the pervasive view that material blessing was a sign of divine favour, and misfortune evidence of divine punishment. One such misfortune was premature death, since God blessed his righteous ones with long life in the land (Deut. 30:19–20; Psalms 112; 127). This became particularly problematic during times of persecution, when young Israelites began to die precisely for their fidelity to God and the Law. It was in such contexts that a Jewish theology of martyrdom seems to have flourished: these deaths were not the deaths of the wicked, but the undeserved deaths of the righteous. Ultimately, God would vindicate them and show them to have been in the right.

Not only do the martyrs articulate the conviction that God will **11** ultimately vindicate them for their untimely deaths; the response to their cry, presumably from a heavenly voice, proclaims the notion found in other apocalyptic writings whereby there is a predetermined number of righteous deaths (e.g. *1 En.* 47:3–4; *4 Ez.* 4:35–37), a **full number** which must be **completed** before the end. Others of their **brothers and sisters** will have **to be killed like them**. Again, John raises the stakes and arouses expectation of dark days to come (for the evidence from the seven messages suggests that actual martyrs in the Asia of his time were few and far between: see on 2:13). But this claim of a full number is no cold fatalism. It issues from the profound conviction that, from the divine perspective on the world, these apparently futile deaths play a crucial role in the overcoming of injustice and evil. The slaughter of the righteous is ultimately not in vain.

Nor is their present state one of futile waiting. Although, unlike the slaughtered Lamb, they have not yet attained the fullness of resurrection life (that will happen at 20:4), **each of them is given a shining white robe**. White robes are symbols of victory achieved: the attire of victorious Christians (3:4–5; 7:9, 13; cf. 3:18), the twenty-four elders (4:4) and the armies of heaven (19:14). In anticipation of their resurrection glory, the martyrs exchange their blood-stained garments for new garments washed gleaming white in the Lamb's blood (7:14). But the juxtaposition of the altar with the specific word John uses for robe (στολή, used in the LXX of priestly vestments: e.g. Exod. 28:4; 29:21; Ezek. 44:19; 2 Macc. 3:15) may suggest an additional priestly role: they fulfil the priestly role of intercession on behalf of the world, their prayers being especially effective because of their proximity to God's throne. This interpretation is reflected in the iconographical tradition, especially in the West. In the Bamberg Apocalypse, for example, they are given the stoles of Christian priests, following the Vulgate translation *stolae albae* (Kovacs and Rowland 2004: 89).

Finally, they are **told to rest**: given their location in the heavenly sanctuary, this is surely a reference to the sabbatical rest in the presence of God, which they now experience in an anticipatory manner (cf. Heb. 3:7–19). The promise of rest from labour will be made at 14:13 to 'the dead who die in the Lord from now on', one of the seven beatitudes in the Apocalypse (contrast 14:11). In a book so noted for its emphasis upon the future, we should not downplay the extent to which Revelation presents salvation as 'realised' in the present. Nevertheless, this realisation anticipates greater things yet to come, though not very far in the future: they are to wait for just **a little while longer**. Suffering, injustice and martyrdom will have their end.

The Opening of the Sixth Seal (6:12–17)

(12) Then I looked when it opened the sixth seal, and there was a great earthquake, the sun turned as black as hairy sackcloth, and the whole moon became like blood. (13) The stars of heaven fell down upon the earth, like a fig-tree shedding its late figs when shaken by a strong wind. (14) Heaven split open like a scroll rolling up, and all the mountains and islands were removed from their places. (15) Then earth's kings, high-ranking officials and generals, the rich and those in power, every slave and freedman, all hid themselves in caves and among the rocks of the mountains. (16) They said to the mountains and the rocks: 'Fall on us, and hide us from the presence of the one seated on the throne and from the Lamb's anger. (17) For the great day of their anger has come, and who can stand before it?'

The scene shifts once again as the Lamb opens **the sixth seal**. What 12
John now sees contains a standard checklist of apocalyptic imagery
associated with the End itself, involving not only natural disasters
such as earthquakes but the very fabric of the cosmos, heaven no less
than earth. Two questions are posed by this vision. First, how does
this scene relate to the five seals which precede it, and the cycles of
trumpets and bowls which follow? Second, how are we to take this
disturbing imagery, which seems to point to the divinely ordained
destruction of God's creation?

Commentators have located this scene within the drama of the
book in a number of ways. Some see it as simply the next stage in a
neat chronological sequence running from chapter 4 to the end of the
book. For others, building on Victorinus' proposal of recapitulation,
the contents of the seals sequence will re-emerge, albeit in different
patterns, in the trumpets and bowls septets. The three sections, in
other words, essentially describe the same eschatological events;
hence all three septets climax in the same divine judgement, marked
by thunder, lightning and an earthquake (8:5; 11:19; 16:18). In broad
outline this is an attractive proposition, though there are indications
that the ensuing trumpets sequence is especially related to the sixth
and seventh seals. First, there is significant overlap between the
contents of the sixth seal and the more detailed descriptions of the
seven trumpet-plagues (both involving signs in the sun and moon,
and stars falling from heaven). Second, the opening of the seventh
seal results directly in the emergence of seven trumpet-angels
(8:1–2).

Parallels with the Synoptic Apocalypse confirm that, with the
opening of the sixth seal, things have moved on in the eschatological
timetable from the 'beginning of the birthpangs' marked by the four
horsemen, and the persecution of God's people. We are now presented with the shaking of the cosmos, which will herald the final
coming of the Son of Man in judgement (Mk 13:24–25). In other
words, it is particularly this section of the seals sequence which will
be recapitulated, and viewed from different angles, in the visions yet
to come.

From the perspective of Revelation's narrative flow, however, this
recapitulation will come as something of a shock. The cosmic signs
described by John are stock elements of the final Day of the Lord,
envisaged by the prophets as a reversal of God's original creative act,
from order to chaos, in response to human sinfulness and arrogance
(Sweet 1979: 143; cf. Isa. 13:9–11; 24:21–23; Joel 2:30–31; *1 En.*
102:2–3). Indeed, an early Christian reader would probably associate
such signs (as does Mark) with the imminent coming of Christ. But
the end is not yet. In Revelation, Christ's coming will be delayed for
several more chapters.

The **great earthquake** will become more prominent as the Apocalypse unfolds (see on 8:5); earthquakes are part of the expected signs of the End (e.g. Joel 2:10; Ezek. 38:19; Mk 13:8; *T. Mos.* 10:4), and the succession of significant earthquakes in first-century Roman Asia may have heightened the eschatological tension for at least some Jews and Christians. The loss of light from **the sun** and **moon** is likewise attested in a range of Jewish eschatological texts (see Charles 1920: I, 180–81).

13–14 Other Old Testament echoes suggest the intimate connection between the heavenly and earthly realms. The falling of **the stars of heaven**, as well as suggesting a reversal of creation, may also describe the fall of angelic powers (as at 8:10 and 9:1–2). Isaiah 34, whose language is echoed at several points in this vision, seems to link the disorder of life on earth with the activity of the 'host of heaven' lying behind and influencing it, who will rot away and fall like figs. This reminds us that the battle of the Lamb is not confined to the human realm, but is a cosmic battle also involving the angelic world. The description of **heaven split open like a scroll rolling up** also echoes Isa. 34:4. But we should beware of treating passages such as this as a mere pastiche of Old Testament texts: instead, prophetic descriptions of the End have entered into John's visionary imagination, such that they form new patterns to challenge John's own world. Indeed, the reference to **all the mountains and islands** being **removed** may also betray John's physical location on Patmos, from which both are in clear view. The island exile views the world from his marginal perspective, fragmented by the sea of chaos into islands and volcanic mountains.

Some have wanted to link this vision to specific historical events, whether in John's own day or in subsequent centuries. Among historical-critical commentators it is common to detect allusions, either here or more often at 8:8, to the eruption of Vesuvius in 79 CE, which devastated the towns of Pompeii and Herculaneum (e.g. Witherington 2003: 136). An alternative which is rather closer to home, and fits the earlier dating of Revelation, proposes that the seer is describing the eruption of volcanic Thera or Santorini, visible from Patmos, which began in 60 CE (Bent 1888). However, the stock apocalyptic imagery employed by John might not allow such precision.

15–17 The terrified reaction of humanity to this cosmic collapse, echoing Old Testament passages such as Hos. 10:8 and Isa. 2:19, is striking. As will become clear (e.g. 9:20; 16:11), such terrifying signs are meant to lead people to repentance. Here, however, the response is only fear and a desire to hide. While those who **hid themselves in**

caves and among the rocks include the lower echelons of Roman society (**every slave**), the list is dominated by the wealthy and powerful. **Earth's kings** will reappear as the enemies of the Lamb and allies of Babylon later in the book (16:14; 17:2, 18; 18:3, 9; 19:19; though cf. 21:24). Other political and military leaders and those who have profited economically from the present world are also explicitly listed. They look on in horror as the world which has made them great now collapses upon them (compare Lk. 21:26, which recounts how people will faint from fear and foreboding). As artistic representations from Dürer's woodcut to John Martin's *The Great Day of His Wrath* have recognised, this vision of judgement is a great leveller. All, rich and poor, weak and powerful, slave and free, stand on equal terms before the judgement seat of God. They wish to be hidden **from the presence of the one seated on the throne**, the day of whose coming has now dawned. Now, however, the enthroned one is closely associated with the Lamb, such that they fear **the Lamb's anger**, and the Day of the Lord is now **the great day of their anger** (some manuscripts heighten the connection of the Lord's Day with the Lamb's Day by reading *his* instead of *their*).

What is distinctive about this anger being **the Lamb's anger**? Some detect here a softening of the terrifying concept of divine anger (e.g. Rossing 2004: 135–40) or a reminder that the Lion has been reinterpreted in terms of the Lamb (Caird 1966: 91–93; but contrast Moyise 2001: 181–94). The Lamb, after all, is the slaughtered Christ, who wins the victory through non-violent self-sacrifice and invites his followers to do the same. This is an important consideration: Christ's weapons are words rather than military arms, and the blood shed his own rather than that of his enemies. Nevertheless, one should not downplay the fact that the victorious Lamb is engaged in a battle, which has disastrous consequences for all that opposes its victory. Nor should one fail to recognise that this cry is not that of a heavenly voice, but from the lips of **earth's kings** and their associates. For those whose hearts are set on the world which is passing away, the outworking of the Lamb's victory is experienced as an anger which is only too real (cf. Rom. 1:18). For them, the sacrificial Lamb bears the terrifying features of the warrior Lamb.

Interlude 1: The Sealing and Preservation of   (7:1–17)
God's People

(1) After this I saw four angels, standing at the four corners of the earth. They were restraining the earth's four winds, preventing them from blowing over the earth or on the sea or on any tree. (2) Then I saw another angel ascending from where the sun rises, with the seal of the living God. He cried out in a

loud voice to the four angels who were permitted to harm earth and sea: (3) 'Refrain from harming the earth or the sea or the trees, until we have sealed the foreheads of the servants of our God.'

(4) I then heard how many were sealed, one hundred and forty-four thousand, sealed from all the tribes of the children of Israel.

(5) From the tribe of Judah twelve thousand were sealed;
from the tribe of Reuben twelve thousand;
from the tribe of Gad twelve thousand;
(6) from the tribe of Asher twelve thousand;
from the tribe of Naphtali twelve thousand;
from the tribe of Manasseh twelve thousand;
(7) from the tribe of Simeon twelve thousand;
from the tribe of Levi twelve thousand;
from the tribe of Issachar twelve thousand;
(8) from the tribe of Zebulun twelve thousand;
from the tribe of Joseph twelve thousand;
from the tribe of Benjamin twelve thousand were sealed.

(9) After this I looked, and there was a vast crowd, too large to be counted, from every nation and tribe, from every people and language. They were standing in front of the throne and in front of the Lamb, dressed in shining white robes and with palm-branches in their hands. (10) They cried out in a loud voice:

'Salvation to our God,
who is seated on the throne,
and to the Lamb.'

(11) Then all the angels stood around the throne and around the elders and the four creatures, and they fell down on their faces in front of the throne to worship God with these words:

(12) 'Amen! Praise and glory, wisdom and thanks,
honour and power and strength
be to our God for ever and ever. Amen!'

(13) Then one of the elders asked me: 'Who are these people who are dressed in shining white robes, and where have they come from?' (14) I answered him: 'My lord, you know the answer.' Then he told me: 'These are the ones who pass safely through the great tribulation, who have washed their robes white in the blood of the Lamb. (15) Therefore they now stand in front of God's throne and minister to him day and night in his sanctuary, and the one seated on the throne will pitch his tent over them. (16) They will never again be hungry or thirsty, and sun or heat will no longer harm them. (17) For the Lamb who is in the middle of the throne will be their

shepherd; it will lead them to the springs of the water of life. And God himself will remove every tear from their eyes.'

The climax to the sixth seal brought the apparently futile question from those fleeing from the day of the Lamb's wrath: 'who can stand before it?' At this point, the action is halted, and we are given a vision of those who are indeed able to 'stand': first, the **four angels** (v. 1), and then the **vast crowd, too large to be counted** (v. 9). The halting of Revelation's dramatic action by an interlude or intercalation between the sixth and seventh elements in a septet is a recurring feature (see also the lengthy intercalation at 10:1—11:14). It serves to heighten the dramatic tension in the narrative, leading the reader to expectant anticipation of the End only to find that End delayed. The reader, and hearers, are encouraged by the text to locate themselves in that crucial 'in-between' time between the sixth stage and the eschatological seventh, when salvation is finally accomplished. John, no less than Paul, presents the Church as experiencing that eschatological tension between the 'already' and the 'not yet'. This is an insight grasped again and again in Revelation's history of reception, as a succession of commentators (e.g. Joachim of Fiore) have regarded their time as the expectant sixth period.

John sees **four angels, standing at the four corners of the earth**. 1 These are probably angels charged with carrying out judgement and destruction, a common feature in Jewish apocalypses (e.g. *1 En.* 66:1– 2; *2 Bar.* 6:4ff.; cf. Ezekiel 9). Whatever destructive forces there are in the world, John sees them as ultimately under the control of God and God's angelic agents. At present, however, they are **restraining the earth's four winds**. Some might recall the four winds of heaven which stirred up the sea in Daniel's vision, enabling the terrifying monsters to emerge (Dan. 7:1–3). John too will see a monster from the sea that will threaten the lives of God's people (Revelation 13). Others might remember that Zechariah's four chariots with their horses were identified with the four winds/spirits of heaven (Zech. 6:5). Perhaps, then, we are seeing again John's four horsemen: before they can finally ride out to wreak their havoc on the earth, something else is yet to be done. In the meantime, they are held in check by the restraining angels (for the destructive power of the four winds, see also Jer. 49:36).

That 'something' is the sealing of **the servants of our God** by a fifth 2–3 **angel** who ascends **from where the sun rises** (that is, the east). The precise identity of this angelic figure is obscure, allowing a variety of suggestions from Elijah through Francis of Assisi to Elizabeth I (Kovacs and Rowland 2004: 100–01). The background to this scene is provided by two Old Testament narratives. First is the story of the Exodus, which has been a recurring motif throughout Revelation (e.g. 1:5; 5:6–12; 12:14; 15:2–4). The sealing of God's servants here echoes the marking out of the houses of the Israelites in Egypt by lamb's blood, ensuring protection from the Destroying Angel (Exod. 12:13, 23). Given the wider context, **the servants of our God** are no longer the ancient Israelites but God's people of the New Exodus, who like John (1:1) are servants or slaves of God and followers of the true Lamb. The language of sealing, the mark of ownership, may suggest early Christian baptismal practice (e.g. 2 Cor. 1:22; Eph. 1:13; 4:30).

But Ezekiel has also been a key text for John, and a more specific antecedent is Ezekiel 9. Here the prophet witnesses the marking on **the foreheads** of those who sigh and groan over all the abominable things done in Jerusalem (Ezek. 9:4; cf. Rev. 14:1). Those marked with this sign (Hebrew *taw*, sometimes written as a cross) are, like the Exodus generation before them, spared from death (for the seal and *taw* in Jewish Christianity, see Sweet 1979: 148). In John's visionary world, the faithful Christians of the seven Asian congregations are part of that ongoing story of the redemption of God's faithful people.

But there is a fundamental difference between the sealing in John's vision and in his antecedents. Although at 9:4 those with God's seal will be divinely protected from the plague of demonic locusts, the sealing in Revelation does not render God's people immune from suffering, or even death, per se (e.g. 2:10; 6:9–11; 7:14; 11:7–8; 12:11; 13:7; 17:6; 20:4; see above on 3:10). The powers of evil will do their utmost to attack the Lamb's followers, and martyrdom may result. The idea of a pre-tribulation Rapture, widespread in popular readings of Revelation, ignores the extent to which the victorious have trodden the path of the slaughtered Lamb. What their sealing does do is mark them out as God's servants, sustained through the great tribulation, and destined for ultimate salvation.

4–8 John now hears the number of those sealed: **one hundred and forty-four thousand**. Given the echo of Ezekiel's sealing vision, the huge number of those involved is striking. From the perspective of small, vulnerable churches such as those in Smyrna and Philadelphia, the canvas is broad indeed. Moreover, they are sealed **from all the tribes of the children of Israel**. Three questions have often engaged commentators on this section. First, how is one to account for the order and selection of the twelve tribes? Second, is the number 144,000 literal or symbolic? Third (but closely related to the second), what is the relationship between the 144,000 and the 'vast crowd' of verse 9?

Commentators often stumble over John's order of Israel's twelve tribes here. R. H. Charles, following Buchanan Gray, posited a process of dislocation, with verses 5c–6 originally belonging after verse 8 (Charles 1920: I, 207). Yet this may be unnecessary once we remember that the biblical lists of the tribes vary considerably, both in the order of the tribes and in the names they include (cf. Gen. 35:23–26; 49:1ff.; Exodus 1:2–4; Num. 1:5–15; Numbers 26; 1 Chron. 2:1–2; 1 Chron. 2:3—8:40; see Table 3). The tribes are sometimes ordered according to mother, sometimes not; occasionally the sons of Joseph, Manasseh and Ephraim (Gen. 41:50–52) replace one or two of Jacob's sons in the list (Numbers 26: Levi; Num. 1:5–15: Levi and Joseph). In this regard John's somewhat different order should not surprise us. One ingenious proposal is that the Galilean tribes, the sons of the handmaids Zilpah and Bilhah (Gad, Asher, Naphtali [and Manasseh, replacing Dan]) have been moved up the list by John as a sign of the inclusion of the Gentiles (Smith 1990: 114f.).

However, John's list does have two distinctive features. First, the initial name in his list is **Judah**, whereas almost all the other lists begin with the first-born Reuben (but cf. 1 Chron. 2:3—8:40). Almost certainly John gives Judah a pre-eminent place because it is David's tribe, and therefore the tribe of the messianic Lion/Lamb (5:5; cf. Rom. 1:3; Heb. 7:14). Second, Dan is missing from the list completely (replaced by **Manasseh**). The reason for this is less clear, although it may be related to that tribe's association with idolatry (Lev. 24:11; Judg. 5:17; 1 Kgs 12:25–33) and apostasy (*T. Dan* 5:6, which lists Dan's angelic prince as Satan; cf. Gen. 49:17). In the second century CE, Irenaeus cites a tradition that the Antichrist would arise from Dan (*Adv. Haer.* 5.30.2, citing Jer. 8:16), although we cannot be sure how early that belief emerged (Bauckham 1991: 100).

The meaning of the number 144,000, and the relation of this group to the group described in vv. 9–17, is also disputed. If one takes the number literally, then it is a restrictive, limited number, and serves to differentiate the 144,000 from the 'vast crowd'. On a surface reading the text would seem to support this, given that it claims different ethnic origins for the two groups ('from the twelve tribes' versus 'from every nation and tribe'), and explicitly states that the second group could not be counted (verse 9). Typical of this literal reading is the exegesis of the Jehovah's Witnesses, according to which only 144,000 of 'spiritual Israel' will participate in the millennial reign of Christ, while a larger number will have a share in the new heavens and the new earth (Watch Tower 1988: 113–29). Dispensationalist readings correlate this and similar visions with the fate of the contemporary state of Israel, often with powerful effects on the political stage (on this see e.g. Sizer 2004). In more mainstream exegesis, the 144,000 are sometimes regarded as Jewish Christians as opposed to

Table 3: Order of the Twelve Tribes

Gen 35:23–25	Genesis 49:1ff.	Exod. 1:2–4	Num. 1:5–15
Reuben [Leah]	Reuben	Reuben	Reuben
Simeon	Simeon	Simeon	Simeon
Levi	Levi	Levi	Judah
Judah	Judah	Judah	Issachar
Issachar	Zebulun	Issachar	Zebulun
Zebulun	Issachar	Zebulun	Ephraim
Joseph [Rachel]	Dan	Benjamin	Manasseh
Benjamin	Gad	Dan	Benjamin
Dan [Bilhah]	Asher	Naphtali	Dan
Naphtali	Naphtali	Gad	Asher
Gad [Zilpah]	Joseph	Asher	Gad
Asher	Benjamin	[Joseph]	Naphtali

Numbers 26	1 Chron. 2:1–2	1 Chron. 2:3—8:40	Rev. 7:5–8
Reuben	Reuben	Judah	Judah
Simeon	Simeon	Simeon	Reuben
Gad	Levi	Reuben	Gad
Judah	Judah	Gad	Asher
Issachar	Issachar	Levi	Naphtali
Zebulun	Zebulun	Issachar	Manasseh
Joseph	Dan	Benjamin	Simeon
Ephraim	Joseph	Naphtali	Levi
Benjamin	Benjamin	Manasseh	Issachar
Dan	Naphtali	Ephraim	Zebulun
Asher	Gad	Asher	Joseph
Naphtali	Asher	Benjamin	Benjamin

Gentile Christians (e.g. Draper 1983: 137, arguing for the influence of Zechariah 14), or the restored twelve tribes of typical Jewish eschatological hope (Geyser 1982: 389; cf. *Pss Sol.* 17:26–28, 44; 1QM 2; *4 Ez.* 13:39–47; *2 Baruch* 78—87).

However, there are good grounds for preferring an alternative, symbolic reading. The first is the symbolic use of numbers elsewhere in the book, and in the wider Jewish apocalyptic tradition. If we assume that John is being consistent, then the number 144,000 should also be read symbolically. It represents the square of twelve, a number of completeness, multiplied by a thousand (representing a large number: e.g. Exod. 20:6; Deut. 1:11; Dan. 7:10). In other words, read symbolically this number is 'too large to be counted' (contrast *4 Ez.* 8:1). In a similar way Revelation's vision of the new Jerusalem (21:9—22:5) will also use multiples of twelve and a thousand, to describe a city whose gates are open to all nations and not simply to a remnant of the twelve tribes (21:24–26).

Second, we should attend to the complex relationship between hearing and seeing. Just as John hears of a victorious lion but sees a lamb at 5:5–6, so here too we should expect John's vision to interpret his audition (for a useful table illustrating the relation between seeing and hearing in Revelation, see Rowland 1998: 622–23). In his apocalyptic vision, the expected hope for the restoration of the tribes has been transformed into an ingathering from all the nations of the world. The new Israel is marked now not by descent from Abraham but by allegiance to the slaughtered Lamb (14:3–4; cf. e.g. Gal. 3:28–29; 1 Pet. 2:9–10). It is this multitude, sealed with the seal of the living God, who will be able to come through the tribulation unscathed (Caird 1966: 95).

We are now taken back to the heavenly throne-room and the heavenly 9–10 liturgy. Heavenly time runs on a different track to earthly time, and so we are given a proleptic vision of the 144,000 *after* the great tribulation. Although the Passover-Exodus sealing has been a background motif so far, the scene John now describes echoes the Feast of Tabernacles (see e.g. Draper 1983). An agricultural festival marking the end of the harvest, Tabernacles or Booths also commemorated the dwelling of the Exodus generation in booths (Lev. 23:42–43; Sanders 1992: 140). **Palm-branches**, as well as being used in the construction of booths (Neh. 8:15), were carried together with willow and other branches by pilgrims at the festival (the so-called *lulab*: Lev. 23:40; 2 Macc. 10:7; *Jub.* 16:31; Josephus, *Ant.* 3.245; 13.372; *m. Sukk.* 3). In the hands of this great multitude in festal gathering, they are a sign that the divine protection and victory of Israel's God is no longer confined to the boundaries of the twelve tribes (Zech. 14:16–19 envisages the nations keeping Tabernacles at Jerusalem). Similarly, their **shining white robes** speak of the victory they have achieved (e.g. 3:4; 4:4; 6:11; 19:14).

Yet one question remains: who exactly is this huge throng that John sees? Even if the 144,000 and the **vast crowd** are the same group, albeit viewed from opposite ends of the great tribulation, do they symbolise the whole Church, or just a part of it? The influence of this scene on the literature and liturgy of Christian martyrdom (e.g. *5 Ez.* 2:38–48) might strongly suggest that they are the martyrs, sealed from among God's people and victorious for having shed their blood (Caird 1966: 94–97). But surely that is too precise. While actual martyrs are to be clothed in white (6:11), the call to faithful witness and the promise of white robes is presented as a general call to the churches (e.g. 3:4–5, 10; cf. 11:3ff., where the prophet-witnesses may symbolise the Church's mission). A martyr's death itself is not the determining factor, but following the Lamb in such a way that death becomes a possibility. This is the vocation of the whole Church, and not a particular group within it.

We should recall here the probable 'theatre of reception' of this vision: the liturgical gatherings of the seven Asian congregations. What John sees contrasts dramatically with the actual number of Christians in the seven cities. Yet gathered in their numerically small eucharistic assemblies in back-street villas and hired halls, they would have found themselves caught up into this great multitude and into the heavenly liturgy in which it participates. Their summons to faithful witness, even if that should lead to death in the future (2:10), is an invitation to join a much greater 'cloud of witnesses' (cf. Heb. 12:1). Nor will they lose their own social identity: what John sees is a crowd gathered **from every nation and tribe, from every people and language**. Within the vast multitude he is still able to distinguish between national and tribal groupings, and to hear different languages spoken. The ethnically and linguistically diverse early Christian congregations are a microcosm of the large picture viewed from a heavenly perspective.

What distinguishes this heavenly Tabernacles from its earthly counterpart is the worship of the Lamb along with the one **seated on the throne**. Both are acclaimed for their **salvation**, the safe deliverance of their servants through the great tribulation (including, though not restricted to, the idea of 'victory', for which John uses the νικ-complex of words). The slaughtered paschal Lamb, no less than the enthroned one, has ensured their safe passage through the wilderness.

11–12 The hymn of praise from the human crowd is met with a corresponding liturgical action from the angels: **they fell down on their faces in front of the throne to worship God**. Appropriately their canticle is a sevenfold declaration of adoration (cf. 5:12), reminding Revelation's audiences that the heavenly throne-room rather than any imperial counterfeit is the focus of true worship. The singing of hymns and canticles helps maintain this alternative and subversive vision throughout the Apocalypse. It is particularly appropriate for a liturgical celebration such as Tabernacles. Indeed, rabbinic traditions claim that the shaking of the *lulab* accompanied the recitation of the great *Hallel* Psalm 118 (*m. Sukk.* 3.9), which proclaims God's salvation or victory for his people. Interestingly, verbal echoes of Psalm 118 are to be found both in the cry of **salvation** (σωτηρία, Ps. 118 [LXX 117]:14, 15, 28) and in the angelic response (Ps. 118:15, 16: **power** (δύναμις); Ps. 118:14: **strength** (ἰσχύς); Ps. 118:26: a variation on **praise** (εὐλογία)).

13–17 A common feature of apocalypses is the role of an interpreting angel (*angelus interpres*) who provides an authoritative commentary on the seer's visions or dreams (e.g. Gabriel at Dan. 8:15–17; Uriel in *4*

Ezra; cf. the dialogue form at Zech. 4:4–5; 6:4–5). Revelation, by contrast, is rather sparing in its use of heavenly interpreters (see also 17:7ff.), allowing most of its visions a polyvalency which resists straightforward decoding. The fact that the role of the *angelus interpres* is fulfilled here by **one of the** twenty-four **elders** supports the angelic identification of that group (see on 4:4). The elder asks a rhetorical question about the identity of those **dressed in shining white robes,** to which John responds in words echoing Ezekiel's (Ezek. 37:3). The true meaning of the vision has to be established by the heavenly being, not the human John (cf. Mt. 28:5–6).

The elder's interpretation locates the vast crowd after **the great tribulation,** now standing in the heavenly **sanctuary** and ministering as priests (a reminder that Christ has made all his followers priests to serve his God and Father, 1:5b). Although angels regularly fulfil a liturgical role in Revelation, in this vision all God's people of every tribe (and not just of Levi) exercise a priestly ministry of worship. That it continues **day and night** echoes John's final vision of the new Jerusalem (22:3–5). It is the promise for the **ones who pass safely through** the difficult time which John expects ahead (e.g. 2:10; 11:7; 13:7). Though they may have had to shed their own blood as martyrs, the most important **blood** is that **of the Lamb** (echoing Revelation's sacrificial understanding of Christ's death, e.g. 1:5; 5:6; 12:11); it is this self-sacrificial death which gives meaning to their own following of the Lamb's way. In one of those apocalyptic phrases which stretches our imaginations to the limits, they **have washed their robes white** in the Lamb's red blood (cf. 22:14), fitting them to stand before the presence of God (cf. Exod. 19:10; Zech. 3:3–4).

The **great tribulation** refers to that expected time of trial which, according to Jewish apocalyptic, God's people would undergo in the last days (e.g. Dan. 12:1; Mt. 24:21, 29). For the early Christians, this was believed to have begun with the death and resurrection of Jesus (e.g. Rev. 1:9; 2:10; Jn 16:21; Rom. 8:35). The vision assures the churches that, far from being overwhelmed by this, they will be enabled to **pass safely through** it (the preposition ἐκ suggests they have come out the other side, rather than being rescued from the tribulation before it happens). The present participle (οἱ ἐρχόμενοι) suggests that, from the perspective of John's first readers and audiences, it is to be regarded as an ongoing situation. Their local difficulties, whether actual persecution or less formal hostility, are both thrown into sharper relief and incorporated into a larger picture by what John sees. Generations of Christians ever since have found the same inspiration to hold to the values of the Lamb, despite the hostility and even violence it provokes.

Nor is the goal of the heavenly liturgy simply a vision of the future:

the seven congregations can participate in this heavenly scene *now* through their earthly liturgies. The latter become a point of entry into the heavenly Feast of Tabernacles being played out before John's eyes. Unlike its earthly counterpart, it does not require the building of 'booths' or 'tabernacles' by the worshippers. The one on the throne will provide the tabernacle, pitching **his tent over them** (cf. Jn 1:14). In language evocative of Isaiah's visions of the messianic banquet (Isaiah 25) and the mission of the Servant (Isaiah 49), we hear of the end of that wilderness journey that Tabernacles commemorates, and which Isaiah 40—55 sees re-enacted in the return from Exile. All that threatens the survival of God's people on their journey is now overcome: hunger, thirst, the scorching Middle Eastern **sun** (Isa. 49:10), even the tears of grief and death (Isa. 25:8). Striking too are the parallels with the Fourth Gospel, inviting questions about the relationship between these two texts. Both the Gospel and the Apocalypse describe a Lamb who becomes a shepherd (cf. Jn 1:29, 36; 10:1ff.); both also speak of salvation using the language of **springs** and **water of life**/living water (cf. Jn 4:14; 7:38–39; Rev. 21:6). Moreover, John 7 is certainly set at Tabernacles, and there is debate as to whether the Tabernacles context continues into the Good Shepherd discourse in John 10 (the Feast of Dedication is not explicitly mentioned until Jn 10:22). Indeed, if we are to push these Johannine similarities, there may be eucharistic (e.g. Jn 6:35) as well as baptismal echoes here. If so, this would underline the degree to which participation in these eschatological blessings can be experienced by the churches now through their liturgical celebrations.

The Opening of the Seventh Seal (8:1)

(1) When the Lamb opened the seventh seal, silence reigned in heaven for about half an hour.

The tension in the narrative is palpable, as **the Lamb opened the seventh seal**, completing the sequence (seven being a number of perfection) and leaving the scroll completely open. Surely now the Day of the Lord has come, evil will be overcome, and God's people will experience salvation. But instead, the book continues for another fifteen chapters. The opening of the seventh seal introduces not the expected End, but another set of seven, the seven trumpets (8:2—11:18).

As surprising as the delay of the End is what the opening of this seal actually achieves: **silence reigned in heaven for about half an hour.** The silence has at least two aspects. First, it must mean the silencing of the angelic worshippers. The heavenly liturgy up to this point has been an extremely noisy experience (e.g. 4:11; 5:9–14; 7:10,

12). But now, even the ceaseless Trisagion of the four creatures (4:8) ceases temporarily. Second, this verse also suggests the silencing of the divine voice: the flashes of lightning, voices and claps of thunder (4:5). At this crucial moment in the action, even the God of glory no longer thunders (Ps. 29:3; cf. Ps. 83:1; Isa. 64:12). But this silence remains only for about half an hour, a limited period (e.g. Dan. 7:25; 9:27), half of the 'hour' of divine judgement and salvation (cf. 9:15; 14:7, 15; 18:10).

What is the purpose of this silence? There are three possible explanations, not necessarily mutually exclusive. First, silence is the appropriate creaturely response to the divine (e.g. Hab. 2:20; Zech. 2:13; Amos 8:3). Zephaniah urges God's people to be silent before him because the Day of the Lord is at hand (Zeph. 1:7). The silence here is the profound silence of worship, particularly appropriate as God's saving action reaches its climax. This has some Second Temple antecedents. Aristeas describes the priests sacrificing in silence in the Jerusalem temple (*Ep. Arist.* 95; *T. Adam* 1:12; Wick 1998; but cf. e.g. 2 Chron. 29:27; *m. Tam.* 1:2–4; 3:2, 8; 5:1–2), an earthly echo of the silent angelic liturgy suggested by the Qumran *Songs of the Sabbath Sacrifice* (4Q405 11–13).

A second explanation is that heaven becomes silent in order that the prayers of the saints on earth may be heard at the heavenly throne. The Talmud preserves a tradition that the angels in the fifth heaven cease their praises by day, in order that Israel's prayers may be heard (*Hagigah* 12b; Charles 1920: I, 223). Revelation has already spoken of the prayers of the holy ones, presented in heaven in the golden bowls full of incense (5:8), and these same prayers are about to be mixed with incense on the heavenly altar (8:3–4).

Third, the silence is the lull before the storm, the silence out of which the creative and re-creative Word of God emerges (Sweet 1979: 159). Later Jewish apocalyptic tradition (e.g. *4 Ez.* 6:39) speaks of silence at the dawn of creation, and envisages a restoration of that primeval silence before the resurrection and final judgement (*4 Ez.* 7:30; *2 Bar.* 3:7). But there may be a more specific antecedent for John at this point: gentle silence (σιγή) accompanied the descent of God's all-powerful Word in the Book of Wisdom, the divine Warrior who destroys the first-born of the Egyptians at the Exodus (Wis. 18:14–16). This angelic Destroyer will reappear later in Revelation as the victorious Christ (19:11–16). Moreover, the heavenly silence here is a prelude to the trumpet-plagues, which bear some similarities to the plagues of Egypt (compare Rev. 8:7—11:15 with Exodus 7—12). Yet Revelation's emphasis is not on destruction but on salvation and re-creation. The Word of the Lord is about to be uttered once again, but Christian audiences will recognise in this divine Warrior the features of Jesus the slaughtered Lamb.

3   SEVEN TRUMPETS   (8:2—11:18)

A new section now begins, with a new sequence, of seven trumpets. This section, like the previous one (4:1—8:1), begins with a liturgical action in the heavenly sanctuary/throne-room, including a Sinai-like theophany ('claps of thunder, voices, flashes of lightning, and an earthquake', 8:5; cf. 4:5). It will conclude with a hymn of praise (11:17–18), paralleling the half-hour silence of 8:1. There are other similarities: the first four trumpets are set apart from the fifth and sixth (8:7–13; cf. 6:1–8); there will be an interlude or intercalation between the sixth and seventh trumpets (10:1—11:14; cf. 7:1–17).

Yet in the background is still the activity of the victorious Lamb, opening the scroll in the heavenly throne-room (5:7). There is an intimate connection between the ensuing trumpet sequence and the seals sequence which has preceded it (the link being the opening of the seventh seal). Some have proposed, on the grounds that the opening of this final seal initiates the seven trumpet-plagues, a 'telescopic' theory whereby the seventh seal contains within it the seven trumpets (Desrosiers 2000: 60). Certainly things seemed to have moved on from the 'beginnings of the birthpangs' represented by the four horsemen (6:1–8; Mk 13:5–8 and par.; note the transition from 'a fourth' at 6:8 to 'a third' at 8:7, 9, 11, 12; 9:15, 18). The contents of the trumpet-plagues cannot simply be attributed to dis-ordered human activity, war, bloodshed, famine and death. We are now in the realm of divine judgements, increasingly echoing the plagues of Egypt (Exodus 7—12; cf. Wisdom 11—19), and affecting the whole cosmos.

But sufficient overlap exists between the contents of these trum-pet-plagues and the sixth seal (cf. Mk 13:24–25 and par.) to suggest that the former represent the latter in more detail. The darkening of sun and moon is found in both the sixth seal and the fourth trumpet (6:12; 8:12), while the falling of stars to earth (6:13) is echoed in two fallen stars at the third and fifth trumpets (8:10; 9:1). The reaction of humanity to the day of the Lamb's wrath at 6:15–16 will be echoed in their frustrated longing for death as a result of the locust plague (9:6). In other words, although some progression has taken place in the narrative, John is not describing events in neat chronological sequence. Rather, it is as if the trumpet visions revisit the later seal visions, to describe the final judgements from a different perspective and (in the case of the fifth and sixth trumpets) in greater detail.

Nor will this process stop with Revelation's last trumpet. Like an unfolding tapestry, familiar patterns are beginning to emerge which will be rewoven into the later scenes of the seven bowl-plagues (16:2–21). The trumpet and bowl sequences both echo, though in different ways and in a different order, the plagues of Egypt (see Table 4, at commentary on 16:1). Moreover, there is general agreement in the location affected by the first six in each septet: (i) earth; (ii) sea; (iii) rivers and springs; (iv) heaven; (v) the underworld/'kingdom of the monster'; (vi) the Euphrates (Roloff 1993: 103–05). In John's apocalyptic masterpiece, we are being presented not with a precise diary for Doomsday but with cycles of overlapping visions picturing the same or similar events with increasing visual intensity.

Preparation for the Seven Trumpets (8:2–6)

(2) **Then I saw the seven angels who stand before God; they were given seven trumpets. (3) Then another angel came and stood at the altar, holding a gold thurible. He was given a large amount of incense, to offer together with the prayers of all the holy ones on the gold altar which stands in front of the throne. (4) The smoke of the incense ascended together with the prayers of the holy ones from the hand of the angel before God. (5) Then the angel took the thurible, filled it with burning coals from the altar, and threw it to the earth; and there were claps of thunder, voices, flashes of lightning, and an earthquake. (6) Now the seven angels with the seven trumpets got ready to blow them.**

This transitional passage describes a new stage of the heavenly liturgy after the prolonged silent interlude (8:1). Now is the time for the daily offering of incense, to be burned on the heavenly altar by an angelic priest. Now too is the time for the trumpets to be blown. John has made effective use here of the literary technique of 'interlocking' (A. Y. Collins 1976: 16–19), whereby a passage looks both backward and forward. The angel with the golden thurible, inserted between the introduction of the seven angels at 8:2 and their activity, which begins at verse 6, both refers back to the opening of the fifth seal with its vision of the souls under the altar (6:9–11; also 5:8), and prepares for the seven trumpets which follow.

But the real focus of this section is on **the prayers of the holy ones,** as the following concentric pattern makes clear (a more satisfying explanation than those attempts to 'improve on' this section by placing verse 2 after verse 5, as in Charles 1920: I, 221–22):

  A. Seven angels given trumpets (verse 2)
     B. Angel given incense (verse 3)
        C. Incense smoke rises with prayers of holy ones
          (verse 4)
     B' Angel throws down thurible with incense (verse 5)
  A' Seven angels prepare to blow their trumpets (verse 6)

2 The scene opens with a reference to **the seven angels who stand before God**. This description identifies them as the seven arch-angels, the angels of the Presence or 'the Face' (cf. Tob. 12:15; *Jub.* 2:18; 15:27; 31:14; Lk. 1:19; *T. Levi* 8:2; *1 En.* 81:5; 87:2). They are probably to be identified with the 'seven spirits', who are in a similar position 'before the throne' (see on 1:4; cf. 4:5; 5:6); they are unlikely to be the angels of the seven churches (1:20: a possibility discussed by Beale 1999: 454), for some of these stand under potential judgement. The Greek text of *1 Enoch* 20 gives the names of all seven: Uriel (cf. *4 Ez.* 4:1; 5:20; 10:28), Raphael (cf. Tob. 12:15; *1 En.* 22:2; 40:9), Raguel (cf. *2 En.* 11:25), Michael (cf. Dan. 10:13, 21; 12:1; Jude 9; *1 En.* 40:9), Saraqael (or Sariel, cf. 1QM 9:15), Gabriel (cf. Dan. 8:16; 9:21; Lk. 1:19, 26; *1 En.* 40:9) and Remiel (cf. *2 Bar.* 55:3; probably the Jeremiel of *4 Ez.* 4:36).

Of these seven, only Michael is mentioned by name elsewhere in Revelation, highlighting his particular role as guardian of Israel (12:7; for later traditions about the archangels, see Davidson 1967). Although John's visionary world is permeated with angelic beings and other heavenly powers, he displays surprisingly little interest in either their names or their distinctive functions. More important for him is that even the archangels are now subject to Christ, whose opening of the seventh seal has inaugurated the trumpet section.

Their particular role here is implicit in the fact that **they were given seven trumpets** (the passive verb is a theological passive: they were given them by God). Trumpets were used in the ancient world to announce battles or military victory, to proclaim fasts or announce religious festivals, and to accompany religious worship (e.g. Reddish 2001: 165). Most pertinent to this passage, however, is the prophetic association of the blowing of trumpets with the terrible Day of the Lord, a day of darkness and disaster (e.g. Zeph. 1:14–16; Joel 2:1; cf. *4 Ez.* 6:23; that there are seven trumpets may also recall those which heralded the fall of Jericho at Josh. 6:1–16). There is a specifically Christian version of this connection with eschatological judgement, in which angels or archangels with trumpets herald Christ's return (cf. Mt. 24:31; 1 Thess. 4:16; 1 Cor. 15:52 refers to 'the last trumpet', suggesting a succession of them, as here). For Christian audiences listening to Revelation, this heightens the expectation that the Parousia of Christ is coming next in the narra-tive. Again, our author will use narrative tension to good effect, for any explicit description of the Lord's return will be delayed until the end of chapter 19. In the interim, the archangels' trumpets will announce a succession of warning-plagues.

3–5 An eighth angel now comes on the scene (he is **another angel**, not one of the archangels of the Presence; he is said to be **before God** in verse 4 only because he has now moved temporarily to the altar to carry out his liturgical duties). His location **at the altar**, and the fact that he holds **a gold thurible** (cf. 1 Kgs 7:50; 1 Chron. 9.29; 3 Macc. 5.2), identify him as a priest ministering in the heavenly sanctuary. Probably we are to think of him on duty for offering the daily incense, similar to the role performed in the earthly Temple by John the Baptist's father Zechariah (Lk. 1:5–10; cf. Ps. 141:2; Jdt. 9:1; at Rev. 14:18 the same angel will have responsibility for the altar's fire). Later Jewish sources reveal that the daily morning service in the Temple included the offering of incense by the chosen priest, the throwing of the sacrificial victim onto the fire on the altar of sacrifice, and the blowing of trumpets (*m. Tam.* 5:5; 6:1–3; 7:3; similarly, though in a slightly different order, the evening service: *m. Yom.* 3:5; cf. Ben-Daniel 2003: 38–39, 49–54). In the heavenly temple that John is privileged to visit, the incense-offering is followed by coals from the same altar being thrown to earth, before the trumpets are blown to announce the next stage in the liturgy (the perfect number of seven trumpets rather than the two blown, according to *m. Tam.* 7:3, in the Jerusalem temple). Revelation does not seem to distinguish between the two altars of sacrifice and incense, but envisages one heavenly altar fulfilling both functions (see on 6:9). At this point, the primary focus is on the incense altar, for it is described as **gold** (as in Exod. 30:3), and **stands in front of the throne**.

But the angelic priest does not act on his own behalf. Like Raphael at Tob. 12:12, he is to bring the prayers of human beings before God. Hence **he was given** (another divine passive) **a large amount of incense**: the quantity may evoke the large number of prayers to be heard. The Greek at this point is rather unclear (lit. 'in order that he might give [it] to/for the prayers'), but surely intends to evoke some correlation between the incense being offered and **the prayers of all the holy ones**. It could mean that the incense is offered at the same time as the prayers (Smalley 2005: 201), or as a token of those prayers (e.g. Caird 1966: 103; cf. 5:8, where the prayers are themselves bowls of incense), or as a complement to them (Aune 1998a: 512). The preferred option here, **together with the prayers** (see the parallel ταῖς προσευχαῖς in verse 4), implies some close relationship between the two.

Two related questions remain. First, what precisely are **the prayers of all the holy ones**? Second, what is the theological significance of what they are said to achieve in this heavenly liturgy? The phrase 'holy ones' or 'saints', borrowed by the Christian church from Judaism (e.g. Acts 9:13; 26:10; Rom. 1:7; 1 Cor. 1:2), describes all those who worship God and keep the witness of Jesus (see on 5:8): it cannot therefore simply refer to the prayers of the souls under the altar at 6:9–11, but incorporates all the prayers of God's people, including presumably the songs of praise in which they participate throughout this book (e.g. 5:13; 7:10; 15:3–4; 19:1–3; 6–8). Nevertheless, it must include the 'How long?' of those slaughtered by the great Empire, who provide the paradigm for faithful witness throughout Revelation. The content of those prayers has been explicitly mentioned at 6:10; their deaths have been described in sacrificial terms, as they too are located close to the heavenly altar (6:9); further references to the holy ones associate them particularly with violence and bloodshed (e.g. 13:7; 16:6; 17:6; 18:24; 20:9). It follows that the prayers of the saints are especially prayers for justice to be done, for God to act and bring to an end all that frustrates his plan for creation, which means definitive action against evil, injustice and sin.

Theologically, this vision proclaims the effectiveness of prayer for those who in the world's eyes appear to be voiceless. Prayer is not a futile business, but an activity which, aligned to the perspective of the crucified and risen Jesus, is indeed heard and answered. The upward ascent of the prayers, mingled with the rising **smoke of the incense**, initiates a corresponding downward movement, as the thurible, now filled with **burning coals**, is thrown **to the earth**. Sensitive readers will detect an allusion to Ezek. 10:2, where the man in linen scatters burning coals upon unfaithful Jerusalem, having first marked the servants of God (see also the commentary on 7:2–3): in John's vision, Jerusalem has been expanded to encompass the whole **earth**, just as the servants of God now come from every people and nation. But there is a more ironic aspect which underscores the effectiveness of the prayers of the holy ones: the ascent of the incense smoke is referred to again, more negatively, at 9:2 (the smoke from the Abyss), 14:11 (the smoke from the torments of those who worship the monster), and 19:3 (the smoke of Babylon's burning).

Many interpreters, particularly in the Northern Hemisphere, admit to being disturbed by such a connection, which appears to gloat over the torment of others. Christians encountering oppression, persecution or injustice of various kinds, on the other hand, read a passage such as this as a proclamation of the gospel, refusing to draw a sharp distinction between God's love and God's justice (cf. e.g. Boesak 1987: 75–78). They hear this from the perspective of those who cry 'How long?', rather than from the perspective of those who have a vested interest in the present state of affairs. They challenge more established readings by a heightened awareness of the crucial role of perspective in interpretation, asking whether those who read from the perspective of the marginalised or exiled might be in a better position than others to hear and respond to John's marginal book (e.g. Rhoads 2005).

Moreover, in interpreting a passage such as this we should not lose sight of its liturgical nature (set as it is in the heavenly temple), nor the liturgical 'theatre of reception' in which it was probably first heard. Within the world of the story, it is significant that the altar where the action takes place is located before the throne. As will become clear (e.g. at 22:1), that throne is now occupied by the slaughtered but victorious Lamb, such that the face of the fearsome Judge bears the features of Jesus of Nazareth. Within the real first-century world, it would probably have been heard within the liturgical assemblies of the Asian congregations. Their worship would have been imaginatively caught up into the heavenly liturgy, with the assurance of their prayers being heard at the throne where true power is located. Weak and vulnerable churches such as Smyrna and Philadelphia, and their counterparts in every place and age, would find this compelling.

The liturgical setting of the scene is underlined by the consequence of the thurible being thrown to earth: **there were claps of thunder, voices, flashes of lightning, and an earthquake** (a dramatic contrast to the silence accompanying the seventh seal!). Earthquakes, and the shaking of the cosmos, are often associated with theophanies, not least in an eschatological context (*1 En.* 1:3–9; 102:1–2; *T. Mos.* 10:1–7; *2 Bar.* 32:1). Moreover, the revelation of God on Mount Sinai (e.g. Exod. 19:16–25; Pss 68:8; 77:17–18; Isa. 64:1–3) is particularly associated with the quaking of the earth, together with phenomena such as lightning. God is now making his presence felt, in order to act, as he did for his people at the first Exodus. Further allusions to the Sinai theophany, with increasing intensity, will be found at 11:19 and 16:18–21.

Now that the incense has been offered and the burning thurible 6 thrown down, the next stage in the heavenly liturgy can begin, and with it, a new perspective on the eschatological judgement (viewed now from heaven, from the perspective of the angelic liturgy). **The seven angels with the seven trumpets** now return to centre stage, and prepare **to blow** their trumpets. Again, the dramatic tension rises as the Christian audience expects the story of God's salvation to reach its climax. The appearance of archangels with their trumpets suggests that the Lord's coming is near!

The First Four Trumpets (8:7–13)

(7) The first blew his trumpet, and there came hail and fire mixed with blood, which were thrown to the earth. A third of the earth was burnt up, as were a third of the trees, and every blade of green grass.

(8) Then the second angel blew his trumpet, and what

looked like a huge mountain burning with fire was thrown into the sea. A third of the sea turned to blood, (9) and a third of the creatures that live in the sea died, and a third of all ships were destroyed.

(10) Then the third angel blew his trumpet, and a huge star fell from heaven, burning like a lamp. It fell on a third of the rivers and on the springs of waters. (11) This star's name was Wormwood, and a third of the waters turned to wormwood, so that many people died from the bitter waters.

(12) Then the fourth angel blew his trumpet, and a third of the sun, a third of the moon and a third of the stars were struck. As a result, a third of each was darkened; there was no light for a third of the day, and the same for the night.

(13) Then I looked, and I heard an eagle screeching in a loud voice as it flew high in the sky: 'Woe, woe, woe, to those who make their home on the earth, because of the remaining trumpet-blasts of the three angels yet to blow their trumpets.'

Without further delay, the trumpet sequence begins. As in the seals sequence (6:1–8), the first four of this septet belong together by virtue of their similar structure and their brevity (the fifth and sixth trumpets are given more detailed descriptions). The downward movement (denoted by the verbs **thrown** and **fell**) makes clear in at least the first three trumpet-blasts the close connection between the trumpet-plagues and the ascending of the prayers of the saints mingled with incense. Throughout the Apocalypse, the verbs βάλλω and πίπτω describe either divine judgement towards the earth (e.g. 6:13; 14:16) or God's casting down of hostile powers (e.g. 12:9; 18:2, 21; cf. 2:5; note also the verb καταβαίνω, 'descend': e.g. 10:1ff.; 18:1; 21:2; cf. 3:12).

John's visionary raw materials throughout the seven trumpets, as in the subsequent bowls sequence, seem to be the Egyptian plagues of Exodus 7—12 and their elaboration in Wisdom of Solomon 11—19, together with the terrifying portrayals of the Day of the Lord in Amos and Joel (Amos 5:18–20; 7:1–3; Joel 1—2). No doubt tradition has also been mixed with the memory of particular natural phenomena (Roloff 1993: 110 equates the first trumpet-plague with 'the mysterious red rain, which occurs occasionally in Mediterranean regions with the infiltration of dust from the Sahara') and concrete historical events.

But any attempt to tie these visions down too precisely risks robbing them of their shocking revelatory power and nightmarish quality (for an indication of their capacity to speak to fresh situations and generations, see Kovacs and Rowland 2004: 109–11). 'Nightmare' is an appropriate metaphor, for what is being played out before our eyes (though in symbolic rather than literal form) are the terrifying consequences of a world without God. It is as if the original act of creation, in which the forces of chaos were tamed and restrained, has now been reversed, affecting in turn the earth with its vegetation, the sea and rivers with their creatures, and finally the very sources of light themselves (cf. Genesis 1). In the new Exodus story that John is telling from his Patmos exile, the new oppressor of God's people stands under judgement (cf. 11:8, where one of the names of the 'great city' is Egypt), which is nothing more and nothing less than being brought face to face with the reality of the monster it has created. Yet as in the old story, so in the new: the judgements stand as wake-up calls, trumpet-blasts to alert humanity to the reality of its situation, leading to a change of mind and heart (9:21; cf. Joel 2:15). Also as in the plagues of the old Exodus, their ultimate goal is not destruction, but the liberation of God's people.

The blowing of the first trumpet initiates a shower of **hail**, whose 7 downward movement parallels the throwing down of the thurible (verse 5). The hail evokes the seventh Egyptian plague (Exod. 9:13–35), though the further reference to **fire mixed with blood** heightens its eschatological character and divine origin (cf. Wis. 16:15–23; a similar mixture of fire and hailstones greets Enoch as he ascends to the heavenly throne-room: *1 En.* 14:9–10). This is no freak of nature, but divine judgement writ large (which unlike the unfortunate Laodiceans is both hot and cold). Blood and fire are sometimes associated with the events of the End (e.g. Ezek. 38:22; Joel 2:3, 30). Yet it would not be lost on John's Christian audiences that among the blood shed by the contemporary Egypt/Babylon was the blood of their Lord (of the five references to blood up to this point, three have been to the Lamb's blood and one to that of God's witnesses: 1:5; 5:9; 7:14; 6:10). An empire founded on bloodshed, whether that of Christ (12:11; possibly also 14:20; 19:13), his followers (16:6; 17:6; 18:24; 19:2) or other unnamed victims (18:24), can only reap blood in return (6:12; 8:7–8; 11:6; 16:3, 4, 6). It takes the bloody witness of Jesus to unmask the reality of this senseless scenario, bringing it under the bar of judgement.

The result of this bloody downpour is the burning up of **earth** (probably the land as opposed to the sea: Gen. 1:9–10), **trees** and **green grass**. Two things are to be noted here. First, the collapse of the created order is very much in view here, with the burning of two features associated with the separation of earth and sea on the third day of creation: the vegetation and the fruit-bearing trees (Gen. 1:11–12). While no human beings are killed at this stage, it does mean the destruction of a substantial part of the food chain vital for human survival. Second, despite the overlapping of seals, trumpets and bowls, some progression can be detected. The explicit reference to a third of earth and trees (every blade of green grass may be simply a stylistic variation: Smalley 2005: 220) moves us on from the 'fourth' associated with the fourth seal (6:8); the bowl-plagues will move us on further still (16:2–21). Yet even here the divine hand of restraint is in evidence: only a third is destroyed. The End is not yet, and there is still time for the horrific vision to bring humanity to its senses.

8–9 With the second trumpet-warning, what looked like a huge mountain burning with fire was thrown into the sea (the omission of 'with fire' in some late readings does not affect the meaning). The earth having been affected by the first trumpet-plague, now it is the turn of the sea. The prominence of the sea, and Rome's dominance over it, would have been particularly evident to the seer on the island of Patmos (Revelation has 24 references to θάλασσα, including several which evoke its chaotic, untamed character: e.g. 13:1; 15:2; 21:1). Those attentive to historical allusions in the Apocalypse have often understood the huge mountain as a reference to Vesuvius, whose dramatic eruption in 79 CE was witnessed by the younger Pliny. But such a reference presupposes the later, Domitianic dating for Revelation, and there are other possibilities closer to Patmos, such as the eruption of Thera (the island of the 'monster', θηρίον) or Santorini, which began in 60 CE (Bent 1888). However, on closer inspection neither eruption is a perfect fit, for what John witnesses is the *whole* mountain which is thrown into the sea, rather than a shower of burning rocks and pumice stone.

More likely, we are to think of the mountain-like object as a fallen angel, as are the seven stars 'like great burning mountains' that Enoch witnesses at the end of heaven and earth (*1 En.* 18:13–14; 21:3; cf. 108:4; the similarity of John's description to a meteorite has been noted by Roloff 1993: 110). The verb used of this fallen star/angel (was thrown) places it in the same league as Satan, the monster, and the false prophet (12:9, 10, 13; 19:20; 20:10, 14, 15). But perhaps we can be even more precise about its identity. Jeremiah 51:25 speaks of the oppressive city Babylon as a destroying mountain, and warns that it will become a 'burned-out mountain'. This echoes Rev. 18:21, where a great millstone, representing the contemporary Babylon, is thrown into the sea (cf. *Sib. Or.* 5:158–61, telling of a great star which will burn the sea and Babylon). Perhaps, then, the mountain-like angel is the heavenly representative of Babylon (like Egypt, now to be identified with Rome), facing divine judgement in John's visionary kaleidoscope. It is a brief, long-distance shot, preparing us for the close-up, more detailed vision of Babylon's downfall in chapters 17—18.

The effect of this fallen mountain/angel is that a third of the sea

turned to blood (see on verse 7), resulting in the deaths of **a third of the creatures that live in the sea** (a reversal of Gen. 1:21). The direct role played by Babylon's angel in the destruction underscores the extent to which the great empire brings judgement upon itself. The Exodus motif is continued with an allusion to the first Egyptian plague, which turned the water of the Nile to blood and killed all the fish (Exod. 7:14–24). But the trumpet-plague goes further (perhaps underlining the demonic nature of Babylon's fallen angel): not only were the fish killed, as in Exod. 7:21, but **a third of all ships were destroyed**. Ironically, Babylon's angel strikes at the very source of Rome's current dominance on the high seas (cf. 18:17–19, where a chorus of seafarers and naval officers lament over Babylon's fall and their consequent loss of wealth).

The third trumpet heralds an event not dissimilar to that just   10–11 described. John tells how **a huge star fell from heaven, burning like a lamp**. Falling stars are equated elsewhere in Jewish apocalyptic with fallen angels (e.g. *1 En.* 86:1–6, which is a symbolic description of the fall of the Watchers; cf. Gen. 6:1–4; *1 Enoch* 6—8), and Revelation will later refer to the casting down of Satan (12:9–10; cf. Lk. 10:18). If Isa. 14:12 is an appropriate background, then this falling star may be the angelic personification of the king of Babylon, falling like the Day Star from its exalted place down to Sheol. This would then reiterate the warning of the second trumpet that arrogant Babylon, or its present incarnation in imperial Rome, faces divine judgement (the verb ἔπεσεν is also used of Babylon's fall at 14:8 and 18:2; cf. 11:13). Rather cryptically, we are told that this angel's name is **Wormwood**, a name appropriate to the effects it will cause (probably the bitter plant *Artemisia absinthium*, oil from which was used to treat worms: Aune 1998a: 521f.). Wormwood itself, though unpleasant to the taste, does not kill. In these exaggerated and nightmarish trumpet-plagues, however, what was simply unpleasant becomes deadly poisonous, the consequence of demonic activity.

The burning star **fell on a third of the rivers and on the springs of waters** (cf. the third bowl-plague at 16:4), causing them to turn to **wormwood** (cf. Jer. 9:15; 23:15; Lam. 3:15, 19; Amos 5:7). Here there is a partial echo of the first Egyptian plague already alluded to in the previous trumpet, for that plague affected the Nile and the other rivers, canals and ponds of Egypt (Exod. 7:19). More striking, however, is the dramatic reversal here of Moses' sweetening of the bitter water at Marah (Exod. 15:22–25), enabling the people of Israel to quench their thirst. The idolatrous empire Babylon can bring only bitterness and death to humanity, a point also made by the reference to the springs of waters, which for the followers of the Lamb are a source not of bitterness but of blessing and spiritual refreshment (7:17). In Babylon's hands, by contrast, the waters lead to the deaths of **many people.**

12 The fourth trumpet-plague echoes the ninth Exodus plague, in which a dense darkness descends over the land of Egypt for three days (Exod. 10:21–29; cf. Ezek. 32:7–8). In Revelation, however, the 'three days' have become a third: the darkness affects **a third of the sun, a third of the moon and a third of the stars** (the heavenly luminaries which emerged on the fourth day of creation, Gen. 1:14–19). Unnatural darkness over the earth is a frequent accompaniment to the Day of the Lord (e.g. Amos 5:18–20; Joel 2:31; 3:15), and is picked up by early Christian writers (e.g. Mk 13:24–25; Mt. 24:29). The second half of the verse clarifies the first: the result is not a reduction in the heavenly bodies' brightness, but in the length of their operation: **there was no light for a third of the day.** Indeed, the darkening of **a third of the stars** may even contain an echo of angelic fall (a feature of the previous two trumpets). If so, we have a further indication that the trumpets confront us with the terrible consequences of rebellion against God in both heavenly and earthly realms. Yet Christian audiences ought to detect a note of hope and restraint, even in this darkest of scenes. Despite the negative connotations of darkness, the domain of malevolent powers, God is shown to be in ultimate control.

13 As if to mark off the first four trumpets from those yet to come, and also to heighten the dramatic tension as we await those remaining three, **an eagle** appears flying **high in the sky,** at the zenith (perhaps the fourth living creature, which was described as like a flying eagle, 4:7). The eagle is a creature of swiftness and strength, but also evokes doom (the Greek ἀετός may also be translated 'vulture', heightening the sense of foreboding: e.g. Hos. 8:1 LXX; Lk. 17:37). The phrase **high in the sky** (ἐν μεσουρανήματι) will be used of a flying angel with an eternal gospel at 14:6. Perhaps the variant reading 'angel' in some witnesses (reflected in the AV) is an early attempt to identify the two flying figures; alternatively, it may result from scribal unease over an unclean bird apparently fulfilling a divine function (in other apocalypses, the eagle is negatively associated with Rome: e.g. *4 Ez.* 11:1; 12:11; *T. Mos.* 10:8).

The human-like voice of the eagle reiterates the function of these visions to warn and to provoke a change of heart, with its threefold **Woe, woe, woe** (see also 12:12; 18:10, 16, 19) upon **those who make their home on the earth** (for this group see on 3:10). The Greek οὐαὶ οὐαὶ οὐαὶ is onomatopoeic, reflecting the sound made by the eagle (conveyed in this translation by the verb **screeching**). The logic of this passage would suggest that the three woes or coming disasters will correspond to the three remaining trumpet-plagues: **because of the remaining trumpet-blasts of the three angels yet to blow their trumpets.** However, as the narrative progresses, the reader is left guessing. The locust plague inaugurated by the fifth trumpet is indeed explicitly identified as the first woe at 9:12. The statement that the second woe has come is not made until 11:14: although we could identify it with the sixth trumpet-plague (9:13–21), we are probably meant to understand the whole section from 9:13 to 11:13. This would mean that John's own prophesying 'about many peoples and nations, languages and kings' (10:1–11), and the Church's prophetic witness (11:3–13), are themselves part of the woe. Faithful witness, to the point of death, represents disaster for the world, which cannot accept it.

There is, however, no further mention of the third woe. Knight suggests, on the basis of 11:14b and the structural similarities between 11:19 and 15:5, that this woe occupies the whole section between the blowing of the seventh trumpet and the appearance of the seven angels with the bowl-plagues (11:15—15:4: Knight 1999: 80). For others, it is the seventh trumpet, which marks the transition from the 'royal rule of this world' to that of 'our Lord and of his Christ' (11:15: e.g. Murphy 1988: 241f.). Perhaps, however, the silence about the third woe functions as a reminder of the cyclic and spiralling nature of John's book, in which the same climactic judgements reappear with ever greater intensity and detail. It may, then, be no coincidence that the fall of Babylon is also accompanied by a repeated cry of 'woe' (three sets of two: 18:10, 16, 19). The final judgement of Babylon/the great city in chapters 17—18 is the detailed canvas portraying what is implicit in the seventh trumpet and the seventh bowl (and anticipated proleptically by the second flying angel at 14:8).

The Fifth Trumpet   (9:1–12)

(1) Then the fifth angel blew his trumpet, and I saw a star which had fallen from heaven to the earth. It was given the key to the shaft which led to the Abyss. (2) It opened the shaft of the Abyss, and smoke ascended from the shaft, like the smoke produced by a huge furnace. The sun and the air were darkened by the smoke from the shaft. (3) Then out of the smoke there came locusts onto the earth, and they were given the same power as earthly scorpions. (4) But they were commanded not to harm any of the earth's grass, no greenery nor any tree, but only those people who do not have the seal of God on their foreheads. (5) They were not permitted to kill them, but only to torment them for five months. Their

torment was to be like a scorpion's sting. (6) At that time human beings will search out Death, but will fail to find it; they will long to die, but Death will elude them. (7) The locusts looked like horses ready for battle, with what looked like gold wreaths on their heads, and their faces were like human faces. (8) They had hair like that of women, and teeth like those of lions. (9) Their breastplates looked as if they were made of iron, and the sound of their wings was like the noise of chariots pulled by many horses, charging into battle. (10) They had tails like scorpions' tails, with stings; it was with their tails that they were able to harm people for five months. (11) They have as king over them the angel of the Abyss: his name is in Hebrew 'Abaddon', and in Greek 'Apollyon'. (12) The first woe has passed; there are two more woes still to come!

1–2 The threefold pronouncement of woes (8:13) has warned us to expect the nightmare to intensify, and so it does as the fifth and sixth angels blow their trumpets. At the trumpet-blast of the **fifth angel**, John sees **a star which had fallen from heaven to the earth**. This star is almost certainly an angelic being: stars have already been equated with angels in this book (e.g. 1:20; 3:1; probably 8:10–11). There is, however, considerable disagreement as to his precise identity: is he to be identified with the 'angel of the Abyss' in verse 11, and is he a positive agent of God or a demonic figure paradoxically used by God to bring about his purposes? In favour of his being in the divine service is the fact that the star **was given the key to the shaft which led to the Abyss** (at 20:1 the angel who binds Satan is also given the key to the Abyss; elsewhere it is only Christ who possesses keys: 1:18; 3:7). Ancient readers might detect a sideswipe at the goddess Hekate, who held the keys to the underworld in Greek mythology.

Yet this star-angel has already **fallen** (cf. *1 En.* 86:1–6): the same verb describes the fall of the Ephesian angel (2:5), the stars of heaven (6:13), Wormwood (8:10), Babylon the great (11:13; 14:8; 18:2), the cities of the nations (16:19), and five Roman kings (17:10). But then God can use even hostile and rebellious forces to accomplish his ultimate will. This fallen angel is probably to be differentiated from the 'angel of the Abyss', Abaddon, for that figure seems to belong down below with the locust army he heads, whereas this one opens the Abyss from the outside.

The fallen angel **opened the shaft of the Abyss**, allowing **smoke** to escape, which darkens **the sun and the air**. The demonic nature of this judgement is clear, for **smoke ascended from the shaft** (ἀναβαίνω is also used of monsters at 11:7; 13:1, 11 and 17:8), infecting the light by which human beings see and the air by which they breathe. The **Abyss** (Greek ἄβυσσος, meaning 'without bottom') is used in the LXX to denote the Hebrew *tehom*, the watery deeps held back at creation (e.g. Gen. 1:2; 7:11; Ps. 104:6; Ezek. 26:19; Amos 7:4; Job 28:14), or the depths under the earth (e.g. Pss 71:20; 88:6). It also comes to be associated with the dwelling-place of the dead (e.g. Rom. 10:7) and the location of demons (e.g. *1 Enoch* 18—21; Lk. 8:31; see the discussion in Charles 1920: I, 239–42). Elsewhere in Revelation it denotes the place of origin of the monster (11:7; 17:8) and Satan's temporary place of imprisonment (20:1, 3; contrast the 'lake of fire' at 19:20; 20:14, 15; 21:8). It is probably to be identified with the sea of chaos, from which the monster ascends at 13:1.

The divine permission for the shaft to be opened, albeit temporarily, 3–5 unleashes a demonic plague of **locusts onto the earth**. The scene is reminiscent of the eighth Egyptian plague (Exod. 10:1–20), though Joel's vision of a terrifying locust attack heralding the Day of the Lord (Joel 1:4–7) is a vital added ingredient in John's visionary melting-pot. Locusts were legendary in the ancient world for their ability to destroy crops, and therefore the human food-chain, in a short space of time. John would be hard-pressed to find a more satisfying symbol of utter havoc and devastation: a single migrating swarm can contain millions of locusts, create a phalanx several miles in width, and devastate a nation's food supply in a matter of days.

But this is no natural swarm of locusts, which would normally attack vegetation: this army is expressly **commanded not to harm any of the earth's grass, no greenery nor any tree** (contrast the first trumpet at 8:7; but see 7:3). Moreover, the locusts **were given** scorpion-like stings (another divine passive), accentuating their supernatural identity. Hybrid creatures evoke fear in all cultures, standing as they do on the wrong side of the line demarcating order from chaos. Yet again God's restraining hand seems to be active, not permitting them to kill **but only to torment ... for five months** (five being a natural round number having the sense of 'a few', and therefore denoting a limited period: Aune 1998a: 530).

The scorpion-like stings, however, are able to affect **only those people who do not have the seal of God on their foreheads** ('those who make their home on the earth' of 8:13). The symbolic 144,000 were sealed back at 7:4–8, not to render them immune from suffering (that is to be expected by those who hold the witness of Jesus), but to mark them out as God's servants and preserve them through the great tribulation. In the present vision they are protected from the worst excesses of the demonic onslaught, just as the generation of the first Exodus were unharmed by the locust plague which affected the land of Egypt (cf. Lk. 10:18–19, where those sent out by Jesus trample on snakes and scorpions unharmed). In contrast, those marked with the mark of the monster (13:16, 17; 14:9, 11; 16:2; 19:20; 20:4) will reap the only fruits that the beastly empire can produce.

6   In words reminiscent of humanity's reaction to the sixth seal (6:15–17), John describes their reaction to the onslaught on locusts. Far from the hoped-for response of repentance, we learn that **human beings will search out Death** (that terrifying fourth rider, influenced by the Greek Thanatos and the Canaanite god Mot: see on 6:8). It is an understandable human reaction. Yet in parallel poetic couplets (either of the narrator or of a heavenly voice), we discover the futility of such a quest (cf. Job 3:21; *Sib. Or.* 2.307–08; on this, see Aune 1998a: 531). Ironically, the figure of Death, whose sickly green horse could not be avoided when the Lamb opened the fourth seal, now eludes humanity when directly sought out.

7–10   The mutation of these demonic locusts continues with a further description of their ghastly appearance. Under the influence of Joel 2:2–9, they are now transformed into a formidable army of would-be warhorses (as elsewhere in this visionary book, the seer piles simile upon simile in order to describe what he sees). There is emphasis upon their strength and warlike character: **ready for battle**, with **breastplates** (presumably their scaly bodies) which **looked as if they were made of iron**. The huge number of locusts is implied by **the sound of their wings**, likened to **the noise of chariots pulled by many horses, charging into battle**. We have come to expect extreme loudness in this book (e.g. 1:15; 4:5; 5:11–14), but this noise is terrifying in its intensity and ferocity. The comparison of their **teeth to those of lions** highlights the ferocity with which they attack their prey, as well as setting up a contrast with the true Lion of the tribe of Judah, the slaughtered Lamb (5:5–6), whose battle plan is very different from theirs.

The reference to their headgear (**wreaths**, στέφανοι) is rather ambiguous, for it would seem to suggest not only a victorious army, but one that is allied to God: elsewhere in the Apocalypse, στέφανοι are symbols of victory worn by faithful Christians or their angels (2:10; 3:11), the twenty-four elders (4:4, 10), the woman clothed with the sun (12:1), and 'someone like a son of man' (14:14; 6:2 probably refers to a demonic parody). Yet we are simply told that they had **what looked like gold wreaths on their heads**: they are no more true victors than they are real horses. Their apparent victory is a counterfeit victory, for it is established on the torments produced by their scorpion-like **stings**.

Two further and related features of their description are worthy of note: **their faces were like human faces**, and **they had hair like that of women**. Located within this beastly mix of locust, horse and scorpion are human characteristics. For all the demonic, otherworldly dimensions of this locust plague, it has a human face. Evil and chaos may manifest itself in our world in superhuman proportions, yet ultimately it needs human cooperation in order to function, and cannot finally be dislocated from human sinfulness and rebellion. But can we be more precise as to where these locusts' human side is to be located? A clue may be detected in the reference to their women-like hair, probably alluding to its length (cf. 1 Cor. 11:15). This may be another tantalising allusion to Rome's sworn enemy on its eastern borders, the Parthian Empire (cf. 6:2; 9:14; 16:12), whose warriors were known for their long hair (Plut. *Crass.* 24.2; cf. Suet. *Vesp.* 23.4). It was to Parthia that the arrogant Nero was believed by some to have fled in 68 CE, in order to raise an army and return to destroy his enemies (on this see Aune 1998a: 737–40). John's visionary nightmare plays upon residual fears and hopes to evoke the destruction of the great empire at the instigation of one of its own, which is judgement under another name.

This evocation may be confirmed by the description of the locusts' **11–12** **king** or 'emperor' (βασιλεύς). Of course, he is an angel, **the angel of the Abyss** (not mentioned elsewhere in Revelation, but known from 4Q280 as the '[Ange]l of the Pit and Spir[it of Aba]ddon': Aune 1998a: 534). The Hebrew and Greek versions of his name, **Abaddon** and **Apollyon**, evoke his character as 'Destroyer', indicative of the disastrous consequences of following this particular king (cf. Prov. 15:11; in Job 26:6, Abaddon is associated with Sheol/Hades, the abode of the dead, and in 4Q504 with the Abyss). But the king/ emperor also has a human face. The name Apollyon would have prompted association with the similar-sounding Apollo, particularly for John, given Patmos' thriving cult of that god and its strong cultural and political links with Apollo's oracle shrine at Didyma. Apollo was the god with whom the emperor Nero was explicitly identified (for an illustration of coins depicting Nero as Apollo the lyre-player, see Kreitzer 1996: 208). Some at least would have pictured the vision in terms of Nero riding at the head of a great and destructive Parthian army, the human façade of a demonic, destructive and ultimately self-destructive invasion.

The first woe, then, has given an indication of what is still on the horizon: judgement against the great city, whether known as Egypt, Babylon or even Rome, will come about not from without but from within. For evil and injustice bear within themselves the seeds of their own destruction. Abaddon is even more appropriate a name than might at first have appeared.

The Sixth Trumpet (9:13–21)

(13) Then the sixth angel blew his trumpet, and I heard a voice coming from the four horns of the gold altar which is before God, (14) saying to the sixth angel with the trumpet: 'Release the four angels tied up at the great river Euphrates.' (15) The four angels, who had been prepared for this hour and day, this month and year, were released, to kill a third of humanity. (16) I heard the number of this army of cavalry: twenty thousand times ten thousand. (17) I saw these horses in my vision, and their riders wearing breastplates of fiery red, dark blue and sulphur-yellow. The heads of the horses were like lions' heads, and fire, smoke and sulphur came out of their mouths. (18) It was by these three plagues that they killed a third of humanity: by the fire, the smoke and the sulphur which came out of their mouths. (19) The horses' power was in their mouths and in their tails; for their tails were like serpents, with heads by which they inflicted harm.

(20) But the rest of humanity, who were not killed by these plagues, would not repent of what they had made, nor stop worshipping demons and idols made of gold and silver, bronze, stone and wood, which cannot see or hear or walk. (21) Nor would they repent of their murdering, their sorcery, their sexual infidelity, or their robbery.

13–15 The trumpet-blast of **the sixth angel** reminds us that John is describing events from heaven's perspective, for we find ourselves back in the heavenly temple. John hears **a voice coming from the four horns of the gold altar which is before God**. Again, the emphasis is upon the altar of incense (which was made of gold, 8:3: cf. Exod. 30:3), maintaining the link between the trumpet-visions and the prayers of the holy ones. Altars in Israel had **four horns** (the number 'four' is lacking in some manuscripts) on their corners, the symbols of divine power (see Ford 1975: illus. 15, for an example found at Megiddo). 1 Kings 2:28–35 suggests that holding onto the horns of an altar guaranteed asylum: ironically, from these horns comes **a voice** which allows forces of destruction to be released. We are not told whose voice can be heard. As it comes from the altar **before God**, it is presumably not the divine voice itself. Because it is associated with the altar, it might be one of the souls of the slain (6:9–11). However, these cry out for their blood to be avenged, whereas this single voice seems to be part of the answer to that prayer. A more promising solution is that this is one of the four living creatures, or all four of them speaking as of 'one voice' from each of the four corners (one variant reading at this point has 'a voice from the four living creatures which were before the altar of God'). The single voice of each of these creatures has been heard in turn before, also provoking activity on the earth (6:1, 3, 5, 7). Now their voices are heard again, linked this time not with the throne but with the altar before it (such shifts of location are commonly found in apocalyptic visions, as in dreams).

The sixth archangel has a further task to perform, besides blowing his trumpet: **'Release the four angels tied up at the great river Euphrates.'** The Euphrates was one of the four rivers which flowed out of Eden (Gen. 2:14), and had huge symbolic significance for ancient Israel, as the ideal – if not always actual – boundary of the Promised Land (Gen. 15:18; Exod. 23:31; Deut. 1:7; 11:24; Josh. 1:4). This meant that in the religious consciousness of Jews and Jewish Christians, the invading enemies of God's people (e.g. the Assyrians, the Babylonians) would have come from beyond the Euphrates. The river will be mentioned again at the pouring out of the sixth bowl (16:12), strengthening the case for essentially the same events being alluded to in the trumpet- and bowl-septets. But as in the fifth trumpet-plague, first-century audiences may have detected a more immediate resonance. In John's day, the Euphrates marked the eastern boundary of the Roman Empire with Parthia.

The identity of the four angels is not made explicit (though some detect parallels with the punishing angels of *1 En.* 66:1, or the destructive angel-winds of Dan. 7:2, Zech. 6:5–8 and *2 Bar.* 6:4). Four angels have been met before in Revelation at the four corners of the earth (7:1). Those angels, however, were restraining the four winds/horsemen from damaging the earth prior to the sealing of God's servants; the four angels here are themselves being restrained, and must be a different quartet. The fact that they have been **tied up** and now **released** points to their demonic character, as does their ability **to kill a third of humanity** (note the striking parallels between this scene and 20:7–9, where Satan is temporarily released from the Abyss, where he has been tied up, to gather for battle the innumerable armies of Gog and Magog). The verbs used suggest divine permission rather than the active pursuit of the divine will: nothing happens in this world outside the divine purpose, not even those things which are ultimately contrary to that purpose (Harrington 1993: 112). This is implied in the claim that these rebellious angels **had been prepared for this hour and day, this month and year.** This is not the fatalistic determinism so often attributed to the apocalyptic mentality, but a proclamation, even in the face of those most horrendous outworkings of evil, that God is in control of God's universe.

The beastly mutation we encountered in the fifth trumpet-plague 16–19 continues here, with the transformation of the four angels into a vast

army of cavalry, emphasising the great devastation they are to wreak: to kill **a third of humanity**. This is a striking reminder that what the Apocalypse sets before us are not primarily coded descriptions of actual historical events, but kaleidoscopic and poly-valent visions, which work by their evocative power, stretching our imaginations to their limits. Perhaps we are to think of these angels as the driving forces behind human armies, particularly the human enemies of God's people and those that will eventually bring the great city to its knees (see the similar scene in *1 Enoch* 56). As with numbers elsewhere in Revelation, the **twenty thousand times ten thousand** is not a literal number (though two hundred million certainly does the trick), but a symbolic number expressing the immensity of this army (cf. the number of angels around the throne at 5:11, or that of Gog and Magog at 20:8).

The description of this mighty cavalry is strangely evocative of the locusts of the fifth trumpet, even though what John saw are clearly **horses** (note again the complex relationship between what John 'sees' and what he 'hears': cf. 5:5–6; 7:4, 9). In both trumpet-plagues we seem to be seeing something similar. As befits their demonic origin, these horses have the same hybrid nature as the locusts (Joel's vision of the Day of the Lord has influenced both: e.g. Joel 2:4–5; cf. Ezek. 38:14–16). Their heads are **like lions' heads** (again perhaps a parody of the true messianic Lion: 5:5; cf. 9:8), and **their tails were like serpents, with heads by which they inflicted harm** (cf. the scorpion-like tails of the locusts at 9:10, which also cause harm; at 12:9 Satan will be identified as the ancient serpent). The **heads** on the tails are probably to be envisaged as serpent-heads biting their victims.

In contrast to the locusts, attention is also focused on the **riders** of these horses (anticipating 'earth's kings', who will play a key role in the various battle scenes: e.g. 16:14; 19:19). The **breastplates** are not on the horses but on the riders (contrast verse 9, which describes the locusts' breastplates). Given Revelation's attention to often-vivid colours, it is not surprising that these are colourful breastplates, **of fiery red, dark blue and sulphur-yellow**. These colours parallel **the fire, the smoke** (by implication a blue shade, like jacinth) **and the sulphur** which come out of their mouths (note the parallels with Leviathian in Job 41:19–21). **These three plagues** are the char-acteristics of the Abyss, contrasted with the ordered lamps and sweet-smelling incense smoke of heaven. It is not surprising that it is these, **which came out of their mouths**, that kill, for the Abyss is ulti-mately the abode of the dead (contrast the double-edged sword coming out of the mouth of 'someone like a son of man', the only weapon allowed to his army: 1:16; 2:12, 16; 19:15, 21).

This sixth trumpet ends with a reminder of the purpose of all the 20–21
trumpet-plagues, and indeed of the Exodus plagues which they
evoke: to bring humanity to repentance, to a change of heart due to
being confronted with the reality of their situation. The apocalypse
genre is ultimately a genre which lifts the veil on the world,
unmasking its delusion and its arrogance by presenting it with the
divine perspective.

Yet there is an element of tragedy here, for **the rest of humanity,
who were not killed by these plagues, would not repent**.
Evoking the reinterpretation of the Egyptian plagues in the Wisdom
of Solomon (e.g. Wis. 11:11–20; 14:22–27), Revelation regards the
root of all sin and rebellion to be idolatry, the worship of **idols made
of gold and silver, bronze, stone and wood**. Idolatry is humanity's refusal to acknowledge its Creator and thereby accept its
creaturely status (cf. Rom. 1:18–32). The hybrid creatures let loose
on the earth by the fifth and sixth trumpets manifest in their bodies
the consequent chaotic breakdown of the created order. John's words
echo the mocking tones with which the Jewish tradition character-
istically attacks Gentile worship, as centring their lives on objects
which cannot see or hear or walk (e.g. Isa. 44:9–20; Ps. 115:4–8;
Wis. 15:15–17). John's first audiences would have been only too
aware of the images of pagan gods, and even deified emperors, in the
temples and streets of their own cities. They may even have picked
up an allusion to the imperial minting process, which worked in
gold, silver and **bronze** (Janzen 1994: 650f.). Some may have been
shocked by John's visions into reconsidering their own commitment
to their cities, and the extent to which they were themselves implicated, perhaps unwittingly, in such worship. Subsequent generations
of readers have had to ask what subtler forms of idolatry they
themselves have embraced.

Yet Revelation is not simply in the business of mockery, but
recognises a darker side (as there is also a darker side to the monstrous armies of locusts and horses). It shares the apocalyptic insight
that the worship of apparently inanimate objects is tantamount to
worshipping demons (*Jub.* 11:4; *1 En.* 99:6–7; cf. 1 Cor. 10:20).
This analysis would have implications for those, like 'the followers of
Balaam' in Pergamum or 'Jezebel' in Thyatira, who argued for a
closer engagement of Church with society, including membership of
the guilds. There is one further consequence of idolatry: it turns
humanity in on itself, and thus not only away from its Creator but
also from its fellow-creatures. Hence the passage concludes with a list
of vices believed to spring from the root of idolatry, reflecting that
breakdown in respect for humanity and its property (stock lists of
vices were commonly found in Greek philosophical writings as well
as in Jewish and early Christian texts). The list of vices here is

selective (cf. 21:8; 22:15), but prepares us in particular for the crimes of that archetypal model of idolatry, the great city Babylon (**mur-dering, sorcery, sexual infidelity**: e.g. 17:2, 4, 6; 18:3, 9, 23, 24; 19:2).

Interlude 2a: John's Commissioning as Prophet (10:1–11)

(1) Then I saw another angel, a powerful one, descending from heaven, dressed in a cloud, with a rainbow over his head. His face was like the sun, and his feet were like fiery pillars. (2) He had a little scroll open in his hand. The angel set his right foot on the sea, and his left on the earth. (3) Then he shouted in a loud voice, like a lion roaring. When he had shouted, seven thunderclaps sounded out. (4) When the seven thunderclaps had sounded, I prepared to write. But I heard a voice from heaven which told me: 'Seal up what the seven thunderclaps have said! Do not write them down!' (5) Then the angel whom I had seen standing on the sea and the earth raised his right hand to heaven (6) and swore an oath by the one who lives for ever and ever, who created heaven and everything it contains, the earth and everything it contains, and the sea and every-thing it contains. This is what he swore: 'There is no time left to wait! (7) But at the time when the seventh angel prepares to blow his trumpet, then will God's secret plan be brought to completion, as he proclaimed the good news to his servants the prophets.' (8) Then the voice I had heard out of heaven spoke to me again: 'Go and take the scroll which is open in the hand of the angel standing on the sea and the earth.' (9) I approached the angel and asked him to give me the little scroll. He said to me: 'Take it and eat it up! It will make your stomach bitter, although to your mouth it will taste as sweet as honey.' (10) So I took the little scroll from the angel's hand and ate it up. It tasted as sweet as honey in my mouth, but when I had swallowed it, my stomach became bitter. (11) Then I was told: 'You must prophesy again about many peoples and nations, languages and kings.'

The dramatic tension created by the first six, increasingly outlandish trumpets has apparently brought us to the brink of the seventh, the 'last trumpet' which will now announce the coming of the Lord himself (cf. 1 Cor. 15:52; 1 Thess. 4:16). Yet again, however, the narrative presents us with a frustrating delay. As after the sixth seal, when we witnessed the sealing and proleptic preservation of God's servants (7:1–17), there is a two-part interlude or intercalation at this point also (though an even longer one, comprising 10:1—11:14).

Again, the focus is upon God's people in the woes of the last days. Back in chapter 7, we saw them sealed prior to the tribulation, and gloriously rescued through it. Here the Church's ministry of prophecy and faithful witness comes to the fore, beginning (10:1–11) with the prophet John himself. The purpose is twofold: to assure God's people that whatever sufferings they are to face in the short term have meaning within the eschatological plan of God, and to reiterate that sense that the Church has a crucial prophetic role to play in this penultimate sixth period, enabling the final, seventh period of God's salvation to come to birth. To those Christians hopelessly compromised by their accommodation to the kingdoms of this world, this comes as a clarion call to embrace a more radical form of discipleship, characterised by faithful witness and active endurance. To those crying out 'How long?', John's commissioning and subsequent prophesying offers reassurance that following the Lamb's way will not be in vain. Heavenly plagues may not lead humanity to change its mind and return to its Creator; the witnessing Church, however, may just be able to turn the tide.

Once more we are reminded of the extent to which John the exiled visionary is indebted to the prophet-exiles Daniel and especially Ezekiel. The opening chapters of Ezekiel, which formed the backdrop to John's throne-vision in Revelation 4—5, are picked up here again with a renewed mention of a scroll, soon to be devoured by John as he is recommissioned as a prophet for the last days (compare 10:9–11 with Ezek. 2:8—3:3, and the whole section 10:1—11:14 with Ezekiel 11—14). The scene here is one of prophetic commissioning in Ezekiel's mould, highlighting the book's unself-conscious claim to be a work of prophecy, the re-envisaging of ancient prophetic visions by one who regards himself as exiled to the new Babylon of the last days. But if Ezekiel's book continues to provide the main framework for Revelation, the latter is shot through with echoes of Daniel's visions – here, in particular, the final vision of the 'man clothed in linen' of Dan. 12:5–13.

John describes how he sees **another angel, a powerful one, des-** 1 **cending from heaven.** Descent from heaven functions in the Apocalypse to describe God's movement or action towards humanity (e.g. 3:12; 21:2, 10, of God's heavenly city; 20:9 of fire from heaven), or, as here, to describe divine revelation at the hand of an angelic messenger (cf. 18:1; 20:1; though note the demonic parodies at 12:12 and 13:13; 'descent from heaven' is to be distinguished from 'falling from heaven', e.g. 9:1). The Greek could also be translated 'another powerful angel', but the word **another** is not meant to contrast this messenger with the first 'powerful angel' referred to at 5:2 (also 18:21). Rather, in its immediate literary context, it distinguishes him from the seven archangels with the trumpets, and the four bound angels just mentioned at 9:14–15 (reflected in the translation here). Most likely, John is describing the second appearance of this angelic figure first introduced in the heavenly throne-room prior to the appearance of the Lamb. Both here and at Revelation 5, the mighty angel is associated with a scroll (5:2); the angel's rainbow picks up on the rainbow around the throne at 4:3.

But who is this **powerful** angel? The similarities between his description here and that of the angelomorphic 'someone like a son of man' in 1:13–16 are pronounced, and have led to the suggestion that this is Christ himself (for a detailed comparison, see Gundry 1994). The angel's **feet were like fiery pillars**, paralleling Christ's feet 'like polished bronze that had been refined in a furnace' (1:15; cf. Dan. 10:6). **His face was like the sun**, echoing that of the son of man figure at 1:16. The clothing of the **cloud** matches Christ's heavenly mode of transport at 1:7 (cf. Dan. 7:13; Ps. 104:3). It is an identification that has been made again and again in Revelation's reception history, from Victorinus onwards. The marginal notes to the sixteenth-century Geneva Bible, for example, interpret this angel as the glorified Jesus, coming to comfort his persecuted people with the Gospel he holds in his hand (Kovacs and Rowland 2004: 118–19).

John's description certainly makes clear that this is no ordinary angel. Andreas of Caesarea proposed that he was 'one of the Seraphim adorned with the glory of the Lord' (Tauschev and Rose 1995: 159; compare the description of the exalted angel Yahoel in *Apoc. Abr.* 11:1–3). Indeed, features of his appearance also reflect that of the one on the throne, suggesting an exalted heavenly being capable of representing God directly (e.g. the **rainbow**, a reminder of the divine mercy promised to Noah at Gen. 9:8–17, is linked to the *Merkavah* at 4:3; cf. Ezek. 1:28). The strong echoes of the 'man clothed in linen' of Daniel 10 and 12 – often identified with Gabriel – also point to an exalted angel. On the basis of Rev. 1:1, however, he is most likely Christ's angel (cf. 5:2, where the powerful angel is to be distinguished from the Lamb of 5:6). In the Apocalypse's opening verse, the promise was made that the revelation given by God to Jesus Christ, of 'what must soon come to pass', was made known to John by 'his angel'. The giving of that revelation to Christ the Lamb was described back in Revelation 5; here the second part of that revelatory process is now being described with the reappearance of his angelic messenger. He looks like Jesus because he represents him (hence the parallels with the vision of 'someone like a son of man', itself also influenced by Daniel 10); but the two are not identical.

2 The identification of this powerful angel with the one encountered at 5:2 strengthens the case for the **scroll** he holds being the same one

taken and opened by the Lamb (Mazzaferri 1989; Bauckham 1993a: 243–57; for arguments against this, see Garrow 1997: 26–32: he sees the little scroll, to the contrary, as foreshadowing the contents of the Lamb's scroll). The Lamb's scroll is the only one referred to so far as having been opened, hence it is now **open in his hand** (the other scroll previously mentioned is the one in which John is told to write his apocalypse, 1:11). True, here it is described as **a little scroll** (βιβλαρίδιον, a diminutive of a diminutive (βιβλάριον) of a diminutive (βιβλίον): Smalley 2005: 258), and we should probably not treat this as insignificant. But this is not sufficient to distinguish it from the scroll of 5:1 (indeed, it will be called a βιβλίον in verse 8, and some witnesses have that reading here too, including P⁴⁷). Rather, the open scroll is **little** because it needs to be accommodated to the situation and capacity of John. In terms of the narrative, John is now back on earth, presumably on Patmos. In order for him to receive the Lamb's heavenly scroll and devour it, it has to be reduced to a manageable size. The things of God, and especially the mysteries of God, are too awesome to be conveyed to mortals in an unmediated fashion.

If the scrolls of 5:1 and 10:2 are one and the same, then at last we are on the verge of the contents of this scroll, of 'what must soon come to pass', being revealed. This will begin, albeit in nutshell form, at 11:1–13, though we must wait for the second half of the book for the details to be spelt out. Made known by the angel to God's servant John, they can be divulged to the whole Church, represented by the seven congregations, as recipients of his prophetic book. Again, dramatic tension created by the raising of expectations is built into the very structure of the book.

As if to underline the contrast between heavenly and earthly realms which requires the shrinking of the Lamb's scroll, **the angel set his right foot on the sea, and his left on the earth**. This is a colossal figure, whose heavenly origin enables him to transgress the laws of physics rather than sink into the waters of the Abyss. In contrast to the disintegration of creation manifested in some of the preceding trumpet-visions, the angel's position exemplifies God's ultimate control over his whole creation, including the sea with its connotations of evil. Jewish and early Christian tradition occasionally alludes to the unusual stature of angels: *1 Enoch* hints at this when it describes the race of giants fathered by the fallen Watchers (*1 En.* 7:2), while the *Gospel of Peter* describes two men with their heads reaching to heaven, accompanying the risen Christ out of the tomb (*Gos. Pet.* 10.40).

The angel's impressive size is matched by the volume of his voice: **he** 3–4 **shouted in a loud voice, like a lion roaring**. The prophets Hosea and Amos speak of God roaring like a lion, in Amos's case as a prelude to prophecy (e.g. Hos. 11:10; Amos 3:8). But there are also christological echoes here. The Messiah is sometimes envisaged as a roaring lion (e.g. *4 Ez.* 12:31–32; cf. Rev. 5:5), and it is appropriate that his angel speaks with the same terrifying voice. The response to this deafening roar, as if by way of multiple echo throughout the earth, is that **seven thunderclaps sounded out** (Ps. 29:3 speaks of the God of glory thundering). Again, the perfect number seven makes an appearance, raising the expectation that Revelation is about to embark on a new septet, following on from the seven trumpets.

But this expectation is short-lived (the next explicit set of sevens, that of the bowls, will not begin until 15:5). John obviously found **the seven thunderclaps** intelligible, for he **prepared to write**, presumably to preserve their message for the seven congregations. But we are given no hint whatsoever of their content. Instead a **voice from heaven** utters the following command: '**Seal up what the seven thunderclaps have said! Do not write them down!**' This voice may be the same one that spoke from the horns of the altar at 9:13; on the other hand, the presence of the scroll suggests that this is the voice of Christ, who first commanded John to write in a scroll at 1:11, and called John up to heaven at 4:1 to witness the Lamb opening the scroll containing 'what must soon come to pass'. Frustratingly, even in a revelatory book like the Apocalypse, there are some things which human beings are not privileged to know but are to be sealed. Revelation stands in that tradition – humbling for humanity with its often optimistic belief in the inevitability of human progress – which believes that there is far more in heaven and earth than the human mind can grasp (e.g. Job 42:3; *4 Ez.* 4:21). This has not stopped commentators from speculating about the content of the seven thunderclaps: their thunderous nature has often been interpreted as threatening a new set of plagues, which are then immediately withdrawn in line with the Gospel view that God shortens the time for the sake of the elect (e.g. Mk 13:20). This may be implicit in the angel's words in verse 6. Unfortunately, John is not sufficiently forthcoming to allow us to know for sure.

The double command to seal but not to write is odd (contrast 22:10, where John is explicitly forbidden to seal up the words of his prophecy; cf. 1:19). In other apocalypses, the act of sealing is related to things which have been written, so that they can be revealed at the opportune time to the 'future' generation to whom they apply (pseudonymity presenting the sealer as a figure of the distant past, thus investing the message with authority: e.g. Dan. 8:26; 9:24; 12:4, 9; *4 Ez.* 14:26, 46). John's more metaphorical sealing, however, is to guarantee that the content of the thunderclaps is never divulged. The literary tension between disclosure and non-disclosure is palpable here, to be echoed by the giving of the scroll (verses 8–11), whose contents remain indeterminate, at least until John begins to prophesy (Ruiz 1994: 201).

At this point, John's vision consciously evokes the closing scene of 5–7 the book of Daniel (Dan. 12:5–13). Daniel describes how he sees the angelic 'man clothed in linen', accompanied by two others standing on either bank of the river, swearing an oath **by the one who lives for ever and ever**. The raising of the **hand** is recognisable even today as the appropriate gesture for taking an oath: it has a biblical precedent at Deut. 32:40 (see also commentary on 5:1). In Daniel, the oath made by the angel is an answer to the question about the amount of time left before the end. He declares that there will be a delay of 'a time, times and half a time' (Dan. 12:7: half of the symbolic period of seven years), that is, a limited period of persecution for God's people before the End finally comes. Until that time is over, the words of Daniel's revelations must be kept sealed and secret (Dan. 12:9). Variants of three and a half years will fascinate John in the remainder of his book (e.g. 11:2, 3; 12:6, 14; 13:5).

The angel seen by John gives a rather different answer, picking up on the 'How long?' of the souls under the altar at 6:9–11. Instead of an announcement of a further period of hostility and a further sealing of 'what must soon come to pass', he declares that there will be no further delay. The Greek here is somewhat ambiguous (χρόνος οὐκέτι ἔσται), and the similar phrase about the sea at 21:1 (ἡ θάλασσα οὐκ ἔστιν ἔτι) might suggest that it should be translated 'there shall be no more time'. In this case, the angel is speaking about the disappearance of earthly chronological time. It is an interpretation found in some of Revelation's earliest commentators, such as Andreas of Caesarea. However, the wider context of this passage and its parallel in Daniel urge a somewhat different meaning: 'There is no time left to wait!' The seals and trumpets, together with their time for repentance (ineffectual as it has turned out), have delayed things enough. What for Daniel had to be stored up for the future is now about to be revealed, because it is about to come to pass. We can only conclude that it is contained in the open scroll now in the hand of the powerful angel.

The particular significance of this angel's gesture lies in its linking all three levels of Revelation's symbolic universe (heaven, earth, the sea/waters under the earth). Like Daniel's angel, John's powerful angel swears **by the one who lives for ever and ever**. This appeal to God himself underlines the truthfulness of what the angel proclaims (4:9, 10; 15:7; cf. Dan. 12:7). Yet earlier in Revelation Christ was also described as living for ever and ever, by virtue of the resurrection (1:18). We are reminded once more that it is precisely through Jesus' faithful witness and violent death that the powers have been defeated and the last days are now able to descend. To this divine title is added that of Creator, encompassing the whole universe momentarily linked by this huge angelic being: **who created the heaven and everything it contains, the earth and everything it contains, and the sea and everything it contains.** The threefold repetition is appropriate here, for three is the divine number. This emphasis upon God as Creator, so central to the Old Testament witness, is instructive and theologically significant, not least because of the pervasive readings of the Apocalypse which understand its God as hell-bent on destroying this world (see also 3:14; 4:11; 5:13; 14:7; 21:5). Contrary to such interpretations, the Creator here claims sovereignty over all areas of his creation, and later in John's visions will move to overcome all fragmentation and rebellion within it (in the uniting of earth and heaven, and the departure of the rebellious sea, at 21:1–4).

The Greek of verse 7 is difficult. It clearly links in a general sense the activity of the seventh trumpet-angel with the completion or fulfilment of **God's secret plan.** But it is less clear whether the two events are to coincide, for the text literally reads 'in the days of the sound of the seventh angel, when he is about to sound the trumpet ...' This could mean that the plan has been fulfilled *before* the seventh trumpet is blown. This possible nuance is reflected in the translation: **when the seventh angel prepares to blow his trumpet, then will God's secret plan be brought to completion** (ἐτελέσθη is an aorist passive, literally meaning 'was completed'; however, it is almost certainly proleptic, appropriately translated with a future sense: Smalley 2005: 265). The translation may have a bearing on the question of when the contents of the Lamb's scroll are finally revealed: that may well begin when John begins to act as a prophet in chapter 11, prior to the sounding of the seventh trumpet at 11:15. On the other hand, it could refer to the proclamation of God's Kingdom, which the seventh trumpet heralds.

God's secret plan (Greek μυστήριον: cf. 1:20; 17:5, 7) is a popular apocalyptic term for heavenly secrets made known to a privileged seer (e.g. Dan. 2:28, 29, 47; *1 En.* 40:2; 46:2). In the New Testament it often refers to the hidden mystery of what God has done in Christ, now revealed in the gospel (e.g. 1 Cor. 2:1; Eph. 3:3ff.; Col. 1:26). Here it is clear that what is about to be completed is God's plan, made known when he previously **proclaimed the good news to his servants the prophets** (cf. 14:6), but sealed then and only now revealed with clarity. It is as if, like the Teacher of Righteousness before him (1QpHab. 7:1–6), John has been given privileged insight into the true meaning of the veiled words of his prophetic predecessors. The mysterious scroll of Ezekiel, the sealed scroll of Daniel, and other prophetic revelations, are now becoming clear in the light of 'the revelation of Jesus Christ'.

Although the early Church believed that the spirit of prophecy had now been renewed in the Church and one could speak of distinctly Christian prophets (e.g. Acts 11:27; 13:1; 1 Cor. 12:10, 29; 14:29–33; *Did.* 11:3–12), **his servants the prophets** here must include the canonical prophets of Hebrew tradition. John does not clearly distinguish between the two (see e.g. 11:18; 16:6; 18:20, 24; 22:6, 9), although 11:10 seems to have Christian prophets in mind. God indeed does nothing without revealing his secret purposes to his servants the prophets (Amos 3:7). This passage is important for understanding the self-presentation of John, whose book is described elsewhere as 'prophecy' (1:3; 22:18–19). He sets himself at the end of a long line of those privileged to know the divine mysteries, as a prophet like them. His sense of exile on Patmos seems to have evoked a particular sympathy for his exiled predecessors, notably Daniel and Ezekiel.

John's association with his prophetic forebears is confirmed by a **8–10** scene of prophetic commissioning, modelled on that of Ezekiel (Ezek. 2:1—3:3). He is commanded by the voice he had heard out of heaven (the voice of verse 4) in the following words: **'Go and take the scroll which is open in the hand of the angel standing on the sea and the earth.'** Having been promised that the secret purposes of God will be completed, the open scroll promises at least both the revelation and the execution of those purposes. Like Ezekiel, and perhaps as a second Ezekiel, John is further told: **'Take it and eat it up!'** (λάβε καὶ κατάφαγε). Revelation's first audiences, probably hearing this read out during a eucharistic celebration, might detect echoes of Jesus' command at the Last Supper (esp. Mt. 26:26: λάβετε φάγετε; Ezek. 3:1 has just one imperative, 'Eat!'). The Lord's words, no less than his body and blood, are to be taken and devoured. This is especially the case for prophets, who must inwardly digest the word they are to utter. Dürer's famous woodcut of this scene vividly portrays John, kneeling before the angel, furiously devouring the book like a ravenous animal. But this episode may not simply be a literary device to symbolise the prophetic ingesting of God's word. A number of apocalypses hint at careful preparations undertaken by Jewish seers prior to visionary experience. These preparations include both eating and drinking. Ezra eats flowers growing in the field of Ardat prior to his vision of the woman-city Zion (*4 Ez.* 9:26). Later he is bidden to drink a cup of fiery water before dictating ninety-four books to his scribes (*4 Ez.* 14:38–39). We cannot rule out the possibility that physical eating either prior to or during the visionary state underlies this verse also.

There are two differences between the commissionings of Ezekiel and John as prophets. First, the scroll that John devours is not only **sweet as honey** in his mouth (Ezek. 3:3), but is **bitter** in his stomach (though the latter effect may be implicit in Ezek. 3:4–11, which suggests that the prophet's ministry will be rejected). The word of God, though sweeter than honey to his servants (Ps. 119:103), nevertheless has its bitter side. Moreover, its bitterness is twofold. It is bitter for the prophet, who must be prepared to suffer for it (and Revelation 11 will describe the working out of this in detail). It is also bitter for those who hear, for it is a word of judgement no less than salvation.

11 The second difference from Ezekiel's commissioning concerns the recipients of John's prophetic message. Ezekiel's scroll contains words of lamentation, mourning and woe for the house of Israel. Revelation, however, has already addressed the prophetic word to God's people in the seven churches (Revelation 2—3), following the first commissioning of John. He must now **prophesy again** for a different audience, who will be the focus of the second half of the book. Having prepared the churches for their role in the last days, he now turns his attention to **many peoples and nations, languages and kings** (a phrase which sets him also in the mould of that other exilic prophet, Jeremiah: e.g. Jer. 25:13–14, 30). The fourfold phrase (four being the number of the universe) echoes similar phrases used elsewhere (e.g. 5:9; 7:9; 11:9; 13:7; 14:6; 17:15). Here is the only occurrence of this phrase which explicitly mentions **kings**. But standing before kings and rulers is an expected eschatological role for God's faithful ones (e.g. Mk 13:9 and par.), and particularly appropriate for one who is to prophesy on behalf of Christ, the 'ruler of earth's kings' (1:5). Moreover, 'earth's kings' will play an increasingly prominent role in the remaining visions of this book, as the visionary onslaught on Christ's people gains momentum (e.g. 16:14; 17:2, 18; 18:3, 9; 19:19; but note their hopeful transformation at 21:24).

Interlude 2b: The Church's Prophetic Witness (11:1–14)

(1) Then I was given a measuring reed like a sceptre, and told: 'Get up and measure the sanctuary of God, the altar and those who worship in it. (2) But exclude the outer courtyard of the sanctuary. Do not measure that, because it has been given to the nations, who will tread on the holy city for forty-two months. (3) Then I will permit my two witnesses to prophesy for one thousand two hundred and sixty days, dressed in sackcloth.'
(4) These are the two olive trees and the two menorahs

which stand before the Lord of the earth. (5) If anyone wants to harm them, fire comes out of their mouths and eats up their enemies. Yes, if anyone should want to harm them, that person must be killed in this way. (6) These have power to shut up heaven, to prevent rain from falling during the time of their prophesying. They also have power over the waters, to turn them to blood and to strike the earth with every plague whenever they want. (7) When they have completed their witness, the monster that ascends from the Abyss will wage war with them, conquer them and kill them. (8) Then their corpses will be in the public square of the great city, which is called in spiritual terms 'Sodom' and 'Egypt', the city where their Lord was crucified. (9) Some of the peoples and tribes, languages and nations gaze on their corpses for three and a half days, but do not allow their corpses to be placed in a tomb. (10) And those who make their home on the earth rejoice over them, and celebrate by sending each other presents, because these two prophets have tormented those who make their home on the earth. (11) Then after the three and a half days a spirit of life from God entered into them, they stood up on their feet, and great fear fell upon all those who saw them. (12) And they heard a loud voice from heaven commanding them: 'Come up here!' They ascended into heaven in a cloud, and their enemies saw them go. (13) At that very hour there was a great earthquake, and a tenth of the city fell. Seven thousand people were killed in the earthquake, and the rest became terrified, and gave glory to the God of heaven.

(14) The second woe has passed! Look! The third woe is coming soon!

The second part of the interlude between the sixth and seventh trumpets is dominated by the theme of prophetic witness, prepared for by John's own commissioning as a prophet in the previous chapter. Having eaten the sweet yet bitter scroll, John now begins to act as a prophet. He is commanded to measure the sanctuary of God (verses 1–2), and then utters the prophetic words of God, or Christ, about his two witnesses (verse 3; cf. his transcribing of Christ's words in Revelation 2—3). This is followed by a detailed description of the fate of these prophet-witnesses in verses 4–13, and a concluding reminder of the ongoing series of woes at verse 14 (in favour of the integral role of 11:1–14 in Revelation, see Giblin 1984).

Towards the end of Revelation, John will witness an angel measuring the new Jerusalem, a scene influenced by Ezekiel's vision of an angel measuring the ideal restored Temple in Jerusalem (Ezekiel 40—42). But the city that John sees will have no temple in it, because it will have become redundant. At this point in the narrative, John himself is commanded to measure the interim sanctuary, which will play a crucial role in the tribulation inaugurating the End (since eating the scroll, he is no longer a passive observer of his visions, but like his mentor Ezekiel an active participant in them).

Given 10:11, we should expect this section to begin to divulge the contents of the Lamb's scroll containing 'what must soon come to pass', which John has just devoured. That indeed is what happens, for 11:1–13 offers a kind of summary of the scroll's contents. It introduces themes to be spelt out in more detail in the remainder of the book: the protection of God's people (11:1–2, anticipating the divine protection of the woman in chapter 12); the emergence of the monster from the Abyss (11:7, heralding the onslaught on the Church by the monster in chapter 13); the persecution, martyrdom and resurrection of God's witnesses (11:4–13, a type of the visions of salvation through suffering with which Revelation will climax); the partial fall of the 'great city' (11:13, prefiguring the ultimate demise of Babylon the great in chapters 17 and 18).

1 Like Ezekiel's angel (Ezek. 40:3, 5), John is **given a measuring reed** which he likens to **a sceptre** or staff (cf. the iron sceptre wielded by the victorious Son: 2:27; 12:5). The rod Ezekiel describes is six cubits, or approximately ten feet, in length, but John makes no comment about its size here. His task is to **measure the sanctuary of God, the altar and those who worship in it**. Measuring the sanctuary seems to function to mark it out as belonging to God (e.g. Ezekiel 40—42) and therefore subject to divine protection (compare the protective measuring of Jerusalem at Zech. 2:1–5; cf. *1 En.* 61:1–4). It parallels the sealing of the one hundred and forty-four thousand, which comes at the same point in the seals septet (7:1–8).

The similarity with the sealing helps solve one of this passage's key interpretative issues: the identity of **the sanctuary of God** and its **outer courtyard**. There are three principal ways in which these references can be interpreted. First, John is being commanded – albeit in a visionary state – to measure historical Jerusalem and its temple. The reference to the trampling of the outer court has been understood as alluding to the traumatic events in and around Jerusalem in 70 CE, events which have left their mark on the Synoptic Gospel tradition (cf. the similar phrase at Lk. 21:24). However, we have repeated grounds for reading John's visionary descriptions in a symbolic way, including those which apply priestly, temple language to the earthly realm (e.g. 1:6, 20; 3:12). In the light of this, a literal interpretation in terms of the earthly Temple in Jerusalem would appear out of place.

Second, the reference is to the heavenly sanctuary, whose liturgy has been witnessed regularly throughout Revelation. But John has been back on earth since at least 10:1, from which he witnesses the descent of the powerful angel from heaven. The logic of the narrative suggests that the sanctuary too is located on earth. Indeed, its outer courtyard **has been given to the nations**, which could not be said of the temple in heaven. Furthermore, at 21:15 it is an angel, not John himself, who must measure the holy city which comes down from heaven: here, however, the earthly John is able to perform the measuring himself.

The third and most likely explanation is that, whatever sources our author has used, the sanctuary and its worshippers are now symbols for the Church. Followers of the Lamb have already been described in priestly terms, and their worship as a participation in the angelic liturgy of heaven, where Christ officiates as high priest. The symbolism, of course, depends upon the literal geography of the earthly Temple: **the sanctuary** (ναός) referring to the actual shrine comprising the Holy of Holies and the Holy Place with its altar of incense, **the altar** probably referring to the altar of sacrifice in the Court of the Priests, and **those who worship in it** including the Court of the Israelites, reserved to male members of the nation, and the Court of the Women. But in John's visionary world the sanctuary itself has a human face. The New Testament, building on precedents within Second Temple Judaism, had come to understand the Church as a living temple and a priestly people (e.g. Rom. 12:1–2; 1 Cor. 3:16–17; 1 Pet. 2:5), and this enables John to envisage God's people, both Jewish and Gentile, as a sanctuary where sacrifices are offered and true worship rendered to God. The story of the holy city, and the onslaught upon its temple by Babylon, has become the story of God's temple, his vulnerable people in the last days. As in the sealing vision in chapter 7, they are here assured of God's care and presence in the difficult times ahead (though not of exemption from suffering or hostility).

If the sanctuary of God and its worshippers symbolise the Church 2 protected by God, then what does **the outer courtyard** represent? The imagery is almost certainly drawn from the Court of the Gentiles, that vast open space bordered by porticoes, and separated from the inner courts, accessible only to Jews, by a dividing wall and the Beautiful Gate. But in John's vision, it must represent a group of people. Moreover, in its present context, it has negative connotations: although the Court of the Gentiles was essentially positive, reserved for God-fearing pagans, it has here been given to the nations who will tread on the holy city. The simplest solution is that **the outer courtyard** symbolises those no longer associated with the one on the throne and the Lamb. As it has been **given to the nations**, this group must be differentiated from the nations and so is unlikely to represent the unbelieving world. Rather, **the outer courtyard** represents Christians who are themselves unfaithful in their witness, and possibly also non-Christian Jews. These believe themselves to be worshippers in the sanctuary, but find themselves in John's apocalyptic unveiling not only consigned to the Court of the Gentiles, but in the power of those Gentile nations. It may be no coincidence that John's prophetic rivals in the seven churches are given the nicknames of notorious Gentiles, outsiders to the priestly people of Israel (Balaam and Jezebel, 2:14, 20). In Revelation's apocalyptic name-calling, their right to enter God's temple has been dramatically removed. The alternative proposal – that the outer courtyard represents the Church in its relationship to the world, facing persecution, just as the sanctuary itself symbolises the Church as protected by God (Caird 1966: 132) – adds an unnecessary complication to this vision.

John then changes his metaphor from the sanctuary itself to the whole city: the nations **will tread on the holy city for forty-two months** (the treading of the winepress may be a direct divine response to this: 14:20; 19:15). Since later in the Apocalypse the term **holy city** will be used of the new Jerusalem, in contrast to Babylon (21:2, 10; 22:19), those who are trampled must be the true worshippers, not the outer courtyard (in the same way that being a pillar in God's sanctuary merges into citizenship of the heavenly city at 3:12). The sanctuary, with its inner courts, and the holy city are two ways of speaking of the same reality. Being measured does not guarantee physical security (at 20:9 the nations will surround the camp of the holy ones and the beloved city). But any suffering and persecution will be limited and short-lived. The **forty-two months** are a variation of Daniel's 'a time, times and half a time', which represents the length of the persecution of God's people under the tyrant Antiochus Epiphanes (Dan. 7:25; 12:7: three and a half years, i.e. half the perfect period of seven years; cf. the 'half a week' of Dan. 9:27).

Not surprisingly, Rev. 11:1–2 has been important in discussion of Revelation's dating. These verses have been used in support of an earlier dating, since if taken literally, they seem to presuppose that the Jerusalem Temple is still standing (e.g. Robinson 1976: 238–42). Indeed, the statement in verse 13 that only 'a tenth of the city fell' betrays no knowledge of the traumatic events of 70 CE, which resulted in the fall of the entire city to the Roman forces. Those who posit a Domitianic dating for Revelation tend to regard verses 1–2 as a reused fragment of a Jewish apocalyptic text or zealot oracle. This would have originally been spoken during the siege of Jerusalem but prior to its final destruction, and now reworked symbolically for the present context (e.g. Charles 1920: I, 274). But such an explanation is unnecessary, presuming that John can only interpret symbolically what someone else has already understood literally (see the comment of Caird 1966: 131). Moreover, it fails to do justice to the visionary mindset, which is quite capable of taking up disparate historical allusions into a visionary whole.

The 'I' in the previous two verses is clearly John. However, now the 3 first person takes on a divine persona, as if John is directly uttering the prophetic word of the Lord: **Then I will permit my two witnesses to prophesy for one thousand two hundred and sixty days, dressed in sackcloth.** The 'I' could be either the one on the throne or Jesus Christ: the two witnesses would then be **my two witnesses** either because they bear witness to the truth of God, as Jesus did (e.g. 1:2; cf. Jn 18:37; 1 Tim. 6:13), or because they continue Jesus' own witness. The identity of the two witnesses has fascinated and intrigued commentators for centuries (for a fine survey of the history of its interpretation, see Turner 2004). Their number almost certainly reflects the Israelite requirement for two or three witnesses in legal cases (e.g. Deut. 19:15). The **sackcloth** that they wear is the traditional clothing for mourning and repentance (e.g. Gen. 37:34; 2 Sam. 3:31; 1 Kgs 21:27; 1 Chron. 21:16; Neh. 9:1; Jer. 4:8; Mt. 11:21). It is appropriate garb given that their mission is one of proclaiming the bittersweet word of God, which calls the world to repentance. Because their work has not yet finished, their clothing contrasts with the white robes of the heavenly multitude or the twenty-four elders, the sign of victory achieved (4:4; 7:9; cf. 19:14). The length of the prophesying, **one thousand two hundred and sixty days,** matches exactly the time of trampling for God's holy city, the satanic onslaught on God's people (given a calendar with months consisting of thirty days: cf. 12:6, 14).

Are these two witnesses two particular individuals, or representative 4–6 figures? Revelation's reception history provides plenty of interpretations favouring the former, whether as two specific eschatological figures (Moses and Elijah, or Elijah and Enoch) or as two historical personages of the commentator's own age. That they are recognisable individuals seems to be confirmed by the specific allusion to Old Testament figures in John's description. First, they are identified as **the two olive trees and the two menorahs which stand before the Lord of the earth.** John's allusion is to Zechariah's vision of two olive trees flanking a seven-lamped menorah, a branch of each pouring out olive oil into the menorah (Zech. 4:1–14, a passage which has already influenced John's description of the heavenly throne-room in Revelation 4). Zechariah's angel identifies the two branches of the olive trees as 'the two anointed ones who stand by the Lord of the whole earth' (Zech. 4:14). In other words, they are the prince Zerubbabel, governor of Judah after the return from exile, and the high priest Joshua.

The further description of the activities of the two witnesses in verse 6 echoes the stories of Moses and Elijah. Like Elijah, they have **power to shut up heaven, to prevent rain from falling during the time of their prophesying** (1 Kgs 17:1–7; 18:1, 41–46). Like Moses, they **have power over the waters, to turn them to blood and to strike the earth with every plague whenever they want** (echoing the plagues of Egypt: Exodus 7—12, esp. Exod. 7:14–25). Both Elijah and Moses were figures expected by Jews and early Christians to return in the last days (e.g. Mk 1:2; Mt. 17:9–13; Acts 3:22; based on Deut. 18:18; Mal. 4:5–6).

However, these allusions are not enough to exhaust their significance, and there are grounds for interpreting them as representative figures. In verse 5 the power of their prophetic word is likened to **fire** which **comes out of their mouths and eats up their enemies**. While Elijah's ability to call down fire from heaven (e.g. 1 Kgs 18:36) is often cited as a parallel, a closer fit is with Jeremiah (Jer. 5:14). The fire-like breath of the Messiah (Isa. 11:4; *4 Ez.* 13:10; cf. Rev. 1:16; 19:15) may also lie in the background. In other words, a multiplicity of biblical figures and roles, primarily prophetic, underlies the description of the witnesses (indeed, Enoch rather than Moses was a favourite companion to Elijah for earlier commentators, and some have detected echoes of Peter and Paul, who shed their blood for Christ in the very heart of Nero's Rome: Sweet 1979: 185). Moreover, far from one being a returned Elijah and the other a prophet like Moses, both of them exhibit all of the characteristics described. What they do, they do together (see Strand 1981).

It is perhaps better, then, to view them as representative figures of the prophetic ministry of the Church. The **menorahs** have already been explicitly interpreted as symbolising the Christian congregations (1:20). That there are only **two menorahs** (of the complete number of seven) may point to the prophetic ministry being reserved to only part of the Church (note the distinctive charism of prophet at 1 Cor. 12:10, 28). On the other hand, it may be a sign that only a fraction of the Church lives up to the Church's prophetic vocation (only two menorahs, the congregations of Smyrna and Philadelphia, receive untarnished praise in Revelation 2—3). The allusion to Zerubbabel and Joshua, **the two olive trees**, evokes the royal and priestly dimension of the Church, here linked to the prophetic ministry. Similarly, the eschatological figures Moses and Elijah are appropriate models for the Church's witness in the last days. Indeed, they may serve as particular inspiration for John himself: his two prophetic rivals in Pergamum and Thyatira, 'Balaam' and 'Jezebel', are named after figures active in the times of Moses and Elijah respectively. Finally, there may be a particular twist in the image of the two olive trees. The olive is traditionally a symbol of peace (e.g. Gen. 8:11; Hos. 14:6); yet little peace will be promised in the short term for the prophetic witnessing Church.

Most importantly, however, the life of the witnessing Church is to be **7–9** closely patterned on that of the Lord. The details of their story are a repetition of the gospel story: witnessing to the truth, thus provoking hostility; death at the hands of a beastly power; vindication through death. The reference to **the monster that ascends from the Abyss** prepares the ground for the monster from the sea, which will threaten God's people in chapter 13. Like the protomartyr Stephen (Acts 7:54–60), like Paul, who bears in his body the marks of the crucified Christ (Gal. 6:17), like Antipas of Pergamum, who was killed where Satan's throne is (2:13), the Church is called to speak the prophetic word of truth even if that ends in persecution and death. Later Jewish traditions about the prophets came to regard them as martyrs who gave their lives for speaking God's word (e.g. Mt. 23:29–36). Revelation is clear that the same will be the case for those who continue the witness that Jesus bore. The world, and even many within the Church, will respond to the word of truth not with joyful acceptance but with hatred and violence.

The harsh treatment of these witnesses is particularly highlighted by their treatment after death: **their corpses will be in the public square of the great city**, but will lie unburied **for three and a half days** (a variation on Daniel's three and a half years, perhaps adapted to conform more closely to the period between Christ's death and his resurrection). The Jewish horror of not being buried, but left as prey to vultures and other carnivorous creatures, is reflected in Tobit's pious concern (Tob. 1:16—2:8). The identity of this **great city** has been the subject of great debate. Given the phrase **where their Lord was crucified**, historical Jerusalem has often been the prime candidate, suggesting a holy city turned sour, now rejected by the Lord whom it once rejected (e.g. Lk. 19:41–44). Yet later on, **the great city** will be Revelation's term for 'Babylon', with all its resonances of imperial Rome (16:19; 18:10, 16, 18–19, 21; cf. 14:8; 17:5; 18:2: see Feuillet 1965: 60–62 for the view that the identity of the 'great city' changes from unbelieving Jerusalem in chapter 11 to Rome in chapters 16—18). The citizens of this city who attack the witnesses are not Jewish citizens of Jerusalem but derived from **peoples and tribes, languages and nations**. It is not Jerusalem nor is it Rome, though its citizens can be found in both locations. Revelation's great

city can never be located on a terrestrial map, though its characteristics are those of **Sodom** and **Egypt**, both symbols of rebellion
against God and, in the case of Egypt, oppression of God's people.
The great city can manifest itself in any city in the world where
God's sanctuary is attacked, where the Church is giving faithful
witness: from Jerusalem to Rome, from Ephesus to Laodicea, from
London to Beijing to New York. Almost certainly John's visionary
imagination has been particularly fired by the memory of what
happened to Jesus in Jerusalem, and what happened to God's people
in Rome under Nero. But he also imagines the horrifying prospects
of what might happen in any of the seven cities (and indeed in any
city). The only antidote to this great city is the City of God, the new
Jerusalem (see 21:9—22:5).

10–12 The patterning of the witnesses' story on that of Jesus continues.
With their deaths, their enemies – **those who make their home on
the earth**: see on 3:10 – act in a manner which combines gleeful
relief (**rejoice over them**) with childish excitement (**sending each
other presents**). They have experienced the witnesses' ministry as
torment (compare the 'torment' of the scorpion-serpents at 9:5): the
prophetic word burns like fire (verse 5), consuming with its searing
heat the lies and injustices which stand in its way.

But like Jesus, the prophetic witnesses will be vindicated beyond
death. The church of martyrs can never lie dead for long. In a
description which echoes Ezekiel's vision of the dry bones (Ezekiel
37), John describes how **a spirit of life from God entered into
them** and **they stood up on their feet**. The vindication theme
continues with the statement that **great fear fell upon all those
who saw them** (cf. the reaction of the righteous man's enemies
when they see him vindicated at the judgement: Wis. 5:1–2). Having
been raised, the two witnesses now complete Christ's victory by
imitating his ascension to heaven: **And they heard a loud voice
from heaven commanding them: 'Come up here!' They
ascended into heaven in a cloud, and their enemies saw them
go** (the minority reading 'their fifteen enemies' is due to scribal
duplication of the two Greek letters ιε, an easy mistake in *scriptio
continua*: Royse 1980). Again, traditions about Moses and Elijah are
evoked, this time their miraculous ascents to heaven (2 Kgs 2:11;
Josephus, *Ant.* 4.326). There are also echoes of John's privileged call
to 'Come up here!' at 4:1, the basis of the heavenly visions currently
unfolding in this book.

13 The result of all this is full of ambiguity. Is the earthquake the
eschatological earthquake, the sign that the final judgement has come
(note the earthquake surrounding Jesus' death and resurrection in

Matthew 27—28)? The proportion affected suggests that we have not reached that stage: **a tenth of the city fell** and **seven thousand people were killed.** Moreover, the death of seven thousand parallels the faithful remnant of seven thousand whom Elijah hears will not be killed (1 Kgs 19:18). The remnant number here (and the implication that nine-tenths of the city survive) point to greater possibilities for 'those who make their home on the earth'. Finally, what motivates the response of the remainder, who **became terrified, and gave glory to the God of heaven?** Is this purely negative fear, as a number of commentators have suggested? Or do we have the beginnings of a positive turning to God, the first-fruits of repentance, a reorienting of human lives from earth-centred to heaven-centred existence? If this is the case, then the trumpet-plagues are placed in a new context. They were aimed at leading humanity to repent but were ultimately ineffective. In contrast, however, the prophetic testimony and martyrdom of the witnessing Church may just have done what is required.

Before the action moves on, we are reminded finally from where we 14 have come. The fifth trumpet-plague had been identified explicitly with the first woe (9:12), and two more were promised. But the announcement that **the second woe has passed** is delayed until now. It is possible that we should regard this simply as looking back to the sixth trumpet-plague of 9:13–21, and that is almost certainly to be included in it. But its delay until now is surely significant. It suggests that **the second woe** is incomplete until John has begun to prophesy, and tell us about the work of the two prophet-witnesses. The Church's prophetic witness – so sweet and yet so bitter – is part of the woe which is capable of bringing humanity to its senses, so that it gives **glory to the God of heaven.**

The Seventh Trumpet   (11:15–18)

(15) Then the seventh angel blew his trumpet, and loud voices resounded in heaven, saying:
    '**The royal rule of this world**
    has become the royal rule of our Lord and of his Christ,
    and he will reign for ever and ever.'
(16) Then the twenty-four elders seated on their thrones before God fell down on their faces and worshipped God, (17) saying:
    '**We give thanks to you, Lord God Almighty,**
    who are and who were,
    because you have taken up your great power
    and begun your royal rule!

> (18) The nations became angry,
> but your anger came,
> the opportune time for the dead to be judged,
> for rewarding your servants, the prophets and holy ones,
> and those who fear your name,
> both the little ones and the great,
> and for destroying those who destroy the earth!'

After the substantial interlude of 10:1—11:14, the seventh trumpet is blown, accompanied by a proclamation from loud heavenly voices. The contrast with the silence which followed the opening of the seventh seal is palpable. Yet such a dramatic proclamation is to be expected. The heightening of literary tension in previous chapters has led the reader to expect 'no more delay' (10:6), the completion of the 'secret purpose' of God (10:7), and therefore the End. What is proclaimed at this point is indeed the End: the transition from the kingdom of this world to the Kingdom of God. Yet perhaps surprisingly, given that the seventh trumpet is almost certainly to be identified with the 'third woe' (8:13; cf. 9:12; 11:14), it brings with it no explicit plague or punishment (though see verse 18). Instead, it provokes a heavenly hymn of praise and victory, almost a coronation or enthronement scene. The key to this surprising aspect may lie in the sudden change of location: John, so recently on earth, now finds himself again in the heavenly throne-room, with the twenty-four elders again gathered around the throne (see 4:4; 5:8; 7:11). What may be experienced as divine plagues from the perspective of earth are signs of God's victory and an answer to prayer for divine justice when viewed from heaven.

Psalm 2, a coronation psalm interpreted as the enthronement of the Messiah, runs like a thread throughout this section (and will echo again and again through the ensuing chapters: 12:5; 14:1; 16:14; 17:18; 19:15, 19). The psalm tells of the plot by earth's kings against the Lord and his Anointed One (LXX Χριστός), the response of divine wrath and the Lord's establishing of his king on 'Zion, my holy hill'. The kingly Messiah is proclaimed as God's son, and given power over the nations, to rule them or break them with an iron rod or sceptre (Ps. 2:2, 5–6, 7–9). Juxtaposed with the story of the Lamb, slaughtered by the 'great city' yet vindicated by God and now sharing God's throne, the psalm takes on added poignancy.

15 The opening phrases pick up where we left off prior to the interlude: **the seventh angel blew his trumpet**. The identities of the heavenly **loud voices** are not spelt out. Hitherto, we have encountered singular heavenly voices (e.g. the loud voice of 'someone like a son of man' at 1:10 and 4:1; the thunderous voice of each of the living

creatures at 6:1, 3, 5 and 7; the voice from the four horns of the altar at 9:13). It is unlikely that Christ's voice is among the voices here, for it is his enthronement which is being proclaimed. Nor are these the voices of the twenty-four elders, for they will take up the refrain in verse 17. Perhaps we are hearing again the angelic choirs who in their thousands upon thousands sang of the victory of the Lamb in the first throne-room scene (5:11–12; cf. 7:12), or the victorious great multitude clothed in heavenly white, who proclaimed the salvation of God and the Lamb at 7:10.

The heart of the proclamation, as of Psalm 2, is the enthronement of the Messiah and the defeat of earth's rebellious rulers. There are also strong echoes of Ps. 99:1, proclaiming the Lord as King (see also Pss 93:1; 96:10; 97:1). But the precise translation of the verb which John uses is uncertain (it is the aorist ἐγένετο lit. 'became', though often translated elsewhere in Revelation simply as 'was'). It is possible that what is being proclaimed is simply a statement of what has always been the case, even though humanity has largely been unable to see it: that 'the kingdom of the world was our Lord's and his Christ's', i.e. it belonged to them (Rowland 1998: 643). **The royal rule** has never been anyone else's, despite futile attempts to steal the throne. But the Apocalypse can use ἐγένετο to mean 'became' (e.g. 6:12; 8:8, 11; 16:3, 4; 18:2), and the close parallel at 12:10, where it clearly has that sense, may be decisive. What we have heard instead is a proclamation of the passing of the royal rule from the **world** which has usurped it (note the Johannine use of the word to describe humanity hostile to God: cf. Jn 1:10; 3:17; 12:31; 17:6–19) to **our Lord** and to **his Christ**.

The particular wording of Ps. 2:2 has influenced the phrase **of our Lord and of his Christ**. Nevertheless, following Old Testament antecedents, Revelation does use the title 'Lord' most often of the one on the throne (e.g. 1:8; 4:8, 11; 11:4, 17; 15:3, 4; 16:7; 18:8; 19:6; 21:22; 22:5, 6; it is used of Jesus at 11:8; 17:14; 19:16; 22:20, 21 and possibly 14:13). **Christ** is rarely used of Jesus in Revelation: the only other occurrences are at 1:1, 2 and 5 (as part of the phrase 'Jesus Christ'), and 20:4 and 6 (speaking of the millennium, and therefore as having explicit messianic overtones). What is more striking is the switch to the singular verb at the end of the verse: **and he will reign for ever and ever**. The antecedent here may be Christ, the last mentioned, emphasizing that his reigning along with God is dependent upon his death and exaltation (see e.g. Rom. 1:4; Acts 2:36). However, the throne where the Lamb sits is ultimately the Father's throne, and the singular should probably be understood as incorporating both, thus emphasising their essential unity of purpose and will (note the variant reading to 6:17 above; cf. 22:5).

16–18 **The twenty-four elders** now take up the refrain in response to this proclamation of divine sovereignty. Their opening words, **We give thanks to you**, identify this as a hymn of thanksgiving. The addressee is **Lord God Almighty**, a phrase which, like other titles of God and the Lamb, occurs the perfect number of seven times in Revelation (also at 1:8; 4:8; 15:3; 16:7; 19:6; 21:22: see Bauckham 1993a: 33–35). The now familiar triad (e.g. 1:4, 8; 4:8) has become simply **who are and who were** (the small number of manuscripts which include καὶ ὁ ἐρχόμενος almost certainly reflect scribal correction). Now that God's royal rule has finally been established, there is no coming still to await.

Instead, the thanksgiving hymn provides the outline of how that rule is achieved: the raging of **the nations** (Ps. 2:1 LXX), which has led to the cries of the martyrs (6:9–11), is itself met by the coming of God's righteous **anger, and the opportune time for the dead to be judged**. Much of this outline has already been played out in visionary detail in John's narrative. It will be revisited again in the chapters to follow. But there is a strong sense of the End anticipated, for the judging of the dead will not be explicitly described until 20:11–15. The difficulty is overcome if one recalls the Apocalypse's 'theatre of reception', most likely during the eucharistic liturgy. It is precisely in the Eucharist that the End breaks into the present, as the Lamb's marriage feast is anticipated. So too in this eucharistic prayer of the heavenly elders (its opening verb is εὐχαριστοῦμέν: cf. 4:9; 7:12), the Lord's coming judgement is made present.

The coming-but-present judgement not only promises justice against the oppressive rulers of the earth; it also promises reward for **your servants, the prophets and holy ones, and those who fear your name**. The reference to God's servants the prophets at 10:7 (cf. 22:9) has included Israelite prophets like Ezekiel and Daniel; in the light of the preceding chapter, however, it most likely focuses here upon the prophetic witness of the Church (thus prophets and holy ones may denote two aspects of the same group of God's servants). However, unless the καὶ is epexegetical (an explanatory 'i.e.' or 'that is'), another group is also mentioned as recipient of the reward: **those who fear your name, both the little ones and the great**. This group seems to refer to former members of 'those who make their home on the earth', who have woken up to their position and begun to fear God's name. The little ones and the great will be forced to receive the monster's mark at 13:16, and their flesh will be among that offered to the birds at 19:18. But they have the opportunity to repent and fear God, irrespective of their economic or social standing (19:5). The juxtaposition of this group, now experiencing reward, and the former citizens of the 'great city' who were terrified and gave glory to God at 11:13 is unlikely to be coincidental. A hopeful door remains open for such people on the judgement day of God.

Finally, the Day of Judgement will be the time **for destroying those who destroy the earth**. The repeated concern of the Creator for his creation is striking in a text which has so often been read as a blueprint for the destruction of that creation. The apocalyptic imagery of destruction and cosmic collapse is shown rather to function as a challenge to all that would itself destroy the creation, all that keeps it out of kilter and removed from its divinely ordained destiny. But is this straightforwardly a proclamation of the divine destruction of human beings? Certainly Gen. 6:5 saw the evil of humanity as so great that it needed to be obliterated. Yet again, there are indications that Revelation's solution is more subtle (the presence of the rainbow at 4:3 has already been noted: cf. Gen. 9:12–16). The primary destroyers up to now have been demonic forces, such as those led by the king of the Abyss Apollyon, whose name literally means 'Destroyer' (9:1–11). Moreover, those whose destruction will ultimately bring an end to the pillaging of the earth are the satanic trinity of the dragon, the monster and the false prophet (19:20; 20:10). Revelation may ultimately share the view of *1 Enoch* that the fall of the angels had a devastating effect on the earthly realm: 'And the world was changed' (*1 En.* 8:2).

With the judgement proclaimed, now at last the Apocalypse can end. The final trumpet has been blown, the secret plan of God has been brought to completion (a plan which involved God's slaughtered yet victorious Messiah), and God's royal rule has been definitively established. Yet we are still only halfway through John's visionary book. The story now unfolds again, in rather more detail. What John's audiences are left with is a sure vantage point from which to view the remaining story, in which God's people will be particularly involved: the knowledge that **you have taken up your great power and begun your royal rule**.

Part II The Unveiling of the Lamb's Scroll and the Church's Witness (11:19—22:11)

4   SEVEN VISIONS (11:19—15:4)

Despite the proleptic proclamation of the End following the seventh trumpet, the Apocalypse continues with a new series of visions, focusing particularly upon the Church's witness during the last days. Although (as I shall argue) this section represents the fourth section in a series of six, it also marks the start of the second half of the book, which in many ways revisits the themes of Rev. 1:9—11:18. Here we are reminded of that challenge made by the son of man figure to the seven congregations in chapters 2—3: to be faithful in a world of subtle deception and compromise, of external pressure and threat and the dangers of false prophecy. The character of these threats and dangers will be spelt out in visions of the monsters, unveiled as earthly puppets of the dragon, while the alternative possibility of following the Lamb will run alongside like a subversive thread.

At this point, the structural marker of sevens which has explicitly dominated the first half of the book (the seven messages, seals and trumpets) breaks down, and will not emerge explicitly again until the seven bowl-plagues which commence at 15:5. This might be accounted for by the fact that (after the summary in chapter 11) the contents of the Lamb's scroll are now being revealed in more detail, and that these contents become the determining factor for the following four chapters. However, John is quite capable of sustaining sets of seven without explicitly drawing attention to them (the seven beatitudes, scattered throughout the book from 1:3 onwards, have already been noted, as have the sevenfold occurrences of divine titles such as 'Lord God Almighty': see on 11:17). Having established the pattern with three explicit septets, it is not at all unlikely that such a sophisticated text now continues that pattern, though below the surface. The following is a possible outline of what now follows:

1. The woman and the dragon (11:19—12:18)
2. The monster from the sea (13:1–10)
3. The monster from the earth (13:11–18)

173

4. The Lamb and its followers on Mount Zion (14:1–5)
Interlude: three angels (14:6–13; cf. the eagle with the three woes at 8:13)
5. The harvest of 'someone like a son of man' (14:14–16)
6. The grape harvest (14:17–20)
7. The song of the new Exodus (15:1–4)

First Vision: The Woman and the Dragon   (11:19—12:18)

(11:19) Then the sanctuary of God which is in heaven was opened, and the Ark of his Covenant appeared in his sanctuary. There were flashes of lightning, voices, claps of thunder, an earthquake and heavy hail.

(12:1) And a great sign appeared in heaven, a woman dressed in the sun, with the moon under her feet, and on her head a wreath of twelve stars. (2) She was pregnant, and she cried out in intense labour pains as she prepared to give birth.

(3) Then another sign appeared in heaven, a great fiery red dragon, which had seven heads and ten horns. On its heads were seven diadems, (4) and its tail dragged a third of the stars from heaven and threw them to the earth. The dragon stood before the woman, who was on the verge of giving birth, so that it might eat her child up as soon as she gave birth. (5) She gave birth to a male child, the son who would shepherd all the nations with an iron sceptre. But her child was snatched up to God and to his throne, (6) while the woman fled into the wilderness, where a place had been prepared for her by God, so that she might be fed there for one thousand, two hundred and sixty days.

(7) Then a war broke out in heaven: Michael and his angels had to wage war with the dragon. The dragon and his angels fought back, (8) but it was not powerful enough, and they could no longer keep their place in heaven. (9) It was thrown down, the great dragon, that ancient serpent, who is known as 'Devil' and 'the Satan', the deceiver of the whole world. It was thrown down to the earth, and its angels were thrown down with it. (10) Then I heard a loud voice in heaven saying:

'Now have come the salvation and the power,
and the royal rule of our God,
and the authority of his Christ!
For the accuser of our brothers and sisters has been thrown down,
the one who accuses them before our God day and night.
(11) These have conquered him
as a result of the blood of the Lamb,

and as a result of their witness,
for they did not love their life even in the face of death.
(12) Therefore celebrate, you heavens,
and you who shelter there!
But woe to you, earth and sea,
because the devil has descended to you,
in a furious rage,
knowing that he has little time left!'
(13) Now when the dragon saw that it had been thrown down to the earth, it pursued the woman who had given birth to the male child. (14) But the woman was given the two wings of a great eagle, so as to fly into the wilderness to her place, where she was fed, for a time, times and half a time, and protected from the presence of the serpent. (15) The serpent spewed a river of water out of its mouth after the woman, to sweep her away. (16) But Mother Earth came to the aid of the woman, opening her mouth and swallowing up the river which the dragon spewed out of its mouth. (17) So the dragon became angry with the woman, and went off to wage war with the rest of her children, those who keep God's commandments and continue the witness of Jesus.

(18) Then it took its stand on the shore of the sea.

Many commentators follow the standard chapter divisions and take 11:19 as the conclusion to the seventh trumpet. There are good grounds for making the break a verse earlier, however, as does the Roman Lectionary in its reading for the feast of the Assumption of Our Lady (Rev. 11:19—12:6, 10). The opening of a door in heaven inaugurated the vision of the heavenly liturgy in Revelation 4, accompanied by lightning, voices and thunder from the throne (4:5); the trumpets sequence also began with a liturgical action in the heavenly sanctuary, accompanied by thunder, voices, lightning and an earthquake (8:5; note the 'opening' of the seventh seal, which seems to serve as both the conclusion to the seals and the beginning of the trumpets). It is appropriate that a new section should begin in the same way (the septet of bowls at 15:5–8 will also begin with an opening in the heavenly sanctuary).

After the scene-setting of 11:19 the passage falls neatly into three sections: 12:1–6 begins the story of the woman and the dragon; 12:7–12 recounts the battle between Satan and the archangel Michael in heaven, with a canticle reinterpreting the action in verses 10–12; the story of the woman and the dragon resumes in verses 13–18. No doubt two sources have been combined here (see e.g. Harrington 1993: 129). What is important, however, is not the literary prehistory of this vision but its present form. John's sandwich technique suggests some correlation between the activity of the woman and her offspring, and the defeat of the dragon Satan (for the history of interpretation of Revelation 12, see Prigent 1959).

This chapter provides one of the Apocalypse's richest and most evocative visions, which has left a powerful impression in Western art, from Dürer's woodcut of St Michael slaying the dragon to Velázquez's famous *Immaculate Conception*, which highlights the passage's importance for that Marian doctrine in seventeenth-century Spain. If the metaphor of the kaleidoscope is an appropriate one for understanding Revelation, it is perhaps most so for this particular vision. To grasp its significance, one needs to be aware that it presents a series of interconnecting stories, each of which contributes something significant to the whole. There are echoes of the story of Eve and the serpent, whose head her offspring would eventually bruise (Gen. 3:15); of Israel, pursued into the wilderness by Pharaoh but borne on eagle's wings (Exod. 14:1–31; 19:4; see the likening of Pharaoh to a dragon at Ezek. 29:3; 32:2); of mother Zion, who like a pregnant woman struggles to be rescued from the twisting serpent Leviathan (Isa. 26:16—27:1; cf. Mic. 4:10); of Mary, that faithful Israelite who gave birth to Israel's Messiah; and Satan's opposition to her son's royal rule.

Underlying all these is a much more ancient story, which took different forms throughout the ancient Near East and Mediterranean world: the so-called combat myth. Myths, contrary to popular parlance, are not necessarily untruths but potent stories which may express truth more forcefully and meaningfully than other forms of discourse. Cultural variations of this combat myth can be found throughout the ancient world, describing in different ways the cosmic struggle between the forces of good and evil, order and chaos, rival gods battling for supremacy. Israel had already reworked such traditions to express its conviction that YHWH had defeated the forces of chaos (e.g. Gen. 1:1—2:3; Ps. 74:13–14; Isa. 27:1; 51:9–10), and John is almost certainly drawing on this biblical tradition.

Nevertheless, there are also strong echoes here of pagan forms of the myth (A. Y. Collins 1976: 57–71). Given the geographical location of both author and first recipients of Revelation, the best-known form of this myth would have been that of the birth of Apollo, brother of Artemis and son of Zeus, to the pregnant Leto. Asia contained one of the ancient world's major shrines to Apollo, the oracle of Didyma. Moreover, through Didyma's political dependence on Miletos, its cult would have particularly influenced the imagination of an inhabitant of Patmos, itself a fortress-island of Miletos (see Saffrey 1975 for evidence of thriving cults of both Apollo and Artemis on Patmos in John's day). In this Greek version of the myth, Leto, pregnant by Zeus, is pursued by the dragon Python, who intends to kill her. Rescued at Zeus' command by the north wind and aided by Poseidon, she makes her way to the Aegean island of Delos, where she safely gives birth to her children Apollo and Artemis. Her son Apollo subsequently defeats the Python and the threat is overcome. It is unlikely that any inhabitant of Roman Asia, hearing Revelation 12, would not pick up resonances of the Leto–Apollo–Python myth. They may also have detected echoes of the Egyptian version, concerning the birth of Horus to Isis, and the attack on them by Seth-Typhon (A. Y. Collins 1976: 62–63; Van Henten 1994: 501). Isis' cult had already made its mark on Asian cities such as Pergamum and Ephesus. What would be most shocking to the first hearers of Revelation, however, is the way in which John's vision retells and radically subverts such myths.

John first recounts how **the sanctuary of God which is heaven** 11:19 **was opened,** and **the Ark of his Covenant** was seen inside it. The Ark (a wooden box supposedly containing the tablets of the Law: Exod. 25:10) signified the saving if terrifying presence of God with his people, both during the wilderness wanderings and when settled in the land (e.g. Num. 10:33–36; Deut. 10:8; 1 Sam. 4:1–4; 7:1; 1 Kgs 8:6). Located in the Holy of Holies of Solomon's Temple, it became the place of encounter and reconciliation between God and Israel. It disappeared at the Exile, and some Jewish traditions claimed that it had been hidden in a cave on Sinai by the prophet Jeremiah, and would be revealed again with the glory of the Lord and the cloud, in the last days (2 Macc. 2:4–8; cf. *2 Bar.* 6:1–9).

When John sees not only the sanctuary opened but also the Ark of the Covenant within it, he is seeing nothing less than the divine Presence. Revelation has been reluctant to describe the Holy God directly (note the absence of anthropomorphisms at 4:2–3), and it exhibits the same reticence here. For John, what is important is that the Holy of Holies now stands open, providing him direct access to the one who dwells there (as if the veil of the Temple has been torn in two from top to bottom: Mk 15:38; though note Rev. 15:8). Just as the first sequence of heavenly visions took their starting point from John's vision of the heavenly *Merkavah*, so this new sequence finds its orientation in the heavenly Ark. That it is **the Ark of his Covenant** stresses God's faithfulness to his people (now the Lamb's people of the new Exodus). Signs which once accompanied the Sinai theophany (Exod. 19:16–18; cf. Rev. 4:5; 8:5) accompany this present theophany: **flashes of lightning, voices, claps of thunder** and **an earthquake.** There is also **heavy hail,** a reminder of the salvific Egyptian plagues (Exod. 9:22–26). The God who saved his people out of Egypt and made a covenant with them at Sinai remains faithful, and is acting to overcome the forces of evil, thus putting the world to rights.

12:1–2 In Isaiah 66:6–9, a voice from the Temple precedes the description of Jerusalem-Zion as a woman in labour. Similarly, John recounts how, after the voices in the heavenly sanctuary, **a great sign appeared in heaven, a woman dressed in the sun, with the moon under her feet, and on her head a wreath of twelve stars**. The word **sign** is used throughout this section to describe heavenly portents (also the dragon at 12:3 and the seven angels with the last plagues at 15:1; cf. Mk 8:11; the plural denotes signs worked by the dragon's earthly accomplices, which lead people astray: 13:13–14; 16:14; 19:20). The woman's location in heaven or 'in the sky', and the reference to the heavenly bodies with which she is adorned, may suggest a further astronomical resonance. Some commentators have understood the woman and the dragon which pursues her as the constellations Virgo and Scorpio (Farrer 1964: 139–45; Malina and Pilch 2000: 155–57), or her starry wreath as all twelve signs of the zodiac (e.g. Aune 1998a: 681).

While one should not rule out such astronomical echoes, there is a more obvious Old Testament background to the **wreath of twelve stars**. The stars are signs of the twelve tribes of Israel, eleven of which bow down, along with **the sun** and **moon**, before Joseph's star in Gen. 37:9 (cf. *T. Naph.* 5:1–5; see Sg Sgs 6:10, where the bride's appearance is likened to both moon and sun). That she is dressed in the sun denotes her heavenly origin (compare the twenty-four elders and the great multitude dressed in heavenly white: 4:4; 7:9, 13; and the powerful angel dressed in a cloud with a face like the sun at 10:1).

This initial description may help us wade through the multiple allusions to biblical texts and pagan myths, in order to identify the woman. She is a heavenly figure, crowned with the tribes of Israel. She sums up in herself many of the maternal figures that God's people have known: Eve, Israel, Jerusalem. Like the other women in the visionary section of Revelation (Babylon; the bride of the Lamb), she has a corporate identity. A further clue is provided in verse 2: **She was pregnant, and she cried out in intense labour pains as she prepared to give birth**. There is a close similarity to Jn 16:20–22, which likens the community of disciples, living through the suffering and glorification of the Son, to a woman in labour (cf. a similar use of the metaphor in 1QH 3). In short, she is the heavenly counterpart of the community of the faithful (and John makes no harsh distinction between Israel and the Church). She represents the community which through a long and often-turbulent history prepared the way for the Messiah's coming and now continues his witness. In her story, John sees the sweep of salvation history from

Eden to new Exodus in Christ. Her labour pains are particularly acute because the dawning of the messianic age brings with it intense tribulation for the people of God (the 'birthpangs' of Mk 13:8 and par.).

This corporate interpretation reflects the earliest patristic exegesis of this passage, the woman as the Church, or God's people of Old and New Covenants (Boxall 1999). This does not render illegitimate the Marian interpretation, which emerged alongside the ecclesial one in the later patristic period and flourished in the Middle Ages. However, it must be regarded as a secondary reading derived from her identification as the heavenly personification of God's people (Le Frois 1954 offers a different, though ultimately unconvincing, reading of the patristic evidence).

Another sign then makes its appearance: **a great fiery red dragon** 3–4 (which will be explicitly identified with the devil in verse 9). Fiery red was the colour of the second horse, whose rider was allowed to remove peace from the earth, highlighting its association with bloodshed and slaughter (6:4; variants of red, 'purple' and 'scarlet' will be worn by Babylon, who is judged for shedding human blood: 17:4; 18:16; scarlet is also the colour of the monster on which she sits: 17:3). As well as the dragon Python or Seth-Typhon in the stories of the birth of Apollo and Horus, Christian Jews would think of the serpent-like Leviathan, the personification of the waters of chaos (the Hebrew equivalent of the Canaanite Litan: Job 41:1; Pss 74:14; 104:26; Isa. 27:1; *4 Ez.* 6:49–52; *2 Bar.* 29:4; *1 En.* 6:7–9, 24; cf. Rahab in Ps. 89:10). The overall effect on the hearer, however, is as important as any antecedents. Fear of dragons and powers that threaten social order and cohesion is a universal phenomenon, and the nightmarish quality of this scene brings residual fears to the surface. Like the most terrifying of nightmares, or the darkest of fairy tales, it calls for satisfactory resolution to assure the audience that such a threat can ultimately be overcome.

The dragon has **seven heads**. This number derives ultimately from ancient traditions about Leviathan/Litan, which according to the Ugarit sources has seven heads (Day 1992). However, the symbolic numerology of the Apocalypse gives it an additional significance. Seven is the number of perfection or completion: thus, to the human eye, it appears perfect. It even has **seven diadems**, symbolising the authority it wields in the political realm (contrast Christ, who wears many diadems: 19:12; cf. the ten diadems of the monster at 13:1). Revelation presents the line separating good from evil as very thin, and many will be seduced by the dragon and the two monsters it spawns (the first monster also has seven heads and ten horns, revealing a striking family resemblance: 13:1; 17:3). But however perfect the dragon may appear, this book unveils its true reality as a terrifying serpent, bringing not order but chaos in its wake.

It also has **ten horns**: the horn is the symbol of power (see on the seven horns of the Lamb at 5:6), and the number suggests that the dragon is powerful indeed. As if to emphasise its power, John tells how **its tail dragged a third of the stars from heaven and threw them to the earth.** Unlike the one who created the stars, the dragon creates chaos even in the ordered heavens (6:13; cf. Dan. 8:10, where the 'little horn', representing the tyrant Antiochus Epiphanes, throws down some of the stars). John has already witnessed such cosmic collapse in the falling of the burning mountain, the star Wormwood and the angel with the key to the Abyss (8:8, 10; 9:1); here it happens on an even grander scale (though the fact that it is only **a third** sets limits to this creature's havoc). Like Python in the Apollo myth, or Seth-Typhon in the story of Horus' birth, **The dragon stood before the woman, who was on the verge of giving birth, so that it might eat her child up as soon as she gave birth.** There is an ironic contrast here with John, who ate up the scroll in order to absorb God's word and pass it on (10:10); the dragon's desire is to eat up the Word of God (19:13) in order that he may be destroyed.

5–6 The woman **gave birth to a male child, the son who would shepherd all the nations with an iron sceptre.** The Greek is literally 'a son, a male', the latter word being effectively redundant: the translation here attempts to retain both by picking up on the significance of God's Son in Psalm 2, which is obviously being evoked, as it was at the seventh trumpet of 11:15–18 (here esp. Ps. 2:9; also Isa. 66:7 LXX). The verb translated **shepherd** could also mean 'rule', while the **iron sceptre** may be the shepherd's rod or crook, used for both rescue and reproof. This ambiguity is appropriate for the kingly Lamb, whose action can be experienced either as careful shepherding or terrifying judgement (cf. 2:27; 19:15).

Though many commentators have understood the **birth** to be Christ's historical birth in Bethlehem, and the woman's flight **into the wilderness** as the flight of the Holy Family into Egypt (Mt. 2:1, 13–18), this is problematic given that the birth is immediately followed by the child being **snatched up to God and to his throne.** Rather we are hearing, in mythological terms, of the death and resurrection of Christ, by which he became 'first to be born from the dead' (1:5; cf. Col. 1:18), and his ascension or exaltation to God's right hand (e.g. Acts 2:33; Rom. 1:4; Heb. 1:3). Psalm 2:7 speaks of the Messiah becoming God's Son on his enthronement, and this is interpreted in terms of Jesus' resurrection at Acts 13:33. By virtue of his death and resurrection, this child overcomes the attacking dragon and comes to share God's throne and therefore God's royal rule. The verb for **snatched up** is ἡρπάσθη, which may be translated 'was raptured'. Given the huge popularity of the doctrine of the so-called pre-tribulation 'Rapture', whereby the faithful will be caught up to heaven prior to the great tribulation, it is notable that Christ alone in the whole Apocalypse is said to be 'raptured', and only after suffering, while God's people are pursued by the dragon into the wilderness.

For John's first audiences, this story of the male child's rescue from the dragon would also have had reverberations on the contemporary political scene. A number of early emperors, including Nero, who has left his mark on Revelation elsewhere (e.g. 6:2; 9:11; 13:3, 18), presented themselves in the mould of Apollo. According to one contemporary source, Nero's special corps of soldiers, the Augustiani, acclaimed him in the following manner: 'Glorious Caesar! Apollo! Augustus! Unmatched, like Pythios! By thyself we swear, O Caesar, none surpasses you' (Cassius Dio 62.20.5; cited by Van Henten 1994: 506). The story of Leto, Apollo and Python would come to have imperial overtones: the emperor is the Saviour who establishes peace by overcoming the dragon of chaos. With such overtly political connotations, Revelation's vision becomes politically subversive. In John's retelling, the tables are turned. It is Christ, rather than Apollo or any imperial incarnation of that deity, who has won the victory. The arrogant emperor finds himself identified not with the divine Son, but with the destroying dragon. The victim of Rome, crucified under Pontius Pilate, is revealed as the true victor.

The woman fled into the wilderness, where a place had been prepared for her by God. Rather than representing the flight of Mary and Joseph into Egypt, the flight of the woman into the wilderness evokes that journey in reverse, out of Egypt at the Exodus (cf. Ezek. 29:3, where Pharaoh is likened to a dragon). It is a reminder that the story of God's people as John witnesses it is the story of a new Exodus. Though the wilderness is often viewed as a place of danger and desolation (hence Babylon is there at 17:3), it is also the place of preparation, where God cared for his people prior to their entering the promised land. The **place ... prepared for her by God** echoes the sealing of the one hundred and forty-four thousand, or the measuring of God's sanctuary and its worshippers (7:1–7; 11:1–2). It offers assurance of divine care, though not exemption from suffering. She is **fed there** (cf. the story of Hagar, Gen. 21:14, 19) **for one thousand, two hundred and sixty days** (see on 11:2 and 3). The ecclesial interpretation of the woman has sometimes suggested a eucharistic reading of her being fed or 'nourished' (picking up on the relationship between the manna and the eucharistic bread: e.g. John 6). The illustration in the thirteenth-century

Trinity Apocalypse, for example, shows an angel approaching the woman with the host and a chalice (van der Meer 1978: 159).

7–9 Sandwiched between the two parts of the story about the woman and her flight into the wilderness is a description (though not a vision) of **a war ... in heaven** between **the dragon** and the archangel **Michael,** together with their respective armies of **angels.** Michael has already appeared at 8:2 among the angels of the Presence, but this is the only place in Revelation where he is explicitly named. In Jewish apocalyptic he is the angelic protector of God's people Israel (e.g. Dan. 10:21; 12:1; *1 En.* 20:5; cf. Jude 9). Cosmic battles between angelic forces are known elsewhere in Jewish tradition (e.g. the eschatological war underlying the Qumran War Scroll, which also involves Michael and his troops as heavenly counterparts to the earthly forces of Israel: 1QM 17). This heavenly war heightens that sense of threat and chaos caused by the dragon's onslaught on the woman and her child, and promises to resolve it. Faced with Michael and his troops, the dragon **was not powerful enough** to sustain that onslaught. We have already been reminded of the constant threat to God's creative ordering of the cosmos which is posed by the demonic realm of the sea or the Abyss. This threat lurks even in heaven itself, where John has seen 'something like a sea of glass, like crystal' (4:6); it will only be resolved with the destruction of the sea at 21:1.

But here we are confronted with the beginning of that end, for we learn that the dragon and its army **could no longer keep their place in heaven** (contrast the woman, who has a place 'prepared for her by God' in verse 6). Rather, the dragon **was thrown down**, like the burning mountain of 8:8, Babylon at 18:21, and the monster and false prophet at 19:20 (the dragon itself will ultimately be thrown into the lake of fire: 20:10). Some tradition of a fall or expulsion of Satan from God's presence, or of rebellious angels like the Watchers of *1 Enoch* 6—9, may well underlie what John now describes (e.g. Isa. 14:12–15; *2 Enoch* 29:3–5(J)), for '**Satan**' is revealed as one of the dragon's aliases. The list piles up familiar yet infamous names designed to instil fear and anxiety: the dragon is also **that ancient serpent** (evoking not only Leviathan but the serpent of Eden, Gen. 3:1), **who is known as 'Devil'** (the serpent and the devil are identified at Wis. 2:24) **and 'the Satan'.** The use of the term **the Satan** evokes its more primitive usage to refer to God's chief prosecutor (Job 1:6ff.; Zech. 3:1; cf. Lk. 22:31). Despite this, however, its juxtaposition with other titles highlights its more sinister aspect: it is **the deceiver of the whole world** ('deceiving' or 'leading astray' being one of the greatest crimes in Revelation: e.g. 2:20; 13:14). The throwing down is not simply out of heaven, where God is now in complete control, but **to the earth** (contrast the *2 Enoch* passage, where Satanail and his angels are consigned to flying in the air above the Abyss). Revelation has already told us of the serpent's activity at Pergamum, 'where Satan's throne is' (2:13; cf. 2:9; 3:9); the warning is now broadened to embrace the whole earth.

Yet whatever antecedents underlie this passage, Revelation has 10–12 transformed them into something very different. Here as elsewhere in this book, the canticle proclaimed by **a loud voice in heaven** provides the interpretative key to the surrounding action, rather like the chorus in a Greek drama (Le Moignan 2000: 85). In a reversal of apocalyptic expectation, the really significant story is not that of Michael and Satan in heaven, or a primeval fall of Satan, but the earthly story of Jesus Christ and his followers. In Lk. 10:18, Jesus connects the fall of Satan like lightning from heaven with the proclamation of God's Kingdom in his own ministry and that of his followers. John 12:27–32 speaks of the 'hour' of Christ's death and resurrection as the definitive time at which the ruler of this world will be thrown out. So also the Apocalypse presents the crucial battle as a hard-won human battle involving Jesus and his faithful witnesses. Picking up again on the enthronement psalm, Psalm 2, the canticle declares: **Now have come the salvation and the power, and the royal rule of our God, and the authority of his Christ!** Typically, the attributes of God are threefold, reflecting the divine number. The defeat of the Evil One coincides with the coming of God's Kingdom (Mt. 6:10, 13; 12:28; 2 Thess. 2:8–10; cf. Rev. 11:15).

Again, the early notion of the Satan as **the accuser** appears. Echoing the prophecy uttered to the congregation in Smyrna (2:10), the prospect of specific hostility and legal action against Christians is raised (he is **the accuser of our brothers and sisters**). But in the legal processes, they have won the day; victory has been achieved in the decisive battle, even if there are individual skirmishes in which followers of Christ will have to engage. Christ has brought Satan's accusatory role to an end in the throwing down of the accuser. The heavenly voice continues: **These have conquered him as a result of the blood of the Lamb.** The Lamb's blood, that is his sacrificial death, represents the definitive defeat of the hostile powers (cf. Col. 2:15). What to casual bystanders outside Jerusalem would have looked like the execution of just another criminal or rebel, from the perspective of heaven is a glorious victory which has unseated evil itself.

But Christ does not stand apart from his people. Nor is martyrdom simply spilt blood. The two witnesses of Revelation 11 are a reminder of the continuation of Christ's witness to which the Church is called. Hence they have also **conquered him as a result of their witness,**

for they did not love their life even in the face of death (the souls of 6:9–11 may be especially in view, although Revelation looks forward to potential hostility in the future as well as back to what has already occurred: cf. 2:10). Speaking the truth, unmasking evil and falsehood, continuing the witness that Jesus bore: such will continue to bear fruit. This heavenly canticle takes up the mundane struggles of possibly tiny congregations of Asian Christians into a struggle of cosmic and cosmos-changing proportions. Theirs is no localised battle, but part of that great battle in which order is re-established over chaos.

At present, however, though the **heavens** may now be free of satanic activity, the same cannot be said of the **earth**, where God's people currently find themselves, nor of the **sea**, from where the newest threat is about to arise (at 13:1). The expulsion from heaven is a reason to **celebrate**, not simply for the heavens themselves, but also for **you who shelter there.** This expression directly parallels the negative 'those who make their home on the earth' (i.e. those hostile to God and his Messiah on account of their disordered priorities). It therefore describes not those specifically located in heaven, such as the angels, or the souls under the altar, but those – including those living on earth – whose lives are oriented toward God and who experience his sheltering presence (cf. 11:1; John 1:14). These have good reason to **celebrate**, for they ultimately belong to that realm from which Satan has been ejected and over which he has no more control (cf. 11:10, where 'those who make their home on the earth' celebrate the deaths of the two witnesses). **Earth and sea,** however, are warned that **the devil** has come down **in a furious rage, knowing that he has little time left!** This echoes the Jewish apocalyptic notion of the 'messianic woes', according to which the approach of the End will see heightened activity on the part of the powers of evil, as their control begins to slip away (probably reflected in Mt. 6:13; cf. Mk 13:20).

13–18   Having been oriented by the heavenly canticle, the story of the woman and the dragon is resumed. Hostility towards God's people emerges again (a theme already highlighted by the attack on the two witnesses of 11:1–13), as the dragon **pursued the woman who had given birth to the male child.** The Exodus story, never far from the surface in the Apocalypse, also re-emerges. **The two wings of a great eagle,** which enables the woman **to fly into the wilderness,** echo Exod. 19:4, where God bears the people on eagle's wings (cf. Deut. 32:10–14; Isa. 40:31). The theme of divine protection **for a time, times and half a time** represents a repetition of the divine protection promised by the sealing of the one hundred and forty-four thousand and the measuring of the sanctuary of God (7:1–7; 11:1–2;

see commentary on 12:6). The persecution she will experience from the dragon will be limited in extent (see 13:5).

Rivers of water are meant to be life-giving (see the 'river containing the water of life' in the new Jerusalem at 22:1), yet the activity of the dragon turns them to destructive use. Here **the serpent spewed a river of water out of its mouth after the woman**, in order to drown her (the juxtaposition of serpent and woman also evokes the Eden story in Genesis 3). But **Mother Earth came to the aid of the woman**: the word 'earth' (Greek γῆ) is personified here, suggesting the goddess Ge of Greek mythology (just as Revelation earlier personified Death and Hades: 1:18; 6:8). If this is a legitimate interpretation, it has implications for the generally negative assessment of Revelation's portrayal of women as essentially passive (see Additional Note on The Women of Revelation). It suggests that, although now the domain in which Satan is active, the earth recognises her Creator and can cooperate with his salvific purposes, **opening her mouth and swallowing up the river** (cf. Exod. 15:12 and Num. 16:32–34, where the earth swallows up God's enemies). The rage of the dragon, like a creature lashing out in fury, is now directed at the rest of the woman's **children** (lit. 'seed'). These are further defined as **those who keep God's commandments and continue the witness of Jesus** (see on 1:2), that is Christian witnesses. This hints at ominous things to come for the Church, though Christians who recall the story of Eden will detect a more hopeful strand. Genesis 3:15 foresees enmity between the serpent and the woman, its 'seed' and her 'seed'. Nevertheless, although the serpent will bruise the heel of the woman's offspring, the latter will ultimately strike the serpent's head.

The final verse prepares the reader for what is immediately to follow: **it took its stand on the shore of the sea** (this is the reading of the best manuscripts; a variant reading, 'I took my stand', involves the addition of just one extra letter in the Greek, and may well be a scribal accommodation to the verb in 13:1, which is in the first person singular: Smalley 2005: 303). The sea is the Abyss, the natural roaming ground of the serpent Leviathan, which will continue to harbour the forces of evil and chaos until its ultimate defeat in the new heavens and new earth (21:1). In the meantime, the audience is prepared for another of its beastly surprises to emerge.

Second Vision: The Monster from the Sea   (13:1–10)

(1) Then I saw a monster ascending out of the sea, with ten horns and seven heads. On its horns were ten diadems, and on each of its heads a name that blasphemes against God. (2) The monster that I saw looked like a leopard, but its feet were like

a bear's paws, and its mouth like a lion's mouth. The dragon gave its power to this monster, the power derived from its throne, and great authority.
(3) Now one of this monster's heads looked as if it had been slaughtered, fatally wounded, but its fatal wound had been healed. The whole earth went after the monster in amazement; (4) people worshipped the dragon, because it had given authority to the monster, and they worshipped the monster, saying: 'Who is like the monster? Who can wage war with it?' (5) The monster was permitted to utter terrible blasphemous words; it was given authority to do so for forty-two months. (6) So it opened its mouth to utter blasphemous words against God, against God's name and his tabernacle (that is, those who are sheltered in heaven). (7) It was permitted to wage war with the holy ones, and to conquer them. It was also given authority over every tribe and people, language and nation. (8) All those who make their home on the earth worshipped it – everyone whose name is not inscribed in the scroll of life of the Lamb slaughtered since the foundation of the world.
(9) Let anyone who has an ear, listen!
(10) Anyone for captivity, goes into captivity;
Anyone to be killed by a sword, will be killed by the sword.
This calls for the faithful perseverance of the holy ones!

1–2 Nightmares and fairy tales are incomplete without monstrous creatures which threaten destruction, and this is no less the case with many of the apocalypses. Hybrid creatures are clearly on the wrong side of the line marking out order from chaos, and their taming or even destruction addresses the fear that human societies might be overwhelmed by them. Having seen a terrifying dragon expelled from heaven, John now turns his attention to the two lower realms, where the forces of evil and chaos are still at work: first the sea and then the earth. He sees **a monster ascending out of the sea, with ten horns and seven heads**. There is an immediate family resemblance to the dragon, who has the same number of heads and horns (see on 12:3). This reflects the fact that **the dragon gave its power to this monster, the power derived from its throne, and great authority**: this monster, and the one that follows it at 13:11–18, are the agents by which the dragon can persecute the earthly offspring of the woman.

Their association with the sea and the earth respectively suggests that they are modelled on Leviathan and Behemoth (Job 40—41; *1 En.* 60:7–10; *4 Ez.* 6:49–52), who according to some traditions would re-emerge in the messianic age to provide food for those who survive (*2 Bar.* 29:4). Whereas the dragon had seven diadems on its heads, suggesting that the dragon is the source (one possible meaning of κεφαλή) of this counterfeit authority, this monster has **ten diadems on its horns**. Ten is a number of human completeness (though lacking seven's sense of perfection), and its juxtaposition with diadems and horns suggests its complete royal power in the rebellious human realm (cf. Dan. 7:7). At the reappearance of this monster in Revelation 17 its seven heads and ten horns will be explicitly identified as 'seven kings' and 'ten kings' (17:9–10, 12), the latter apparently allies of the monster, perhaps the 'kings from the east' of 16:12. **On each of its heads** there is **a name that blasphemes against God** (this translation follows the singular variant ὄνομα, which literally reads: 'and on its heads a name of blasphemy'). What is meant by this is not immediately clear, but given what follows it may allude to the divine titles claimed by Roman emperors, or ascribed to them by the imperial cult. Such rival claims to be Lord, Divine, or Deserving of Reverence would indeed have been regarded as blasphemous by Jewish and Christian worshippers of the One God.

The reference to the sea recalls not only Leviathan but also the ascent of hideous locusts out of the Abyss at the fifth trumpet (9:1–11; cf. 11:7). Yet there would have been an even more obvious antecedent for John's early Christian audiences: the four monsters which Daniel witnessed ascending from the sea (Dan. 7:1–8). Daniel's first three creatures resembled a lion, a bear and a leopard respectively, while the fourth and most terrifying had ten horns (further, Daniel's four monsters have a total of seven heads and ten horns between them). The interpretation received by Daniel identifies them as a succession of four kings or four empires (Dan. 7:17, 23), generally thought to represent the Babylonians, Medes, Persians and Greeks (and culminating in the persecution of Israel by the 'little horn' Antiochus Epiphanes). John's one monster, with its **ten horns**, is a hideous hybrid of all four: **The monster that I saw looked like a leopard, but its feet were like a bear's paws, and its mouth like a lion's mouth**. It is as though all the evil and beastliness of Daniel's four empires are combined in this one new monstrous empire which has emerged on the scene. In its broadest terms, given its visionary reworking of Daniel's vision, what John sees is the ultimate rebellious and arrogant empire, the incarnation of all that is hostile to God and his people. Hence this vision has had a rich and varied appeal throughout history, exhibiting an impressive ability to speak afresh to new generations (see Kovacs and Rowland 2004: 147–59). For first-century readers, however, the name of Rome would be firmly on their lips (cf. *4 Ez.* 12:11, where Rome is identified with Daniel's fourth kingdom; cf. *2 Baruch* 36–40). Indeed, those living in the city of Ephesus would in a very real sense have witnessed Rome

ascending out of the sea, in the person of the Roman proconsul of Asia, arriving by ship at the city's harbour to take up his office in the province.

3–4 First-century allusions continue in the description of one of the monster's heads, which **looked as if it had been slaughtered, fatally wounded** (lit. 'slaughtered to death'), **but its fatal wound had been healed**. The verb **slaughtered** suggests a satanic parody of the slaughtered yet risen Lamb, part of that imperial propaganda which proclaimed the Emperor as Saviour and establisher of universal peace. Such messianic pretensions may also be reflected in the monster's mouth 'like a lion's mouth' (cf. 5:5). The war of words in which Revelation is engaged strikes at the very root of the imperial political machine. The **fatal wound** (literally 'plague of death') echoes the heavenly plagues of the trumpets and two witnesses (9:18, 20; 11:6), and suggests a divine origin. Dürer's woodcut of this scene portrays one of the heads gazing into the sky, where an angel holding a wooden cross prepares to wield the death-blow with his sword. In this interpretation, it is the cross of Christ which delivers the fatal wound (see Smith 2000: 67–71).

But the statement that the monster's **fatal wound had been healed** almost certainly contains a further allusion to contemporary rumours and legends about the emperor Nero. Echoes of this emperor have already been detected in the Antichrist figure riding on the white horse at the opening of the first seal (see on 6:1–2). Nero's flight from Rome and the mysterious circumstances surrounding his suicide ('by the sword': see also verse 14) led to rumours that he had not died but had gone into hiding, probably beyond the Euphrates, until he could regain the imperial throne (e.g. Tacitus, *Hist.* 2.8; Suet., *Nero* 57), thus spawning a succession of 'pretenders' in 69, 80 and *c.* 88/89. In Jewish tradition, the terrifying consequences of his return are elaborated with apocalyptic intensity (e.g. *Sib. Or.* 4:119–24, 137–39; 5:28–34; *Asc. Isa.* 4:2–14); it is even suggested in one late first-century tradition that he would return from beyond the grave (*Sib. Or.* 5:363–73). These diverse traditions also reflect the ambiguity of his memory: popular amongst the Roman populace and well-regarded in the east, not least in Greece and among the Parthians, but offensive to the Roman aristocracy and viewed in more sinister terms by some Roman historians and the Jewish sources (see Bauckham 1993a: 407–23). John's vision draws upon such contemporary residual fears, as well as the Christian memory of what Nero had done against their brothers and sisters in Rome. It proclaims that the evil associated with that tyrant was still alive and well, manifested in that monstrous empire of which Nero was such a cruel exemplar. Although it was one of the heads (Nero) which received a fatal blow, his return meant the monster too had recovered from this mortal wound (hence its, αὐτοῦ, rather than the feminine αὐτῆς, which a reference to the 'head' would require: see 13:12, 14). The use of the Nero tradition in chapter 17 will be somewhat different (for argument against Neronic allusions in this verse, see Minear 1953).

It is salutary to remember that the monster is only seen as monstrous by means of apocalyptic insight. To the naked eye, it looks impressive, beneficent and deserving of gratitude. Hence we hear that **The whole earth went after the monster in amazement** (just as at 17:6 John himself is 'amazed' at Babylon). Power may corrupt, and absolute power may corrupt absolutely: but power also entices and seduces. It is a lesson not restricted to John's first audiences, living under the shadow of imperial Rome. **The whole earth** cannot be the same as Mother Earth (ἡ γῆ) at 12:16, for she acts to protect God's people; rather, it refers here to the 'civilised world' of the Roman Empire, or rather that part of Rome's dominion which is orientated to earth rather than to God. The worship of **the monster** refers to the imperial cult, which far from being imposed from on high seems to have emerged 'from below' within provinces such as Asia (modelled on the local traditional phenomenon of the ruler cult). By the first century CE, all but Thyatira among Revelation's seven cities had temples of the imperial cult, while there is evidence in five for imperial altars and priests (Laodicea and Philadelphia excepted: Thompson 1990: 159). Given its influence on public buildings, statuary, coinage and city festivals, the worship of the emperor, alongside that of the gods, would have pervaded virtually every aspect of life. Non-participation would have been severely frowned upon by the local authorities and probably the local populace. Bold indeed would have been the Christian who attempted to avoid it completely.

The Apocalypse's view is that participation in the worship of the monster is no harmless or empty ritual: rather, those who did so also **worshipped the dragon**, who is the power behind the throne (cf. 1 Cor. 10:20, where idol worship is regarded as the worship of demons). The monster's seduction and deception is complete, reflected in the acclamation placed on the lips of those taken in: **'Who is like the monster? Who can wage war with it?'** This is a cry embedded in the very fabric of cities such as Ephesus and Pergamum, whose architecture, inscriptions and iconography proclaim Rome as the great and invincible empire (though it also manifests itself again and again throughout human history, attached to subsequent powerful and arrogant empires). An ironic contrast is being made with the archangel Michael, whose name means 'Who is like God?' The implied reader, unlike the characters in this vision, will know that Christ's cross has enabled Michael to defeat the dragon and therefore its monstrous offspring. At 11:7 the monster from the Abyss has been foreseen, the one who would wage war with the two witnesses, overcome them and kill them. But the broader canvas presents an alternative victory, achieved not by killing but by being killed. Rome's empire, like Daniel's succession of four monster-empires, may rise but it also ultimately falls.

5–7 The monster's limited reign is described in further detail. The repeated **was permitted** or **was given** (ἐδόθη) may still have the dragon as its antecedent, as in verse 2, where it actively gives its authority to the monster. However, it is more likely that John has moved to a succession of divine passives, with God as the implied agent. However powerful the monster appears to be, and however much it threatens the Church, God is ultimately in control and granting permission for this temporary state of affairs to exist. Revelation ultimately rejects a cosmic dualism which would regard the world as hopelessly locked in a battle between two opposing gods or principles of good and evil. God may not actively will the activity of the monster, but God's world is such that it is allowed to function. The empire's arrogance and assumption of divine prerogatives, like its persecution of God's people, is permitted only for the limited period of **forty-two months** (cf. 11:2–3; 12:6, 14).

Blasphemous words against God and **against God's name** are relatively clear (see on verse 1); what is meant by the final part of verse 6 is less so. If one follows the *lectio difficilior* (rather than the variant reading, 'his tabernacle and those who are sheltered in heaven'), the two phrases **his tabernacle** and **those who are sheltered in heaven** are synonymous. For this reading there are several possible interpretations. First, these phrases mean the natural inhabitants of heaven and the heavenly tabernacle, Michael and the angels. But it is difficult to see what might be meant by uttering blasphemous words against angels (see Caird 1966: 166). Moreover, similar language has been used elsewhere of human worshippers of God rather than the angelic priesthood (e.g. 11:1–2; 12:12). Second, they are explicitly those faithful servants of God who have already been witnessed in heaven: the martyrs, now located under the heavenly altar (6:9–11). They are being blasphemed or slandered on a cosmic level, just as their brethren in Smyrna were in localised legal proceedings (2:9). Yet this might be too restrictive, given the parallels in 11:1 and 12:12. Most likely, we should understand this in its broader sense, to refer to all God's faithful who are oriented towards heaven, that is towards God (in contrast to 'those who make their home on the earth', οἱ κατοικοῦντες ἐπὶ τῆς γῆς, who worship the monster: verse 8; cf. 3:10; 6:10; 8:13; 11:10; 13:12, 14; 14:6; 17:2, 8). They experience even here on earth, and especially during the 'wilderness years' of hostility and persecution, God's tabernacling protection.

Revelation refers here again to **the scroll of life** (3:5; 17:8; 20:12, 15) **8** or **the scroll of life of the Lamb** (as here and at 21:27); such heavenly books or scrolls (cf. 20:12) are typical features of apocalypses. This particular scroll seems to be a heavenly ledger of names, according to which judgement will be made, a challenge to the view that humanity's destiny is in the hands of chance. Nevertheless, such a scroll raises theological difficulties, as it seems to suggest some kind of predestination to eternal life. Yet we are not told the grounds on which someone's name is **inscribed** in that scroll, and the earlier opportunities for repentance challenge the view that being listed on it is predetermined and unrelated to human response (e.g. 2:5, 16, 21; 3:3, 19; 9:20–21; 11:13). All we are told is that it is possible to have one's name removed from it, on the basis of one's infidelity or lack of commitment (see 3:5, where assurance of one's name not being blotted out is dependent on winning the victory; cf. Exod. 32:32–33).

The issue is compounded by debate about the phrase **since the foundation of the world**. It is possible that this should be taken with the verb **inscribed**, hence suggesting that the names have been in the scroll since the beginning of time (as in the parallel at 17:8). Yet this interpretation may simply be a statement of divine foreknowledge rather than divine will: God knows from the beginning those who will choose him, and those who will choose to reject him. The apocalyptic tradition regularly spoke of pre-existent entities, in the mind of God from the beginning (such as the new Temple, the Torah, and even the Messiah). More likely, however, is that one should take seriously the natural order of the Greek in this verse, according to which **the Lamb** has been **slaughtered since the foundation of the world**. In a book which so often presents earthly realities from the perspective of heavenly rather than human time, the decisive salvific act would then be presented from such a perspective.

Indeed, it is the perspective from which Christ's death would have been viewed in Revelation's likely 'theatre of reception', the Eucharist, in which Christ's death is proclaimed until he comes (1 Cor. 11:26). There is a close parallel at 1 Pet. 1:19–20, which speaks of Christ the spotless Lamb being destined 'before the foundation of the world'; similarly, Peter's Pentecost speech envisages Christ's death as according to the plan and foreknowledge of God (Acts 2:23). The slaughter of the Lamb, and its salvific effects, are not some late afterthought, but were central to God's plan from the beginning.

The vision of this terrifying monster concludes with a call to listen, a **9–10** proverb, and a challenge. The call to attention picks up on the conclusion to the seven messages, and echoes a synoptic saying of Jesus (e.g. Mk 4:9, 23): **Let anyone who has an ear, listen!** The command serves as a literary device alerting the reader, and therefore the audience, to a saying which requires particular attention. Given the Gospel parallel, and its earlier occurrences in Revelation on the lips of the 'someone like a son of man', we should perhaps understand the voice of the exalted Christ to be interrupting at this point also.

The proverb which begins verse 10 is closely modelled on Jer. 15:2 (cf. Jer. 43:11). In its present context, it serves to emphasise the strand running through the preceding chapters that God's people, though spiritually protected, cannot be immune from suffering. If imprisonment and even martyrdom are required by their prophetic calling, so be it. The background in Jeremiah, and the parallelism between the two parts of the proverb, suggest that we should prefer the minority reading **Anyone to be killed by a sword**, found in the important fifth-century Codex Alexandrinus. Other readings are variations on 'if anyone kills by the sword', apparently scribal attempts at clarification, influenced by Jesus' words in Mt. 26:52. Whichever reading is preferred, it is significant that the word used here for 'sword' is μαχαίρα (as in Jer. 15:2; contrast 43:11, which has ῥομφαία): the Apocalypse seems to use μαχαίρα of violent death (e.g. 6:4; 13:14), as opposed to the sword of God's word (ῥομφαία: 1:16; 2:12, 16; 19:15, 21).

Finally, there is a call **for the faithful perseverance of the holy ones**. The virtue of **perseverance**, a more active attitude than the normal translation 'endurance' might suggest, is one shared between John and his fellow-Christians (1:9). It eschews violence on the part of Christians, but suggests that perseverance in the face of suffering, and even martyrdom, is effective (on the various forms of resistance to foreign powers available to Jews, see A. Y. Collins 1977). Further calls to attention will occur at 13:18 (in relation to the number of the monster), 14:12 (following the pronouncements of the three angels), and 17:9 (preceding the explanation of the monster's seven heads). It is a call that has resounded across the centuries. Against the backdrop of Nazi dominance in 1930s Germany, Dietrich Bonhoeffer urged the German churches to become a distinctive community which listened to the Apocalypse (Bonhoeffer 1965: 324). Such a call will be all the more important as the narrative continues.

Third Vision: The Monster from the Earth (13:11–18)

(11) Then I saw another monster ascending out of the earth, which had two horns like a lamb's horns, but which spoke like a dragon. (12) It exercised the full authority of the first

monster, in the presence of that monster, forcing the earth and those who make their home in it to worship the first monster, whose fatal wound had been healed. (13) It also performed great miraculous signs, even making fire descend from heaven to the earth before people's eyes, (14) and it led astray those who make their home on the earth by the miraculous signs it was permitted to perform in the presence of the monster. It told those who make their home on the earth to make a statue for the monster, which was wounded by the sword but came back to life. (15) It was also permitted to breathe a spirit of life into the statue of the monster, so that the monster's statue could speak. And it was permitted to have all those who refused to worship the monster's statue killed. (16) It forced everyone – the little ones and the great, the rich and poor, freedmen and slaves – to receive a branded mark on their right hand or on their forehead, (17) so that no-one could buy or sell anything unless they had the branded mark showing the name of the monster or the number of its name. (18) This calls for wisdom! Let the one who has insight figure out the number of the monster, for it is the number of a human being: its number is six hundred and sixty-six.

11–12 A second monster now emerges, this time **ascending out of the earth**, suggesting the male Behemoth, separated at creation from the female Leviathan (e.g. *4 Ez.* 6:47–54; *1 En.* 60:7–10; *2 Bar.* 29:4); in Dan. 7:17 the four monsters from the sea (Dan. 7:3) are interpreted as four kings who are said to arise 'from the earth'. The phrase **out of the earth** suggests a subterranean creature, paralleling the first monster's emergence 'out of the sea', and the locusts' coming out of the Abyss at 9:3. Nevertheless, it belongs to the realm of human activity, the 'earth' (and possibly more specifically the 'land' of Roman Asia).

John's description of this second monster anticipates its ability to lead human beings astray (verse 14). First, it has **two horns like a lamb's horns** (as opposed to the 'ten horns' of the first monster, suggesting its more limited power and its dependence on its predecessor). Hence it is another satanic parody of the slaughtered yet risen Lamb: its lamb-like appearance, without the assistance of apocalyptic insight, could easily lead to a case of mistaken identity, even amongst Christians (cf. 2:20–23). When it opens its mouth, however, it speaks **like a dragon**. Its ultimate dependence upon Satan, whose words it utters rather than the true words of God, becomes clear.

The twofold function of the second monster is elaborated on in verse 12. First, it acts on behalf of and with **the full authority** of the monster from the sea, presumably towards the earth or the 'land'. Second, it promotes the **worship of the first monster** among **those who make their home in** the earth (for this phrase see on 3:10). The Greek construction used suggests a strong element of compulsion. Overshadowed by this monster, and still more by the first monster and the furious dragon, humanity is not free.

With whom should this second monster be identified? There are three main possibilities. The most obvious is that this monster represents the local lackeys of the arrogant empire (in John's eyes incarnated in Rome). This could be specifically the priests of the imperial cult, or, given the interpenetration of religion, culture and politics, the wider local elite who profited from Rome's local dominance and considered it their duty to promote the grateful worship of Rome and her emperors. The emphasis upon worship favours this solution in some form.

A second interpretation emphasises the later description of this monster as the 'false prophet' (16:13; 19:20; 20:10). Some commentators note that, elsewhere in the New Testament, false prophecy is largely an internal problem for the Church (Garrow 1997: 88–91). And elsewhere in Revelation, 'false prophets' have emerged within the seven congregations in the persons of 'Balaam' and 'Jezebel' (2:14, 20). Both renegade Christians have re-emerged here in the person of the second monster. This explanation is appealing insofar as it recognises the extent to which this monster will be associated with false prophecy. On its own, however, it fails to do justice to the wide appeal of the monster to the dominant population outside the churches, or the strong echoes of the imperial cult. 'Balaam' and 'Jezebel' are rather examples of how easily Christians can be implicated in the work of the second monster/false prophet, rather than representing that monster *in toto* (if that were correct, then it would follow that 'Jezebel' is to be equated with Babylon in Revelation 17, for there are also strong similarities between these two). It does serve, however, as an important secondary reading, a potent warning that Christian religion can become false and even demonic, if it loses its ability to speak the prophetic word.

Third, some commentators have opted for a more general interpretation, which picks up on elements of the other two, but avoids the restrictions of either. In the words of Eugene Boring: 'All who support and promote the cultural religion, in or out of the church, however Lamb-like they may appear, are agents of the monster. All propaganda that entices humanity to idolize human empire is an expression of this beastly power that wants to appear Lamb-like' (Boring 1989: 157; see also Smalley 2005: 345f.). Given the way in which Roman allusions have attached themselves to visionary creatures such as Daniel's four monsters, which already had a prehistory and life of their own, this wider reading of the false prophet's identity is an appealing one.

Being a false prophet as well as a parody of Christ, this monster **13–15** evidences the appropriate tools of the trade. Jewish and early Christian tradition expected evil eschatological figures as well as good, figures would deceive many by performing miraculous deeds. Mark 13:22 specifically envisages that false messiahs and false prophets would arise in the last days to perform signs and wonders (cf. 2 Thess. 2:9). There were even such traditions associated with the returning Nero (*Sib. Or.* 3:63–67). Revelation's false prophet emulates John's great hero Elijah, by **making fire descend from heaven to the earth before people's eyes** (1 Kgs 18:38; cf. Rev. 11:5–6). As in the Gospel tradition, the discernment of true and false prophecy is a particularly difficult task: it certainly cannot be decided on the basis of miraculous signs, but is judged more acutely by the fruits which it bears (Mt. 7:15–23; cf. 1 Cor. 14:26–33; *Did.* 11:3–6).

In what appear to be allusions to the corrupting influence of Asia's emperor cult, as well as the shameful episode of the golden calf (Exod. 32:1–35), the monster from the earth encourages the making of **a statue for the monster** from the sea. The word used is literally 'image' (Greek εἰκών), although it almost certainly refers here to a cult statue of the emperor, examples of which would have adorned temples across the empire (the word can also refer to the image of the emperor on coins, which may be significant for verses 16–17). In a shocking parody of the divine action in relation to the two witnesses (11:11), **It was also permitted to breathe a spirit of life into the statue of the monster, so that the monster's statue could speak.** Steven Scherrer has provided detailed evidence for elaborate hoaxes associated with pagan cults: statues which were able to 'speak' by a combination of puppetry, subdued lighting and ventriloquism (e.g. Lucian, *Alex.* 12—26). He also hypothesises that lightning machines designed for use in the theatre may have been used in a cultic setting, specifically the imperial cult (Scherrer 1984). There is every indication, however, that Revelation regards this as the work of Satan via his minion, rather than just an elaborate trick. The claim that **it was permitted to have all those who refused to worship the monster's statue killed** may be an allusion to the past martyrdoms under Nero, or, on the other hand, a visionary account of terrors yet to come.

Idolatry is subtle, and eventually affects every area of human life, as **16–18** the worshippers find themselves under a new lordship. Thus those persuaded to worship the monster are forced **to receive a branded mark** (Greek χάραγμα) **on their right hand** or **on their** forehead. Although some have suggested that χάραγμα refers here to the emperor's image on coins (Caird 1966: 173), its location on the right hand and forehead would seem to rule this out. It is probably an allusion to the branded mark or tattoo imposed on slaves or prisoners of war, often made on the forehead, which proclaimed that its recipient now belonged to another. The Jewish John would probably also detect a demonic parody of contemporary Jewish practice, whereby phylacteries containing words of the *Shema* were bound on the forehead and the left hand (Charles 1920: I, 362). The mark imposed on the worshippers of the monster is the antithesis of the true worship of Israel's One God. Nor does it distinguish between social or economic groupings; all of rebellious humanity is affected: **the little ones and the great, the rich and poor, freedmen and slaves.** The irony of the last doublet is that freedmen find themselves once again under slavery, though this time of a more pervasive and far-reaching kind.

But whatever allusions underlie this description, the branded mark is not a physical mark but a symbolic one. It cannot be seen by the naked eye (any more than the sealing of God's servants), but only in apocalyptic vision. It is the demonic counterpart to those who have the name or seal of God or the Lamb on their foreheads (7:3; 14:1). It is a mark of ownership, a reminder that where your treasure is, there will your heart be also (Mt. 6:21). It marks out those who belong to this earth from those who belong to heaven.

Yet if idolatry is so all-consuming, it will have an inevitable economic aspect too. In John's day, the branded mark revealed a family resemblance between those who possessed it and its presence on imperial coinage. Revelation's earlier reference to the silver denarius (6:6) shows that Roman coins bearing images of and inscriptions to the heads of the monster were well known to the audiences to whom his book was first addressed. Now the monster from the earth takes one further step: the emperor cult, along with the worship of traditional gods, was so thoroughly integrated into the lives of the cities, including their commercial and economic lives, that participation in one aspect necessitated participation in all others: **no-one could buy or sell anything unless they had the branded mark showing the name of the monster or the number of its name.** There have already been hints of this in the messages to Pergamum and Thyatira, where the extent of Christian participation in the trade guilds and wider civic life seems to be the issue in hand (2:12–29). Revelation utters a warning about the slippery slope that such involvement entailed. It echoes one interpretation of the 'taxes to Caesar' pericope of Mk 12:13–17 and parallels, whereby Jesus, by not possessing an imperial coin himself, shows his opponents implicated in an economic system by which he is untouched.

The branded mark is now accompanied by **the number of its name**. This wording suggests that some kind of *gematria* is called for (the practice, common in the ancient world, of arriving at a person's number by adding together the numerical equivalent of each letter of their name). That this requires careful reflection is highlighted by another call to attention (cf. 13:10; 14:12; 17:9): **This calls for wisdom! The one who has insight** is invited to **figure out the number of the monster**: it is possible that the singular ὁ ἔχων refers to the reader of the Apocalypse in the liturgical assembly, who would be expected to stop reading at this point and explain the number's significance (cf. 1:3; Neh. 8:8; Mk 13:14). Alternatively, it is an indication that Revelation was not designed to be read only once, but to be reread and carefully studied for its deeper secrets to be unveiled. The number is given: **six hundred and sixty-six** (a variant reading found in P[54] and known to Irenaeus (Iren. Adv. Haer. 5.30.1) is 616). What is required is to correlate the number, the monster, and the name **of a human being** (though the Greek could just mean 'a human number', i.e. an earthly mode of calculation: cf. the similar phrase at 21:17, of the system of measurement used by the angel). The most likely solution, which explains both numbers, is Nero Caesar.

Additional Note 2: The number of the monster

Almost every generation has been fascinated with the invitation of Rev. 13:18 to calculate 'the number of the monster' or 'the number of the beast'. The number 666 has left a vivid impression on Western culture far beyond the boundaries of the Christian Church. History is littered with now-discredited attempts to uncover the name behind the number. Candidates have included Julian the Apostate, Pope Innocent IV and Pope Benedict XI (the Latin *Innocentius Papa* and the Greek βενεδικτος both give the required number, as does the papal title *Vicarius Filii Dei*), Napoleon Bonaparte, and Patriarch Nikon of Moscow, scourge of the Russian Old Believers. In more recent times, Adolf Hitler, Ronald Wilson Reagan (whose three names each contains six letters), Bill Gates III and Saddam Hussein have added to the roll-call. Others prefer a less personal solution: the number 666, it is claimed, is hidden in barcodes of the Uniform Product Code System, or in the word COMPUTER itself (according to the numerical alphabet employed by the World Bank).

Where all these interpretations fail, of course, is in their unintelligibility either to John himself or to the members of the seven congregations to whom Revelation was first read. However, many of them have correctly recognised that there is a correlation between numbers and letters of the alphabet, such that adding up the numerical value of the letters will give the number of the name or word they spell. Almost certainly Revelation's cryptic number represents an ancient example of this process, known to later Jews as *gematria* and to the Greeks as ἰσοψηφία. In both Hebrew and Greek alphabets, letters are given their numerical equivalent (e.g. in Greek, $\alpha = 1$, $\beta = 2$, $\gamma = 3$, etc. up to ten, with alphabetical equivalents also for the tens and the hundreds).

A famous Greek example of *gematria* or ἰσοψηφία is the following graffito from Pompeii: 'I love her whose name is φμε' (i.e. 545). The puzzle for the Pompeian passerby would be to work back from this number to the correct name. More seriously, the Jewish *Sibylline Oracles* engage in *gematria* to describe a succession of Roman emperors (*Sib. Or.* 5:12–51). Lines 28–29, for example, read: 'One who has fifty as an initial will be commander, a terrible snake, breathing out grievous war' (Charlesworth 1983: 393). The letter for fifty in the Greek alphabet is N, and Nero is almost certainly meant. In contrast, the number of Ἰησοῦς or Jesus is 888 (*Sib. Or.* 1:324–29).

The difficulty for the interpreter of Rev. 13:18 is that a given number could be the sum of any number of different letters. John probably presumes that his first audiences would already know the name behind the number. The mystery, then, would not be the number, but its association with the monster (indeed, the numerical value of the Greek word for 'monster' or 'beast', θηρίον, when transliterated into the Hebrew alphabet as *trywn*, is 666: Bauckham 1993a: 389). At least two constraints seem to be placed on interpretation: first, the name represented by this number should be that of a human being (the most natural reading of ἀριθμὸς γὰρ ἀνθρώπου ἐστίν: though see e.g. Smalley 2005: 351 for a different view); second, it should be a name known to John's first-century Asian Christian audiences. The wider context of Revelation 13 (the visions of the two monsters) suggests that the Roman imperial context will be a key factor in interpretation.

One of the earliest exegetes of this passage, Irenaeus of Lyons (*Adv. Haer.* 5.30.3), detected the Roman resonances of this number. But he was reluctant to identify a particular individual, preferring generalities such as ΛΑΤΕΙΝΟΣ (the Latin one) and ΤΕΙΤΑΝ (Titan). More recent commentators have opted for a particular Roman emperor: the suggestions have included Gaius, Nero and Domitian.

The most likely solution identifies 666 as the number of Nero Caesar. Sufficient echoes of traditions surrounding Nero have been detected in Revelation to suggest that this emperor was on John's mind (e.g. 6:2; 13:3, 12; 16:12–16; 17:8, 11). This solution requires that John is thinking in Hebrew though writing in Greek, not in itself surprising for one who seems more comfortable in a Semitic language. Moreover, this difficulty is ameliorated if John is alluding to a name–number correspondence already well known to early Jewish Christians. Working in the Hebrew alphabet, the number of the name *Neron K(ai)sar* is 666, with 'Nero' spelt as in its Greek form as *Neron* and 'Caesar' in a rather unusual shortened form (this Hebrew form of *Neron K(ai)sar* is attested in a first-century Jewish document found in the Judaean desert: Klauck 2001: 692f.).

There is, however, a variant reading of 13:18, in which the monster's number is given as 616. This was known in the late second century to Irenaeus, who dismissed it as a scribal error (*Adv. Haer.* 5.30.1). Concrete manuscript evidence for this variant is found in P[54] among the Oxyrhynchus papyri. This is the number of the emperor Gaius (Caligula), written in the Greek alphabet as Γαιος Καισαρ. However, the variant also works for Nero: the Latin form *Nero Caesar* (without a final *n* as in the Greek) written in the Hebrew alphabet gives 616.

Nevertheless, the number of the monster may have a further significance. Although Revelation encourages speculation about an individual here by the at worst ambiguous 'number of a human being' or 'a human number', numbers elsewhere have symbolic significance, as I note throughout this volume. Six, being one less than the number seven, is a number which falls short of completeness (though note the reservations expressed by A. Y. Collins 1996). The repeated six hundred and sixty-six would then accentuate the ultimate imperfection of the monster, despite appearances to the contrary. It would represent yet another apocalyptic reminder that what looks good and perfect (and this monster has seven heads: 13:1) is not necessarily so.

Fourth Vision: The Lamb and Its Followers on Mount Zion (14:1–5)

(1) I looked, and there was the Lamb standing on Mount Zion. With it were one hundred and forty-four thousand people possessing its name, that is its Father's name, written on their foreheads. (2) Then I heard a sound from heaven like the sound made by many waters and like the sound of a loud thunderclap; indeed, the sound which I heard was like that of harpists playing on their harps. (3) They were singing something like a new song before the throne and the four creatures and the elders. No-one could learn this song except the one hundred and forty-four thousand, who had been redeemed from the earth. (4) These are the ones who have not made themselves ritually unclean with women, for they are chaste; they follow the Lamb wherever it goes. They have been

redeemed from among humanity as first-fruits offered to God
and to the Lamb. (5) No lie is found in their mouths, but they
are without blemish.

1 Psalm 2, which has been running like a golden thread through the
past couple of chapters, declares in the face of the rebellion of earth's
kings that God has set his anointed king on Zion, his holy hill (Ps.
2:6). So it is not surprising that, after the preceding monstrous
manifestations of political and religious rebellion, John now describes
how he saw **the Lamb standing on Mount Zion**. Mount Zion in
the Bible refers not to the south-western hill of Herodian Jerusalem
known by this name today (the result of a mistake in the fourth
century CE), but the eastern hill, the 'city of David' (2 Sam. 5:7).
Given the building of Solomon's Temple on the Temple Mount to
the north, the latter came to be known as Mount Zion (e.g. Pss 9:11;
50:2; 76:2; Isa. 8:18), and this is probably what is referred to here (cf.
4 Ez. 13:35–36, where the Messiah stands on Mount Zion to judge
the nations).

But John is not concerned with physical geography: where the
Lamb is standing is not the Temple Mount or even the heavenly
Mount Zion (cf. Heb. 12:22), but that spiritual Zion which is
nowhere and everywhere. It describes that state of openness to God
and protection by him which has been referred to elsewhere as the
measured sanctuary (11:1) or the 'holy city' (11:2). It is that place of
true spiritual worship which takes place neither on Mount Gerizim
nor in Jerusalem (John 4:21–24). Understood in this way, the question as to whether this scene is located on earth or in heaven is
superfluous (although the voice 'from heaven' in verse 2 seems to
count against the latter).

If Psalm 2 is indeed in the background, then several features of
John's description are significant. First, the Lamb is **standing**, just
as it was 'standing as if it had been slaughtered' when John first
encountered it at 5:6. The king victoriously enthroned on Mount
Zion is the king who has gained his throne by allowing himself to be
killed by his enemies. Such royal training overturns all human
expectations and qualifications for kingship. Second, this king does
not stand alone, but shares his royal rule with others (cf. 5:10): **With
it were one hundred and forty-four thousand people possessing its name, that is its Father's name, written on their
foreheads.** The Lamb is accompanied by the huge number of the
redeemed (for this interpretation of the one hundred and forty-four
thousand, see on 7:4–8), those who in the previous two chapters faced
the hostile onslaught of the dragon and its monstrous cronies. Far
from being overcome by the dragon and monsters, they are presented
as a victorious army. The Lamb's **name, that is its Father's name**

(taking the second phrase as epexegetical), is **written on their foreheads**. In other words, they are marked out as belonging to the one God, whose name 'Lord' is transferred to his Son throughout the New Testament (e.g. Jn 5:43; 17:11; 1 Cor. 8:4–6; Phil. 2:9–11; Heb. 1:4). They have the same divine protection that was promised by their sealing in 7:1–8. The literary juxtaposition of this vision to the preceding one highlights the direct contrast between the seal or name of God and the branded mark or name of the monster (13:16–17; cf. 3:12).

Heaven now breaks in on Mount Zion, just as heaven regularly 2–3 breaks in wherever God's servants are gathered in his name for worship. The earthly assemblies of Christians are caught up once again in the heavenly liturgy. The **sound** (φωνή), **from heaven** here is probably a heavenly sound (contrast 4:1; 6:6; 9:13; 10:8; 11:12; 12:10; 14:13; 16:1, 17; 18:4; 19:5; 21:3), **loud**, as one has come to expect from the heavenly realm, but melodious nonetheless, for it is **like that of harpists playing on their harps**. Many waters describes the voice of 'someone like a son of man' at 1:15, and the **loud thunderclap** has hitherto described the divine Presence (4:5; 8:5; 11:19; see also 16:18). But the sound of heavenly worshippers, rather than God himself, is more appropriate here (cf. 19:6, where the Hallelujahs of a great multitude will be described in this way). Those heavenly beings making this heavenly music **were singing something like a new song before the throne and the four creatures and the elders**. At 5:8–9, the twenty-four elders (and possibly also the four creatures) possessed harps and were singing a new song: however, they cannot be the singers here. The choir could include the souls of the martyrs under the altar (6:9–11), or the great multitude before the throne (7:9–10), but probably incorporates the whole host of heaven (5:11–12; 7:11–12), and possibly also the whole creation (5:13). Its ear-splitting volume matches that of the thunderous voice of the Lord (Ps. 29:3).

But the song is not heard only in heaven. Rather, it is sung on earth also by **the one hundred and forty-four thousand, who had been redeemed from the earth**. The language of 'purchase' or 'redemption' recalls again the new Exodus story, particularly pertinent in connection with rescue from the dragon and its monsters (see also 15:2–4, where the people of the new Exodus will sing the Song of Moses and the Lamb). Only those who have been described elsewhere as dwelling in heaven rather than earth (e.g. 12:12) **could learn this song**. This does not imply divine predetermination, an exclusion of a section of humanity from the heavenly chorus. Rather, the emphasis of the **could** is upon human response. It is not insignificant that a derivative of the verb **learn** (μανθάνω) is used by the New Testament to describe disciples of Jesus (μαθητής). To learn this song demands a particular disposition of discipleship, a sympathy for its sentiments. One who is enslaved to the monster, whose priorities are elsewhere, cannot begin to understand it, let alone learn its words. It is as impossible as saying 'Jesus is Lord' without the Holy Spirit (1 Cor. 12:3).

Is it possible to be any clearer about the content of this new song? Two antecedents may help here. The first is Ps. 96:1–3, where the 'new song' describes the saving deeds of Israel's king. The second is within the pages of the Apocalypse itself. At 5:9–10 we hear the content of the new song sung by the twenty-four elders: it is a song in praise of the Lamb who redeemed them by being slaughtered, and who made human beings sharers in God's royal rule and priests, to reign on earth (cf. 15:3–4). The content of that heavenly song has now come to pass in what John sees, and is manifested on earth in the liturgical assemblies of the followers of the Lamb. The Lamb on Mount Zion is accompanied by his worshippers, who are reigning with it in its spiritual capital, and (as will become clear) ministering as priests.

It is only appropriate that the Lamb's new world order should be proclaimed in song. Song has been an important part of the heavenly, angelic liturgy so far. Moreover, it had for centuries been a central part of the worship of God's people Israel, both in the psalms of the Temple cult and in the laments of the Exile. On a wider canvas, singing has often played a central role in sustaining an alternative vision in the face of political and religious oppression. Protest songs continue to nourish the souls of nations and the beliefs of threatened minorities. The followers of the Lamb too sing a potent if subversive song of the Kingdom of God.

4–5 The subsequent description of the one hundred and forty-four thousand is ambiguous and, on the surface at least, highly problematic. First, they are described as **the ones who have not made themselves ritually unclean** (or 'have not polluted themselves': cf. the unsoiled garments of the faithful Sardians at 3:4) **with women.** If this is taken literally, as it often has been in the text's reception history, it can have the effect either of disparaging Christian marriage or of demeaning women. Patristic commentators sometimes understood this passage as privileging celibates over ordinary Christians, regarding the former as a higher calling (Kovacs and Rowland 2004: 161f.). They took the Greek παρθένοι, here translated **chaste,** in its more usual sense of 'virgins'.

Difficulties with this kind of literal reading underlie the comment of R. H. Charles that the bulk of verses 4–5 is to be regarded as the work of a 'monkish interpolator' (Charles 1920: II, 9). More recently, attention has focused on the negative potential of such a verse for attitudes towards and even action against women (e.g. Pippin 1994: 119). If read in a literal way, even female Christians would be excluded from the one hundred and forty-four thousand, and therefore from the new Jerusalem. These critical concerns cannot be ignored, nor the wider question of whether ultimately the Apocalypse is bad news for women, producing effects which are destructive and even violent (for further discussion, see Additional Note 3, pp. 249–251).

However, a symbolic reinterpretation of the one hundred and forty-four thousand has already been argued for in the commentary on Revelation 7. Moreover, there are two further resonances to this language (conveyed in the translation **ritually unclean**), both of which are susceptible to a non-literal reading. The first picks up on the location on Mount Zion, where the Temple cult is performed. In this web of associations, those with the Lamb on Mount Zion are priests, in a state of ritual purity to perform their sacrificial duties (cf. Lev. 15:18). Those ransomed by the Lamb have already been described as 'priests' as well as kings (1:6; 5:10). However, within the symbolic world which Revelation creates, the sacrifice they offer is nothing less than their own lives. Hence, they are also described in terms associated with the sacrifices themselves. They are **first-fruits offered to God and to the Lamb**, the first crop of the harvest, or the first-born of the flock, offered in sacrifice to God (Exod. 23:19; Lev. 23:9–14; Deut. 18:4; 26:1–11). In the New Testament, the phrase 'first-fruits' contains the hope of more yet to come (e.g. Rom. 16:5; 1 Cor. 15:20, 23; 16:15), and here too one might detect a hopeful sign that the apparent dominance of the monster over humanity will be transformed into a glorious and universal victory of the Lamb. The one hundred and forty-four thousand are also **without blemish**: the Greek adjective ἄμωμος is used in cultic contexts of sacrificial animals (e.g. in the LXX of Lev. 1:3; 9:2; Num. 28:19; and Ezek. 43:25; Lev. 23:9–14 combines the notion of the first-fruits with an unblemished lamb). In a Christian context, 1 Pet. 1:19 uses the same word to speak of Christ's death as like that of a lamb without blemish. The call of Christians to faithful witness requires a state of readiness appropriate to that of the temple priesthood, while the possibility that witness will end in death transforms the priests into sacrificial victims.

The second, complementary resonance is that of holy war. A battle is under way, between the monster and the Lamb's followers. It is primarily a war of words: the truth spoken by the Lamb and its followers versus the lies spouted by the dragon and its accomplices. Hence it is said of the one hundred and forty-four thousand that **no lie is found in their mouths** (cf. 1 Pet. 2:22, where a similar claim is made for Christ, quoting from Isa. 53:9). The lie is that idolatry is harmless, that compromise is possible and even beneficial, that it does not destroy the soul. Idolatry is often described metaphorically in the biblical tradition as sexual immorality or infidelity (e.g. Jer. 2:1–4; Ezekiel 16; 23; Hosea 1—3; 'Jezebel' in Thyatira), and the avoidance of such idolatrous liaisons is implied here. But the holy war tradition is not far in the background. The list of the tribes at 7:4–8, when the one hundred and forty-four thousand were sealed, is essentially a military roll-call. In their second appearance here they are again ready for battle, fulfilling the purity regulations required as much for participation in the holy war as for maintaining the Temple cult (e.g. Deuteronomy 20; 23:9–10; 1 Sam. 21:5; 2 Sam. 11:11; A. Y. Collins 1977: 248). The Qumran War Scroll puts it this way, setting out the requirements for human participation in the great battle between good and evil:

> No boy or woman shall enter their camps, from the time they leave Jerusalem and march out to war until they return. No man who is lame, or blind, or crippled, or afflicted with a lasting bodily blemish, or smitten with a bodily impurity, none of these shall march out to war with them. They shall all be freely enlisted for war, perfect in spirit and body and prepared for the Day of Vengeance. And no man shall go down with them on the day of battle who is impure because of his 'fount', for the holy angels shall be their hosts. (1QM 7:3–6; Vermes 1997: 170)

Similarly, the Apocalypse places harsh demands on those who would join the Lamb's army. Taken literally, these would be celibate male Israelites; in the symbolic world of Revelation, these are males and females, adults and children, rich and poor, Jew and Gentile, called from every people and tribe, language and nation. What they have in common is that they are prepared to **follow the Lamb wherever it goes**, even into battle, out of which they might not come with their lives intact. Even if Revelation does not presuppose a contemporary situation of violent persecution and martyrdom, it certainly represents a call to arms whereby martyrdom might become a greater possibility. Hence it is appropriate that among the earliest interpretations of this passage there is one which links it to actual martyrdom: the death of Vettius Epagathus, in the *Letter from Vienne and Lyons* (cited in Eus. *H. E.* 5.1.10). The meeting with the Lamb on Mount Zion is at one and the same time a call-up to a military barracks and a summons to offer temple sacrifice. But it is a call which, as Vettius Epagathus discovered, could cost nothing less than one's life.

Interlude 3: The Three Angels   (14:6–13)

(6) Then I saw another angel flying high in the sky, with an eternal gospel to announce to those whose seat is on the earth, to every nation and tribe, language and people. (7) He called out in a loud voice: 'Fear God, and give him glory, because the hour for his judgement has arrived! Worship the one who made heaven and earth, the sea and the springs of waters!'

(8) Then another angel, a second one, followed him crying: 'She has fallen! Babylon the great has fallen! She who made all the nations drink the wine of her flagrant sexual immorality!'

(9) Yet another angel, a third, followed these two, crying in a loud voice: 'Anyone who worships the monster or its statue, or receives a branded mark on the forehead or the hand, (10) will drink the wine of God's fury, poured unmixed into the cup of his anger. Such a one will be tormented in fire and sulphur in the presence of the holy angels and of the Lamb. (11) The smoke from their torment ascends for ever and ever; those who worship the monster and its statue, or receive the branded mark showing its name, will enjoy no rest either by day or by night.'

(12) This calls for the perseverance of the holy ones, that is, those who keep God's commandments and continue the faithfulness of Jesus!

(13) Then I heard a voice from heaven saying: 'Write this: happy are the dead who die in the Lord from now on!' The Spirit responded: 'Yes indeed! They shall have rest from their hard work! For what they have done follows them.'

The fourth and fifth trumpet visions had been separated by an interlude describing an eagle 'flying high in the sky', which proclaimed the three forthcoming woes. This had the effect of heightening the dramatic tension, and raising certain expectations about what was to follow in the three remaining trumpets. At the same point in this new sequence of visions, three angels emerge, the first of which maintains the same position **high in the sky** as the eagle of 8:13. They anticipate the coming judgement, summarising events which will be described in more detail in the remainder of the book: the bittersweet gospel of God's Kingdom – and the hour for his judgement – which is still being proclaimed to those attached to the earth (experienced negatively in the plagues of 15:5—16:21); the fall of Babylon (17:1—19:10); the destruction of the monster and the judgement of those associated with it (19:11—20:15).

6–7 The first angel is **another angel**: if we leave aside Michael and his angels at 12:7–9, and the vague allusion to angelic choirs in 14:1–5, the last angel mentioned was the archangel with the seventh trumpet (11:15). This description differentiates him from that trumpet-angel (and possibly also from the previous six), though no more is stated about his identity. Perhaps more significant is the fact that he is the first of a group of three, the number of the divine (e.g. 1:4, 8; 4:8; cf. 21:13). Although all unfallen angels act on behalf of God, here their role as 'messengers' (the root meaning of ἄγγελος) is stressed: it is appropriate that there are three of them, given the directness and importance of the divine message they announce.

Like the eagle of the three woes, this first angel is **flying high in the sky** (in the zenith, literally 'in mid-heaven'), presumably where he can be readily seen by all. Although the Judaeo-Christian tradition, and popular imagination, envisages angels as flying beings, this is the only angel in the whole book explicitly described as in flight. He has **an eternal gospel to announce**: 'eternal' (αἰώνιον) perhaps denoting its enduring quality, like the one whose message it is, who lives εἰς τοὺς αἰῶνας τῶν αἰώνων (10:6). This is the sole occurrence of the noun εὐαγγέλιον in Revelation. However, the related verb εὐαγγελίζω was found on the lips of the powerful angel with the little scroll at 10:7, describing God's secret plan revealed to the prophets. Thus the content of this **eternal gospel** must be essentially the same as that made known (though perhaps not made clear) to God's servants like Ezekiel and Daniel. In other words, it must encapsulate God's secret purposes of 'what must soon take place', now made possible by the slaughter and resurrection of the Lamb. The contents of the Lamb's scroll have begun to unfold in visionary form since John devoured it at 10:10 (see especially the summary of it in 11:1–13). Here it is summarised in the angel's message: **the hour for his judgement has arrived!** The 'good news' of the establishment of God's royal rule of peace and justice is a message of judgement (κρίσις), for it divides humanity into those who joyfully embrace it and those whose world and commitments fall apart in its wake (Jn 9:39; 12:31). For those whose world needs turning around, it brings with it a call to repentance (Mk 1:15).

Thus the **eternal gospel** is addressed specifically **to those whose seat is on the earth** (a variant on the more usual 'those who make their home on the earth'). The phrase describes those whose world is rooted to earth, currently being ravaged by the dragon and its monsters, rather than directed to heaven, where God reigns on the throne. Elsewhere in Revelation those seated in the earthly realm are those hostile to God: the destructive horsemen seated on horses (albeit used for God's ultimate purposes: 6:2, 4, 5, 8; 9:17); Babylon seated on many waters (17:1, 15) and on the seven-headed monster

(17:3, 9; 18:7). In contrast are those seated in heaven: God and the twenty-four elders, seated on thrones (4:2, 3, 4, 9; 5:1, 7, 13; 6:16; 7:10, 15; 11:16; 19:4; 20:4, 11; 21:5); 'someone like a son of man' seated on a cloud (14:14, 16); Christ the heavenly warrior seated on his white horse (19:11, 19, 21). The addressees of the message are further defined as belonging **to every nation and tribe, language and people**. These are the groups from which the diverse followers of the Lamb are called (e.g. 5:9; 7:9). The repetition of this phrase here, in the context of a call to **Fear God, and give him glory** (cf. 11:13), suggests that the work of redemption has not yet been completed. Even on the verge of the Judgement, the urgent voice of heaven still calls out to humanity to think again and acknowledge the God for whom it was made and in whom it finds its true destiny: **the one who made heaven and earth, the sea and the springs of waters** (a variation on Revelation's normal threefold division of creation into heaven, earth and sea).

There may be a further dimension to the **eternal gospel**, particularly pertinent to those Christians hearing this book in the great Roman cities of Asia. The language of 'good tidings' or 'gospels' was regularly used as part of the imperial propaganda, especially in relation to the emperor himself. A famous inscription from the first century, first discovered at Priene south of Ephesus but subsequently attested also in four other cities of Asia Minor, refers to the 'birthday of our god' (Augustus) as signalling the 'beginning of good news' (using the plural εὐαγγέλια: Stanton 2004: 25–33). It is unbelievable that those living in the urban centres of proconsular Asia would not hear John's echoes of this language loud and clear, particularly after a succession of visions which have unmasked Rome and its associates as in league with Satan himself. Again, the Apocalypse shows itself a highly subversive book, proclaiming a rival and eternal gospel besides which those transitory and ultimately dehumanising 'good tidings' of the empire fade into oblivion.

The **second** herald-angel now makes his appearance. His task is to **8** announce the fall of Babylon the great, whose identity and demise will be presented in great visionary detail in Revelation 17 and 18. The announcement here is a proleptic one, assuring God's people of the future certainty of what is being proclaimed in the Greek past tense. In chapter 17, Babylon will particularly bear the features of the city and empire of Rome. Yet Rome was only the latest incarnation of this oppressive and idolatrous city, and cannot exhaust her meaning. The angel's opening words – **She has fallen! Babylon the great has fallen!** – evoke Isa. 21:9, although Revelation's preference for the Greek aorist over Isaiah's perfect tense accentuates the completed nature – proleptically described – of the city's fall. It is a reminder that Babylon already had a long history before imperial Rome emerged on the scene (the author of Daniel had already seen her in the persecutory activity of the Greek Antiochus Epiphanes). Moreover, **Babylon is the great**, identifying her as the 'great city' which can be encountered in every age and in every location on the face of the earth (see on 11:8).

Great emphasis will be placed in Revelation 17 upon Babylon's drunkenness and debauchery. The metaphorical nature of such charges will be clear, focusing especially on her idolatrous claims and her thirst for shedding innocent blood (e.g. 17:2, 4, 6). Power and the adulation of power are, like wine, addictive, and here the angel exploits this fact to liken the cause of Babylon's fall to a drunken orgy: **She has made all the nations drink the wine of her flagrant sexual immorality!** Again, the language is scriptural. Jeremiah 51:7 spoke of Babylon as an instrument of God's judgement, a gold cup in his hand from which the nations drank, causing them to go mad. On the one hand, Revelation views Babylon not as an instrument of God but God's archetypal enemy, institutionalised in a political system. On the other hand, there may be a hint that Babylon's wine – which is her extravagant and arrogant idolatry (the metaphorical use of πορνεία) – does indeed become the vehicle of divine judgement. The phrase **her flagrant sexual immorality** is literally 'the fury of her fornication', evoking the fury (θυμός) of God, which will react against what Babylon has done not only to herself but to the world's population by forcing them to drink her wine (14:10, 19; 15:1, 7; 16:1, 19; 19:15). The whole world idolises her, but ultimately not by free choice. Nor, however, is Babylon free: the web of seduction and mutual dependence between city and allies – here designated by **all the nations** – will be a repeated aspect of the Babylon motif in chapters to follow.

Feminist critics have made the present generation acutely sensitive to the way in which feminine language and imagery function in passages such as this (e.g. Pippin 1992; Fiorenza 1991: 12–15). On the one hand, there is a need to be attuned to ancient conventions whereby cities were regularly portrayed in female terms. Contemporary parallels are the British tendency to use the feminine pronoun of ships, or the well-established male personification of 'Old Father Thames'. On the other, there is a need to attend to the negative effects of Revelation's androcentric stereotyping of women. This is particularly so in the case of Babylon, who is described from an overtly misogynist perspective as a drunken yet seductive prostitute: the object simultaneously of male desire and male revulsion. To ignore the metaphorical nature of the language here is to open the door to readings which are at best irresponsible, at worst downright dangerous.

The **third** and final herald-angel now follows them, proclaiming his 9–11
message in an equally **loud voice**, ensuring that it is heard by all
humanity. It is the ultimate word of warning, setting out the dire
consequences of worshipping the monster, whether in the political
system itself (**the monster**) or its religious (**statue**) or economic
aspects (**branded mark**). Those who participate to any degree in
such worship will not only find themselves sucked into the drunken
debauchery associated with Babylon; they will also find themselves
drinking **the wine of God's fury, poured unmixed into the cup
of his anger**. In the Old Testament, drinking from a cup is a frequent symbol of anger and judgement (cf. Job 21:20; Ps. 75:8; Isa.
51:17; Jer. 25:15–26; 49:12; Ezek. 23:31–34). It is **unmixed** in that it
is undiluted, not watered down as wine so often was, but full
strength. Furious indeed is the divine reaction to idolatrous worship
(although the **anger** of God, ὀργή, as opposed to the more emotive
fury, θυμός, describes his impersonal reaction against what should
not be: cf. Rom. 1:18; 3:5). It requires endless torments. Many indeed
have found this passage a passage too far, morally objectionable and
unworthy of the gospel of Christ. D. H. Lawrence famously put it
thus: 'They could not be happy in heaven unless they *knew* their
enemies were unhappy in hell' (Lawrence 1931: 186; italics his).

Understanding the rhetorical function of this angelic announcement is crucial. Revelation employs shock tactics to dissuade faithful
Christian hearers from even the hint of compromise, and to wake up
the compromisers to the reality of the dangerous road on which they
have embarked. False gods will tolerate no rivals, but demand
wholehearted submission, as does the true God. Even dipping one's
toe into an idolatrous system is a perilous step. Sooner or later one
will find oneself enmeshed in the whole web, implicated in the same
immorality, injustice and idolatrous self-absorption for which the
monster must ultimately be destroyed. John articulates the shocking
consequences with such rhetorical panache that one would be fool-
hardy to ignore it: **Such a one will be tormented in fire and
sulphur in the presence of the holy angels and of the Lamb**
(the imagery has been influenced by that of the destruction of Sodom
and Gomorrah: Gen. 19:24–26; cf. Isa. 30:33; Ezek. 38:22). The
contrast with the prayers of the holy ones is obvious. The latter
ascend with the smoke of sweet-smelling incense before the throne
(8:4), around which the four creatures sing the Trisagion ceaselessly
day and night (4:8). Those tormented in the fire and foul-smelling
sulphur **enjoy no rest either by day or by night; the smoke
from their torment ascends for ever and ever**. The juxtaposition
of the two suggests an intimate connection between the prayers being
heard and the torments of those associated with the monster (cf. 6:9–
11). Unlike some apocalypses, however, Revelation holds back from

allowing the redeemed themselves to witnesses the torments of their oppressors (contrast *1 En.* 27:3; *Apocalypse of Peter* 7—8; and implicitly *4 Ez.* 7:36–38, 88–93).

Yet it is not as if the angel's warning presents God's desire for humanity. Rather it reveals, albeit in non-literal, visionary language, the bitter fruit which idolatry ultimately bears. What is not God – however much it presents itself as God – cannot deliver what only God can offer: freedom from enslavement, peaceful rest, eternal life. It can only pull humanity down into its own destructive destiny, the lake of fire and sulphur (19:20; 20:10; 21:8).

12–13 The sense of urgency raised by the three angels is backed up by another call for **perseverance** (see 13:10; cf. 13:18; 17:9), and the second of Revelation's seven beatitudes. **The holy ones**, those 'set apart' by their faithful witness to God and rejection of the monster, must exhibit the same perseverance as John (1:9) on his island exile. Temptations to waver and compromise must be resisted. The wording is similar to the call at 13:10, but expanded as it spells out what this perseverance means. The 'faithfulness' of the holy ones is interpreted as **the faithfulness of Jesus**, his fidelity to his mission (τὴν πίστιν 'Ιησοῦ understood as a subjective genitive: so also 'the witness of Jesus' at 1:2, 9; 19:10; 20:4; cf. 6:9). Moreover, it also involves keeping **God's commandments**. Death in fidelity to the commandments of God is a regular feature of Jewish stories about the martyrs (e.g. 4 Macc. 9:1; 16:24); in the present context, the first commandment, with its rejection of idolatry (Exod. 20:1–6; Deut. 5:6–10), would be particularly to the fore.

The beatitude in verse 13 is the first since the prologue at 1:3. As if to emphasise the note of urgency as the book reaches its conclusion, they will appear with increasing regularity from now on (16:15; 19:9; 20:6; 22:7, 14). This beatitude is introduced by an unnamed **voice from heaven**, which commands John to **write**. That this is the voice of Christ is suggested by the parallel at 1:11, where the voice of the 'someone like a son of man' commands John to 'write' in a scroll (cf. also 10:4, where the voice, possibly the voice of Christ, orders John *not* to write). The punctuation around the phrase **from now on** (ἀπ' ἄρτι) is unclear, but the phrase is probably to be taken with the preceding clause. Hence the beatitude runs: **happy are the dead who die in the Lord from now on!** But even this is difficult, for it might imply that only those 'from this point' are blessed, ruling out even the 'souls under the altar'. Yet the latter must be included, because they have already been granted rest (6:11). Rather, 'from now on' must refer to the eschatological 'now', that is, from the time of the death and resurrection of the Lamb. This Lamb is now identified as **the Lord** (11:8; 17:14; 19:16; 22:20, 21), who offers rest to all his faithful dead. It is a word of reassurance to early Christian communities, for whom the deaths of loved ones prior to the Lord's return raised difficult questions (see e.g. 1 Thess. 4:13–18); it has particular poignancy for those confronted with the onslaught of the monster.

In a kind of liturgical dialogue, **the Spirit** responds, for the first time since the sevenfold voice of the Spirit in the messages to the seven congregations (2:7, 11, 17, 29; 3:6, 13, 22), and the last until 22:17. The dead, associated with their slaughtered but risen Lord, **shall have rest from their hard work.** Again, Revelation's 'realised eschatology' breaks through, as they are promised an experience already of the eschatological sabbath rest (e.g. Heb. 4:1–3; *2 Bar.* 85:9). Emphasis has been placed upon work as maintaining faithful witness in the messages to the seven congregations (2:2, 19; 3:1, 8, 15), the appropriate response to the call of God. Working to maintain that witness, even in the face of the fiercest opposition, is not in vain: **For what they have done follows them.**

Fifth Vision: The Harvest of Someone Like a (14:14–16)
Son of Man

(14) Then I looked, and there was a white cloud, with someone like a son of man seated on it. He had a golden wreath on his head, and in his hand there was a sharp sickle. (15) Then another angel came out of the sanctuary, crying out in a loud voice to the one seated on the cloud: 'Use your sickle and reap the harvest, because the hour for harvesting has arrived, and the earth's crop is ripe for harvest!' (16) So the one seated on the cloud put his sickle to work over the earth, and the earth was harvested.

This sequence of visions continues with two very similar scenes, picking up on the well-established imagery of harvesting to describe the Judgement. The first suggests a grain harvest, for it involves the use of a sickle. The second (in verses 17–20) concerns a harvest of grapes. The two may have been suggested by a passage from Joel: 'Send in the sickle, for the harvest is ripe. Come, trample, for the winepress is full' (Joel 3:13). But they both also evoke a rich interpretative tradition within early Christianity, traceable to Jesus himself, for which the language of harvesting was a potent symbol both for the judgement of Israel and of humanity, consequent upon the arrival of God's eschatological kingdom (e.g. Mt. 9:37; 13:30, 39; Mk 4:29; Jn 4:35).

14–16 But if Joel has inspired the subject matter, Daniel has once again provided much of the imagery. The vision of 'someone like a son of man' coming to the Ancient of Days is clearly in the background (Dan. 7:13–14). Two main interpretative questions are raised by this vision. The first is the identity of the figure described as **someone like a son of man**. Is he the same as the heavenly son of man figure at 1:12–20, who is to be identified with Jesus Christ? Or is he a lesser angelic figure, described in this way because he resembles a human being (the original meaning of this phrase at Dan. 7:13)? Some might find it problematic that Christ could apparently take orders from a lesser being (the angel from the sanctuary), and thus prefer the angelic identification. Yet this becomes less problematic if we understand the angel as coming **out of the sanctuary**, that is directly from the presence of God, to give an order to the expectant Christ from the throne itself. Others note that there are six angels referred to as such in 14:6–20, and that therefore the son of man figure must be a seventh angel, or that the description of this particular figure differs significantly from other portrayals of Christ (e.g. Kiddle 1940: 275–77).

Yet there are good reasons for preferring the identification of this son of man figure with Christ himself. First, there are the obvious echoes of Daniel 7: not only the 'someone like a son of man' phrase but also the mention of **a white cloud** ('someone like a son of man' comes with the clouds of heaven at Dan. 7:13). The Danielic figure has been identified with Christ in Revelation 1, and this provides the interpretative framework within which this vision would most readily be interpreted. Second, the portrayal of Christ as the Son of Man coming with, in or on clouds or a cloud is clearly found elsewhere in the New Testament (e.g. Mt. 24:30; 26:64; Mk 13:26; 14:62; Lk. 21:27). Moreover, in one of these parallels the Son of Man is said to be **seated**, albeit at the right hand of God rather than on a cloud (Mk 14:62, probably under the influence of Ps. 110:1: Smalley 2005: 371). All these parallels present Christ in a parousia context, as he comes in judgement and vindication, sometimes with his angels (cf. 1 Thess. 4:16–17). They cohere with this vision's harvest motif, which is associated with the coming judgement.

Moreover, although the description of this figure does not quite match the description of 'someone like a son of man' at 1:12–20, that is not decisive given the diversity of portrayals of Christ throughout the Apocalypse (e.g. 5:6–7; 12:5; 14:1–5; 19:11–16). On the contrary, the **white cloud** and **gold wreath** are both appropriate accompaniments to a Christophany. White elsewhere in the Apocalypse is the colour of heaven and victory: either could be the resonance here, although the fact that he also wears a gold wreath on his head favours the latter. He is a heavenly figure of victory, like the returning Christ who comes to initiate the judgement on God's behalf. The **sharp sickle** is an appropriate tool for the harvesting Christ, who will wield a 'sharp sword' in the battle scene at 19:15 (the sickle is derived from the judgement scene at Joel 3:13; cf. Mk 4:29).

The second main question about this vision is the nature of the harvest being reaped. What is happening when **the one seated on the cloud** puts **his sickle to work over the earth?** That the Judgement is implied is clear: there is a strong literary parallel between the phrase **the hour for harvesting has arrived** and the announcement of the first herald-angel that 'the hour for his judgement has arrived' at 14:7. But who are being harvested: the righteous, the wicked (as in verses 17–20), or both?

The Matthean parable of the wheat and the tares offers a vision of eschatological harvesting in which, in the reaping of a grain crop, righteous and unrighteous are harvested/judged simultaneously (Mt. 13:41–43). It is possible that John, without knowledge of Matthew, has understood the harvest motif in a similar way, and that both elect and wicked are being judged together. Alternatively, the wicked alone may be at issue here also. **The earth's crop** is specifically mentioned as **ripe for harvest**, and 'earth' has often functioned in Revelation to mark those who are rebellious towards God (e.g. 'those who make their home on the earth'; 'earth's kings'; the 'whole earth' associated with the monster at 13:3, 12).

However, there are good grounds for viewing this first harvest scene as the harvesting of the righteous. First, a number of New Testament passages use harvesting imagery to describe the successful preaching of the Church (e.g. Lk. 10:2; Jn 4:35–38), while Mk 13:26–27 envisages a gathering in of the elect when the Son of Man comes in clouds. Second, this harvest scene and that of the grape harvest have different antecedents earlier in this chapter. The harvest of the earth picks up on the description of the one hundred and forty-four thousand as 'first-fruits' for God and the Lamb (14:4), while the treading of the winepress associated with the grape harvest explicitly picks up on the wine of Babylon, and the corresponding cup of God's anger (14:8, 10). Third, the grain harvest is a one-stage affair, involving reaping, which is not a negative image of judgement, whereas the grape harvest involves both gathering and trampling (see 16:14 and 19:15; cf. 19:17–21). Finally, it is Christ as the son of man figure who performs the (positive) reaping of the grain harvest, whereas in the grape harvest Christ performs only the second stage, that of judgement after the gathering-in (Bauckham 1993b: 94–98). In short, the vision described here is a vision of salvation, in contrast to what is yet to come.

Nonetheless, it is important to recall the wider literary context within which this harvesting is set. It has been heralded by a wake-up call from three flying angels, the first of whom explicitly prepares the earth for the approaching judgement. The reader of the Apocalypse might reasonably ask whether that call had gone totally unheeded, or whether the reaping of the earth might after all have been more successful in its wake, despite the best efforts to the contrary of the dragon and its monstrous accomplices.

Sixth Vision: The Grape Harvest (14:17–20)

(17) Then another angel came out of the sanctuary which is in heaven, and he also had a sharp sickle. (18) Yet another angel came out from the area of the altar (the one who has authority over the fire), and called in a loud voice to the one with the sharp sickle: 'Use your sharp sickle and gather the bunches of grapes from the vineyard which is the earth, for its grapes are ripe.' (19) So the angel put his sickle to work on the earth, and gathered the vintage of the earth. He threw it into the great winepress of God's fury. (20) The winepress was trodden outside the city; blood flowed out from the winepress, as high as horses' bridles, for a distance of one thousand six hundred stadia.

17–18 After the victory comes the description of judgement. The prophecy of Joel has pointed to the negative aspect of this scene: 'The wine-vats are overflowing, for great is their wickedness' (Joel 3:13c). It is inaugurated by **another angel** who comes **out of the sanctuary which is in heaven**. This may suggest that he has some priestly role (and there may be a hint that his mission is in response to the prayers of the holy ones, still rising before the throne in that sanctuary). Just as significantly, like his counterpart in verse 15, he comes directly out from God, from whom presumably he has received his **sharp sickle**. The specific command for him to **gather the bunches of grapes** comes from yet another angel, who emerges **from the area of the altar** (literally 'from the altar'), synonymous with the sanctuary itself. This angel is further identified as **the one who has authority over the fire**. *Jubilees.* 2:2 lists a number of angels and their appointed tasks, among them 'angels of the spirit of fire'. But the reference here is probably more specific. At 8:3–5 we have already encountered an angel associated with fire: the angel who takes fiery coals from the altar and throws them to the earth, heralding the seven trumpet-plagues. This priestly angel, closely associated with the prayers of the holy ones, makes his appearance once again at this crucial stage of the eschatological gathering and judgement.

The fire angel gives the authoritative command, presumably received from the throne (hence his **loud voice**): '**Use your sharp** sickle and gather the bunches of grapes from the vineyard which is the earth, for its grapes are ripe.' Jewish-Christian audiences might be somewhat taken aback by the description of the vineyard as 'the earth', given the well-established association of the vineyard with Israel (e.g. Isa. 5:1–10; 27:2; Jer. 12:10; Ezek. 19:10). Revelation's canvas is a broad canvas indeed, embracing the whole earth in terms of both judgement and salvation.

The vintage of the earth, once harvested, has to be trampled. The 19–20 winepress being used, however, is **the great winepress of God's fury** (19:15; cf. Isa. 63:3; Lam. 1:15). This description recalls the messages of the last two herald-angels, who spoke respectively of the wine of Babylon's fornication, and 'the wine of God's fury' that the worshippers of the monster will be forced to drink. The trampling judgement of those who have rejected such a last-minute call to repentance is being played out in technicolour: **blood flowed out from the winepress, as high as horses' bridles, for a distance of one thousand six hundred stadia.** One stade is the length of a Greek athletics stadium, approximately 185 metres, giving a wildly extravagant distance for the flow of red blood which the grapes produce. The precise significance of this number is unclear, though it has been noted that 1,600 is the square of 40, a number associated with punishment in the forty days and nights of Noah's flood. Alternatively, it reflects humanity, whose blood it measures, being the square of the universe's number 4 multiplied by the square of 10. Given John's complex numerology elsewhere, one should not be swift to rule this out (on this see Bauckham 1993a: 384–407). The treading of the winepress here represents a direct response to the trampling of the holy city by the nations at 11:2.

Nevertheless, there are hints of a more subtle thread running through this vision. Strangely, we are told that **the winepress was trodden outside the city.** Is it located here because it is a direct punishment for the crucifixion of Jesus 'outside the city' of Jerusalem (cf. Heb. 13:12)? Or are we witnessing in visionary terms that crucifixion itself? Is the **blood** pouring out from the winepress in impossible amounts the blood of the damned, or is it Christ's own blood? Christians hearing this read out as part of a eucharistic assembly might well raise this as a possibility. The same question will raise its head at 19:13, where the Word of God will ride out with his robe dipped in blood even before battle has been engaged. That judgement is taking place in this scene is not in doubt. But is that judgement supplementary to the cross of Christ, or is his cross itself, and the blood of his witnesses, judgement enough?

Seventh Vision: The Song of the New Exodus (15:1–4)

(1) Then I saw another sign in heaven, a great and marvellous sign: seven angels with seven plagues! These are the last plagues, because by them God's fury has been brought to completion. (2) I also saw something like a sea of glass mixed with fire, and standing on the sea of glass those who conquer the monster and its statue and the number of its name. They held harps given to them by God, (3) and they sang the song of God's servant Moses, and the song of the Lamb:

'Great and marvellous are your deeds,
Lord, God Almighty!
Just and true are your ways,
King of the nations!
(4) Who will not revere, Lord,
and glorify your name?
For you only are holy.
All the nations will come
and worship before you,
For your just judgements have been made clear!'

This latest sequence of visions began with the opening of the heavenly sanctuary, and the appearance of a 'great sign' (11:19—12:1). It is appropriate that this cycle should draw to its close with the appearance of another **great and marvellous sign**. Both visions recall the story of the (new) Exodus, which runs as a key thread through the Apocalypse tapestry: the woman has been pursued by the dragon into the wilderness, where she is nourished by God in the place prepared for her; here the victorious followers of the Lamb stand beside a glassy sea recalling the song which Moses sang after the glorious deliverance through another sea (Exod. 15:1–18; cf. Deut. 32:1–43). But just as the seals and trumpets sequences were intimately bound together (8:1–6), with the trumpets emerging out of the seventh seal and overlapping significantly with the sixth, so the reference to the **seven angels with seven plagues** prepares John's audiences for the new sequence of bowls (15:5—19:10). This new sequence has already been anticipated in the calls of the three herald-angels, which reviewed the final judgement which the bowls will represent (14:6–7; cf. 15:5—16:21), announced proleptically the fall of Babylon (14:8; cf. 17:1—19:10), and foretold the dire consequences of worshipping the monster (14:9–11; cf. 19:11—20:15). Now the familiar cycle – known especially from the trumpet-plagues and made clearer in the revelation of the Lamb's scroll – is about to begin once more.

Again the action is taking in place **in heaven**, from which per- 1
spective (the only true perspective) the earthly battle with the
monster is now being viewed. The sense that the Apocalypse is, after
so many false alarms, at last reaching its climax is marked by the
description of this new sign as **great and marvellous**. We are not
told whether the **seven angels** are the same as the seven archangels
with the trumpets (8:2—11:18), though there is nothing to rule this
out. It would be appropriate for the archangels to perform this
function also, particularly given the key role of Michael in expelling
Satan from heaven (12:7–9).

The plagues of the seven angels are **the last plagues, because by
them God's fury has been brought to completion** (the aorist
ἐτελέσθη is proleptic, describing the plagues as if they have already
taken place). The reference to God's fury evokes 'the wine of God's
fury', which is the inevitable divine response to a world seduced by
the monster into a web of idolatry and injustice (see on 14:9–11).
Such things cannot be allowed to stand, and the prayers of the holy
ones have called for just such a divine response. But in what sense are
these plagues **the last plagues?** This adjective might be regarded as
supporting a chronological reading of Revelation: these are last in that
they follow sequentially on the seals and trumpets. Yet the difficulties
with this view have been noted already. More likely, 'last' describes
the nature of these plagues: they are the eschatological plagues
(whether or not they have been described before), about to be presented in this book for the final time.

The seven angels have been introduced in order to prepare for what 2
is to follow. Yet before that action begins to unfold, John's narrative
pauses and he presents another scene, which is intended to put the
ensuing plagues into their proper perspective. He describes how he
saw something like a sea of glass mixed with fire. This is the
heavenly 'sea of glass, like crystal' that John first saw before the
throne, suggesting the tamed yet threatening presence of evil close to
that throne (see on 4:6). Here it is described as **mixed with fire**,
presumably giving it a reddish glow. Fire is regularly associated with
the presence of God (e.g. Exod. 24:17; Ezek. 1:27), and in an
interesting parallel Enoch describes passing through a heavenly
palace of fire and snow into the throne-room containing a sea of fire
(*1 En.* 14:13, 22). But this may not be the whole explanation. The fire
may also symbolise the judgements of the plagues about to unfold
(fire is linked with judgement at 8:7, 8; 9:17, 18; 11:5; 14:10; 16:8;
17:16; 18:8; 19:20; 20:10, 14, 15; 21:8). Alternatively, it may evoke the
fiery purging that the Lamb's witnesses have had to undergo as
sacrificial victims (fire is associated with the altar at 8:5 and 14:18).
But however threatening the heavenly sea might have been,

something crucial has happened. At 12:9 Satan was thrown down from heaven, the expulsion of that residual evil lurking near God's throne. Picking up on the Exodus motif which surrounded the vision of the dragon and the woman, the sea has become the Sea of Reeds, through which the people of Israel passed unharmed on their Exodus journey from slavery to freedom. Hence John sees **standing on the sea of glass those who conquer the monster and its statue and the number of its name**. The preposition ἐπὶ, whose root meaning is 'upon', is sometimes translated 'beside' here in conformity with Exodus 15, where Moses and the Israelites sing their song after having passed through the sea. But the translation **on** is preferable here, suggesting the victory achieved over the sea of chaos and, by implication, the dragon and **monster** who belong there. Those **standing on the sea of glass** are the one hundred and forty-four thousand, who have held onto the name marked on their foreheads rather than compromise with the monster in any shape or form, politically, religiously or economically. They are the victorious people of the new Exodus, who in every age and culture maintain their faithful witness.

As a consequence of their victory, they have **harps given to them by God** (literally 'harps of God'), and therefore have gained membership of the angelic choirs (harps are held by the twenty-four elders at 4:8, and played by the unnamed heavenly harpists at 14:2; in contrast, the sound of harpists will no longer be heard in fallen Babylon, 18:22). As members of the heavenly chorus, they are able to sing heavenly songs, most especially the 'new song' of Christ's victory which they learned with the Lamb on Mount Zion (14:1–5).

3–4 Now they sing another song: **the song of God's servant Moses, and the song of the Lamb**. This is not the 'new song' previously learned, for it has no explicitly christological content (unlike the 'new song' of 5:9–10). This suggests that the genitive in the additional phrase **and the song of the Lamb** should be understood, like the previous genitive 'of Moses', as a subjective genitive: both Moses and the Lamb sing this song. In this interpretation, perhaps Christ is being presented as a new Moses, who 'leads' his people to salvation (for the Lamb as leading, see 7:17; cf. 14:4). It is possible that here Christ is the leader of the heavenly choir (Knight 1999: 108; see *Asc. Isa.* 9:1, 4, where an angel is set over the praises of the sixth heaven). Though not explicitly stated as being present, the Lamb may be implied as part of that group which is victorious over the monster.

The song is a song of God's victory and righteous action. In terms of context, the Old Testament antecedent is the song sung by **God's servant Moses** and the Israelites after their triumphant passage through the sea and the destruction of their enemies (Exod. 15:1–18;

for Moses as God's servant, see e.g. Exod. 4:10; 14:31; Dan. 9:11). This after all is the position in which the Lamb's followers now find themselves, brought safely through the sea of the Abyss from which the monster had emerged. The conclusion to this song of Moses has already been alluded to in the heavenly canticle following the seventh trumpet (11:15; cf. Exod. 15:18). Here it is evoked again, and provides the basic thematic outline for the song of the victors (Bauckham 1993b: 99).

But the actual content of Revelation's song is closer to the second song of Moses, uttered prior to his death (Deut. 32:1–43). There is a particularly close parallel between Deut. 32:4 LXX, which speaks of God's deeds as 'true' (ἀληθινὰ), 'his ways' (αἱ ὁδοὶ αὐτοῦ) as judgements, and his character as 'righteous and holy' (δίκαιος καὶ ὅσιος). But the canticle John hears is no mere repetition of Deuteronomy 32, and commentators have detected a wide range of additional echoes of and allusions to Old Testament texts (for a detailed chart, see Reddish 2001: 293).

The song begins by proclaiming the saving actions of God in a parallelism reminiscent of Hebrew poetry: **Great and marvellous are your deeds ... Just and true are your ways**. That they are **great and marvellous** (a phrase which has just been used to describe the heavenly sign of the seven bowl-angels) suggests that the deeds particularly in mind are the plagues that are about to unfold. Moses' song followed on from the plagues of Egypt: the song of Moses and the Lamb is presented before these plagues, though as if they have already taken place. One of Revelation's favourite titles for the one on the throne, **Lord God Almighty** (seven times; also 1:8; 4:8; 11:17; 16:7; 19:6; 21:22), is paralleled by **King of the nations** (Jer. 10:7), proclaiming God's ultimate royal rule even over those who currently resist that rule (e.g. 2:26; 11:2, 18; 12:5; 14:8; 16:19; 19:15; 20:3, 8). Ultimately they will experience the just and wise rule of the true king (21:24, 26; 22:2). The main variant reading 'King of the ages' may well be due to harmonisation under the influence of 1 Tim. 1:17 (the alternative reading 'King of saints', adopted by the AV, does not have strong manuscript support, and could be due to confusing Latin abbreviations for 'ages' and 'saints': see Metzger 1971: 756).

The 'Who is like you, O Lord ...?' of Exod. 15:11 (taken up and parodied by worshippers of the monster at 13:4) has become in the Lamb's song a question about the expected human response to that divine greatness: **Who will not revere, Lord, and glorify your name?** (influenced by two passages with a strongly universalistic strain: Jer. 10:6–7a and Ps. 86:8–10). Far from instilling terror and dismay in the hearts of the pagan nations (Exod. 15:14–16), the song sung by the followers of the Lamb regards the saving acts of God as leading the nations away from worshipping the monster to true worship. Whereas Moses' original song climaxed with Israel coming to worship in the sanctuary on God's holy mountain (Exod. 15:17), Revelation's song envisages that **All the nations will come and worship before you, for your just judgements have been made clear.**

The effect of all this, as Bauckham has shown, is to reinterpret Moses' song in a dramatically universalistic way (Bauckham 1993b: 98–104). *Pace* Bauckham, however, this makes its location *prior* to the bowl-plagues all the more significant. For this song, like other songs in the Apocalypse (e.g. 12:10–12), provides an authoritative commentary on the surrounding action, not least the action about to unfold. This has two implications. First, it encourages the reader to view the new Egyptian plagues from the perspective of the redeemed rather than from that of the punished oppressors. Just as contemporary Christians sing the first song of Moses annually at Easter, not in order to gloat over the destruction of real Egyptians but to give voice to their sense of being set free from universal slavery, so this second song of Moses also articulates the thankfulness of the victors. It functions liturgically in a manner very different from a report of an actual battle. Second, and equally important, it points to the function of these plagues not to punish but to reveal yet again the madness of worshipping the monster, and to lead the nations instead to true worship of the true God. Their vision may be of total destruction; but the proleptic description of them, like a vast and terrifying Apocalypse tapestry, retains the possibility of repentance before it is too late.

5 SEVEN BOWLS   (15:5—19:10)

The climax of John's visionary book is at hand. The previous section concluded with the appearance of the seven bowl-angels, and a statement to the effect that the seven last plagues were at hand. It also reiterated the assurance that God's people would be brought safe through the other side of the turbulent sea, ultimately unscathed by the monster despite physical suffering and perhaps even death. But now the words of the powerful angel that there would be no more delay (10:6) find their (ironically delayed) narrative accomplishment. John will describe another series of seven plagues, in quick succession, and without the element of interruption that has marked the previous septets of the book. On reaching the seventh and final plague, he will then focus in on one major aspect of that plague, and paint a great visionary canvas describing in fascinating detail the fall of the great city Babylon.

Preparation for the Seven Bowl-Plagues   (15:5–8)

(5) After this I looked, and the sanctuary was opened, that is the tabernacle of witness in heaven, (6) and out from the sanctuary came the seven angels with the seven plagues. They were dressed in clean, shining linen, with gold belts wrapped around their breasts. (7) Then one of the four creatures gave the seven angels seven gold bowls full of the fury of God who lives for ever and ever. (8) The sanctuary was filled with smoke from the glory of God and from his power, and no-one could go into the sanctuary until the seven plagues of the seven angels had been brought to completion.

The previous sections have begun with an 'opening' in heaven (4:1; 11:19; cf. 8:1), and concluded with either a liturgical silence or a liturgical hymn (8:1; 11:15–18; 15:3–4). This new sequence of bowl-plagues also starts with an 'opening', that of the heavenly **sanctuary**, which John last saw wide open at 11:19. In the interim, priestly angels have moved in and out of it performing their required tasks (14:15, 17, 18). Now the sanctuary stands open again, allowing John a direct vision of the divine Presence. Lest we forget that the new Exodus of God's people is still under way, Revelation uses an unusual term for the heavenly sanctuary: **the tabernacle of witness** (see e.g. Num. 17:7; 18:2; cf. 17:4 LXX). This is an alternative name for the 'tabernacle [*or* tent] of meeting', where Moses went in before the Lord (described in some detail at Exod. 33:7–11). This earthly tabernacle was a portable shrine carried around by the Exodus generation in the wilderness, marking God's presence with them. The tabernacle that John sees, however, is **in heaven**, where the new Exodus generation has arrived victorious: that there was believed to be a heavenly tabernacle on which the earthly one was modelled is implied at Exod. 25:8–9, and explicitly stated by Heb. 8:5 (cf. Acts 7:44).

The seven angels introduced at 15:1 now emerge **from the sanctuary**, where they have apparently been attired for the task they are to perform. They are **dressed in clean, shining linen, with gold belts wrapped around their breasts**. This is the priestly clothing of Aaron and his sons, appropriate to ministering in the tabernacle (e.g. Exod. 28:39–43; cf. the attire of 'someone like a son of man' at 1:13, whose belt was also gold). Later, the Lamb's bride and his heavenly armies will be clothed in clean shining linen (19:8, 14: though in both these verses βύσσινον rather than λίνον). A variant reading has them wearing a 'stone', like the king of Tyre at Ezek. 28:13, adorned with every precious stone (λίθον instead of λίνον, though this is easily accounted for as a scribal error).

221

7–8 At this point **one of the four creatures** gives the angels **seven gold bowls**. The four creatures played a role in the opening of the first four seals (6:1–8); one of their number appears again here to help inaugurate the bowls sequence, perhaps because these plagues will ultimately affect the whole created order which the four represent in the heavenly realm (one possible reading of 5:8 is that both the four creatures and the twenty-four elders held gold bowls). The gold bowls are those used in cultic worship, for libations or for holding the ashes from the sacrifices (e.g. Exod. 25:29; 27:3; 38:3; Num. 4:14; 1 Chron. 28:17; Zech. 14:20; 1 Macc. 1:22). The bowls here are **full of the fury of God who lives for ever and ever**, highlighting their role as judgements. But their designation as **gold bowls**, and the priestly dress of the seven angels, would suggest that these are not a different set of gold bowls from those originally held by the twenty-four elders, which were explicitly identified as 'the prayers of the holy ones' (5:8). The angels are involved in a complex priestly liturgy whereby 'the prayers of the holy ones' are heard in the heavenly sanctuary, and responded to in the action towards the earth about to take place. This liturgy was first performed at 8:3–5, when the angel with the fire threw the burning thurible to the earth, inaugurating the series of the seven trumpets. It was echoed again at 14:18, when the angel with the fire inaugurated the grape harvest. Now it is to occur once more with the same urgent prayers, now transformed into God's righteous and indignant fury, in the gold bowls of the seven priestly angels.

As when Isaiah saw the Lord enthroned in the Temple (Isa. 6:1–4), the heavenly sanctuary is **filled with smoke from the glory of God and from his power**. The smoke here is presumably the pungent smoke of incense, in contrast to the choking smoke of sulphur (14:10–11), appropriate to a manifestation of the divine glory or Presence. Moses too witnessed the tent of meeting being covered in a cloud and filled with the glory of the Lord, preventing him from entering it (Exod. 40:34–38). As the new Exodus continues, the same smoky cloud fills the heavenly tabernacle, preventing access to it. There must be no interruption now until the prayers of the holy ones are answered and God has decisively acted against wickedness and injustice: **no-one could go into the sanctuary until the seven plagues of the seven angels had been brought to completion.**

The Seven Bowl-Plagues (16:1–21)

(1) Then I heard a loud voice coming from the sanctuary, saying to the seven angels: 'Go and empty out the seven bowls of God's fury onto the earth.'

(2) The first angel went off and emptied out his bowl onto

the earth, and a foul and painful sore erupted on those who had the branded mark of the monster and who worshipped its statue.

(3) The second angel emptied out his bowl into the sea, and it turned to blood, like the blood of a corpse; every living thing in the sea died.

(4) The third angel emptied out his bowl into the rivers and the springs of waters, and they turned to blood.

(5) Then I heard the angel of the waters saying:

'You are just, O Holy One, who are and who were,
because you have made these judgements!
(6) For they shed the blood of holy ones and prophets,
And you have given them blood to drink.
For my holy ones and prophets are worthy!'

(7) Then I heard the altar cry out:

'Yes indeed, Lord God Almighty,
your judgements are true and just!'

(8) The fourth angel emptied out his bowl upon the sun, and it was permitted to scorch people with fire. (9) They were scorched with the intense heat, and blasphemed the name of God who had control over these plagues. But they would not repent or give him glory.

(10) The fifth angel emptied out his bowl upon the throne of the monster; the monster's royal rule was thrown into darkness. People bit their tongues in pain, (11) and they blasphemed the God of heaven for their pain and their sores. But they would not repent of what they had done.

(12) The sixth angel emptied out his bowl upon the great river, the Euphrates; and its water was dried up, making a way for the kings from the rising sun. (13) Then I saw coming out of the mouth of the dragon, out of the mouth of the monster, and out of the mouth of the false prophet three unclean spirits, like frogs. (14) These are demonic spirits, which perform miraculous signs. They come out upon the kings of the whole world, to assemble them for the battle to take place on the great Day of God Almighty.

(15) 'Look! I am coming like a thief!

Happy is the one who stays awake and protects his clothes, so that he does not go around naked and people see his shame!'

(16) The spirits gathered the kings at the place which in Hebrew is called 'Har-Magedon'.

(17) The seventh angel emptied out his bowl into the air, and a loud voice issued forth from the sanctuary – from the throne itself – saying: 'It has happened!'

(18) Then there were flashes of lightning, voices, and claps of thunder; and there was a mighty earthquake, the like of which had not occurred since human beings populated the earth, so great and violent it was! (19) The great city was split into three parts, and the cities of the nations fell. Then Babylon the great was called to mind in God's presence, so that she was given the cup containing the wine of his furious anger. (20) Every island fled, and no mountains were to be found. (21) Then great hailstones, weighing about a talent each, descended from heaven upon the people. But the people blasphemed against God because of the plague of hailstones, for terrible indeed was that plague.

1 At the command of **a loud voice coming from the sanctuary**, the **seven angels** begin to empty out their bowls in rapid succession, with no interlude between the sixth and seven bowls (contrast 7:1–17 and 10:1—11:14). There are just two brief interruptions, both with a liturgical feel. The first is a dialogue between 'the angel of the waters' and the altar, in praise of God's just actions (verses 5–7); the second is an unannounced interjection, apparently by Christ himself, in verse 15. Neither of these serve to slow down the action, however, but rather speed it up with their strong note of urgency.

The **loud voice** here is surely the voice of God himself, since the previous verse has ruled out anyone else from entering the heavenly sanctuary. The command to **empty out** or 'pour out' makes another link between these **seven bowls of God's fury** and 'the prayers of the holy ones', especially the cries of the martyrs (6:9–11; 8:3–5), for the same verb is used of the shedding or pouring out of the blood of holy ones and prophets in verse 6 (ἐξέχεαν; cf. 17:6; 18:24). The command is to empty them out **onto the earth**: this is not strictly accurate, however, for they will affect the sea, the Abyss and the sky as well. But it marks out the primary focus of these plagues as the realm where humanity dwells, currently overrun with demonic forces in league with the dragon but destined to be restored to its primeval state, united to heaven in a renewed creation where God will be all in all (21:1–5, 22–26; 22:1–2).

There have already been striking parallels between several of the trumpet-plagues and the plagues of Egypt, preparing us for the emergence of the Pharaoh-like dragon, its pursuit of the woman into the wilderness, and the safe passage of the Lamb's followers through the sea. The parallels are even more pronounced in this new sequence of seven bowls, each one of which echoes a particular plague in the Exodus story, though not in order, and with some repetition (see Table 4). There is some progression or intensification: the trumpet-plagues affected 'a third' (8:7, 9, 10–11, 12; 9:15, 18), whereas the

Table 4: Trumpets, Bowls and Exodus Plagues

Trumpets	*Bowls*
1. Location: earth Content: hail and fire *Seventh Egyptian plague*	1. Location: earth Content: bodily sores *Sixth Egyptian plague*
2. Location: sea Content: sea turns to blood *First Egyptian plague*	2. Location: sea Content: sea turns to blood *First Egyptian plague*
3. Location: rivers and springs of water Content: waters turn bitter (Cf. Exod. 15:22–25)	3. Location: rivers and springs of water Content: waters turn to blood *First Egyptian plague*
4. Location: heaven Content: third of light darkened *Ninth Egyptian plague*	4. Location: heaven Content: sun scorches people *Variation on ninth Egyptian plague*
5. Location: Abyss Content: locusts *Eighth Egyptian plague*	5. Location: kingdom of monster Content: kingdom darkened *Ninth Egyptian plague*
6. Location: Euphrates Content: army of horses	6. Location: Euphrates Content: frog-like spirits *Second Egyptian plague*
7. Kingdom of God arrives (Cf. following theophany at 11:19, which includes thunder and hail, evoking *Seventh Egyptian plague*)	7. Great city destroyed Content: thunder, earthquake, hail *Seventh Egyptian plague*

effects of these bowl-plagues are complete. This progression does not point straightforwardly to a chronological progression, however. There is also considerable overlap, suggested not least by the common location of the trumpets and bowls (1. earth; 2. sea; 3. rivers and springs of water; 4. heaven; 5. the Abyss/the monster's kingdom; 6. the Euphrates). What John's hearers are presented with is a repeated proclamation, with ever greater intensity, that humanity must ultimately be held accountable for the choices it has made, if God is indeed the God of justice and faithfulness.

The action of **the first angel** establishes a literary pattern which will 2 be repeated in a stereotypical manner for the remaining six bowls (though with rather more detail for the sixth and seventh):

(a) a reference to the angel;

(b) the phrase **emptied out his bowl;**
(c) the location of that emptying;
(d) a statement of its consequences.

Here it is emptied out **onto the earth,** the primary focus of all these plagues, aimed as they are at judging and unmasking the folly of idolatry, the following and worshipping of the monster and its satanic puppet-master. The consequence of this first bowl is that **a foul and painful sore erupted on those who had the branded mark of the monster and who worshipped its statue.** This recalls the sixth Egyptian plague, which brought festering boils on the Egyptians and their livestock (Exod. 9:8–12: the same word for **sore** is used here and at Exod. 9:11 LXX: ἕλκος). As if to suggest an intimate connection between the judgements and that which provoked them, this horrid physical mark echoes the invisible but far more destructive **branded mark of the monster** (13:16–17). Association with the monster, and the worship of **its statue** (whether wittingly through active participation in the emperor cult or the more subtle and seductive worship which goes under the acceptable title of accommodation and compromise), is a dehumanising state which in John's prophetic vision erupts to the surface in all its disfiguring horror.

3–4 The actions of the **second** and **third angel** together reflect the first Egyptian plague, in which the River Nile, and the other waters of Egypt (its rivers, canals, ponds and pools of water) turned to blood, killing all the fish (Exod. 7:14–24). In John's account, the pouring out of the second bowl causes **the sea** to turn **to blood,** while the third bowl has the same effect on **the rivers and the springs of waters.** There is an equally close parallel with the second and third trumpets, which resulted respectively in the turning of a third of the sea to blood and a third of the waters bitter (8:8–11). Now the devastation is complete. As if to accentuate this, the bloody waters of the sea are described as **like the blood of a corpse:** not the flowing, pulsating blood of a living person but the cold, coagulating blood of the dead. But this is only to be expected for those associated with the living death of the monster's regime, founded on the shedding of innocent blood (e.g. 6:10; 16:6; 17:6; 18:24; 19:2). It stands in striking contrast to the life-giving blood of the Lamb, the fruit of self-giving sacrifice and the means to true liberation from enslaving powers (e.g. 1:5; 5:9; 7:14; 12:11; cf. 14:20; 19:13). If Revelation's theatre of reception was indeed the eucharistic celebration of the early congregations, it would also stand in stark contrast to the eucharistic blood which promises eternal life to all who drink it (Jn 6:54–56).

As a result of this corpse-like blood, **every living thing in the**

sea died (contrast the 'third' at 8:9). This would include the fish, an important source of food in the Mediterranean world, and crucial on such a small and otherwise inhospitable island as Patmos. But one should not forget the extent to which the sea, both mythologically (e.g. Gen. 1:10; Job 26:12; Ps. 74:13) and historically (e.g. Ps. 107:23–31; Mk 5:13), was a dangerous place. Until the departure of the sea in the new heavens and new earth (21:1), it will remain a threat, the dwelling-place of chaotic sea monsters. Its close relationship with the Abyss has been suggested by the association of the monster with both (11:7; 13:1). But in this final cycle of plagues the writing is on the wall for this realm of evil and chaos: **every living thing** must include those dark creatures lurking in the deep, threatening the order of creation and the peace of humanity.

The third bowl (and possibly all three emptied out so far) now **5–7** provokes another heavenly canticle, this time from **the angel of the waters**. This angel is presumably in charge of the waters under the earth, rather than the heavenly sea, for the third bowl has been poured out on the former. This strange statement is a reminder of the extent to which John's visionary world is populated with innumerable spiritual beings, influencing the earthly realm for good as well as for ill. Chapters 2—3 revealed the extent to which the lives of individual Christian congregations are underpinned by angelic activity. The same holds for the waters: *1 En.* 66:1 refers to angels of punishment who have authority to release the waters under the earth for judgement and destruction, and this angel may have a similar role here (cf. Rev. 7:1, where four angels restrain the four winds; see also *1 En.* 60:11–25).

The canticle itself offers the authoritative heavenly perspective on what is unfolding in the mythological language of Revelation's vision. God is acting justly, especially in response to the plaintiff cry of the martyrs and holy ones (6:10). This song picks up on the themes and actual wording of 'the song of Moses and of the Lamb' (15:3–4): **You are just, O Holy One, who are and who were, because you have made these judgements!** The first title of God here, 'Holy One', is derived from the second Song of Moses at Deut. 32:4. The second title is a more familiar one in Revelation, although elsewhere it has had a threefold pattern (1:8; 4:8). Here God is simply **who are and who were**: he is no longer described as 'who is coming', for in these last plagues God is already coming in judgement (cf. 11:17).

The 'emptying out' of the bowls (ἐξέχεεν) matches directly the claim that **they shed** (ἐξέχεαν) **the blood of holy ones and prophets**. Like is matched by like. The holy ones are God's holy people, sealed with the name of God and the Lamb, and symbolised by the heavenly woman (see e.g. 5:8; 7:1–17; 12:1). The Church's prophetic vocation has been articulated in Rev. 11:1–13, and so there is a sense in which all God's holy ones are called to be prophets, whose prophetic witness might well require the shedding of their blood. But John may also have a distinct group of prophets in mind, given the extent to which Israel's prophets came to be regarded as martyrs (e.g. Mt. 23:35; the souls under the altar at 6:9–11 are probably not restricted to Christian martyrs). John's book presents him in the mould of the exiled prophet, in a manner which sets him apart from his brothers and sisters (and distinguishes him from 'false prophets' such as Thyatira's 'Jezebel': 2:20).

The translation of the final phrase in verse 6 is difficult. It literally reads: 'They are worthy' (ἄξιοί εἰσιν). But who are 'they'? And what precisely does 'worthy' mean in this case? The phrase is generally translated along the lines of 'it is what they deserve!' This is based on the reasonable assumption that the most obvious antecedent is the group last mentioned: those who have shed innocent blood (whether directly or indirectly through association with the monster and Babylon). Some have found this statement morally objectionable, on the grounds that it presents a God who demands punishment, and delights in seeing that punishment meted out. This is not, however, the view of those who hear Revelation from the perspective of violence, persecution and other forms of oppression (e.g. Boesak 1987; Richard 1995). What is being meted out is not unjust, or out of proportion to the injustice done. Rather, it is the only appropriate response to the cries of the slaughtered. This would fit in with the principle of *lex talionis* (Exod. 21:24) articulated in this section: the bloody water they are drinking is in direct relation to the blood they themselves have 'drunk' (the latter verb to be understood metaphorically, reflecting the 'drunken' behaviour of Babylon and her allies: 14:8; 17:2, 6).

However, an alternative reading may fit the evidence better. 'It is what they deserve' is not the most natural rendering of the Greek (though see Lk. 12:48; Rom. 1:32). Moreover, all other occurrences of ἄξιος in Revelation are utterly positive, referring to God (4:11), the Lamb (5:9, 12; and, by implication, 5:2, 4), or the Lamb's faithful (3:4). The words should probably be read, not as a judgement on the oppressors, but a statement of the worthiness of the oppressed, 'the holy ones and prophets'. Because they are judged worthy, like the Lamb that they followed even to death, their bloody deaths have now been vindicated in the heavenly hall of judgement.

The interpretative canticle of the angel finds a liturgical response in the cry of the personified **altar**, presumably the altar in the heavenly sanctuary (6:9; 8:3, 5; 9:13; 14:18). It too picks up on phrases from 'the Song of Moses and of the Lamb', proclaiming that the **judgements** of God are **just**, to be trusted, that is, in character with the Judge himself (compare especially 15:3). But how can an inanimate altar speak? One should not push the difficulties too far, for Revelation is a visionary text which makes an impact by its surprising and often shocking images and metaphors. However, greater precision may be possible. The voice here is probably not the same referred to at 9:13, for that came from the four horns on the exterior of the altar (and may be the united voice of the four creatures). Rather, the altar may be articulating here the cries of the martyred souls which dwell underneath it (6:9–11). To their oppressors and murderers, they may well have been regarded as the voiceless and the dispensable. Indeed, at times they may have felt the same themselves. Yet the Apocalypse, through the sacrificial altar which receives their blood and integrates it into the heavenly liturgy, provides them with a voice. When John first heard them, their cry was the desperate 'How long?' to the Master who is 'holy and true'. Now their shout has been transformed into the affirmative voice of the vindicated, whose prayer has been answered by God's 'trustworthy and just' judgements: **Yes indeed, Lord God Almighty** ('Yes', Ναὶ, is a cry of heavenly assurance: see also 1:7; 14:13; 22:20).

The fourth bowl-plague with its focus on **the sun** echoes the fourth **8–9** trumpet-plague, which also affected the heavenly bodies (the sun, moon and stars, 8:12). There the diminution of their light explicitly recalled the ninth plague of Egypt, in which darkness covered the land for three days (Exod. 10:21–29). When **the fourth angel** empties out his bowl upon the sun, however, the opposite effect occurs. Rather than the sun being darkened, **it was permitted** (another divine passive, expressing God's ultimate control) **to scorch people with fire**. Fire appears elsewhere as a sign of judgement (e.g. 8:5, 7, 8; 9:17, 18; 11:5; 14:10; 17:16; 18:8; 19:20; 20:9, 10, 14, 15; 21:8; possibly 15:2); here the scorching seems to have the same judging effect. John's early audiences, whether raised like him in the Middle East or natives of Asia Minor, would know at first hand the destructive effects of the sun's searing heat. Those associated with the monster rather than God's tabernacle have no shelter from its harmful rays, while those associated with God and the Lamb will be sheltered by the one on the throne, and shielded by him from both sun and heat (7:15–16).

Again, humanity is portrayed in its most hardened, impenitent state. It seems incapable of seeing the judgement for what it is: the working out of commitments directed away from the Creator and its fellow-creatures. Instead of renouncing the monster and the satanic dragon, it **blasphemed the name of God who had control over these plagues** (see on 14:1 for 'the name of God'). Blaspheming will be one of the signs of the ungodly in the last days (cf. 2 Tim. 3:2; 2

Pet. 2:2). However, the purpose of these Exodus-like plagues – to cause a change of heart – is not achieved: **they would not repent or give him glory.** It would appear that only the prophetic witness of the Church – proclaiming the truth not only with one's lips but with one's very life – is capable of achieving that (cf. 11:13).

10–11 **The fifth angel** pours his bowl **upon the throne of the monster.** The result of this, namely that **the monster's royal rule was thrown into darkness,** is a much closer parallel to the ninth Exodus plague (Exod. 10:21–29; cf. Wis. 17:1–21) than was the fourth bowl. But what or where precisely is the throne of the monster? The related fourth trumpet saw a swarm of hideous locusts emerge from the Abyss (9:1–11), and this might suggest that the same realm is the throne spoken of here. After all, this is the monster's place of origin, an appropriate location for its royal seat (cf. Abaddon, the king of the Abyss: 9:11). However, with the monster's emergence from the sea/Abyss (11:7; 13:1), its royal rule has extended onto the earth, where it has seduced many. Hence, just as 'Satan's throne' may be located at Pergamum, the seat of Roman juridical power in the province (2:13), so too can the throne of the monster be located on earth (the dragon gave its 'throne' to the monster at 13:2). But it is not restricted to any one geographical location, unlike the darkness which enveloped the land of Egypt. Rather, the throne of the monster vies with 'the sanctuary of God' or 'the holy city' (11:1–2) for the hearts and minds of humanity.

Yet even this lightning-strike on the very heart of the monster's deceptive rule is incapable of awakening the most hardened of its victims. They refuse to believe that their choices and commitments can only leave them further shackled to a cruel and demanding master. They cannot see that the plague of **darkness** sheds the most profound of lights upon the nature of this kingdom, which is dark through and through. But then those who belong to the dark not only hate the light; they cannot even comprehend the light but choose rather to remain where they are (a profoundly Johannine insight: see e.g. Jn 1:5; 3:19–21). Hence their response is the same here as it was to the fourth bowl: **People bit their tongues in pain** (inflicting harm upon themselves), **and they blasphemed the God of heaven for their pain and their sores. But they would not repent of what they had done.**

12–16 The sixth and seventh bowl-plagues are described in rather more detail. The action of **the sixth angel,** like the blowing of the sixth trumpet (9:13–21), affects **the great river, the Euphrates.** The consequences of this bowl evoke two scenes from the original Exodus narrative: the drying up of the waters of the Sea of Reeds (Exod.

14:21–25), and the second Egyptian plague, which brought a plague of frogs (Exod. 8:1–15). The only other references to frogs in the Bible are in relation to this Exodus plague (Pss 78:45; 105:30; Wis. 19:10). Hearers of the Apocalypse would be in no doubt that the new Exodus journey, in which the Lamb leads a new people from 'every nation and tribe, people and language', had reached its climax.

The Euphrates had great symbolic significance for God's people Israel, representing the eastern boundary of the promised land (see on 9:14). Hence a reference to it here would suggest that the eschatological battle between God's holy ones and their enemies is about to take place. The Qumran War Scroll provides a vivid description of this great and terrible final war between the sons of light and the sons of darkness (see esp. 1QM 1). It reflects the Judaeo-Christian conviction that evil cannot continue to struggle with good indefinitely, but will ultimately be defeated. However, the picture is complicated by the reference here to **the kings from the rising sun** (or 'from the east'), for whom **a way** is made by the drying up of the Euphrates (see also the drying up of the Jordan, enabling Joshua and the Israelites to enter Canaan: Josh. 3:14–17). Asian Christians hearing this read in the wake of Nero's demise would almost certainly detect echoes of the myth of Nero's return, according to which 'the kings from the rising sun' would be the Parthians. In this contemporary expectation – a fearful threat to some, a hopeful desire for others – the return of Nero at the head of a Parthian army would herald the end of Rome's current domination, or at the very least an end to the turbulent months of bitter civil war and social collapse (cf. 6:2; 9:14; see esp. on 13:3). So there are sinister resonances here both for imperial Rome, the current incarnation of Babylon, and for God's faithful people.

The sinister connotations are strengthened by the appearance of **three unclean spirits, like frogs**, who will orchestrate the military manoeuvres of earthly armies from now on. The belief that behind human rulers and terrestrial political powers are spiritual forces is well documented in Jewish apocalyptic, and finds echoes in the New Testament at 1 Cor. 2:8 and Eph. 6:12. These frog-like creatures emerge **out of the mouth of the dragon, out of the mouth of the monster, and out of the mouth of the false prophet** (the latter being the name by which 'the monster from the earth' will henceforth be known: 19:20; 20:10). In contrast to Christ, from whose mouth comes the double-edged sword which is God's word of truth (1:16; 2:16; 19:15, 21; cf. 11:5), these three can only produce **unclean spirits**, of demonic origin (cf. 18:2). Their threefold description echoes, and shamelessly parodies, the threefold description of the one on the throne, the seven spirits and Jesus Christ at 1:4–5. The capacity of this satanic triad to deceive and lead astray runs like a shocking thread throughout the second half of this book. It is Revelation's bold claim that, far from being crystal clear to the undiscerning eye, the dividing line between good and evil, truth and falsehood, is very subtle indeed. True discernment requires divine revelation, an apocalyptic unveiling of the true state of affairs such as this book claims to mediate. It may even reveal a fault-line running through the middle of the Church itself, for the activity of the false prophet is not restricted to outsiders.

There is a question over the precise relationship between the kings from the rising sun and the kings of the whole world. There are two main possibilities. First, both titles could describe the same group, or, more likely, the former could be a subset of the latter. The drying up of the Euphrates has enabled kings of east and west to muster together before their attack. Both sets of kings would then be raised up together against the great city Babylon. The role of the 'ten kings' at 17:16, allies of Babylon who subsequently turn against her, makes this a possibility. Second, the two sets of kings might belong to opposing sides of the battle, with 'the kings of the whole world' (understood as a pseudonym for the 'ten kings' of Revelation 17) still allied to Babylon/Rome at this point. However, there is no clear indication that the two groups are on opposing sides of the battlefield, nor that only one is under the influence of the demonic spirits.

The wider context (and later descriptions of what is probably the same battle: 17:13–14; 19:17–21; 20:7–10) suggests that what we have here are the preparations for the final battle between the forces of evil and rebellion and those of God and the Lamb. The battle is to take place on the great Day of God Almighty, the eschatological Day of the Lord (6:17). Moreover, the strong echoes of Ezekiel's prophecy about the invasion of Israel by Gog of the land of Magog (Ezekiel 38—39, a passage to which John will return in Revelation 19—20) supports this reading (cf. Zechariah 14; Ps. 2:1–2). Looking beyond the fall of Babylon herself, John's visionary kaleidoscope focuses on the one really decisive battle. This is the battle for which the kings are gathered together at the place which in Hebrew is called 'Har-Magedon'.

Har-Magedon, or its more popular spelling Armageddon, contains associations which run deep in the collective psyche of Western culture. In popular imagination it is associated with cosmic destruction and, since the middle of the twentieth century, nuclear war. Located literally on a map of the Middle East, it plays a prominent role in futurist 'end-time' scenarios which have serious implications in the political arena (Sizer 2004: 193–99). This is not a battle instigated by humanity, however. And in line with Revelation's symbolic geography (e.g. 11:1–2, 8; 14:1, 8), it is not to be located at any particular spot on the earth's surface. Rather, Revelation evokes memories of battles won and lost, anxieties about enemies still around, and traditions about the great battle yet to come. All these coalesce in the evocative name Har-Magedon.

Nevertheless, it does evoke a particular location in the geography of the Holy Land. The most likely interpretation of the Greek name Ἁρμαγεδών is that it is a transliteration of the Hebrew *har megiddon* or 'Mountain of Megiddo' (Day 1994, who provides a judicious survey of the alternatives). The main alternative proposal is that the name derives from *har mo'ed* or 'Mount of Assembly', the mountain of the gods which the king of Babylon boastfully claimed to be able to climb (Isa. 14:13: it is difficult, however, to see how this Hebrew phrase would give rise to the Greek name Revelation uses). Megiddo was a city strategically placed near the narrow Megiddo Pass through the Carmel range, which provided entry into the wide Jezreel Valley in southern Galilee. It was, moreover, the location of a number of crucial battles which would have been etched deeply in the collective Jewish memory: e.g. the defeat of the Canaanites by Deborah and Barak (Judg. 5:19), and the battle between Judah and Pharaoh Neco, in which the righteous king Josiah was killed (2 Kgs 23:29). Megiddo was also the place where King Ahaziah of Judah died after fleeing there from battle (2 Kgs 9:27). Megiddo, or the broad Plain of Jezreel in which it stands, was the site both of glorious victory and of bitter defeat for God's people.

But there is a problem with the designation *har megiddon* or 'Mountain of Megiddo'. For the city of Megiddo is not built on a mountain. Even today, the archaeological tell of Megiddo rises to no more than seventy feet above the plain. Some have proposed that the nearby Mount Carmel may be meant: this would be significant, given that Carmel was especially associated with the prophet Elijah, who has functioned as one of John's role models in Revelation (especially in his confrontation with Thyatira's 'Jezebel': 2:20; cf. 1 Kings 18). But Carmel is still some distance from Megiddo, and there is no other evidence that it was ever named after that city.

The solution may be in the combination of prophetic texts which seem to lie in the background of John's description. The first is Ezekiel 38—39, mentioned above, which John will return to again in chapter 19 (from that point, his beloved Ezekiel will provide the structure and order for Revelation's remaining visions). This explicitly locates the battle between God's forces and those of Gog 'on the mountains of Israel' (Ezek. 38:8; 39:2, 4, 17). But John has combined it with Zech. 12:11, which speaks of mourning in the plain of Megiddo, in the context of a prophecy about the end-time battle. Zechariah 12:10 has been explicitly evoked, in relation to Jesus, at Rev. 1:7. Zechariah 12:11 is the only place prior to the Apocalypse where Megiddo is mentioned in an end-time context; moreover, it is the only place in the MT where the city is spelt as *megiddon* (which would explain the form Revelation uses, which Rev. 16:16 claims is derived from the *Hebrew*: Day 1994). Read in the light of Ezekiel, Zechariah's eschatological war, in which the nations of the earth gather together to attack God's holy city, takes place at the Mountain of Megiddo.

The details of this battle are not described until later (19:17–21; possibly also 20:7–10). Yet before Revelation moves on, there is an interjection, either from the narrator or, more likely, from an unnamed heavenly voice: **Look, I am coming like a thief!** The use of the first person singular, and the parallels elsewhere in the New Testament, make the voice of Christ the most likely candidate. Variants on the thief saying occur on the lips of Jesus at Mt. 24:43 = Lk. 12:39 (in an eschatological context); the Day of the Lord is said to come like a thief at 1 Thess. 5:2 and at 2 Pet. 3:10 (cf. Rev. 3:3).

Given that this saying interrupts the description of the final battle here, a number of commentators have wanted to treat it, and the beatitude which accompanies it, as an interpolation (though without any textual evidence for such a conclusion). This does not do justice to the literary skill of the Apocalypse, however. The breaking in of Christ's warning voice – as abrupt as will be his final breaking in on the Day of the Lord – functions to steady the nerves of Christian audiences as they hear the disturbing description of the final onslaught by the forces of evil. Thieves come unexpectedly, suddenly, and often violently. A state of readiness, of active perseverance and faithful witness, is what continues to be required. Moreover, in the light of preceding visions, hearers of Revelation will recall that the one who comes like a thief has already won the decisive battle. The defeat of the powers of evil, achieved on the cross of the slaughtered Lamb (e.g. 1:5; 12:10–12), removes the sting from the tail of the battle at Har-Magedon.

Similar sentiments are found in the beatitude, the third in a series of seven. The thief saying is all about watchfulness for the Lord's coming, and the beatitude reiterates this: **Happy is the one who stays awake.** But it also picks up on references in the messages to the seven congregations (3:4, 5, 17–18), which use the image of clothing to denote a state of readiness. The Greek phrase literally translated as 'keeping his garments' possibly has the sense of **protects his clothes** (underlining the theme of watchfulness). However, there is more: the faithful are to be like those few in Sardis 'who have not soiled their garments' (3:4) through the subtle temptation to compromise their witness; they are to eschew the economic and political prosperity of the Laodiceans, which may leave them **naked** in the eyes of the God who sees all. **Shame** is a terrible thing, particularly in a society such as John's where honour was prized above all else. But the shame of being naked, as Adam and Eve discovered, is as old as humanity itself (Gen. 3:7). When humanity seeks to be like God, or to worship that which is not God, it loses respect even for itself. The call to guard one's clothing is ultimately a rallying cry against the seductions of the dragon, the monster and the false prophet.

Finally, and without the delay which marked both the seventh seal **17–21** and the seventh trumpet, **the seventh angel emptied out his bowl into the air**. The thematic parallels with the blowing of the seventh trumpet (11:15–18) are striking, for both announce the time of final judgement. The focus on the air here may be a reflection of the cosmic effects of this ultimate plague. More likely, however, John is invoking the association of the air with the activity of malevolent spiritual forces (cf. Eph. 2:2, which speaks of 'the ruler of the power of the air'): the only other instance of ἀήρ in the Apocalypse is in reference to the demonic locusts from the Abyss (9:2). The cosmic powers are about to see their stranglehold broken.

As if to accentuate the finality of this seventh plague, before its effects are described John tells of **a loud voice** coming forth **from the sanctuary – from the throne itself**. A voice from the sanctuary has been heard at 16:1; one will be heard from the throne at 19:5. But in John's visionary heaven, the two are essentially different ways of describing the one location of the divine Presence. The temple and the throne-room are one and the same. Whether mediated through an angel or not, this is the authoritative divine voice, which gives the definitive commentary on what is taking place. The voice proclaims **'It has happened!'** (Γέγονεν), a declaration which echoes the cry of the Johannine Jesus from the cross: 'It is accomplished' (Jn 19:30). The Greek perfect tense used here has the sense of a past event which has ongoing implications in the present. Though it could be a proleptic perfect, indications earlier in the Apocalypse suggest that it is a declaration of what has been achieved in the death and resurrection of the Lamb (e.g. 12:10–11). The long-awaited saving judgement of God (cf. 10:6–7) has already arrived and is being worked out systematically on earth as in heaven.

The remainder of the passage describes the consequences of this bowl. First, signs of the Sinai theophany are described: **flashes of lightning, voices, and claps of thunder** (cf. 4:5; 8:5; 11:19; Exod. 19:16). The Sinai echoes may be a sign that what is taking place is no more than God acting in accordance with his loving covenant faithfulness. But this is the fullest of Revelation's four echoes of the Sinai theophany: the other signs are accompanied by **a mighty earthquake, the like of which had not occurred since human** beings populated the earth. Early audiences in Roman Asia, like their modern counterparts in contemporary western Turkey, knew from bitter experience the unpredictable nature of earthquakes and their capacity to destroy human lives and communities. Several of the cities where the seven congregations lived had themselves been devastated by recent earthquakes (Sardis and Philadelphia in 17 CE; Laodicea in *c.* 60 CE). But unimaginable devastation is implied in this description of an unprecedented earthquake. A great cosmic earthquake was regularly associated with the coming of God on the last day, often viewed as a new Sinai theophany (e.g. *1 En.* 1:3–9; 102:1–2; *T. Mos.* 10:1–7; *2 Bar.* 32:1; see Bauckham 1993a: 199–209). What God did in the past, God would do again at the End, as he shakes the heavens and comes down.

The effect of God's earth-shaking appearance is that **the great city was split into three parts**. **The great city** is often treated by commentators simply as a cipher for Rome. For others, on the grounds of its designation at 11:8 as 'where their Lord was crucified', it is Jerusalem. But both these readings restrict the meaning of the phrase unduly. It is the ultimate symbol of the arrogant and oppressive city, which sets itself up against God and which can manifest itself in any place on the globe, Rome and Jerusalem included (see on 11:8). Hence it can also be called **Babylon**, the city and empire which exhibited such traits in Israel's past, and which continues to replicate itself in subsequent generations, especially from John's perspective in imperial Rome. The splitting of this city also brings down **the cities of the nations**, which have become politically and economically dependent upon her. **The nations** are described elsewhere as those who have been led astray by Babylon and Satan (e.g. 14:8; 18:23; 20:3, 8). This is not their last appearance, however, for they will have a place in the new Jerusalem (21:24–26; 22:2).

The reason for the collapse of the great city is that **Babylon the great was called to mind in God's presence**. The idea that God remembers, both to save and to judge, is well established in the biblical tradition (e.g. Gen. 9:15; Lev. 26:45; Ps. 137:7; Hos. 7:2; 8:13). This is not because God is some unforgiving tyrant who harbours grudges and stores them up for the future. Rather it is because ultimately God does not forget his people, and what they have had to endure. There are times when earth calls to heaven for justice: genocide or violent rape, terrorism or cruel and dehumanising dictatorships, are regarded as unacceptable even by fragile human standards of justice. Arrogance and oppression must not be allowed to go unchecked indefinitely (a theme picked up in the reference to **the cup containing the wine of his furious anger**: see on 14:10). Here the final collapse of Babylon is announced. But John's apocalyptic tapestry also pays attention to the individual scene. Hence the narrative will now pause to provide a description of this city and its fall in the next two chapters.

The violence of God's theophanic earthquake has cosmic effect: **Every island fled, and no mountains were to be found.** Such a statement, echoing other descriptions of apocalyptic disaster (e.g. *1 En.* 1:6; *T. Mos.* 10:4), particularly reflects the perspective of the Patmos exile. Stranded on the small Aegean island, John's visible world would be that of islands in a threatening sea, and in the distance the mountains of Samos and the mainland. It is as though the whole of John's physical landscape is swallowed up. Finally, there is a torrential downpour of **great hailstones**, explicitly called a **plague**, reminiscent of the seventh Egyptian plague (Exod. 9:13–35; cf. Josh. 10:11; the word πληγή is used at Exod. 11:1; 12:13 LXX). The sheer destructive force of these hailstones is expressed by their unnatural weight: **weighing about a talent each**, that is, approximately ninety pounds.

Yet tragically, even this ultimate action against wickedness and injustice is presented as incapable of penetrating and remoulding hardened human hearts. The reaction here is only too reminiscent of the reaction to the fifth and sixth bowl-plagues, and in possible contrast to the human response following the preaching, death and vindication of the two witnesses (11:13): **the people blasphemed against God because of the plague of hailstones, for terrible indeed was that plague.**

Detailed Vision: Babylon   (17:1—19:10)

Description of Babylon the Great   (17:1–18)

(1) One of the seven angels who had the seven bowls came and spoke with me: 'Come, I will reveal to you the condemnation of the great prostitute, who has her seat over many waters, (2) with whom earth's kings have been sexually unfaithful, and on the wine of whose sexual immorality those who make their home on the earth have become drunk.'

(3) He carried me away in a spiritual trance to a wilderness, and I saw a woman seated on a scarlet monster, full of names that blaspheme against God. It had seven heads and ten horns. (4) The woman was dressed in purple and scarlet, and gleamed with gold, precious stones and pearls. She held a gold cup in her hand which was full of detestable things, the uncleanness of her sexual immorality. (5) On her forehead there was a name written, a secret: 'Babylon the great, the mother of prostitutes and earth's detestable things.' (6) Then I

saw that the woman was drunk on the blood of the holy ones, that is, of the witnesses of Jesus.

When I saw her, I was utterly amazed. (7) But the angel said to me: 'Why are you amazed? I shall tell you the secret of the woman and the monster with seven heads and ten horns which is carrying her. (8) The monster that you saw once was, but does not now exist, and yet is about to ascend from the Abyss and go off to destruction. Those who make their home on the earth – whose names have not been written in the scroll of life since the foundation of the world – will be amazed when they see the monster that once was, but does not now exist, and yet will come again.

(9) 'This calls for understanding with wisdom! The seven heads are seven mountains, on which the woman has her seat. They are also seven kings, (10) of whom five have fallen, one is now reigning, and the other has not yet come. When he comes, he must remain for only a short time. (11) As for the monster which once was but does not now exist, he is an eighth and one of the seven, and is going off to destruction. (12) The ten horns which you saw are also ten kings, who have not yet received royal power; they will receive authority as kings, along with the monster, for one hour. (13) These are of one mind in giving their power and authority to the monster. (14) They will wage war with the Lamb, but the Lamb will conquer them, because he is Lord of lords and King of kings. Those who accompany him are called, chosen and trustworthy.'

(15) Then the angel said to me: 'The waters which you saw, on which the prostitute is seated, are large numbers of peoples, nations and languages. (16) But the ten horns which you saw, and the monster, they will hate the prostitute; they will lay her waste, leave her naked, eat up her flesh and burn her with fire. (17) For God has put it into their hearts to fulfil his purpose, to be of one mind in giving their royal rule to the monster until God's words have been brought to completion. (18) The woman whom you saw is the great city whose royal rule extends over earth's kings.'

The literary parallels between the visions relating to Babylon (17:1—19:10), which conclude the seven-bowls section, and that of the new Jerusalem (21:9ff.), which concludes the series of final visions, are striking. Both are introduced by the same phrase describing **one of the seven angels who had the seven bowls** (17:1; 21:9). This angel will function in both sections as the *angelus interpres* who will expound the mysteries of what the seer sees. Both visions conclude with a failed attempt on the part of John to worship this angel (19:10; 22:8–9). But this Babylon section is no mere 'appendix' to the bowls section (*pace* Farrer 1949: 55). Rather it represents the detailed climax to those bowls of judgement: **the condemnation of the great prostitute,** Babylon the great (whose demise has been prepared for at 14:8 and 16:19). In the description of this idolatrous city and its ultimate downfall, the Apocalypse sets before its hearers the full drama and pathos of the Day of Judgement and the salvation that Day brings for God's people.

This opening vision of Babylon falls into several sections: an introductory statement from the angel (verses 1–2); a detailed description of a prostitute, identified as Babylon (verses 3–6); an explanation of the details of this vision by the interpreting angel (verses 7–18). The angel's interpretation can itself be subdivided: the monster (verses 7–8); an interjected call for wisdom, which lies at the centre of the whole vision (verse 9a); the seven heads and ten horns (verses 9b–14, 16–17); the waters on which the woman sits (verse 15); the woman herself (verse 18). As noted earlier, interpreting angels play a crucial role in a number of other apocalypses (see especially Daniel 7—12 and *4 Ezra*, both of which combine vision and interpretation in a fairly systematic way). Such step-by-step interpretation is relatively rare in Revelation, however (elsewhere only at 1:20; 7:13–17), which should caution us against adopting a 'decoding' method as the appropriate reading strategy. The general fluidity and polyvalence of its visions and images suggests that, even in this vision with its clear allusions to the first-century political climate, the symbolism must be allowed wider resonances.

Indeed, the detailed explanations given by the angel are themselves complex and may suggest a process of ongoing reflection by the seer (e.g. in verses 9–10 the seven heads of the monster are revealed as both seven mountains and seven kings). Combined with the diverse associations of Babylon and harlot-cities, this has given Revelation 17 a very rich reception history indeed. Over the centuries, Revelation's 'Babylon' has been associated both with imperial Rome and with historical fallen Jerusalem. It has been viewed in non-historical terms as a symbol of the human tendency towards idolatry, the antithesis to the City of God, or as the personification of luxury and indulgence. Dürer's woodcut of this scene portrays Babylon in the guise of a seductive Venetian woman, reflecting Venice's political and commercial influence in the late fifteenth century and its dominance on the seas.

Once the Church was transformed from a vulnerable minority within the empire to the majority stakeholder in political as well as religious power, elements in this vision that warned of Christian compromise came to the fore in interpretation: Babylon as the apostate church, the church of heretics or even of Antichrist himself. Following seeds sown by the radical Franciscans of the late Middle Ages, a full-blown anti-papal reading of this vision served a potent polemical purpose during the Reformation. Ancient associations with the city of Rome were revitalised, but this time stressing not so much its imperial past as its papal present. Within a few decades of the publication of Dürer's Apocalypse woodcuts, German illustrated Bibles began to portray 'Babylon' wearing the papal triple tiara, while the Pope's residence of Castel Sant'Angelo joined the pagan Capitol among the collapsing buildings in depictions of Babylon's fall (Scribner 1981: 174–75). This anti-Catholic, anti-papal interpretation has come to be regarded as the most natural by generations of Protestant Christians ever since. John's vision of Babylon has represented a dire warning of 'the drunken bliss of the strumpet kiss of the Jezebel of Rome' (Walsh 1899: 372). The two main sixteenth-century Catholic responses, either to stress the identification of Babylon with historical, imperial Rome, or to focus the vision on a city of the eschatological future, both have their followers among contemporary interpreters (for further details of this chapter's reception history, see Boxall 2001; Kovacs and Rowland 2004: 177–89). We shall return to this question of Babylon's identity as the commentary proceeds.

1–2   The opening of the vision (paralleling the new Jerusalem vision at 21:9) introduces John's heavenly guide: **one of the seven angels who had the seven bowls.** Just as nothing was said at 15:1 to clarify whether the seven bowl-angels are to be identified with the seven archangels who blew the trumpets (8:2), so no further identification of this particular angel is made here. All that is implied is that he is an *angelus interpres*, who fulfils for John the role played by Uriel for Ezra (e.g. *4 Ez.* 4:1; 5:31), Yahoel for Abraham (*Apoc. Abr.* 10:3–9), and Gabriel for Daniel (Dan. 8:15–27; 9:22–27; cf. Rev. 5:5 and 7:13–17, where this role is performed by one of the twenty-four elders).

His invitation to John is to **Come**, echoing the command of the heavenly voice to ascend into the heavenly throne-room at 4:1 (cf. 21:9). What the angel promises to reveal to him is **the condemnation of the great prostitute**: this is not actually the subject of this chapter (though hinted at in verses 16–17), but is reserved for Revelation 18. Nevertheless, this introduction sets the scene, bringing in a note of impending judgement which hangs over the description of this woman in what unfolds. The imagery of the prostitute may have been influenced by Israel's prophets, who use this of Jerusalem (e.g. Isa. 1:21; Jer. 13:27; Ezek. 16:15ff.; 23:1–4) and Tyre (e.g. Isa. 23:16). At this stage we are not told even the symbolic name of this prostitute; rather, a portrayal of the woman is built up which seems set to evoke a negative response when that name is finally unveiled. A description is given of illicit sexual relationships, evoking the metaphorical use of **sexual immorality** for idolatry (e.g. Hos. 3:3; Ezek. 6:9). But there are subtle clues provided as to her true identity. Hints of a political dimension are implied by the reference to **earth's kings**, the earthly rulers not yet responsive to the Kingdom of God (cf. 1:5; 6:15; 17:18; 18:3, 9; 19:19), and the statement that the prostitute **has her seat over many waters** (a phrase used of Babylon at Jer. 51:13). The mention of her **wine** recalls the announcement of Babylon's fall at 14:8. The seductive nature of idolatry, and its alcohol-like ability to desensitise the faculties, are parodied in a dramatic fashion. Revelation's literary strategy is clearly designed to shock. Like an astute political cartoon, which satirises its target by juxtaposing unexpected and often unlikely images, Revelation's vision is setting Babylon up to look at best ridiculous, at worst downright destructive.

Reliving the experience of his mentor Ezekiel, who was carried off 'in 3–6a spirit' to the place of exile in Chaldaea (Ezek. 11:24; cf. 37:1, 9), John describes how the angel **carried me away in a spiritual trance** (literally 'in spirit': cf. 1:10; 4:2) **to a wilderness**. It is unclear whether the wilderness is the location of the prostitute, or simply the vantage point from which John views her (cf. 21:10, where John views the new Jerusalem from a high mountain). The woman clothed with the sun was pursued by the dragon into the wilderness, but she encountered it as a place of refuge and nourishment (12:6, 14). If the wilderness is the location of the prostitute here, it does not have the same positive connotations. If it is John's situation, then it is the place to which he must go in order to learn true discernment, albeit with angelic assistance (some might detect parallels with Jesus' wilderness experience, and that of the Exodus people of Israel). Even he will have some difficulty resisting the allurements of the prostitute (see verse 6b).

John's first view of the prostitute is of **a woman seated on a scarlet monster, full of names that blaspheme against God.** Scarlet is a vivid variant of red, already associated with the bloodshed unleashed by the second horseman (6:4), and with the Satanic dragon (12:3). It also had connotations of luxury, being an expensive pigment (it is one of Babylon's luxury imports listed at 18:12). This monster will be the cause of bloodshed, and is associated with Satan; it also undergirds the opulence of the woman who rides it. The fact that it is **full of names that blaspheme against God,** and that it has **seven heads and ten horns,** identifies it as the 'monster from the sea' of 13:1 (verse 8 states that it will 'ascend from the Abyss': cf. 11:7). The monster of Revelation 13 symbolised the rebellious and arrogant empire, in which John particularly saw the features of imperial Rome and its emperors. Its reappearance here will renew visionary interest in at least some of its imperial rulers.

The attire of the woman accentuates her seductive appearance as a prostitute. Extravagance and opulence are the order of the day. Like the monster on which she rides, she is wearing expensive **scarlet**, as well as the equally rare **purple** (cf. 18:12, 16), which had associations with royalty (e.g. Dan. 5:7; 1 Macc. 10:20; cf. Mk 15:17). This ostentatious clothing is meant to contrast with the simple but gleaming white clothing of victorious Christians (3:4, 5, 18; 6:11; 7:9, 13, 14; 19:14) and the twenty-four elders (4:4). The participle κεχρυσωμένη (literally 'gilded' or 'covered in gold') could mean that her whole body is painted with gold. However, that would render the additional **with gold** (χρυσίῳ) superfluous, and also upset the balance it creates with the two further phrases **precious stones and pearls**. We are probably to think of her as wearing jewellery made of all three. This accentuates the close similarities between her and the new Jerusalem, which will be made of pure gold, its walls founded on twelve precious stones, and its gates composed of twelve pearls (21:18–21). This means that Revelation's difficulty with Babylon cannot be with material wealth per se, but rather the exploitative means by which is it achieved, and to which it is put. It will be taken up, redeemed, along with so much else of human culture and creativity, in the new heavens and new earth. But the similarities between the two women underscores the Apocalypse's claim that what is evil and unjust can so easily be taken for what is good and beneficial. It requires an apocalyptic unveiling such as this to reveal the true state of affairs.

The shocking features of the prostitute are religious as well as economic. The **gold cup in her hand** (cf. 14:8, 10) is **full of detestable things** or 'abominations' (βδελύγματα), a word clearly associated with idolatry. In Daniel, the singular form refers to the pagan altar to Zeus set up by Antiochus IV Epiphanes in the Jerusalem Temple (LXX Dan. 9:27; 11:31; 12:11; cf. Mk 13:14). This idolatrous association is reiterated by the metaphorical use of sexual imagery: **the uncleanness of her sexual immorality**. The woman is being held responsible for the powerful human drift away from the true God to that which can only be a pale and unsatisfying imitation. Again, there are echoes of historical Babylon, who is described by the prophet Jeremiah as a gold cup in the Lord's hand, making the whole earth drunk (Jer. 51:7).

Hence it comes as no surprise when the prostitute's name is confirmed, written **on her forehead** (contrast 14:1, where the one hundred and forty-four thousand have the name of God and the Lamb written on their forehead; cf. 13:16): **Babylon the great**. But deeper insight is required, marked by the fact that the name is a

secret or 'mystery' (μυστήριον). The word has been used elsewhere of the secret of the seven menorahs (1:10), and of the secret
eschatological purposes of God (10:7). It suggests that the name
Babylon too has a secret, hidden meaning (see verse 7, where
μυστήριον introduces the interpretation of both the woman and the
monster). This is confirmed by two additional statements. First, she
has a universal role as **the mother of prostitutes and earth's
detestable things**, a 'metropolis' in the true sense of the word.
Second, she is **drunk on the blood of the holy ones, that is, of
the witnesses of Jesus** (taking the καὶ as epexegetical). While the
first phrase could apply to historical Babylon, responsible for the
destruction of Jerusalem and its first Temple, that city cannot be so
easily associated with the witnesses of Jesus. The reference is plainly
to those who have died for their testimony; the genitive of Jesus in
this case (unlike the related μαρτυρία 'Ιησοῦ at 1:2, 9; 12:17; 19:10;
20:4; cf. 6:9) is probably an objective genitive: they are witnesses to
Jesus through the shedding of their blood. The word μάρτυς comes
very close here to its later meaning of 'martyr'.

In the light of all this, who does Babylon symbolise? Given her
name, she clearly represents a city, for which the ancient world
conventionally used feminine imagery and pronouns. Leaving aside
the ancient city and empire of Babylon, by John's time a shadow of its
former glory (cf. Dio Cassius, 68.30), and the Egyptian military
outpost of the same name, there are three main possibilities. First,
Babylon is a symbol for Jerusalem. This has had a number of
defenders (e.g. Ford 1975; most recently Barker 2000: 279–87). A
number of the prophetic oracles which seem to have influenced John
here are portrayals of unfaithful Jerusalem as a prostitute (see on
verse 1). Further, Babylon is seated on, and therefore to be differentiated from, the monster which bears the features of Rome. Indeed,
it is sometimes claimed, on the basis of *1 Enoch* 24, that Jerusalem is
appropriately described as seated on 'seven mountains' (verse 9).

This is not as decisive as at first appears, however. The 'great city
whose royal rule extends over earth's kings' (verse 18) is not the most
obvious description of Jerusalem. Moreover, there are other antecedents of Revelation's 'prostitute', not least the pagan city of Tyre
(Isaiah 23, an oracle which seems to have influenced Revelation 18).
In Enoch's vision, Jerusalem is strictly speaking built on one
mountain, and surrounded by the other six; there is, however, a
better explanation of the 'seven mountains'.

This second interpretation, which represents the consensus view of
contemporary critical scholars, picks up on the virtually unanimous
conclusion of patristic exegetes that she is to be equated with ancient
Rome. Her location on 'seven mountains' reflects the ancient designation of Rome as the city built on seven 'hills' (see Virg. *Georg.*

2.535; Horace, *Carm. Saec.* 7; Propertius, 3.11.57) or 'mountains' (*de septem montibus*: Tibullus, *Eleg.* 2.5.55; Ovid, *Trist.* 1.5.69). The memory of Babylon as foreign oppressor of God's people (e.g. Jeremiah 51, which seems to underlie this chapter; Isaiah 47), and as place and instrument of exile (e.g. Ps. 137:1), could have appropriately been applied by a Jewish Christian to imperial Rome, even prior to Rome's Babylon-like destruction of Jerusalem in 70 CE (cf. 1 Pet. 5:13). Babylon's location 'over many waters' (verse 1), although not a literal description of Rome, expresses well Rome's dominance over many peoples. Indeed, from John's vantage point of Patmos, her control over the waters would have been only too visible. The description of a woman seated on seven hills, moreover, mirrors the iconography of the goddess Roma, the personification of the city worshipped enthusiastically throughout proconsular Asia. Roma was often portrayed seated, occasionally on Rome's seven hills. First-century Christians would pick up on these resonances, only to be shocked by their juxtaposition with the description of a drunken prostitute. Finally, the claim that this prostitute is intoxicated on the blood of the witnesses of Jesus probably betrays knowledge of the memory of what Nero did to Roman Christians in 64 CE, as a dire warning of what Rome had the capacity to become in the future.

However, to say that Babylon equals Rome is to fail to do justice to the richness of John's vision. More satisfying is the third interpretation, which acknowledges the echoes of imperial Rome, but does not regard such echoes as exhausting the meaning of this woman-city. Babylon is not Rome; rather Rome represents the latest incarnation of the oppressive and idolatrous city, 'the great city', which originally bore the features of Mesopotamian Babylon. The image of 'Babylon' has a long history in the biblical tradition: the author of Daniel saw her resurgence in the kingdoms of the Greeks, not least in the idolatrous activity of the Seleucid Antiochus IV; John the visionary is given insight from his island exile to recognise her once again, clothed this time in the garb of Roma. But take away the Roman attire, and Babylon remains. Ultimately, Revelation is confronting its hearers with two visionary cities which promise very different destinies to humanity: 'the great city' enthroned over the waters of chaos, and 'the holy city' or City of God, in which flows the river of the water of life (22:1).

6b–8 John tells of his response on seeing her: **I was utterly amazed.** The use of the verb θαυμάζω elsewhere in the book (13:3; 17:8) would strongly suggest that John is not simply perplexed by what he sees, or astounded that such evil could exist (contra Smalley 2005: 433), but on the verge of succumbing to her charms. Even though he has been warned that this is a scene of condemnation, and he has described

Babylon (at least with hindsight) in shocking terms, even he wavers momentarily. Thus he receives an angelic rebuke: **Why are you amazed?** This question provides the prompt for the interpreting angel to perform his role, explaining the alluring vision step by step (again it is described as a **secret** (μυστήριον)). Mentioning first **the woman** and then **the monster**, his interpretation is given in reverse order.

In addition to the interpretation of the monster as the rebellious and arrogant empire, particularly manifest in imperial Rome, the apocalyptic angel unveils another. This alludes once more to the myth of returning Nero, which in its most sinister form proclaimed that the emperor had died but would return from the dead (Klauck 2001; cf. 13:3): **The monster that you saw once was, but does not now exist, and yet is about to ascend from the Abyss and go off to destruction.** The Nero connection is an early one, already picked up in Victorinus' Latin commentary (Dulaey 1997: 106–07). It is further clarified in verse 11, where the angel tells John that the monster is one of the seven kings represented by its heads, and also an eighth (i.e. one to rule in the future). Hence it appears that **the monster** has a dual identity. First, it is the satanic imperial power which supports the 'great city' Babylon. Second, it symbolises that emperor who particularly manifested its monstrous nature, Nero himself. The reiterated description at the end of verse 8 – **the monster that once was, but does not now exist, and yet will come again** – sets Nero up as a monstrous parody of the one who is, who was and who is coming (1:4, 8; 4:8). Yet there is a further revelation in the claim that this monster is to **go off to destruction.** Christians are warned not to be seduced by a monstrous counterfeit whose days are already numbered. To be so seduced is a mark of **those who make their home on the earth** (for the **scroll of life,** see on 13:8).

Before the angel goes on to interpret the heads and horns of the 9–11 monster, there is a call **for understanding with wisdom,** either from the angel himself or from an unnamed heavenly voice (cf. 13:10, 18; 14:12). Though this could refer back to what preceded, it is probably a call to careful attention and discernment of what is about to be divulged (as at 13:18). The interpretation of **the seven heads,** as of the monster itself, is twofold. First, they **are seven mountains.** The allusion, as stated above, is almost certainly to the *septem montes* of Rome, providing a local colouring to John's vision. Second, **they are also seven kings** or emperors (the Greek βασιλεύς can denote either). The much-debated explanation which springs from this has been important in discussions of the dating of Revelation: **five have fallen, one is now reigning, and the other has not yet** come. The number seven is clearly symbolic, as it has been throughout the book: the number of perfection and completeness. Hence, a group of seven kings is not unexpected. But the fact that the angel further subdivides them has led to the conclusion that Revelation has a particular set of Roman emperors in mind (for a similar linkage of body-parts to successive rulers, see Dan. 7:7–8; *4 Ezra* 11), and that John is providing clues as to the time of writing. Five are former emperors, presumably dead (they have 'fallen' from their thrones); the sixth is now reigning; the seventh yet to come **must remain for only a short time** (because another, **an eighth and one of the seven** – also to be equated with the monster itself – will return shortly to bring the complete sequence of seven to an end: another allusion to Nero returning, signalled by the shift to the masculine pronoun he). There are a number of different ways of understanding this verse, of which (a) is preferable:

(a) John is describing a succession of Roman emperors within the expected set of seven, in the knowledge that he himself is writing in the reign of the sixth, who **is now reigning**. This is the most obvious interpretation; however, commentators differ widely as to where the list should begin, and whether any rulers should be left out of the list. Should one begin with Julius Caesar, whom Suetonius includes in his *Life of the Twelve Caesars* (cf. *Sib. Or.* 5:12), or with Augustus (Octavian), with whom, strictly speaking, the empire began? Or should one start later in the list, perhaps with Gaius because of his idolatrous pretensions, or with Nero, given his identification with **the monster** in verse 11? Should one include the short-lived Galba, Otho and Vitellius (these are also included among Suetonius' twelve Caesars)? Such strategies are often employed in order to tally this passage with Irenaeus' claim that the visions of the Apocalypse were seen during the end of Domitian's reign, i.e. the mid-90s (Iren. *Adv. Haer.* 5.30.3). Victorinus' Latin commentary, for example, starts counting with Galba, thus arriving at Domitian as the current, sixth emperor (Dulaey 1997: 104–07). However, the most straightforward approach is to begin with Augustus, and count each emperor in turn (see Table 5): this would make Galba (68–69) the sixth king, reigning when John is writing. If the three short-lived rulers are omitted, the sixth king would be Vespasian (69–79).

(b) John is using an apocalyptic convention of 'antedating' his prophecy to make it look as if it had been received at an earlier stage. If this is the case, the passage in question will only reveal the seer's fictional dating (akin to the author of Daniel locating his hero during the Babylonian exile rather than the second century BCE).

(c) John has reused an earlier apocalyptic interpretation, incorporating it into a text written at a later date (this explanation is sometimes appealed to by those who wish to maintain Irenaeus'

Table 5: Succession of Roman Emperors

[d. 44 BCE	Julius Caesar]
27 BCE–14 CE	Augustus
14–37	Tiberius
37–41	Gaius (Caligula)
41–54	Claudius
54–68	Nero
68–69	Galba
69	Otho
69	Vitellius
69–79	Vespasian
79–81	Titus
81–96	Domitian
96–98	Nerva
98–117	Trajan

Domitianic dating at all costs). But one should only appeal to this kind of explanation if alternatives present insurmountable difficulties. That is not so in this case.

(d) John intends no allusion to specific emperors but highlights the symbolic significance of seven as a complete or perfect set. However, while the number seven surely does have such significance, this explanation on its own fails to do justice to the urgency of the call in verse 9, and the careful subdivision of those seven in verse 10.

After an identification of the monster (see on verse 8), attention turns to the monster's **ten horns**. These are also **kings** (cf. Dan. 7:24), though these ten **have not yet received royal power**. Given that they are horns of the monster, one might assume that they too are Roman emperors (although their natural round number, ten, lacks the precision of the five–one–one of verse 10 and suggests that particular individuals are not in mind). However, these ten seem to be kings who will rule simultaneously, for they **are of one mind in giving their power and authority to the monster**. Furthermore, **they will receive authority as kings, along with the monster**, whether in its present form as imperial Rome, or as its returning head. Another possibility therefore makes good sense: these are close allies of Rome, or (in the light of verse 16) of the returning Nero. This agrees with certain strands in the Nero myth, which saw Nero and his allies from beyond the Euphrates as a threat to the dominance of Rome (e.g. *Sib. Or.* 5:93–110). Echoes of expected Parthian allies (the 'kings from the rising sun' of 16:12) may well have been detected by first-century audiences.

Yet there is more here than first-century political allusion. Rather, these horns, like the monster itself, are part of the final onslaught of

12–14

evil, the conspiring of the nations against the Lord and his Anointed (Ps. 2:1–3). The nations are amassing for the final battle in which **they will wage war with the Lamb** (the battle which has been announced at 16:14, 16, and which will be described at 19:11–21 and 20:7–10). However, the outcome of this battle is assured from the outset: **the Lamb will conquer them, because he is Lord of lords and King of kings.** This is surely an allusion to Christ's victorious death and resurrection, by which he was crowned as King (cf. 12:5, 10) and received the name of Lord (Κύριος: e.g. Acts 2:36; Phil. 2:9). The title 'Lord of lords and King of kings', a variant of which is used of Christ at 19:16, is probably influenced by the LXX of Dan. 4:37 (Beale 1985; cf. *1 En.* 9:4). Because of Christ's victory, the influence of these kings will be short-lived (they will receive authority only **for one hour**, the time of the judgement of Babylon: 18:10, 17, 19). But Christ does not win his victory alone; rather he is accompanied by his great band of faithful witnesses, who form his powerful army: they are described as **called, chosen and trustworthy.** They too are victorious over the monster and its allies, even if in human terms their victory initially appears as defeat (see 11:7, where the two witnesses are conquered and killed by the monster).

15–18   Finally the interpreting angel returns to the woman. In verse 1 he has described her as having her seat 'over many waters'. **The waters** evoke the waters of chaos, the realm from which the monster she rides has emerged. Here further precision is given to them: they **are large numbers of peoples** (literally 'peoples and multitudes'), **nations and languages.** Rome of the first century was supreme not only over the waters of the Mediterranean and beyond; Rome was also supreme over large sections of the earth's population, **the great city whose royal rule extends over earth's kings.** Yet Rome's dominance simply continued the political and religious dominance of Babylon throughout history. But the perceptive listener will recall that it is from the peoples, nations and languages that the Lamb has redeemed people for God (5:9). Babylon's dominance is not a foregone conclusion.

On the contrary, in a description which recalls Ezekiel's portrayal of the destruction of the prostitutes Samaria and Jerusalem (Ezekiel 23), **the ten horns** and **the monster** turn on **the prostitute** out of hatred and destroy her. Few can fail to be shocked and embarrassed by the highly charged sexual language here, which takes the visual form of the violent rape and murder of a woman by a collection of bloodthirsty male rulers, not without a hint of cannibalism: **they will lay her waste, leave her naked, eat up her flesh and burn her with fire.** Of course, one must appreciate that the feminine description of Babylon reflects ancient conventional language which portrayed cities in female terms. One needs also to bear in mind the metaphorical use of the language of harlotry and sexual immorality in relation to idolatry. The scene is not one of literal sexual assault. Yet contemporary readers cannot be blind to this passage's 'history of effects', nor the ongoing negative potential inherent within it. The violent sexual aspects are vividly portrayed in certain artistic representations of this scene (e.g. the sixteenth-century engraving by Jean Duvet). In large part, the scene functions on the association of the female with the alluring, seductive whore (see Additional Note 3 below).

Yet this analysis, while correct so far as it goes, scarcely does justice to the complexity of John's vision. First, both Babylon and the ten kings are presented as victims of the monstrous system with which they are associated. The scene is essentially one of the self-destructive nature of evil, a truth which has been proclaimed throughout the Apocalypse from the four horsemen onwards. Evil and injustice bear within themselves the seeds of their own destruction, and ultimately the whole edifice will come tumbling down. Second, there are also echoes of the story of Jezebel's demise (2 Kgs 9:30–37), just one of a number of echoes in Revelation 17—18 (compare 2 Kgs 9:22 with Rev. 17:1–6; 18:23). These establish a triangular link between the Old Testament queen, Revelation's Babylon, and the prophetess of Thyatira, who is likewise accused of sexual immorality/idolatry (2:20). This does not mean (*pace* Duff 2001) that Thyatira's 'Jezebel' and Babylon are one and the same. But it does represent a warning to Christians of how easily Babylon's influence can impinge even on the churches, and a wake-up call to reassess their own commitments as a result. Third, the unholy onslaught on the woman is itself set within the wider frame of God's **purpose**, the **completion** of **God's words** of judgement (especially those explicitly connected with the fall of Babylon: e.g. 14:8; 16:19). In the theological vision of the Apocalypse, all is ultimately held within the controlling hand of God – even, paradoxically, evil itself.

Additional Note 3: The Women of Revelation

An issue which has received heightened attention in recent decades is the portrayal of women in the Apocalypse. On the one hand, female *dramatis personae* play substantial roles in the action (the woman clothed with the sun of Revelation 12, the great prostitute Babylon of Revelation 17—18, the bride of the Lamb/heavenly Jerusalem of Revelation 21—22). On the other, feminist critics have argued that these characters are little more than androcentric stereotypes which encourage the perpetuation of misogynist attitudes (e.g. Fiorenza 1991; Pippin 1992, 1994, 1999; Thimmes 2003). Those feminine figures presented by the text in positive terms are those whose identity is defined by the male other: the passive pregnant woman, whose role as 'mother' is central and whose male child will take centre stage; the new Jerusalem, who has been prepared for her husband and waits patiently for the wedding day to be announced (19:6–8; 21:2). Those who attempt to assert their own independence over men, however, are condemned as whores, like the sinister Babylon, portrayed in terms at once comical and shocking as a drunken prostitute and a vampire-like sorceress. This negativity is found not simply in the visionary sections of Revelation: John's prophetic rival in the Thyatiran congregation is cast as a second 'Jezebel', whose sexual immorality parallels that of Babylon herself (2:20–23), and who is threatened with the same fate as her Old Testament namesake. We listen in vain, however, for this Jezebel's voice to be heard (see Boxall 2004), or indeed the voice of any of these female characters. In Fiorenza's words, the only positive female characters are 'silent, passive, powerless, sexually controlled, and pure' (Fiorenza 1991: 13).

In addition, scholarly interest in the 'history of effects' or *Wirkungsgeschichte* has made readers acutely aware of the negative as well as the positive effects of biblical texts, particularly pertinent to these passages from Revelation (on this in relation to Revelation 17, see Boxall 2001). Contemporary readers are consequently more likely to regard the description given of Babylon's destruction at 17:16–17 as bordering on the pornographic. The potential negative effects of this passage are thrown into sharp visual relief by the sixteenth-century engraving of this scene by Jean Duvet, in which a bare-breasted woman is thrown from the monster on which she sits and violently attacked by male onlookers. On the other hand, Duvet's depiction needs to be set alongside more standard visual portrayals of this scene, in which Babylon is clearly a collapsing city (e.g. his contemporary Dürer; the fourteenth-century Angers Tapestry).

Such reflections highlight the extent to which Revelation, marked like all texts by the assumptions and constraints of its human author, is open to negative as well as positive consequences. Nevertheless, other considerations place this in a broader perspective. Fiorenza and others, for example, have developed reading strategies which recognise the presence of conventional generic language, and refuse to identify grammatical gender with 'natural' gender (Fiorenza 1991: 12–15). When Rev. 14:4 speaks of the 144,000 as an army of priest-soldiers who have not defiled themselves with women, for example, this need not be read in a literal sense as gender-specific, such that only males will be able to enter into the new Jerusalem, but can be construed as a symbolic presentation of the Christian vocation as participation in a holy war (see the commentary on this verse above).

Further, the ancient convention of describing cities and nations in female terms need not be understood as presenting Babylon and the new Jerusalem as literally female (though the negative effects of such description should not be ignored).

Similarly, the language of sexual infidelity or 'playing the whore' throughout Revelation is not literal but metaphorical. Drawing upon Old Testament usage, it uses such language to speak of idolatry, the seduction and attraction of commitments to that which is not God and therefore cannot ultimately satisfy. It points to the single-hearted commitment demanded of those who follow God and the Lamb (e.g. 14:4), which applies to male characters no less than female. Indeed, 'Jezebel' of Thyatira is not rejected because she is a literal prostitute, still less because she is a woman; rather, her compromise with Roman culture is such that she is guilty of idolatry, and therefore a false prophet (like the masculine 'Balaam' in Pergamum and the equally masculine 'false prophet': 2:14; 16:13).

Moreover, there is greater complexity in Revelation's portrayal of feminine figures than at first appears. The woman clothed with the sun (12:1) is presented as exhibiting the same quality of 'perseverance' (ὑπομονή, 1:9) as any of her children, whether male or female. This is vividly portrayed in Diego Velázquez's *St John the Evangelist on the Island of Patmos*, in which the lone woman figure confidently confronts the dragon. Nor is the bride a wholly passive figure (indeed, it is possible that she is the same figure as the woman in Revelation 12): at 19:7 we learn that she has prepared herself, rather than being passively prepared by others (and see commentary on 19: 8). Moreover, unlike Thyatira's 'Jezebel', she does have a voice, and it is the cry not only of the Spirit but of all faithful followers of the Lamb, whatever their gender (22:17). Finally, there is another, often overlooked, female figure in the book. The 'earth' who comes to the aid of the woman at 12:16 is personified in female terms, probably influenced by traditions about the Greek goddess Ge or Gaia. Here we have a female figure who, like the woman she protects, plays an active role in the Lamb's battle against the forces of chaos and destruction.

Judgement of and Lament over Babylon   (18:1–24)

(1) After this I saw another angel descending from heaven, possessing great authority; the earth was illuminated by his glory. (2) He cried out in a powerful voice:
  'She has fallen! Babylon the great has fallen!
  She has become the haunt of demons,
  a prison for every unclean spirit,
  for every unclean bird,

251

and for every unclean and hated wild beast.
(3) For all the nations have drunk
the wine of her flagrant sexual immorality;
earth's kings have been sexually unfaithful with her,
and earth's traders have made themselves rich
by her excessive luxury.'
(4) Then I heard another voice from heaven, saying:
'Come out of her, my people,
so that you do not share in her sins,
or experience any of her plagues!
(5) For her sins have piled up to heaven,
and God has called her crimes to mind.
(6) Pay her back as she paid others,
match what she herself has done.
Pour her a double measure
in the cup which she herself has poured.
(7) As she has glorified herself and lived in luxury,
in the same measure give her torment and grief.
For she says to herself:
"I sit enthroned as a queen;
I am not a widow,
nor will I ever see grief."
(8) Therefore in one hour will the plagues come upon her:
death, grief and famine;
she will be burned with fire,
for powerful indeed is the Lord God who has judged her.
(9) 'Earth's kings, who were sexually unfaithful with her and shared in her luxury, will weep and mourn over her, when they see the smoke of her burning.
(10) Standing far off out of fear of her torment, they will say:
"Woe, woe, the great city,
Babylon the powerful city!
For your judgement has come in one hour!"
(11) 'Earth's traders weep and mourn over her, for no-one buys their cargo any more: (12) cargo of gold and silver, precious stones and pearls, fine linen and purple cloth, silk and scarlet cloth, every kind of scented wood, every article made of ivory, of precious woods, of bronze, iron and marble; (13) cinnamon and spice, incense, aromatic ointment and frankincense, wine and olive oil, fine flour and wheat, cattle and sheep, cargo of horses, chariots, and slaves, that is human lives.
(14) "The fruit you longed for has gone from you,
all your luxuries and glittery things have perished,
never again to be found!"

(15) 'The traders in these things, who made themselves rich by her, will stand far off out of fear of her torment, weeping and mourning, (16) and saying:

"Woe, woe, the great city,
dressed in fine linen, in purple and scarlet,
and gleaming with gold, precious stones and pearls!
(17) For such wealth has been laid waste in one hour!"

'Every sea captain, every passenger, sailors and those who make their living from the sea, stood far off, (18) and they began to cry out when they saw the smoke of her burning:

"What city was like the great city?"

(19) 'They threw dust on their heads and cried out in weeping and mourning:

"Woe, woe, the great city,
where all those who have ships on the sea
made themselves rich on her wealth!
She has been laid waste in one hour!"
(20) Celebrate her fate, O heaven,
holy ones, apostles and prophets,
for God has given judgement for you against her!'

(21) Then a powerful angel picked up a stone, like a great millstone, and threw it into the sea, saying:

'In this way will Babylon the great city
be violently hurled down,
never again to be found!
(22) The sound of harpists and musicians,
of flute-players and trumpeters,
will never be heard in you again.
No craftsman of any craft
will ever be found in you again.
The sound of the millstone
will never be heard in you again.
(23) The light of a lamp
will never shine in you again,
nor will the voices of bridegroom and bride
be heard in you again.
For those who traded with you were the great ones of the earth,
and all the nations were led astray
by your sorcery.
(24) In her the blood of prophets and holy ones was found,
and the blood of all those slaughtered on the earth.'

Following the description of Babylon as a drunken prostitute seated on the scarlet monster, the angelic interpretation of this vision, and a prediction of her fall, Revelation now describes in vivid terms the aftermath and its effects. The fall itself is not described, but left to the imagination of John's audiences, based on the violent announcement of 17:16–17, which will be picked up again in the action of an angel at the end of this chapter (18:21–24). The chapter can be divided into three main parts:

(i) a vision in which an angel announces Babylon's fall (verses 1–3);
(ii) an audition, the words of a heavenly voice, with several subsidiary voices (verses 4–20, which may be further subdivided);
(iii) a narrative of an acted prophecy performed by an angel (verses 21–24).

The response to Babylon's fall will continue into chapter 19 (19:1–10). There, however, things will be viewed from the heavenly vantage point. In this chapter, although heavenly beings and voices are involved, things are viewed from an earthly perspective, with human voices caught up in the drama and pathos of the great city's demise. This juxtaposition of earthly and heavenly perspectives gives Revelation 18 its particular quality and its particular interpretative questions: How are audiences to respond to the laments of Babylon's dependents? Are they genuine expressions of grief, or uttered with irony? Is this chapter focused on joy at salvation achieved, or motivated by revenge and vindictiveness? The answers to such questions depend in part on where inverted commas are placed: the earliest Greek manuscripts lacked punctuation, hence it is not always clear who is speaking in a particular verse.

Those who know their Hebrew scriptures will hear familiar echoes in this chapter, for it is a veritable tapestry of interwoven threads from a range of Old Testament passages (especially the prophetic taunt songs of Isaiah 23—24 and Ezekiel 26—27 against Tyre, and Isaiah 47 and Jeremiah 50—51 against Babylon). Nevertheless, this is no montage of biblical quotations (that is not John's way), but a wealth of allusions and evocations rewoven into something new and creative, to speak powerfully of the arrogant and seductive Babylon that Rome has now become. If this chapter has a backbone, it is Ezekiel's proclamation and lament over the pagan city of Tyre (Ezekiel 26—27), also renowned for commercial prosperity. Ezekiel has been a key text for John throughout, often providing the sequential structure; from this point, the order and themes of Ezekiel's final visions will be particularly prominent (see Table 6). Ironically, Ezekiel's oracle about Tyre envisages her destruction at the hands of the Babylonians coming from the north: now it is Babylon's turn to fall, the climax and summation of all evil cities.

Table 6: The Influence of Ezekiel on Revelation

Entries in italics are out of sequence so far as the order of Ezekiel is concerned.

Revelation 1	Ezekiel 1
Revelation 4	Ezekiel 1
Revelation 5	Ezekiel 2
Revelation 6	Ezekiel 5—7
Rev. 7:1–2	Ezek. 7:2–3
Revelation 7—8	Ezekiel 9—10
Revelation 10	*Ezekiel 2—3*
Revelation 10—13	Ezekiel 11–14 (echoes)
Rev. 11:1–2	*Ezekiel 40*
Rev. 13:11–18	Ezekiel 14
Revelation 17	Ezekiel 16, 23
Revelation 18	Ezekiel 26—28
Rev. 19:11–21	Ezekiel 29, 32 (39)
Rev. 20:1–3	Ezekiel 29, 32
Rev. 20:4–6	Ezekiel 37
Rev. 20:7–10	Ezek. 38:1—39:20
Rev. 20:11–15	Ezek. 39:21–29
Revelation 21—22	Ezekiel 40—48

The chapter begins with the vision of **another angel** (that is, other 1–3 than John's interpreting angel) **descending from heaven**. This angel possesses **great authority**; the same was said of the monster at 13:2, but its authority was derived from the dragon, and is therefore surpassed by the heavenly authority of this angelic being. Moreover, **the earth was illuminated by his glory**: John describes the gradual spreading of an all-encompassing light, dramatically banishing the darkness and allowing the world to be viewed in a new light and with greater clarity. The reference to **his glory** (δόξα), presumably derived from God whose messenger he is, recalls the divine presence or *Shekinah*, which will be the natural state of the new city, the new Jerusalem, when all that Babylon stood for has been finally destroyed (21:11; 22:5).

The angel's proclamation is a dirge over Babylon, which functions not so much as an expression of mourning and grief as an announcement of her judgement (A. Y. Collins 1980), proclaimed as if it has already come to pass: **She has fallen! Babylon the great has fallen!** (cf. Isa. 21:9; Jer. 51:8). This perspective of the heavenly voice reflects the perspective demanded of John's audiences throughout this chapter. Because the opening words repeat those of the flying angel at 14:8, it is possible that the two are to be identified. The eerie description of Babylon which follows is one of a ghost town, a deserted city which once knew so much activity, now reduced

255

to a dwelling for wild and uncivilised beasts. The idea that Babylon would be inhabited by wild animals and even demonic forces is found in various prophetic writings (e.g. Isa. 13:20–22; Jer. 50:39; 51:37; cf. Isa. 34:10–11). These prophetic antecedents list some of the unclean animals to be found there: goat-demons, hawks, ravens, jackals. The angel's list combines the natural with the supernatural, reflecting the satanic power behind Babylon's monstrous throne: **the haunt of demons** and **a prison for every unclean spirit**, as well as the home **for every unclean bird, and for every unclean and hated wild beast**. Babylon has become, as it were, the wilderness from where John is viewing her (17:3). He may not have in mind simply the desolation of the eternal city, although the ruins of the Roman Forum evoke with poignancy the glory that once was. Rather, Babylon's ruin will be evident in whichever cities regarded themselves as her children.

The reason for this desolation is directly related to Babylon's idolatrous arrogance (metaphorically expressed as **her flagrant sexual immorality**) and her **excessive luxury**. Rome's crime is not simply that of political dominance supported by worship of Dea Roma and the deified emperors, in which **earth's kings** are implicated; it is also one of economic dominance and exploitation, necessary to support the extravagant lifestyles of a tiny minority of her population. For this, the complicity of **earth's traders** has been necessary; for them, in their turn, the benefits of such compliance have been immense.

4–5 At this point **another voice from heaven** interjects, uttering a warning-cry to God's people, who will hear this proclamation read out by the 'one who reads' in their liturgical assemblies (1:3). Given the content of the message, this heavenly voice, like that at 1:10 and probably also 10:4, may well be the voice of the exalted Christ. It certainly presents the divine perspective on what is being described. Nor is this divine perspective to be restricted to verses 4–5. Although many translations end the direct speech of the heavenly voice at the end of verse 6, or of verse 8 (and thus understand verses 7–20, or verses 9–20, as the report of John), there are no indications in the text of a change of subject. Almost certainly, the whole section, 18:4–20, represents the words of the heavenly voice. This has important implications for the laments of those who have suffered from Babylon's fall (verses 9–19): although one can sense the profound grief expressed in such laments, the true perspective from which John's hearers are to view such words is the perspective of heaven, which clearly believes that the judgement on Babylon is just, and rejoices over her fall.

The heavenly warning echoes Jeremiah's warning to the exiles in the first Babylon: **Come out of her, my people** (Jer. 51:45; cf. 51:6). It also echoes, though more faintly, the command to Lot to depart from Sodom (Gen. 19:14), Sodom being one of the names given to 'the great city' at 11:8. **My people** here cannot refer to that generation, still less to a group of exiled Judaeans: rather it is a call to God's people of the new Exodus, the followers of the Lamb called 'from every tribe and language, people and nation'. Long before the Apocalypse was written, exilic prophets had come to view the return from exile as a second, more glorious Exodus from Egypt, as God leads his people from Babylon back to Jerusalem (e.g. Isa. 40:1–11; Jeremiah 31). The cry of the heavenly voice here is a cry to begin that return, that new Exodus out of the exile of eschatological Babylon, which will culminate in the arrival at the new Jerusalem (21:9ff.).

To John's first audiences, the effect of this call to come out of Babylon would have been dramatic indeed. It creates the same shocking effect as the messages to the angels of the seven congregations, which unveiled a divided church, divided between those 'holding fast' and those tempted to follow the way of 'Balaam' and 'Jezebel', unduly compromised with the surrounding Roman culture. It is possible for Christians to find themselves belonging to Babylon, implicated **in her sins** and therefore subject to **her plagues**, the heavenly response to the immensity of her sins and crimes, which call to heaven for vengeance.

But what does it mean to 'come out of Babylon'? There is no indication that this is to be taken literally (although Jerome could use it thus to persuade the Roman lady Marcella to flee the dangers of her native city for the spiritual security of Bethlehem: Jerome, *Ep.* 46.12). The Apocalypse does not issue a call for Christians to flee into a literal wilderness; on the contrary, the cities of the world need the continuing presence and prophetic preaching of the faithful witnesses. Rather it is a call to the Lamb's followers, wherever they may find themselves, to abjure that unjust, idolatrous culture which can permeate any city in any age. The values of God's people are to be the values of the new Jerusalem. That is why the visions of these two cities – so similar and yet also so different – are juxtaposed so strikingly in the book of Revelation. Seductive Babylon can easily be mistaken for Jerusalem: it takes a particular quality of apocalyptic discernment to distinguish the two. Many of John's first Christian audiences may well have found themselves profoundly shocked by the Apocalypse's unveiling of the culture in which they had found a home.

If Christian congregations are being directly addressed in verses 4–5, 6–8 the addressee of these verses is less clear. It is unlikely that 'my people' are still intended, for this would give them a direct role in the actual destruction of Babylon (which would be out of keeping with the rest of the Apocalypse, where such a role belongs to heaven). More likely angelic agents of judgement are receiving their orders here from the heavenly voice (cf. Ezek. 9:1). On a number of earlier occasions, it has been made clear that the judgements of Babylon and the monster are appropriate to the crime (e.g. 15:3–4; 16:5–7; cf. 6:10–11; 8:4). The *lex talionis* requires this if justice is to be seen to be done for Babylon's victims: **Pay her back as she paid others**. The following phrase, according to the principles of Hebrew parallelism, ought to express the same sentiments in different words. It literally reads 'Double the double according to her deeds': but that would lose the sense of balance between the injustice and its judgement. Probably, the imperative should be understood in the sense of 'match' or 'duplicate' (cf. Isa. 40:2; Jer. 16:18; 17:18; 50:29): **match what she herself has done**. The **double measure** would then be the appropriate measure to match exactly what Babylon made the nations drink, in her very same cup now transformed into the cup of God's judgement (see 14:8–10). This same motif is picked up at the end of this section, in the announcement that **she will be burned with fire** (this was announced as the appropriate judgement on the worshippers of the monster at 14:11).

Again, we are reminded of Babylon's twofold crime of idolatrous self-exaltation and excessive self-indulgence: **she has glorified herself and lived in luxury** (**torment and grief** being the corresponding punishments, reflecting the torment and grief of Babylon's victims). Most shockingly, she is unaware of her precarious position, like the self-proclaimed *urbs aeterna* which has taken on her characteristics. In words very similar to those attributed to her at Isa. 47:7–8, she declares: **I sit enthroned as a queen; I am not a widow, nor will I ever see grief**. These words express profound self-assurance in her unassailable political dominance, and her ongoing ability to find suitable 'husbands' to support her in the manner to which she has become accustomed. The denial of her widowhood reflects the poverty and powerlessness of this social group, which she cannot contemplate ever belonging to (for the presence of widows as an socio-economic issue within the early Church, see 1 Tim. 5:3–16; Jas 1:27).

The suddenness of the great city's utter desolation runs like a refrain throughout this chapter. It reflects, from an earthly perspective, the shock of how quickly such an apparently indestructible and powerful city can disappear. The dramatic reversal which judgement brings comes **in one hour** (the length of the reign of the ten kings involved in her downfall: 17:12). The eternal city will experience **death**; the queen-turned-widow encounters **grief**; the city groaning under the weight of the world's delicacies is confronted with **famine**. There may be the hint of a military aspect – from a earthly perspective – to her fall, the destruction at the hands of her would-be allies (17:16–17): these three **plagues** are regular consequences of warfare.

In the first century, all roads led to Rome, and that city could not fall **9–10** without bringing down large numbers of dependants with her. Hence at this point, attention is focused upon three groups who have benefited from Babylon in her contemporary manifestation: kings (verses 9–10), merchants (verses 11–17a) and seafarers and others associated with the sea (verses 17b–19). They are presented after the event as those who **weep and mourn over her**, viewing from a distance the ghostly shadow of what the city had once been, and witnessing **the smoke of her burning**. That they weep and mourn suggests a lament over the dead; however, they are probably lamenting not simply her demise but also their own personal loss which that demise has brought. The dramatic tension is heightened by the change in tense as each successive group is described: the future is used of the kings, recognising that what is being described is still a future event; the scene of the merchants (verse 11) is made more immediate by the switch to the present tense (though the future is resumed in verse 15); finally, a mixture of aorists and imperfects are used of the seafarers, as if the whole episode has now passed. From a human perspective, it is difficult not to be moved by the words of these three groups. But there are two reasons for not reading this section as a straightforward lament. First, the words of all three groups involve not only words of woe but also, ironically, declarations of judgement (**in one hour**). Second, the laments are almost certainly being reported by the heavenly voice of verse 4: viewed from a heavenly perspective, the appropriate response is not lament but a cry of 'Hallelujah!' (19:1–3).

The group designated as **earth's kings** have regularly appeared as opponents of God's reign. Here they are described as those **who were sexually unfaithful with her and shared in her luxury**: they have metaphorically toyed with Babylon's affections, not least through worship, and have profited economically from her extravagant prosperity. These are not the ten kings represented by the ten horns of the monster (17:12–14, 16–17), probably the Parthian allies of Nero. Rather, they are rulers from other parts of the empire, and beyond, who have prospered by Rome, made alliances with her, and become client kings or governors on her behalf. Such a scene would have had particular imaginative force when read to groups within the cities of Asia, a number of which were legendary for their own rivalry in promoting the imperial cult and finding other ways of proving their loyalty to Rome.

These kings are **standing far off out of fear of her torment**. The fear may be as much for themselves as for her, a recognition that those implicated in her crimes, however indirectly, face a similar judgement. Their cry, though on the level of the narrative expressing their personal grief, also recalls the cry of the eagle following the fourth trumpet (8:13): **Woe, woe the great city, Babylon the powerful city!** The third woe announced by that eagle, never explicitly mentioned again, is perhaps being played out here in detail, a reminder that Revelation presents the final judgements in a cyclical, spiralling manner and with ever-increasing intensity.

11–13 If all roads led to Rome, then all sea routes led to Ostia, Rome's port, located about twelve miles from the city at the mouth of the Tiber. It was through Ostia that many of Rome's imports passed, and where some of the traders associated with her resided. Yet the merchants that Revelation describes are **earth's traders**: they would have included provincial traders, including some from Asia, who were residents of Ostia and the southern port of Puteoli, as well as those who did business from the provinces (no doubt including members of the seven congregations). But this group also includes merchants from beyond the boundaries of the empire, who likewise prospered economically as a consequence of their involvement with her. On the surface, there is a hint of sorrow that **no-one buys their cargo any more**. Yet on a deeper level, the picture being painted is a tragic one indeed, which calls forth a sense of moral outrage. The heavenly voice describes the wealth of the nations which has been sucked into one city for its own ornamentation and self-aggrandisement, for the benefit of a tiny elite with the emperor at its apex. In the meantime, the rest of the empire, indeed the rest of the world, has been bled dry by such extravagant and unjust exploitation. In a later and contrasting vision, John will witness the 'glory and honour' of the nations being carried into another city, the new Jerusalem (21:26). This city, however, is founded on very different principles, and the characteristics of Babylon are explicitly excluded from it (22:15).

The list of Babylon's cargo shows Ezekiel's influence (specifically the list of Tyre's imports at Ezek. 27:12–24). But Revelation does not slavishly follow Ezekiel. On the contrary, John's list of twenty-eight products specifically reflects the imports of the city of Rome in the first century (Bauckham 1993a: 350–71; cf. Kraybill 1996). Virtually every area of the known world is covered, from Spain to China, Greece to North Africa, Sicily to Egypt (particular focus is on the exotic, mediated from the East via Arabian merchants: **cinnamon and spice, incense, aromatic ointment and frankincense**). So too is almost every area of personal and civic life, at least as it affected the wealthy elite: jewellery, clothing and domestic furnishings (textiles and other cloth, including the extravagantly expensive **purple cloth**), public buildings (**marble**), and entertainment (**horses** and **chariots**). While the list does include items which formed part of the staple diet for the general population (**wine, olive oil, wheat**; see 6:6), as well as animals used for working and breeding (**cattle and sheep**), the emphasis is upon extravagant and luxury goods (hence the separate mention of the luxury **fine flour** imported from Africa). Most shocking is the end of the list, particularly if what is mentioned last reflects its position as the least significant: **slaves, that is human lives** (the καὶ understood as epexegetical). In an economy directed towards the needs of a tiny yet increasingly prosperous elite, slaves have become dispensable commodities (hence they can be described in common parlance simply as 'bodies' (σώματα), the word John uses here). Asia Minor in the first century had a particularly lucrative role in the supply of slaves to Rome, many of whom may have passed through the port-city of Ephesus en route to the great city.

At this point, there is a brief and unexpected change of focus, as 14–17a Babylon herself is addressed. There is no reason to treat verse 14 as out of place, however, as does Charles (who rearranges this section so that this saying occurs after verse 21: Charles 1920: II, 105–08). The theme of **luxuries** has been spelt out in great detail in the preceding verses. It is not totally clear whether the speaker is the heavenly voice, or is reporting the words of the merchants. Most probably the former is the case, with the direct words of the traders beginning at verse 16. The sentiments expressed are more obviously those of heaven. Either way, the general meaning is clear: Babylon has lost that **fruit** she set her heart on but which could never sustain either her or the humans she seduced. Far from pursuing the important matters – justice, peace and integrity – she has wasted her power and wealth on mere fripperies: **luxuries and glittery things** (literally 'all the luxurious and bright things') which have now quickly **perished, never again to be found**. It is a damning indictment of any city or civilisation, obsessed with the accumulation of expensive and extravagant trinkets, while the poor go hungry, fellow human beings are sold into slavery, and innocent blood is shed in that city's name.

If the obscenely rich Babylon has been stripped of her wealth, so too have those reliant on her for their trade. Hence the second group, the huge body of **traders** in that long list of cargoes, take up the lament. The pattern is as for the kings of verses 9–10: a description of their location **far off**, their pronouncement of **woe**, a description of the great city's former glory, and a statement of its judgement **in one hour**. The main focus, however, is on the loss of material wealth. Evoking the vision of the prostitute (17:4) as well as the list of Rome's cargoes, they describe the city in terms of her clothing, personifying the extravagances of her wealthiest citizens: **dressed in fine linen, in purple and scarlet, and gleaming with gold, precious stones and pearls.**

17b–20 The third and final group now takes up the refrain: those associated with the seas. This is a diverse group, including **every sea captain** and **sailors** (those who transported the precious cargoes so lucrative for the earth's traders). It also incorporates **those who make their living from the sea**: ship-owners, and perhaps others whose livelihood came from the waters, such as fishermen. The second category in this group is somewhat ambiguous ('everyone who sails to a place'), but probably means **every passenger**, including the travelling merchants. That this group of seafarers is singled out for special mention reflects not simply the importance of the ports of Ostia and Puteoli, but Rome's dominance on the seas, especially the Mediterranean. An exile on Patmos would have been acutely aware that Roma ruled the waves of the Aegean.

The initial cry of these seafarers reflects the amazement of the earth at the appearance of the monster (13:4): **What city was like the great city?** The burning fate of this city and that of the monster are one and the same (cf. 19:20). Like the mariners in Ezekiel's lament over Tyre, another prominent sea-trading city (Ezek. 27:30–31), **they threw dust on their heads and cried out in weeping and mourning.** Again, the woe focuses on Babylon's lost wealth, though this time the wealth which profited **all those who have ships on the sea.**

Verse 20 brings a swift and somewhat jarring transition from the mourning of the mariners' reported words to the theme of celebration. This would be strange indeed coming from the lips of those seafarers. But it is not at all out of place as the voice of heaven (perhaps the voice of Christ), which has been speaking since verse 4, though sometimes to report the speech of Babylon's lamenters. Heaven is invited to **celebrate her fate** (the only other occurrence of this verb in Revelation describes the celebration of 'those who make their home on the earth' at the deaths of the two witnesses, 11:10). So too are those associated with heaven rather than earth, who have oriented their lives on the heavenly throne: **holy ones, apostles and prophets.** The **apostles** must be the 'twelve apostles of the Lamb' (21:14; cf. the 'false apostles' in Ephesus, 2:2), at least some of whom would have been martyred by the time Revelation was composed. But the reference to **holy ones** and **prophets** suggests that it is addressed as much to those who are still alive and on this earth, though not belonging to it (see on 11:18 and 16:6). The reason for celebration is that **God has given judgement for you against her.** We are reminded of the cry of the martyrs (6:9–11), and all the 'prayers of the holy ones' (8:3–4): in this last great act of judgement, those prayers have been definitively answered in the heavenly court.

The final scene viewed from the perspective of earth is an acted **21–24** prophecy performed by **a powerful angel**. It is not stated whether this is the 'powerful angel' with the scroll, Christ's angel (10:1), though it would be appropriate for Christ's angelic agent to announce the definitive fall of the great city. This angel throws **a stone, like a great millstone, … into the sea**, as if returning the evil city to the realm of evil. The scene is no doubt inspired by Jer. 51:63–64, where a scroll containing the disasters prophesied against Babylon is tied to a stone and thrown into the Euphrates, as a sign of Babylon's own fall. In an even more dramatic way, this angel enacts the fall of Babylon in her current and most monstrous manifestation: **In this way will Babylon the great city be violently hurled down, never again to be found!**

Accompanying the action is a proclamation of judgement. Having begun with a proclamation in the past tense, reflecting the assurance that the Lamb's victory provides, the chapter ends with a return to 'real time', in which that judgement is still in the future. The 'ghost town' description in verse 2 is matched again here at the end of the chapter. As in the laments from Babylon's dependants, this passage also evokes a sense of pathos and tragedy, at least on the surface. The emptiness and eerie silence of the city to come contrasts with the noise and vibrancy of Babylon/Rome as it was, indeed as any thriving metropolis is. At least implicitly, the silence of the city's **millstone** contrasts with the mighty splash of the angel's millstone as it hits the water. Two further contrasts are implied. The first is with the heavenly realm, where **harpists** can be heard (5:8; 14:2), where **trumpeters** herald judgements (e.g. 8:2), and where the announcement will soon take place of the marriage of a **bridegroom** to a **bride** (19:6–8, 9). The second is with that other city, yet to descend from heaven, where **the light of a lamp** will be replaced by the light of God's glory and the lamp which is the Lamb (21:23; cf. 22:5).

Finally, the angel reminds Babylon again of the reason for her fall. First, she is involved in exploitative commerce: the statement that **those who traded with you were the great ones of the earth** might also point to the consequences of such trade for the 'little ones' both inside and outside the empire. Second, her ability to allure and seduce is mentioned once again. Elsewhere, the focus seems to be on idolatry (expressed metaphorically in terms of sexual immorality). Here, however, it is claimed that **all the nations were led astray by your sorcery** (cf. 9:21; 21:8; 22:15). It is unlikely that literal sorcery is at issue, the attempt to manipulate the course of events by spells and potions. More likely, Babylon is being accused of 'casting her spell' over large sections of humanity (Reddish 2001: 349), gaining adulation and even worship as a result. Finally, John's audiences are reminded that Babylon has blood on her hands. This is not simply, however, the blood of God's faithful people, including those recently slaughtered under Nero (**the blood of prophets and holy ones**). Babylon in her Roman incarnation has gone farther than that. Recalling the unnamed multitudes regarded as indispensable in the swift progress of Roman dominance across the Mediterranean world, hinting at the vast numbers of silent deaths necessary to establish the *Pax Romana*, the angel adds a third group to the list. Roman Babylon is answerable no less for **the blood of all those slaughtered on the earth**. That explains why her fall must be so great.

Heavenly Rejoicing (19:1–10)

(1) After this I heard what sounded like the loud voice of a huge crowd in heaven, saying:
    'Hallelujah!
    Salvation, glory and power be to our God,
    (2) for his judgements are true and just!
    For he has judged the great prostitute,
    who was destroying the earth by her sexual immorality.
    He has vindicated the blood of his servants,
    who died at her hands.'
(3) Then a second time they cried:
    'Hallelujah!
    The smoke from her ascends for ever and ever!'
(4) The twenty-four elders and the four creatures fell down and worshipped God who is seated on the throne, saying:
    'Amen! Hallelujah!'
(5) Then a voice issued forth from the throne, saying:
    'Praise our God,
    all his servants,
    you who fear him,
    both the little ones and the great!'
(6) And I heard what sounded like the voice of a vast crowd, like the sound made by many waters, and like the sound of powerful claps of thunder, thundering:
    'Hallelujah!
    For the Lord our God, the Almighty,
    has begun his royal rule!
    (7) Let us rejoice and be glad,
    and give glory to him.

For the Lamb's wedding day has arrived,
and its bride has prepared herself;
(8) she has been permitted to dress herself
in fine linen, shining and clean.'
Now the fine linen is the just deeds of the holy ones.

(9) Then the angel said to me, 'Write this: "Happy are those who have received an invitation to the Lamb's wedding banquet!"' He also said to me, 'These are true words from God.' (10) Then I fell at his feet to worship him. But he said to me, 'Do not do that! I am only a fellow-servant with you and your brothers and sisters who continue the witness of Jesus. Worship God! For the witness that Jesus bore is the essence of prophecy.'

The previous chapter presented the fall of Babylon and its consequences from the vantage point of earth, even if a heavenly perspective on events was provided by the proclamations of the two angels and the omnipresent heavenly voice. The fall of the earthly city was announced, the funeral laments of earthly interest groups were heard, while John on earth witnessed the hurtling down of the massive millstone, and heard again of the 'ghost town' that Babylon would become. In this concluding scene to the bowls sequence the action is firmly back in heaven, where news is received of Babylon's demise. What is described is a heavenly liturgy of praise, in which the judgement of the great prostitute is acclaimed as an act of divine justice, clearing the way for the marriage of the Lamb to its people. Throughout the Apocalypse, the heavenly throne-room has been the sacred space which enables God's people to orientate themselves correctly, the place of true worship where a proper perspective on the world below is gained.

Liturgy, whether earthly or heavenly, involves the singing of canticles and set antiphons, often in a responsorial pattern. Hence, we find here a pattern of canticle and response from various groups of worshippers. Being innately conservative, liturgy also preserves remnants of older languages considered more appropriate to the worship of God. While John describes this heavenly liturgy in Greek, he also hears echoes of a more ancient Jewish liturgy expressed in Hebrew, not surprising for one who seems to spring from a Semitic-speaking Jewish background. This is the only passage in the whole New Testament where the phrase **Hallelujah!** ('Praise Yah': e.g. Pss 105:45; 106:1, 48; 111:1; 148:1; 150:1; Tob. 13:17; 3 Macc. 7:13) is found, and it is used four times within the space of six verses. Similarly, the Hebrew **Amen** is transliterated in verse 4, as the appropriate liturgical response to the canticles from the heavenly choir.

The rapid exchange of praises, and the equally rapid exchange of voices, means that it is not easy to identify the various groups. Two canticles are sung by a heavenly crowd (verses 1–3), to which the twenty-four elders and four creatures respond (verse 4); after a voice from the throne is heard (verse 5), another huge crowd sings a third canticle (verses 6–8). But who are the two choirs? Two earlier passages are relevant for comparison: the liturgical exchange in the heavenly throne-room at 5:11–14, and the vision of the great multitude at 7:9–17. In the first passage, the first choir is angelic (5:11–12), while in the second chorus they are joined by 'every created thing in heaven and on earth, under the earth and in the sea' (5:13), to which the four creatures respond with their 'Amen' and the twenty-four elders with a posture of worship (5:14). This parallel would suggest that the first group of singers in the current passage are the angels, while the second group would include earthly singers too.

But the second parallel in 7:9–17 suggests that the heavenly picture has already altered. There we hear of a choir in heaven which sings, like the first one here, of the **salvation** which belongs **to our God** (7:10). These are the victorious human followers of the Lamb, now in heaven after having passed through the great tribulation. They are then joined by a second heavenly choir, made up of angels, who sing of God's attributes, including his **glory and power** (7:12). The combination of those two canticles in 19:1 suggests that the first choir, though heavenly, is composed of both angels and exalted humans. The faithful witnesses who have now passed from this life, whether their witness led directly to their deaths or not, find themselves among the ranks of the angelic choirs, able to sing this victory song (like those who sing the Song of Moses and the Lamb, 15:3–4). The second choir, though not excluding these, would also incorporate those followers of the Lamb still on earth, celebrating from their earthly vantage point the loss of Babylon's dominance.

1–2 John reminds his audiences of how noisy the heavenly liturgy is: **I heard what sounded like the loud voice of a huge crowd in heaven.** This choir of angels and human followers of the Lamb is able to drown out even the loudest trumpeting of Babylon's victories, and the arrogant self-proclamation of the great city's achievements. The phrase **Hallelujah** occurs regularly in Israel's Psalter, perhaps as a reflection of its pre-exilic Temple liturgy. Revelation then taps into an ancient stream of priestly worship which links early Christian communities with their forebears in God's covenant people. As in earlier canticles, three qualities are ascribed **to our God** (which have also been ascribed to the Lamb: 5:12, 13; 7:10). But these are not general statements of what God is like; rather they are specific proclamations of what God has shown himself to be in this act of judging **the great prostitute**, Roman Babylon. **Salvation** could almost be translated 'Victory!' in this instance. What may look from the perspective of earth's kings, traders and mariners like a cruel and tragic fall is seen from the perspective of heaven, including those humans linked to heaven by the shedding of their innocent blood, as the only just response. Without it, neither God nor God's judgements would be **true and just**. Instead, it would mean that the power which **was destroying the earth** could do so indefinitely and with impunity, while the urgent cry for vindication from **the blood of his servants** (cf. 6:9–11) would be met with a deafening divine silence. The final phrase of verse 2 (ἐκ χειρὸς αὐτῆς) is ambiguous, and has often been translated as referring to Babylon's judgement: God has avenged 'at her hand' or 'on her' the blood of his servants. However, it is probably referring to the manner of his servants' deaths, **at her hands** (see e.g. Gen. 4:11; Exod. 18:4; cf. the close parallel with the story of Jezebel, 2 Kgs 9:7).

The same heavenly choir now sings a second canticle, again begin- **3–4** ning with the psalm-like command to praise Israel's God, **Hallelujah!** This is combined with a declaration of Babylon's fate, which matches directly the ascent of the prayers of the holy ones, together with the sweet smoke of incense, before the divine throne (8:3–4). Again the close link between those prayers and the judgement of the great city is made clear: **The smoke from her ascends for ever and ever!** Yet there are differences as well as similarities: the smoke from Babylon's burning contains the foul, acrid smell of sulphur rather than the pungent incense-smell of true worship; moreover, unlike the prayers, which have now been definitively answered, her smoke goes up **for ever and ever**. Without this assurance, there would remain the residual fear (inherent in the myths surrounding Nero's return, and in Rome's claim to be the 'eternal city') that the corrupt, idolatrous and oppressive city might rise again.

For ever and ever (literally 'into the ages of the ages') is another liturgical phrase, which is answered in Christian liturgy by the Hebrew response **Amen**. This comes from those closest to the throne – **the twenty-four elders**, angelic representatives of God's people, and **the four creatures**, who act on behalf of the whole creation, animals and birds as well as humans. These have a fundamental role to play in the ongoing liturgy of heaven (see 4:8–10). Directing the attention of creation towards the seat of all true power and the focus of true worship, they **fell down and worshipped God who is seated on the throne** with their brief yet powerful response: **Amen! Hallelujah!** (see 5:14).

267

5–8 The next section of this heavenly liturgy begins with a voice issuing **from the throne**, whose call is met with a third canticle, coming from a group which seems to include those on earth as well as in heaven. At 16:17 the voice from the throne was the authoritative divine voice, though perhaps mediated through an angel. An angelic mediator is likely here, for the call is to **Praise our God** (a variation on **Hallelujah** or 'Praise Yah/the Lord'). It is addressed to **all his servants, you who fear him** (the καὶ understood as epexegetical). Fearing God is not to be understood in the negative sense of that word, but in the positive biblical sense of joyful, referential awe towards the one who is worthy of worship (cf. 11:18; 14:7; 15:4). That membership of God's people knows no socio–economic distinctions is made clear by the further description of God's servants, as **both the little ones and the great**.

In response to this divine call, John hears a second choir of ear-splitting intensity. The volume of its singing is evoked by a series of three similes which build upon one another to create a combined dramatic effect. The sound they make is, first of all, **like the voice of a vast crowd** (recalling the 'vast crowd, too large to be counted' of 7:9). Second, it is **like the sound made by many waters**, the deafening, rushing sound of an immense waterfall (which is also the sound made by the exalted son of man figure at 1:15). Third, it is transformed into a choir whose volume matches that of the divine throne, **like the sound of powerful claps of thunder** (see e.g. 4:5; 8:5; 11:19). The identity of this group is likely to include **all his servants** addressed in verse 5, though not excluding the heavenly beings whose songs are recorded in verses 1–3. Heaven and earth sing in harmony that **the Lord our God, the Almighty, has begun his royal rule**. This canticle, along with the similar proclamations which accompanied the blowing of the seventh trumpet (11:15–18), provided George Frederick Handel with the key text for his famous 'Hallelujah Chorus'.

The canticle moves beyond the judgement of Babylon to the positive consequences of that judgement: the establishment of God's royal rule and the arrival of **the Lamb's wedding day**. The prayer attributed by the Evangelists to Jesus (Mt. 6:9–13; Lk. 11:2–4), to be prayed by his followers, is an urgent eschatological prayer that God's kingdom may come and God's will be done not only in heaven but also on earth. The Lord's Prayer is never explicitly cited in the Apocalypse, yet its spirit permeates the whole. This canticle expresses those very same sentiments, as earthly rebellion, the expected 'time of trial' and the wiles of the Evil One give way to God's **royal rule** over all God's creation.

The connection with **the Lamb's wedding day** has also been implicit in the whole Babylon cycle, where one of her greatest crimes

is that of 'sexual immorality' or 'playing the prostitute'. As a metaphor for idolatry, this reflects Israel's conviction that God's people
have been promised to another, betrothed to their one God (e.g. Isa.
54:1–8; Ezek. 16:8–14; Hosea 1—3). In the light of this, the time of
salvation is sometimes compared to the joyful celebration of a wedding (e.g. Isa. 61:10—62:7, which has influenced this passage: Fekkes
1990). Prompted by Jesus himself (e.g. Mk 2:19–20 and par.; Jn 2:1–
11; 3:29), the early Church came to view the messianic age as the time
at which Jesus the Messiah would claim his betrothed, the Church, as
his bride (e.g. 2 Cor. 11:2). Interestingly, marriage is a particularly
prominent image in two early Christian texts associated with Roman
Asia, the Apocalypse and the Letter to the Ephesians (cf. Eph. 5:22–
33). Purged of any compromise associated with the prostitute, the
Lamb's **bride has prepared herself**. Her wedding dress eschews
the obscene extravagances of Babylon's attire, the ludicrously
expensive purple and scarlet. Rather she is adorned **in fine linen,
shining and clean**. This wedding dress has not cost mountains of
silver and gold; yet it has been costly enough, for it is produced from
the just deeds of the holy ones, including those deeds which took
some of them to their deaths in the Lamb's footsteps. The bride's
adornment is that of the ones she personifies, as the heavenly symbol
of the people of God.

This heavenly scene, and with it the whole bowls sequence which **9–10**
began at 15:5, concludes with a stereotyped exchange between John
and the interpreting angel, in which John attempts **to worship him**
(though not specified in verse 9, the subject is certainly the angel who
has been John's guide since 17:1: cf. 22:8). This same sequence will
be repeated at the end of the parallel vision of the new Jerusalem
(22:8–9), a further indication of Revelation's literary pairing. The
exchange begins here with a command to John to **write**, the third
occasion he has received such an order (previously 1:11; 14:13; cf.
1:19). As on the most recent occasion, he is to transcribe a beatitude,
the fourth of seven scattered throughout the book. It is a saying that
has found its place within the Christian Eucharist, reflecting an
understanding of that sacrament as a foreshadowing of the messianic
banquet: **Happy are those who have received an invitation to
the Lamb's wedding banquet!** It is not improbable that early
Christian audiences would have picked up on such eucharistic
resonances. The invited surely include the followers of the Lamb
(17:14), thus making them at one and the same time wedding guests
and part of the bride. Whether others are also invited is left unclear
(though there is no explicit statement that others have *not* been
invited).

The angel tells John that **These are true words from God**. He could be referring specifically to the words of this beatitude, or to all his words in this Babylon cycle. However, a similar phrase at 22:6 could be understood as referring to the whole book, which is a message of 'what must soon come to pass' (cf. 1:1). John's failed attempt to **worship** the angel, and the abrupt rebuke (**Do not do that!**), may function as a warning to the churches against the worship of angels (cf. Col. 2:18), an action which would seriously compromise monotheism. Falling down at an angel's feet is not an uncommon occurrence in Jewish and Christian texts (e.g. Tob. 12:16–21; *3 En.* 1:7; *T. Abr.* 9:1–3), and it is occasionally accompanied, as here, by a rebuke (e.g. *Asc. Isa.* 7:21).

More directly, the scene gives insight into Revelation's perspective on both Christians and Christ. As regards the former, they have been placed on a par with the angelic residents of heaven, an indication of their exalted status already implicit in their designation as 'holy ones': **I am only a fellow-servant with you and your brothers and sisters who continue the witness of Jesus.** Here, μαρτυρία Ἰησοῦ is translated as a subjective genitive: the witness which Jesus bore, now carried on by others (the alternative, the objective genitive, would mean 'testimony to Jesus': see commentary on 1:2). A huge gulf is opening up between the Lamb, whose worship elsewhere (e.g. 5:8, 11–14; 7:9–12; cf. 1:17) provokes no such rebuke, and the angels. Angels should not be worshipped; the worship of the Lamb, however, is not forbidden to those who **worship God.**

The scene concludes with a definition, probably still from the angel, of **the witness of Jesus.** Its precise meaning is rather obscure. Literally it reads 'the witness of Jesus is the spirit of prophecy'. If, as elsewhere (1:2, 9; 12:17; 20:4; cf. 6:9), the witness of Jesus is understood as subjective (the witness that Jesus himself bore), then that suggests that 'the spirit of prophecy' ought to be treated as subjective also. This would mean that **the witness that Jesus bore is the essence** or paradigm **of prophecy** (Mounce 1977: 342): all who speak the prophetic words of God are uttering nothing more, and nothing less, than what Jesus himself witnessed to in his life, in his being slaughtered, and in his rising to new life as a vindication of that message. The angel is simply the vehicle and interpreter of the prophetic message, not its source, who alone is to be worshipped. Alternatively, understood as an objective genitive, it would be a reference to the Holy Spirit, 'the Spirit which inspires prophecy'.

6   SEVEN FINAL VISIONS   (19:11—22:11)

The judgement of the rebellious city, so long anticipated, has now been described. With Babylon's fall, God's royal rule has washed like a powerful wave across the earthly realm where hitherto it was resisted. Babylon was seen seated on a monster, which sustained her and which ultimately brought her down. Yet evil and rebellion has been witnessed in other forms too, in some ways more sinister and more pervasive than its manifestation in the great city. The power behind the monster's throne is still on the loose down in the earthly realm: the dragon which pursues the children of the woman. The sea still exists as the place from which monstrous forces can rise to wreak havoc on the earth. For the Lamb's victory to be complete, there are even greater forces than Babylon to be reckoned with. The final set of seven unnumbered visions will draw upon traditional eschatological scenes and motifs to describe this mopping-up operation. It will climax with the detailed vision of the new Jerusalem (just as the bowls septet concluded with the detailed description of Babylon and her downfall). The exiled prophet Ezekiel, who has been so significant up to this point for the exiled prophet John, seems to have provided the basic thematic and chronological structure for what is about to unfold: the great supper (= Ezek. 29:1–8; Ezekiel 32 (and 39)); the binding of the dragon/Satan (= Ezekiel 29; 32); the first resurrection (= Ezek. 37:1–14); the millennial reign of the Davidic Messiah (Ezek. 37:15–28); Gog and Magog (= Ezek. 38:1—39:20); judgement and restoration (= Ezek. 39:21–29); the new Jerusalem (= Ezekiel 40—48). These seven scenes (all but one of which begin with the phrase 'Then I saw', καὶ εἶδον) form a concentric pattern, at the centre of which is the millennium or thousand-year reign of Christ and his witnesses:

1. The rider on the white horse (19:11–16)
   2. Victory over the monster and the false prophet (19:17–21)
      3. The binding of Satan (20:1–3)
         4. The millennium (20:4–6)
      5. The release of Satan (20:7–10)
   6. The final judgement (20:11–15)
7. The new heavens and new earth (21:1–8)

First Vision: The Rider on the White Horse   (19:11–16)

(11) Then I saw heaven open, and there was a white horse, whose rider was called 'Trustworthy and True'. He judges and wages war in justice. (12) His eyes were like a fiery flame, and

on his head were many diadems; he had a name written on him which no-one else knows. (13) He was dressed in a cloak which had been dipped in blood, and he was called 'The Word of God'. (14) Heavenly armies followed him on white horses, dressed in fine linen, white and clean. (15) Out of his mouth there came a sharp sword, with which to strike the nations. He will shepherd them with an iron sceptre, and he treads the winepress containing the wine of the furious anger of God the Almighty. (16) On his cloak and on his thigh he had a name written: 'King of kings and Lord of lords'.

This opening vision has often been understood as a description of Christ's Parousia, his final coming in glory. This would fit in with the broad eschatological pattern that is established in 19:11—21:8, which takes us through the Messiah's battle and messianic age to the final victory over the evil powers. Yet there are reasons for some hesitation here (McKelvey 1999: 77–80). First, the strong military imagery of this scene is unusual for an early Christian Parousia scene. Second, a number of the features normally associated with Christ's coming again are lacking (though there are similarities with 2 Thess. 1:6–10): the coming with or on the clouds (e.g. 1:7; Mt. 24:30; 26:64; Mk 13:26; 14:62; Lk. 21:27); the gathering of the elect (e.g. Mt. 13:41, 49; 16:27; 24:31; Mk 8:38; 13:27; 1 Thess. 4:15–18). Nor is it clear that the warrior figure here is accompanied by his angels (see on verse 14). If this is a Parousia scene, its primary focus (and that of the second scene in 19:17–21) is not on the coming of Christ or the gathering of God's people but on the battle with God's enemies. These two related scenes are part of a series of battle and other judgement visions in Revelation (e.g. 11:7–10; 12:7–12; 14:14–20; 17:12–14). In particular, 19:11–21 echoes the battle at Har-Magedon, preparations for which were described at 16:12–16, and the full-blooded version of that last battle at 20:7–10, which will result in the definitive defeat of Satan. In the Apocalypse's cyclic pattern, the battle against the forces of evil and chaos is viewed from every conceivable angle, and exploited for every conceivable effect. But it is not a new battle: it is essentially the battle fought and won on the cross, replayed with shocking mythological vividness. Two biblical passages have particularly influenced what John sees: Isaiah's description of YHWH returning from his bloody victory over the Edomites (Isa. 63:1–6), and the descent of the warrior-like Word of God upon the Egyptian first-born (Wis. 18:14–16).

11–13   Previous breaks in the visionary section of Revelation have been marked by some kind of opening in the heavenly realm, highlighting a particular moment of revelation (4:1; 11:19; 15:5; cf. 8:1). This final section also begins with John seeing **heaven open,** enabling him to witness a **rider** on **a white horse.** This is the second such horse in the book: the first emerged at the opening of the first seal, and its rider rode out as a conqueror (6:1–2). This rider too is a conqueror, engaged in a war that he is destined to win. But there are good grounds for distinguishing between the two. Although white is the colour of heaven and of victory, in chapter 6 it is probably a deceptive cover for a figure who is a false Christ, perhaps even Antichrist (see on 6:1–2). The warrior here, however, is clearly Christ: **His eyes were like a fiery flame** (like the son of man figure at 1:14; note also the 'sharp sword' in verse 15: cf. 1:16); the first of his names, **Trustworthy and True,** has already been used as a description of Christ at 3:14. In contrast to the first rider's one wreath of victory, the 'seven diadems' of the dragon (12:3) and the 'ten diadems' of the monster (13:1), Christ the Divine Warrior wears **many diadems** on his head. The diadem is a symbol of royal authority: there are many because Christ has many realms in his universal kingship, in contrast to the arrogant (but limited) assumption of royal power by the dragon and its accomplices.

The contrast between the royal rule of Christ and that of the monster is expressly stated: this royal warrior **judges and wages war in justice.** The words echo Isa. 11:3–4, a passage which had already been interpreted by Jews as a prophecy of the royal Messiah (e.g. 4QpIsaᵃ; *Pss Sol.* 17:24–27). In contrast to the unjust regime of the monster, which sustained the economically exploitative Babylon, and its violent wars against the followers of the Lamb, the reign of that Lamb and the battle in which it engages are marked by justice, which in biblical terms has a particular concern for the poor and meek of the earth (Isa. 11:4). It is a regime utterly appropriate to the one who is called Trustworthy and True.

Yet Trustworthy and True – summing up the character of this figure – is just the first of a number of names by which this Warrior is called. He also **had a name written on him** (presumably on his clothing) **which no-one else knows.** Given that it is unknown to others, it is surely not the name revealed in the following verse, **The Word of God.** It may, however, be 'my new name' which he promised to the victor in the message to Philadelphia's angel (3:12): probably the name 'Lord' given to him by his Father (cf. Phil. 2:9), with which his faithful followers are inscribed (14:1). The emphasis upon its unknowability is significant in a world where possession of someone's name (including that of a deity) gave control over them. Ultimately this Divine Warrior cannot be controlled or tamed, still less brought in to fight personal battles. He remains something of a mystery.

The third name evokes the image of the stern warrior described in chapter 18 of the Wisdom of Solomon: the Word of God who swoops down from heaven during the gentle silence of night, to wreak havoc on the sleeping Egyptians through the last great Exodus plague (Wis. 18:14–16). The Exodus plagues have been a continual theme throughout the trumpets and bowls sequences; in this ultimate scene of judgement, the new Exodus plagues seem to have reached their climax. The Word of God, spoken by God in the beginning to bring order out of chaos, and spoken again and again throughout salvation history, has now returned one last time as a mighty warrior to bring the divine plan to completion.

Yet there are indications here, as there have been elsewhere in Revelation, that traditional patterns have been radically reshaped in the light of the story of Jesus. First, **he was dressed in a cloak which had been dipped in blood.** Jewish-Christian audiences would hear echoes of Isaiah 63, describing God's return from battle against Edom, which he has defeated on Israel's behalf. There too his robes are red with blood; he speaks of having trodden the winepress, a claim which will also be made of the warrior Christ in verse 15 (cf. 14:19–20). In contrast to Isaiah 63, however, Christ is here on his way to the battle, which will not be described until 19:17–21. The logic of the vision suggests that this is not the blood of those he will encounter there, but someone else's. Almost certainly it is his own blood, that of the slaughtered Lamb, by which he sets his people free from their sins (1:5). It may perhaps be mingled with the blood of his faithful witnesses: in a dramatic visionary exchange, the whitening of their robes by Christ's blood (7:14) is achieved by the reddening of his robes by theirs. This then is a vision of the Christ who conquers not by killing his enemies but by allowing himself to be killed, and who invites his followers to do the same.

14–16 The rider is followed by **heavenly armies,** who like him are riding **on white horses.** This suggests that they are engaged in the same battle, and pursuing the same military tactics. Because they belong to heaven, these armies are often understood as the angelic hosts, who were expected to accompany Christ at his return (e.g. Zech. 14:5; Mt. 13:41; 24:30–31; 25:31; *1 En.* 1:9). But the description of their clothing suggests a different interpretation: they are **dressed in fine linen, white and clean.** Angels can wear 'fine linen, shining and clean' (15:6); however, audiences would probably think first of the most recent use of that phrase, to describe 'the just deeds of the holy ones' with which the bride is adorned (19:8). Further, the linen of these armies is white: the colour of the robes worn by the victors in Sardis and Laodicea (3:4–5, 18), the souls of the martyrs (6:11), and the victorious multitude (7:9, 13, 14). These armies are therefore not the angels, but rather faithful human followers of the Lamb, who have fought the Lamb's battle by the word of their witness, even to the point of shedding their own blood. Committed to heaven during their earthly existence, they now find themselves among the heavenly armies. Yet they do not participate at all in the fighting of this last battle; that is left to the one wearing battle-dress, who wields a sharp sword.

The warrior's **sharp sword** reflects the weapon of the descending Word of God (Wis. 18:16). But we misunderstand the apocalyptic imagery if we regard this as a literal weapon of war. Rather it comes **out of his mouth**: the same sword as wielded by 'someone like a son of man' at 1:16, which is the double-edged sword of his word (cf. Heb. 4:12–13). The Wisdom of Solomon has been read in the light of Isaiah 11, and both in the light of the story of Jesus: the word from his mouth is the only weapon that this warrior wields. Yet it is a powerful word, a destructive word with capacity to kill, for it speaks only the truth and unmasks the lie. Before it, all that is based on falsehood will crumble and die. When he strikes the nations enthralled to the monster and Babylon it will have devastating effect, as the monster's house of cards, built on lies, comes tumbling down.

But this figure is not simply a warrior; he is also a messianic ruler whose royal rule is marked by justice in judgement. Psalm 2, a favourite psalm for John, is again in the background: this king will **shepherd them with an iron sceptre** (Rev. 2:26–27; 12:5; Ps. 2:8–9). The ambiguity implicit in the psalm is played on again here, for the protective shepherding of the king could also be understood as severe ruling, and the iron sceptre experienced as a threatening rod (see on 12:5). His fourth and final name, written **on his cloak and on his thigh** (or possibly on that part of his cloak which covers his thigh), reflects his cosmic kingship: **King of kings and Lord of lords** (17:14). This is another example of titles originally addressed to God being transferred to Christ, who acts on God's behalf.

At last the identity of the mysterious figure who trod 'the great winepress of God's fury' (14:19–20) is divulged. Hints that it was Christ were provided by the location of the winepress 'outside the city', where Christ's crucifixion occurred. Now that is confirmed: **he treads the winepress containing the wine of the furious anger of God the Almighty**. Again, Isaiah 63 is in the background: there God tells how he trod the winepress alone, and makes clear that the colour of grape juice on his garments is the blood of peoples whom he has trampled down in his anger. This powerful image of judgement is taken up by Revelation. Once again Revelation forces us to ask who is being trampled. Does the divine judgement require the shedding of additional human blood? Or does the blood of the Lamb slaughtered 'outside the city' bring judgement enough upon those complicit in its death, the whole machinery of the monstrous empire which triumphs by wielding literal swords, thus creating more than enough blood to rise up to a horse's bridle (14:20)?

Second Vision: Victory over the Monster and the False Prophet (19:17–21)

(17) Then I saw an angel standing in the sun. He cried out in a loud voice to all the birds flying high in the sky: 'Come and assemble for God's great banquet, (18) so that you may eat the flesh of kings, generals and those in power, the flesh of horses and their riders, the flesh of all, freedmen and slaves, little ones and great!' (19) Then I saw the monster together with earth's kings and their armies, assembled to wage war with the rider on the horse and with his army. (20) But the monster was captured, and with it the false prophet who performed signs in its presence, by which those who received the branded mark of the monster and worshipped its statue were led astray. These two were thrown still alive into the fiery lake burning with sulphur, (21) while the rest were killed by the sword that came out of the mouth of the rider on the horse, and all the birds feasted on their flesh.

17–18 The arrival of the divine warrior with his armies enables the battle scene to begin. Heaven is in control: earthly armies do not initiate the battle, but must bide heaven's own time. John now sees **an angel standing in the sun**. The angel's location may simply stress his proximity to the birds he is about to address; however, the dazzling appearance which such a location would produce may also be implied (cf. the powerful angel of 10:1, whose face was like the sun). This angel **cried out in a loud voice** to issue his invitation to a **banquet**; a similar phrase is used of the angel who announces Babylon's fall at 18:1, making a strong parallel between the two announcements. The primary background here is Ezekiel's vision of Gog's armies, in which the prophet is bidden to summon the birds and wild animals to a gruesome feast of the slain from those troops (Ezek. 39:17–20). However, if John has been meditating sequentially on Ezekiel's book in preparation for his visionary experience, the theme may already have been suggested by Ezek. 29:1–8 and 32:4–6 (Ezekiel 29 and 32, with their prophecy that the dragon Pharaoh will be captured, underlie the binding of the Satanic dragon at 20:1–3). Gruesome though Revelation's vision is, its primary imagery has been drawn from the deep reservoir of biblical tradition.

This chilling scene is the antithesis of the Lamb's wedding banquet, to which God's people have just been invited (19:9). Christian audiences might also hear it as a gross parody of the eucharistic banquet. In contrast to the meal which enables participation in the Lamb's life-giving body and blood, the consequences of the monster's regime of death is this meal of dead flesh. Whereas Ezekiel's vision summoned both birds and wild animals, the angel's invitation is restricted to **all the birds flying high in the sky** (literally 'in mid-heaven'). This phrase recalls the eagle which also flew high in the sky to announce the impending three woes (8:13; cf. 14:6), suggesting that these predatory birds may in particular be invited. The grisly menu consists of those who resolutely refuse to abandon the monster's army, without distinction on grounds of rank or social status: **the flesh of kings, generals and those in power, the flesh of horses and their riders, the flesh of all, freedmen and slaves, little ones and great.** The list recalls those who attempted to hide from the Lamb's anger at the opening of the sixth seal (6:15–17).

Unlike Ezekiel's prophecy, the announcement of Revelation's banquet occurs even before the battle has taken place. Yet even when the troops finally muster for battle, it is over and done with as soon as it begins. This is no protracted contest, and the conflict is disappointing for those expecting violent and bloody details. We simply hear of **the monster together with earth's kings and their armies** assembling against the forces of **the rider on the horse**, for the battle of Har-Magedon mentioned at 16:16. The allied forces which brought Babylon crashing down now turn their attention on the Lamb and its followers (a battle which has in fact been raging ever since Jesus and his followers first bore witness: see e.g. 11:7). But they are swiftly and definitively dealt with, presumably by the one who has already won the victory on the cross. The earthly manifestation of evil power, enshrined in a political system and those structures by which it is sustained, are finally defeated as **the monster** and **the false prophet** are **captured** and **thrown still alive into the fiery lake burning with sulphur.** This lake, whose very essence is destruction, is the final destination not only of these manifestations of evil, oppression and falsehood, but eventually also of Satan, and the other enemies to be destroyed, Death and Hades (20:10, 14). The imaginative source for this lake may be Gehenna, the burning Hinnom Valley outside Jerusalem which came to typify a place of punishment and exclusion (e.g. Mt. 5:22; 18:9; Jas 3:6); the reference to **sulphur** may evoke the sulphurous area around the Dead Sea (e.g. Gen. 19:24; sulphur is one of the plagues showered on Gog and his troops at Ezek. 38:22). It is to be distinguished from the present realm of evil, the sea or Abyss, which will disappear completely (21:1).

The fate of the monster and false prophet is not the fate of their armies, however. Instead these are **killed by the sword that came**

19–21

out of the mouth of the rider on the horse. They provide the main course for the birds gathered for the banquet. They have to be dealt with, because they are the human agents of the monster's rebellious and arrogant pretensions. All that stands in the way of the Messiah's just and trustworthy reign must be confronted. However, the nature of their deaths remains a question. They are **killed**, not by any weapons that they themselves might use, but **by the sword** from the rider's **mouth**. The word of God, the fiery word of truth issuing forth from the Messiah's mouth, is what effects the death rather than any physical act of slaughter (Isa. 11:4; *4 Ez.* 13:9–11; 2 Thess. 2:8; cf. Heb. 4:12–13). It is the definitive word of judgement: a judicial act phrased in military terms (Beasley-Murray 1974: 284). Whether it also implies the literal deaths of the monster's troops is not made clear; it is perhaps significant, however, that in Revelation's unfolding visionary kaleidoscope the same 'earth's kings' will re-emerge to bring their glory into the new Jerusalem (21:24).

Third Vision: The Binding of Satan (20:1–3)

(1) Then I saw an angel descending from heaven, with the key to the Abyss and a large chain in his hand. (2) He seized the dragon, that ancient serpent, who is 'Devil' and 'the Satan', and chained it up for a thousand years. (3) Then he threw it into the Abyss, which he locked and sealed over it, so that it could not lead the nations astray any more, until the thousand years were over. After this it must be released for a little while.

With the capture of the monster and the false prophet, the deception of the nations and the onslaught on God's people has been brought to an end. Yet until the ultimate power behind the throne has been dealt with, the fear will remain that another monster could emerge Nero-like from the Abyss. At the heart of John's visions of the End, therefore, are the binding (20:1–3) and final defeat (20:7–10) of the real enemy, Satan, and at the very centre between these a vision of the Satan-free millennial reign of Christ (20:4–6). The basic theme for this first part of this visionary triptych has been suggested by those same passages from Ezekiel which may have initially provoked the previous vision: Ezekiel 29 and especially Ezekiel 32. In Ezekiel's visions, the great sprawling dragon, personified in the Pharaoh of Egypt, is drawn out by God, captured in a net, and given as food to the animals and birds (cf. 19:17–21). In Revelation's visionary world, Satan's troops have suffered the fate of becoming food for the birds; now it is the dragon itself which becomes the centre of attention. Another prophetic antecedent is probably Isa. 24:21–22, which speaks of the imprisoning of the host of heaven as well as the kings of the earth (cf. the binding of Azazel by Raphael until the day of judgement at *1 En.* 10:4-6).

This binding of the rebel leader is not unexpected, however. Already in Revelation 12 Satan's expulsion from heaven, and that of his rebellious angels, was described in vivid terms (12:4, 7-9). At that point, as a result of the birth-death and exaltation of the male child, evil lost its foothold in the heavenly realm. The dragon was reduced to activity in the two lower realms: the sea/Abyss and the earth. But even its earthly activity was to be short-lived: its attack on the off-spring of the woman, the followers of the Lamb, was to be for the limited time of three and a half years (cf. 11:2-3; 13:5). It knew even then that its time was short (12:12). The same combat myth that Revelation used to proclaim Satan's expulsion from heaven is now evoked once again as the dragon loses its foothold, at least tem-porarily, on the earth as well. The underworld, the Abyss, is all that remains for it now; yet even that will be temporary (see 20:7-10).

John describes how he sees **an angel descending from heaven**: the 1 angel's heavenly origin marks him out as an agent of God, whose angelic activity will mediate positive effects for the earth. Thus, although he holds **the key to the Abyss**, he cannot be the angel of the Abyss Apollyon (9:11), a Satan-like figure from the lower realm. Nor is he the one who originally opened the Abyss with a key, allowing the demonic plague of locusts to emerge (9:1-2), for that key-holder was one of the fallen angels. Rather, this scene describes a heavenly action which dramatically reverses the fifth trumpet-plague. There the use of the key opened a door which allowed destructive forces to come up onto the earth; here the use of the same key closes that door after the greatest destructive force has been imprisoned below the earth. The angel's role as not only key-holder but also prison warder is confirmed by the **large chain in his hand**, large enough to bind such a dangerous and troublesome captive. His role is first to restrain and then to lock the prisoner securely away, to pre-vent any more crimes being committed. Unlike some modern Wes-tern prisons, however, the purpose of prisons in the ancient world was not to be a long-term place of punishment, but rather a location in which criminals could be detained awaiting trial, which for many meant certain death. So too this prison can only be the temporary resting-place of the rebellious dragon, and the angel only its tem-porary gaoler.

The ancient combat myth so vividly evoked in Revelation 12 func- 2-3 tioned on the knowledge that the forces of evil and chaos are powerful indeed, and can only be defeated in battle by a more powerful opponent. The Israelite version refused to see this as an evenly matched battle: it was one whose outcome was assured. In the Christian retelling of the story in Revelation 12, the definitive victory had been won not in primeval times but on the cross of Christ. That passage is recalled here explicitly, by its reminder that the dragon is **that ancient serpent, who is 'Devil' and 'the Satan'**. This raises a question: is this simply a repeat of the previous vision of Satan's downfall, in different words? One ancient way of understanding this passage and the one which follows it (20:4–6) would answer this in the affirmative. According to Augustine, following the lead set by Tyconius, what we have here is a description of the 'binding of the strong man' which began with the first coming of Christ (Mt. 12:29, reflected in the defeat of the demons in Christ's earthly ministry) and will continue throughout the time of the Church – the millennial age – until the end of the world (Aug. *Civ. Dei* 20.7–8). This interpretation has a certain appeal, reflecting as it does the motifs of the sealing of God's people and the measuring of the sanctuary, offering spiritual protection even in the midst of physical suffering and persecution. Nevertheless, this vision does seem to move one step further: the expulsion of Satan from heaven allowed him to attack the children of the woman clothed with the sun, those who continue the witness of Jesus (12:17); with his binding and temporary expulsion from the earth, even that terrestrial activity has ceased.

The angel **seized the dragon** and **chained it up for a thousand years**. The violence of its arrest not only highlights the divine power invested in the angel, who is strong enough to apprehend such a powerful and dangerous creature; it also reflects the equally violent manner in which agents of the dragon had seized not only Jesus (e.g. Mt. 26:50, 55; Mk 14:1) but some of his followers such as the Neronian martyrs, a pattern which the visionary John saw would repeat itself with ever-increasing violence in the future. But then, only violent restraint is sufficient to ensure that Satan can do no further harm: he is first **seized**, then **chained**, then thrown **into the Abyss** or bottomless pit below the earth. Finally the angel **locked and sealed the Abyss over the dragon**: the sealing of the entrance would have ensured that no attempted escape went unnoticed (Swete 1906: 261). The chaining is to be **for a thousand years**: like Revelation's other numbers, this is to be interpreted symbolically, denoting a long period of time which nevertheless is not indefinite in extent. Augustine noted that a thousand is the cube of the number ten (*Civ. Dei* 20.7), a natural round number signifying completion (e.g. 2:10; cf. 12:3; 13:1). **The thousand years** will be described from their positive perspective in 20:4–6, as the millennial reign of Christ and those who come to life with him. Here it describes the time during which the dragon **could not lead the nations astray** any more (recalling its identity as 'the deceiver of the whole world', 12:9). The temporary, limited nature of this Satan-free state is clear, as John prepares his audiences for a subsequent scene: after the thousand years it must be released for a little while (μικρὸν χρόνον). Its future activity will match its previous activity against the offspring of the woman, where it knew that it had little time left (ὀλίγον καιρὸν, 12:12).

Fourth Vision: The Millennium   (20:4–6)

(4) Then I saw thrones, with people seated on them, and judgement was given in their favour. These were the souls of those who had been beheaded for continuing the witness which Jesus bore, that is God's word, and those who had not worshipped the monster or its statue, and had not received the branded mark on their forehead or hand. They came to life and shared Christ's royal rule for a thousand years. (5) The rest of the dead did not come to life until the thousand years were over. This is the first resurrection. (6) Happy and holy is the one who has a share in the first resurrection. The second death has no power over such people; they will be priests serving God and Christ, and will share his royal rule for the thousand years.

Sandwiched between the imprisonment and release of the dragon lies a passage which has received attention far outweighing its proportionate role in the book as a whole (comprising a mere three verses out of a total of 405): the description of the so-called millennium. It is also one of the most debated and controversial of passages. It has been interpreted as a literal reign of a thousand years, as a terrestrial kingdom without any specific length, and as an allegorical description of the period between individual death and general resurrection. It has been placed chronologically either before Christ's Parousia (post-millennialism) or after it (pre-millennialism). It has been regarded as a gift which only God can grant, and as a goal towards which human effort and Christian faithfulness should strive. It has been located both in heaven and on earth. (For a survey of differing views, see Wainwright 1993: 21–103; McKelvey 1999: 13–41; Kovacs and Rowland 2004: 201–14.)

Though not common, the idea of an interim reign prior to the judgement and the new heavens and new earth can be found elsewhere in Jewish thought (e.g. *1 En.* 91:11–17; *2 Bar.* 29:1—30:5; 40:1–4; 72:1—74:3). This seems to reflect an attempt to hold together the hope for an earthly messianic kingdom with the more apocalyptic hope for the renewal of creation. In certain forms, it gives a key role in this interim period to the Messiah (*4 Ez.* 7:26–44; 12:31–34). However, the Apocalypse's precise focus on a period of **a thousand years** sets it apart from the others: *4 Ezra* envisages a messianic age of four hundred years (*4 Ez.* 7:28). It may be, as early Christian tradition suggests, that the number was derived from a reading of Gen. 2:1 (creation in six days, followed by a seventh day of sabbath rest) in conjunction with Ps. 90:4/2 Pet. 3:8 (a day as a thousand years: e.g. *Ep. Barn.* 15:3–5): the millennium would then represent the sixth day prior to the endless sabbath (see e.g. Aug. *Civ. Dei* 20.7). In John's scheme of things, however, the immediate inspiration for the vision at this point may have been his sequential meditation upon Ezekiel, at this point Ezekiel 37, which describes both the resurrection of God's dead people (Ezek. 37:1–14) and the reign of the Davidic king (Ezek. 37:15–28).

Whatever John's antecedents may be, the question which seems to underlie this vision is the following: who or what will take the place on earth of the now-defeated instruments of rebellion and corrupt rule? Or perhaps more pertinently, what might our world look like governed not by the oppressors but by the victims? The answer provided, which picks up on Ezekiel's two themes along with the courtroom imagery of Dan. 7:9–27, gives a particular role to the martyrs. In a real sense, whether understood as a chronological period at the end of history, or as an alternative state which empowers God's people in any age of the Church's existence, it promises a special place to those prepared to lay down their lives. The reward for would-be martyrs is a place in the millennial reign.

4 The appropriate translation of the first part of verse 4 is not altogether clear. It literally reads: 'And I saw thrones and they sat on them and judgement was given to them, and the souls of those beheaded on account of the witness of Jesus and on account of the word of God and whoever did not worship the monster nor its image and did not receive the branded mark on the forehead and on their hand.' There are at least three issues here for the translator:

   (i) Who precisely are sitting on the thrones?
  (ii) What is meant by 'judgement was given to them'?
 (iii) Are the 'beheaded' and those who 'did not worship the monster' the same group, or two different ones?

The answer to the first question might appear straightforward. Up to now, apart from God and the Lamb (who are surely not meant here, given that God is the implied agent of the verb **was given**), the only positive characters described as seated on thrones have been the twenty-four elders (e.g. 4:4; 11:16; both Satan and the monster have a 'throne': 2:13; 13:2; 16:10). An attentive audience would probably expect the same group here. However, John has hitherto felt no difficulty in mentioning the twenty-four elders explicitly; it would be odd, then, not to do so if they were intended here also. There is, however, an alternative solution: that those on the thrones are in fact **the souls of those who had been beheaded** etc. This would entail taking the καί ('and') epexegetically, that is as an explanatory 'even' or 'that is' ('the souls' are in the accusative because they are 'seen' by John along with the thrones). The ones who **came to life and shared Christ's royal rule** are then not a different group to those seated on thrones, but the same. The promise that they will sit on thrones and rule the nations has already been made to the conquerors in the seven messages (cf. 2:26–27; 3:21).

This is confirmed when the influence of Dan. 7:9–27 is acknowledged, an influence which also helps answer question (ii). In Daniel's vision, thrones are set in place alongside the throne of the Ancient of Days, and judgement is given in favour of the holy ones of the Most High over the fourth monster with its destructive horn. The LXX of Dan. 7:22 is particularly close to the phrase John uses here, and suggests strongly that the latter should be translated not as 'they were permitted to pronounce judgement' but **judgement was given in their favour**. The enthroned ones, then, are not so much judges (though as co-rulers they will also have that responsibility: Mt. 19:28; Lk. 22:30; 1 Cor. 6:2) as those who have received vindication in the heavenly court. The millennium is the state in which those who suffered for their faithful witness find the tables reversed in their favour.

The third issue relates to their precise identity, and again hangs on the interpretation of a καί or 'and'. Are **the souls of those who had been beheaded** also **those who had not worshipped the monster or its statue**? This would restrict participation in the millennial reign to those who have laid down their lives **for continuing the witness which Jesus bore, that is God's word** (for this phrase, see on 1:2). Indeed, it would refer to a more restricted group still, since death by beheading is not explicitly the fate of either Pergamum's Antipas (2:13) or Revelation's two witnesses (11:7), nor was it the fate of many of Nero's victims in the persecution which began in 64 CE (the verb John uses, πελεκίζω, points to official execution by the axe, πέλεκυς, a punishment probably reserved to the *honestiores* or higher echelons of Roman society). Later traditions about the martyrdoms of Peter and Paul have the former being crucified, the latter decapitated by the sword. It is possible that John knew of the fate of Antipas and some other Christian martyrs as decapitation by the axe (Aune 1998b: 1087), and this is reflected in his choice of verb. Whatever the case may be, the fact remains that to restrict the reigning on thrones to those beheaded would restrict it to a limited number even of the martyrs.

But is there more to John's vision? To use later ecclesial distinctions, does it have room for 'confessors' as well as 'martyrs'? There are reasonable grounds for positing more than one group here, so that John sees enthroned not simply the beheaded but others who died by other means, and indeed all those who refused to worship **the monster or its statue, and had not received the branded mark on their forehead or hand**. Perhaps the ambiguity is deliberate: Revelation certainly urges Christian audiences to put themselves in a position where they might find themselves laying down their lives, and indeed sometimes presents death as almost a foregone conclusion (cf. 13:15). The millennial reign is presented as the reward for the martyrs, those serious enough in their Christian witness to shed their blood. But it would be out of character for the Apocalypse to deny it to those whose witness during the time of the monster, although faithful, had fallen short of the supreme sacrifice.

The enthroned witnesses **came to life and shared Christ's royal rule**. This suggests that they have died (although the verb ἔζησαν could simply mean 'they lived'), albeit not necessarily that they died a martyr's death. Yet just as death could not silence the slaughtered Lamb, neither can it keep down the Lamb's followers. The death-dealing rule of the monster and the dragon which promoted it has given way to a very different *modus operandi* marked by a royal rule characterised by life. What is equally different about **Christ's royal rule** is that it is **shared**, unlike the pyramidal, totalitarian regime of the monster, or the extravagant reign of Babylon, which sucks all the world's material wealth into itself. Resistance to such a regime bears fruit in this alternative kingdom, built on very different values.

5–6 The privileged role afforded to the faithful witnesses, whether actual martyrs or not, means that **The rest of the dead did not come to life until the thousand years were over**. The resurrection of the righteous on the Last Day, or of all the dead for the general judgement, was a well-established eschatology believed by many (though by no means all) Jews in the first century. The early Christians had made a partial break with this pattern by claiming that one of the dead, Jesus of Nazareth, had been raised prior to the general resurrection. This unique exception, which provided assurance of the resurrection of all the dead, was interpreted in terms such as 'firstfruits' (1 Cor. 15:20). Revelation introduces yet another new element, by distinguishing between **the first resurrection**, in which the beheaded and other faithful witnesses come to life with Christ to reign with him, and the resurrection of **the rest of the dead** (portrayed at 20:12–13), presumably the 'second resurrection' (although John does not explicitly use that term). On this analogy, it is not necessary to posit that those resurrected here must also participate in the 'second resurrection' (any more than will Christ rise again at the final resurrection on the Last Day), though they will participate in the judgement scene of 20:11–15. Indeed, like Christ, these have already been described in Revelation as 'first-fruits' (14:4).

Those who participate in **the first resurrection**, sharing already in Christ's royal rule, are not subject to the power of **the second death** (cf. 2:11). This phrase is attested in the Targum to Jer. 51:39, 57, meaning exclusion from 'the world to come' (Harrington 1993: 197). It denotes spiritual death, contrasted with 'the first death', presumably natural death, through which the martyrs have already passed. At verse 14, this second death is equated with being thrown into the lake of fire, that state of separation from God in which the powers and structures of evil are destroyed, and which remains an option in God's world for those whose ultimate choice is to reject him. For the faithful witnesses, the final judgement has already taken place and has found in their favour, guaranteeing participation in the new Jerusalem, of which the millennial reign is a glimpse and a foretaste. The book's fifth beatitude is addressed to them: **Happy and holy is the one who has a share in the first resurrection.** The addition of the word **holy** to the traditional macarism formula may evoke the root meaning of its Hebrew equivalent as 'separated', 'set apart'. After all, they have a priestly role **serving God and Christ**, as well as a **share** in the **royal rule** (the genitive pronoun **his**, αὐτοῦ, is an example of the Apocalypse's capacity to speak of God and the Lamb as one). Although in John's vision they already sit on thrones, the two future verbs reflect the fact that what John sees remains a visionary hope: they **will share his royal rule for the thousand years**.

Fifth Vision: The Release of Satan   (20:7–10)

(7) When the thousand years are over, Satan will be released from his prison, (8) and will emerge to lead the nations astray at the four corners of the earth – Gog and Magog – to assemble them for the battle. Their number will be as great as the sand of the sea. (9) They ascended onto the broad plain of the earth and encircled the camp of the holy ones, that is, the beloved city. But fire descended from heaven and ate them up. (10) Then the devil who leads them astray was thrown into the lake of fire and sulphur where the monster and the false prophet already were. They will be tormented day and night for ever and ever.

7 The final part of the triptych describes the post-millennial release of Satan **from his prison**, his own realm of the Abyss. Again, sequential meditation upon Ezekiel may have influenced the scene, for Ezek. 38:1–39:20 describes the invasion of the land by Gog of the land of Magog, and the final defeat of the forces of evil. Revelation too redescribes that final battle, in which satanic armies launch their last desperate attack on God's people. It is in the nature of evil to resurface and perform its old tricks of deception, its tendency to lead astray by promising what it can never ultimately deliver (cf. 12:9; 13:14; 19:20; 20:3). Moreover, Satan must be released because his imprisonment has not dealt with evil definitively. Evil is still lurking, albeit chained; the fiery, glassy sea before the throne has been a reminder of this almost from the beginning of the book (4:6; 15:2).

Yet in the light of what has preceded and what will follow, the release of Satan has lost its gloss. John's alternative vision of a world in which Christ shares his reign with the martyrs has robbed the dragon of its power, and its continuing capacity to instil fear. Moreover, John sees the irony inherent in that release: for its freedom paradoxically brings about its downfall. The last battle the dragon instigates will set the seal on previous lesser battles in which evil, chaos and rebellion had begun to lose their grip through the resistance of those who continue Jesus' testimony.

8–9 This last battle is described with the full panoply of apocalyptic drama, with Ezekiel's vision never far below the surface. Though involving human actors, these are presented as little more than unwitting pawns in the game that Satan is playing, as he emerges **to lead the nations astray**. Their location **at the four corners of the earth** stresses the fact that the dragon's deception will be universal. It might also suggest its destructive intent, for John has previously seen the four winds being restrained at those same four corners before being let loose on the earth (7:1). The appearance of **the nations** again here, after the 'deaths' of earth's kings at 19:21, is a warning against too literal or even chronological a reading of the visions in these last few chapters. They speak of the reality of evil's defeat, rather than offering a precise timetable of events by which that comes to pass.

Indeed, although the language of 'the last battle' is not inappropriate, given that what is being described is the final assault on evil, it is not essentially a different battle from those mentioned before. It is the battle of Har-Magedon, prepared for but not actually described at 16:14–16; it replays, yet with more universal effect, the defeat of the monster and its troops at 19:17–21. Most importantly, it brings to its conclusion the definitive battle won in the heavenly realm – that is, where ultimate decisions are made – as a consequence

of the death and exaltation of the Lamb (12:10–12). Therefore it is
the decisive battle, painted here on a large canvas, which has been
played out in those little victories won wherever people hold faithfully to the witness which Jesus himself bore.

Under Ezekiel's influence, the nations are revealed as **Gog and
Magog**. In fact, Ezek. 38:2 speaks of Gog as a person, the chief
prince of Meshech and Tubal, who leads a coalition of troops against
Israel, while Magog is the land from which he comes (cf. Gen. 10:2,
which speaks of Magog as an individual, the son of Japheth). Later
Jewish tradition had come to speak of Gog and/or Magog as
eschatological enemies of God's people (Bøe 2001: 140–234), and it is
in that sense that John invokes them here in a mythic picture of the
rebellious nations' last battle against the people of God. For those
who have not seen the rival vision of the millennial reign, this scene is
terrifying indeed, as the ancient associations of Gog and Magog
suggest. The hostile armies are huge in extent, their number **as great
as the sand of the sea** (a similar description is given of the armies
which join forces against Israel at Josh. 11:4).

Their monster-like ascent **onto the broad plain of the earth** is
probably meant to suggest a mighty army swarming onto Israel's
greatest battlefield, the broad Jezreel Valley, overlooked by 'the
Mountain of Megiddo' (16:16): the tense changes back from the
future of verses 7–8 to the aorist more frequently used in John's
visionary descriptions. Whereas Ezekiel's armies attacked the people
of Israel, however, John's more universalistic reading regards them as
besieging God's new people gathered 'from every tribe and language,
people and nation'. **The beloved city** (a description of Jerusalem at
Sir. 24:11; cf. Pss 78:68; 87:2) is probably 'the holy city', which has
already been used as a symbol for the Church (11:2), the manifestation of the new Jerusalem which is in the process of coming.
Reminding his audiences that this people is the new Exodus people, a
community still on its journey through the wilderness separating
Babylon from new Jerusalem (see e.g. Isa. 40:1–11), he also calls it
the camp of the holy ones (cf. Heb. 13:11, 13). This is not simply a
military camp, but the encampment of God's pilgrim people, recalling its wilderness wanderings (e.g. Exod. 16:13; Josh. 1:11).

But again, as in Revelation's previous 'battle scenes', an actual
battle is not fought. Rather, the troops are eaten up by **fire** which
descended from heaven. Heavenly fire is a symbol of judgement,
associated with the prophet Elijah (2 Kgs 1:10), and linked to the
destruction of both Gog (Ezek. 38:22) and Magog (Ezek. 39:6).
Judgement certainly occurs; whether this judgement is achieved by
the actual deaths of large sections of humanity depends upon the
degree of literalism extended to visions such as this (cf. 19:21).
Embarrassing though many contemporary readers find it, the

language and symbolism of warfare is fundamental for the Apocalypse, because it takes utterly seriously the reality of evil and the nature of the battle in which the world is engaged. Yet it remains precisely that: military symbolism, not the report of a clairvoyant war correspondent.

10 This vision, and the triptych it forms, concludes with a description of the ultimate fate of the dragon or Satan, here described by his Greek name **devil** or διάβολος (a name which means 'calumniator' or 'slanderer'). Unless evil and chaos are going to remain a lingering fear, able to regroup and emerge to see another day, their defeat needs to be, and to be seen to be, final. Hence the task which was begun with the throwing of the monster and false prophet **into the lake of fire and sulphur** (19:20) is now brought to its logical conclusion. Though what is described is not annihilation (*pace* Harrington 1993: 201), it is all-consuming without the possibility of reversal for any of the monstrous triad: **They will be tormented day and night for ever and ever.** This may sound like gloating over the torments of others; addressed to would-be martyrs, however (and its liturgical ring places its focus on Christian worshippers), it functions as a word of reassurance to those who have experienced at first hand what such evil is capable of.

Sixth Vision: The Final Judgement (20:11–15)

(11) Then I saw a great white throne with someone seated on it. From his presence earth and heaven fled, but they found no place to hide. (12) Then I saw the dead, the great and the little ones, standing before the throne. Scrolls were opened, and then another scroll was opened, which is the scroll of life. The dead were judged according to what was written about their deeds in the scrolls. (13) The sea handed over the dead in it, and Death and Hades handed over the dead in them; each of these was judged according to their deeds. (14) Then Death and Hades were thrown into the lake of fire. This is the second death, the lake of fire. (15) Anyone whose name was not found inscribed in the scroll of life was thrown into the lake of fire.

This dramatic scene presents the other side of the coin to the destruction of the dragon, monster and false prophet: the definitive judgement of humanity. It contains elements associated elsewhere with the final judgement: the appearance before the divine throne (e.g. Mt. 25:31); the resurrection of the dead (e.g. Mt. 12:41–42; Jn 5:21–22); the opening of books or scrolls (e.g. Dan. 7:10); judgement in accordance with human actions (e.g. *1 En.* 1:3–9; Rom. 2:5–11; 2

Cor. 5:10). This does not mean that it is to be regarded as following
on chronologically from the demise of the dragon, still less from the
fiery judgement of the nations (20:9–10). Its position here has again
been suggested by Ezekiel, with his vision of judgement and
restoration (Ezek. 39:21–29). Moreover, this scene presents one
aspect, albeit a very prominent aspect, of Judgement Day: its corporate nature, highlighting the human solidarity both in sin and evil
and in grace and righteous action. But when one goes below the
surface, it is a remarkably restrained and matter-of-fact picture.
Perhaps over the centuries artists have been among the better commentators on such scenes. Visual portrayals of the Last Judgement,
from the portals of medieval cathedrals to the frescoes of Giotto and
Michelangelo, have resorted to combining several of Revelation's
visions (as well as other scriptural passages and in some cases non-
biblical texts) in order to present a rounded and aesthetically satisfying account.

John first sees **a great white throne**, which stands in contrast to the 11
many thrones of 20:4–6. The **someone seated on it** is surely to be
identified with the one on the throne, the figure of God (white has
functioned hitherto as the colour of heaven and of victory; here it
may also connote the dazzling brightness of the throne). There is a
strong parallel with Daniel's vision of the Ancient of Day's throne,
white being the colour of his clothing (Dan. 7:9). The theme of
judgement, and the ultimate vindication of God's holy ones, is clear.
Given the recent use of the singular pronoun to cover both God and
the Lamb, however (20:6), it is possible that the face of Christ is to be
seen on that unnamed enthroned figure (an exegesis reflected in
much of the artistic tradition, where the judgement is carried out by
Christ on the throne).

But where one might have expected universal cataclysm and cosmic disaster, the terrible scenarios often envisaged of nuclear holo-
caust leading to the obliteration of the planet, John resorts to poetic
hyperbole: **From his presence earth and heaven fled, but they
found no place to hide** (cf. 12:8, where no place is found in heaven
for the dragon and its angels). This cannot be a literal description, for
if earth and heaven truly fled the heavenly throne would lose its
location, and the sea would have no shore on which to disgorge its
contents (see verse 13). Rather, Revelation describes in mythological
terms the coming to an end of the old order, that aspect of creation
fatally compromised by its association with evil, chaos and injustice.
Such an order cannot stand before the terrifying presence of God,
whose light exposes the darkness of deception and falsehood. Indeed,
with the flight of earth and heaven, the demarcation between God's
realm and the place where humanity lives is beginning to disappear

(it will lose all significance in the new Jerusalem, where heaven and earth, God and humanity, will be united: 21:3).

12–13 Moving outwards from the throne (as Revelation has done before: 4:1—5:14), John now sees those who are destined to be judged: **the dead, the great and the little ones, standing before the throne.** Death is the great leveller: all must ultimately appear before the judgement seat of God (e.g. Rom. 14:10; 2 Cor. 5:10), without distinction in terms of status or power. That **the great and the little ones** include both God's servants and those in rebellion against him is clear from other uses of this phrase (11:18; 13:16; 19:5, 18): this is a scene of universal judgement. This does not necessarily contradict 20:4–6, however, which presents the faithful martyr-witnesses as having already received judgement in their favour; rather we glimpse here the wider picture, in which their vindication is paralleled by the possibility of unfavourable judgement against other human beings. Ironically, all are **standing before the throne.** Although this is the appropriate posture of suppliants before God, as also in the presence of the emperor, the question had been raised rhetorically at 6:17 in relation to the great day of the Lamb's anger: who is able to stand? Perhaps it is their resurrection state, like that of the Lamb (5:6), which enables them to 'stand' (Smalley 2005: 517).

In Daniel's vision, books or scrolls were opened (Dan. 7:10). So also John sees that **scrolls were opened** (the passive suggesting that they were opened by God, or Christ or the angels on God's behalf). These scrolls clearly contain a record of all human deeds which form the basis of the unfolding judgement, given that **the dead were judged according to what was written about their deeds in the scrolls.** This reflects the tradition of eschatological judgement being made according to the contents of books (3:5; 13:8; 17:8; 21:27; cf. Isa. 4:3; Mal. 3:16; Dan. 12:1). Symbolically, they reveal that nothing which occurs in this world can elude the all-seeing God or the knowledge of the seven-eyed Lamb, whether that be the tiniest act of kindness and heroism or the cruellest act of barbarism and injustice. Reassuring though this is that every attempt at faithful witness will be rewarded, it also declares that every human being, irrespective of their rank or social station, stands under judgement. Those who may have appeared to escape justice in this life now find themselves confronted with the burning, searing eyes of divine judgement beyond the grave.

In order for this to happen, the resurrection of those still bound by death has to take place (the 'second resurrection': cf. 20:5). The martyrs and other faithful witnesses have already been raised with Christ to reign with him (20:4–6); now they are joined by their brothers and sisters in Adam. Jewish beliefs about the nebulous 'half-

life' for the dead in Sheol have come together with Greek notions of
Hades as the underworld abode of the departed. These departed need
to be released from their current deathly abode. Hence **Death and
Hades handed over the dead in them** (these personified figures
have been encountered before, at 6:8). Theologically, they have no
choice, given that by virtue of his victorious resurrection Christ
himself holds the keys of Death and Hades (1:18). But if Christ has
already conquered Death, it has still continued to affect human lives.
Now this 'last enemy' (1 Cor. 15:26) is finally overcome. Along with
Death and Hades, we hear that **the sea** also has **dead** to hand over:
those mariners and others who were drowned in the perilous waters
of this evil Abyss, and who therefore never received an earthly burial.
Their return ensures that all the dead of humanity rise to hear an
account of what they have done.

However, Revelation distinguishes between the plural **scrolls**
(derived from Dan. 7:10; cf. *1 En.* 47:3; *4 Ez.* 6:20) and the separate
scroll of life (possibly the one scroll of Dan. 12:1). The first clearly
reflects the books containing human deeds, a statement that human
deeds have consequences, and humans will be held accountable for
them. The scroll of life would then be that specific ledger containing
the names of God's redeemed people (cf. Exod. 32:32–33; Ps. 69:28),
which earlier has been associated particularly with the Lamb (13:8;
cf. 21:27). It is an assurance, in the midst of a scene of judgement,
that God's faithful people will participate in life with him. It is also a
reminder that, although judgement is not an arbitrary affair but
related to human action, life is ultimately the gift of God, that grace
which makes righteous action and faithful witness a possibility. The
tension between the two types of scroll is a reflection of this very
tension between divine grace and human response.

Given that Death is the last enemy to be destroyed, the end of the   **14–15**
victorious Christ's mopping-up operation, it should come as no
surprise to hear that the mythological figures of **Death and Hades**
are also **thrown into the lake of fire** to join those other cosmic
powers of evil, chaos and injustice which have threatened to destroy
the earth (19:20; 20:10; cf. 11:18). If these are not also thrown into
the enduring place of fiery judgement, then Death's sting may continue to make itself felt (for the lake of fire, see on 19:20). However,
this fiery lake is not simply reserved for mythological figures and
cosmic powers: it remains a possibility also for humanity. It is presented, following conventional imagery, as the place or state to which
those found wanting at the Last Judgement are consigned: **Anyone
whose name was not found inscribed in the scroll of life was
thrown into the lake of fire.**

Some may feel uncomfortable with this statement, which reads

291

rather too much like a threat (although compared with some other descriptions of the punishment of the wicked, Revelation is remarkably restrained: cf. e.g. *Apocalypse of Peter* 5—12). Yet the Apocalypse recognises the very real threat which stubborn allegiance to the dragon represents. It is a path on which one hurtles towards disaster, because the dragon's regime has always been at enmity with order, justice and peace. Nor can Revelation compromise over the basic truth that human actions have consequences, often fatal consequences, and that these must be confronted and judged appropriately. Finally, the presence of this consuming lake of fire, and the possibility of human participation in it, remains a necessity in a Christian worldview which accords any kind of freedom to humanity. It is logically possible to be blotted out, by one's own free action and decision, from the Lamb's scroll of life (cf. 3:5). God calls, God urges, God wills humanity freely to embrace him and his will for their harmony and well-being. Unless God is to coerce, however, his purposes must allow for the tragic possibility of humanity making a definitive choice against him.

Seventh Vision: The New Heavens and New Earth   (21:1–8)

(1) Then I saw a new heaven and a new earth. The former heaven and the former earth had disappeared, and there was no more sea. (2) And I saw the holy city, a new Jerusalem, descending out of heaven from God, prepared like a bride dressed for her husband. (3) Then I heard a loud voice from the throne saying:
'Look! God's tabernacle is among human beings,
and he will pitch his tent with them.
They will be his peoples,
and God himself will be with them, as their God.
(4) He will wipe every tear from their eyes,
and there will be no more death or grief,
no more crying or pain.
For the things of former times have disappeared.'
(5) Then the one seated on the throne said: 'Look! I am making everything new!' He also said, 'Write this: "These words are trustworthy and true!"' (6) He then said to me: 'These things have happened! I am the Alpha and the O, the beginning and the end. The one who is thirsty I will allow to drink without charge from the spring of the water of life. (7) The one who conquers will inherit these things; I will be God to such a person, and he will be my son. (8) However, the cowardly and unfaithful, the detestable and murderers, the sexually unfaithful and sorcerers, idolaters and all liars, will

find their place in the lake burning with fire and sulphur, that is, the second death.'

The Day of Judgement, albeit a fearsome day for those not inscribed in the scroll of life, has not been accompanied by a Big Bang or some other act of cosmic destruction. It is those powers now consigned to the lake of fire which have been intent on destroying the earth. Despite many popular readings of the Apocalypse, such destruction could not be further from the mind of God. Rather, what is revealed in this climactic final vision is that God's mind is intent on re-creation. This is but part of that larger narrative which has been unfolding in previous chapters, a narrative of that new Exodus, modelled on the old, which is a return from Babylonian exile to the new Jerusalem (with Ezekiel 40—48 and Isaiah 40—66 playing an important role: see Mathewson 2003). This motif of an Exodus-like return from exile provides the interpretative lens through which the seven congregations are urged to make sense of their own situation.

Like Isaiah before him (Isa. 65:17; 66:22; cf. *1 En.* 91:16; 2 Pet. 3:13), John recounts how he **saw a new heaven and a new earth**. Yet this is not to be understood in terms of destroying the old or the obsolete in order to replace it with something completely different (neither Isaiah nor John use the language of destruction). Rather, John sees a profound renewal of that which is already there, a heaven and earth which have been judged, purged of those powers which threaten them, now destined to be transformed from the very depths of their being. **The former heaven and the former earth**, which have now disappeared, are the former world order, out of kilter and functioning in a manner contrary to God's original purposes for creation ('the things of former times' spoken of in verse 4). The adjective used, καινός (2:17; 3:12; 5:9; 14:3), has the sense of the restoration or renovation of something old, 'fresh life rising from the decay and wreck of the old world' (Swete 1906: 275; cf. Mt. 19:28; Acts 3:21). The only thing that is destroyed is that which is set on destruction itself.

There is, however, one dramatic difference between the former things and the new or renewed state of affairs: **there was no more sea**. The three-tiered universe has collapsed into two tiers, and almost immediately will collapse into one (21:3), thus overcoming that fundamental separation between God and God's people. Understood literally, this phrase would mean the sad demise of what is in some ways the most beautiful part of the created world: from Patmos, John would have witnessed the Mediterranean sun reflecting brilliantly upon the deep blue waters of the Aegean. Yet Revelation is not speaking literally, but mythologically. The **sea** has been a threatening presence, both in heaven (e.g. 4:6) and in the world below, where it has been associated with the monster, and other demonic forces in its other guise of the Abyss (e.g. 9:1–6; 11:7; 13:1). Given the underlying Exodus imagery, it has also evoked the dangerous Sea of Reeds to be crossed, the necessary passage leading to salvation (e.g. 15:2). Its ultimate departure here replays in different imagery the consigning of the dragon and its accomplices to the lake of fire.

2 Heaven and earth are not the only things to be renewed, however. John also sees **the holy city, a new Jerusalem, descending out of heaven from God**. Isaiah 65:17–18 had linked the new heavens and new earth with the re-creation of Jerusalem, and Revelation picks up on this link. But this is not a totally new city, although it appears utterly renewed and purged of anything that might threaten its purity. We have come across this city before. **The holy city** or 'beloved city' has been a symbol for the faithful Church, particularly in its precarious state of being attacked by enemies (11:2; 20:9). Furthermore, following ancient conventional language, the city is also a woman, **prepared like a bride dressed for her husband** (like Isaiah's Jerusalem: Isa. 49:18; 52:1; 61:10), the Lamb's bride whose wedding day was announced at 19:7–8. She is also, almost certainly, the woman clothed with the sun, the symbol of God's people who gave birth to the male child and was then rescued from the clutches of the dragon (12:1–6). In the fluid symbolism of the Apocalypse, Mother Zion has returned to marry one of her own: Isaiah has provided the precedent for this mother to marry her sons, and for God to rejoice over Jerusalem the bride (Isa. 62:5). Literally, this would represent the most perverse kind of incest; understood apocalyptically, it proclaims the most intimate of relationships between God in Christ, God's people, and the community of which they are part.

It is theologically significant that this city is seen **descending out of heaven from God** (see 3:12). Representing a sharp contrast to human attempts to build the tower of Babel up to heaven (Ellul 1977: 221), this city is God's gift. It is that ideal Jerusalem of Jewish apocalyptic which God's faithful people have attempted to emulate here on earth prior to its revealing (cf. *4 Ez.* 7:26; 13:36; *2 Bar.* 4:2–6). It is nothing that humanity could create of itself, but something whose architect and builder is God (Heb. 11:10; cf. 'the Jerusalem above' of Gal. 4:26). Nevertheless, neither is it unrelated to those human attempts to prepare for it and emulate the principles on which it is built: as John has already discovered, the bride's shining clothing is made up of 'the just deeds of the holy ones' (19:8).

3–4 Hitherto in Revelation, as in other apocalypses, authoritative commentary on events has been provided either by an angelic choir or by a heavenly voice. Once again the **loud voice from the throne** speaks (as in 16:17; 19:5), probably the voice of an angelic mediator, for the divine voice will speak without mediation in verse 5. Evoking a variety of prophetic passages, including Ezek. 37:27 and Isa. 25:8, the definitive interpretation is provided of what the descent of the new Jerusalem means for humanity. First, it obliterates the one division in creation remaining now that the chaotic sea has disappeared: the division between heaven and earth, God and humanity. **God's tabernacle** (σκηνή), that heavenly location of the divine Presence which the wandering people of God approached through their earthly tabernacle (e.g. Exod. 25:9; 2 Sam. 7:6), **is now among human beings**. From now on, **God will pitch his tent with them**, a statement of God's immediate eschatological presence which echoes the Johannine description of the incarnate Word pitching his tent among us (Jn 1:14). Picking up on the language of Ezek. 37:27, Revelation further expresses this new intimacy in terms of covenant relationship: **They will be his peoples, and God himself will be with them, as their God.** The harder reading has the plural **peoples**, representing a universalising of Ezekiel's prophecy to describe the new people of God called from every nation and language (the singular reading λαός could be a scribal correction to bring Rev. 21:3 into conformity with the Ezekiel passage).

As a reminder that the monster's days are over and that Babylon no longer holds sway, Isaiah's promise of the final banquet is also evoked (Isa. 25:8, a promise already alluded to at 7:17): **He will wipe every tear from their eyes, and there will be no more death or grief, no more crying or pain.** Babylon's judgement brought grief and weeping (e.g. 18:8, 9, 11, 19), while pain was associated with the plagues inflicted on those associated with the monster (16:11), and Death previously held sway (20:13–14). In contrast, the holy city will not be associated with such tragedy, which belongs to **the things of former times**: the old order which has now given way to God's new order (cf. *4 Ez.* 8:53). Sickness, grief and ultimately death were never part of God's plan, and have now been defeated in the dawning of God's Kingdom.

The unmediated presence of God among his people allows **the one seated on the throne** to be heard directly, the first time in Revelation's visionary section (it has been heard once before in the prologue to the book at 1:8). This voice serves to confirm what has already been uttered: namely that **I am making everything new!** These words, which echo Isa. 43:19, speak of the renewal of all things, rather than their replacement. The 'new thing' in Isaiah 43 is the glorious return of the exiles from Babylon to Jerusalem, a way through the sea and the wilderness which recalls the Exodus from

5–7

Egypt. Again, that underlying narrative of new Exodus breaks through into Revelation, though with a typically universal slant: not 'a new thing', but **everything new**, the renewal of the whole of creation (cf. Rom. 8:18–25).

John is commanded once again to **write** (cf. 1:11; 14:13; 19:9), highlighting this particular section (although in a wider sense he has 'written' the whole of this book). The Greek ὅτι here is probably introducing a direct statement, although the phrase could be translated 'Write, because these words are trustworthy and true.' The **words** which **are trustworthy and true** are at the very least those just uttered by the one seated on the throne. The same two adjectives have been used of the one who personifies God's word, that is Christ (3:14; 19:11), and have also described the beatitude at 19:9. Here they point to the reliability of these words, the conviction that what they describe (in a prophetic present) will come to pass. But the command may have a wider reference, as a repetition of the earlier commands, to write down his entire vision of 'what must soon come to pass'. The entirety of this book would then be trustworthy and true.

Echoing the words from the throne at the pouring out of the seventh seal (16:17, though in the plural now rather than the singular), the one on the throne now proclaims the solemn words **'These things have happened!'** (one single dramatic word in the Greek). For a book such as the Apocalypse, in which the End has been delayed so often and the cycles of visions have been so repetitive, it seems hard to believe that it has finally arrived. It is appropriate that, just as at the beginning so now towards the end, God reveals himself as **the Alpha and the O**, here further expressed as **the beginning and the end** (cf. 1:8). The God through whom order was brought out of chaos at the first creation is also the one who sees his plan to its completion, having dealt definitively with that chaos in a great act of re-creation.

Anticipating the more detailed canvas yet to come, two promises are made in relation to this renewed creation. The first, to the **thirsty**, is permission **to drink without charge from the spring of the water of life**. This is the promise first made in Isaiah (Isa. 55:1–5), which draws upon the rich resonances of water as both literally and symbolically life-giving. In contrast to the earth dominated by the monster, where people were forced to buy and sell in an idolatrous economic system, the new creation offers the fullness of life without charge. The second, echoing the promises made at the end of each of the seven messages in Revelation 2—3, offers these new things described as an inheritance which is based not on familial blood-ties but on the shedding of blood, whether of the Lamb or of the faithful witnesses. It takes up, and reinterprets, Nathan's prophecy about the descendants of the royal house of David

(Revelation's wording is very close to the LXX of 2 Sam. 7:14). The one of whom God says **he will be my son** is not Christ alone, but everyone (both male and female) who maintains their place in the battle and is ultimately victorious (cf. *Jub.* 1:24). However, while the language of adoption is used here, Revelation is reluctant to have Christians address God as Father: that is restricted to Christ (1:6; 2:28; 3:5, 21; 14:1), whereas to others he is their **God**. Nevertheless, these are powerful promises of what is to come. They remain important, for in 'real time' the audiences of Revelation have not yet arrived at the new Jerusalem in the new creation.

But with the word of promise comes the rhetoric of warning. There **8** are certain groups who must be excluded from the new Jerusalem, in order to ensure that its purged, renewed character is not compromised. This verse states, using the conventional form of the vice list (9:20–21; 22:15; cf. Ezek. 44:9; Rom. 1:29–31; 1 Cor. 5:9–11; Gal. 5:19–21), what has previously been described visually in the previous scene: that some will be found wanting at the judgement, and **will find their place in the lake burning with fire and sulphur** (the **second death**: see 19:20; 20:10, 14–15). The **detestable** (or 'abominable') **and murderers, the sexually unfaithful and sorcerers** are expected members of this list of exclusions, for their sins reflect those of Babylon and her associates (e.g. 17:2, 3, 6; 18:3, 23, 24). **Idolaters and all liars** are those implicated in the worship of the monster and seduced by the lies and deceptions of the false prophet (e.g. 13:8, 11–17). The specific liar at issue here is the one who claims that another apart from God is seated on the throne: such liars contrast with the Christ, who witnesses to the truth, and his followers, on whose lips no lie is found (14:5). **The cowardly and unfaithful** have not been mentioned before in the Apocalypse; yet their lives contrast sharply with the bravery and faithfulness demanded of those who would follow the Lamb. The call to faithful witness remains as necessary as ever for the churches, even as they hear in their liturgical assemblies of what God assuredly has in store. It still remains possible to have one's name blotted out of the Lamb's scroll of life (3:5).

Detailed Vision: The New Jerusalem   (21:9—22:11)

The sequence of seven bowl-plagues (15:5—19:10) concluded with an extensive visionary description of the 'great city' Babylon, and a series of ironical laments over her downfall (17:1—19:10). At the end of this sequence of seven final visions, the same pattern recurs, with a vivid description of that alternative city which has been a rival to Babylon and is destined to replace her: the new Jerusalem. Both 'city-visions' are like grand tapestries at the end of a sequence of shorter 'cartoons', which revisit one of those cartoon scenes in large scale, allowing for at once a much larger and a more detailed visual depiction. There are clear literary parallels between the two sections which suggest that they have a similar function in the book: both are introduced by the appearance of one of the bowl-angels, who will act for John as an *angelus interpres* (17:1–2; 21:9); in both the angel carries John off 'in spirit' to view the city in question (17:3; 21:10); both sections end with a statement about the truth of these words (19:9b; 22:6), a beatitude (19:9a; 22:7), and a failed attempt on the part of John to worship his angelic guide, accompanied by a command to 'Worship God!' (19:10; 22:8–9). Moreover, the two descriptions will set out the profound similarities as well as the shocking differences between these two cities (see Table 7). This serves to remind Revelation's audiences of the thin line separating the evil, idolatrous city from the holy city centred on God's throne. So attractive, beneficent and benevolent can the great city appear, that it is only by a divine apocalypse such as this that her true nature is shockingly unveiled.

Like its counterpart dealing with the great city Babylon, this vision of the new Jerusalem has also had a powerful impact on the theology, culture and visual history of Christendom. Gothic cathedrals were designed to reflect the imagery and splendour of the heavenly city, offering worshippers the possibility of entering already into this new Jerusalem in the present age. Hymns and poems from 'Jerusalem the Golden' and Peter Abelard's 'O quanta qualia' to Blake's 'Jerusalem' have sustained this vision in verse, while the imagery of this celestial city has left its mark in stained glass, illuminated manuscripts, mosaics, frescoes and woodcuts. The power of the vision is at least threefold. First, it evokes those profound hopes for and expectations of a new city to compensate for the failure of the earthly Jerusalem to respond to her vocation or to see ancient promises fulfilled in her. In the light of her population's repeated infidelity followed by the bitter experience of exile, both Ezekiel and Trito-Isaiah had begun to envisage a new or renewed city and sanctuary appropriate to the restoration (Ezekiel 40—48; Isaiah 60). Ezekiel's final visions have strongly influenced what John describes here (following his sequential meditation upon that visionary book), as has the more universalistic strand of Isaiah 60, with its focus upon the place of the nations in God's future plans.

Second, as the literary parallel makes clear, this vision functions powerfully as a contrast to the seductive yet ultimately crushing alternative of life in the unholy city, the oppressor Babylon in any of her reincarnations. John's vision does not envisage the destruction of those human desires which led to the emergence of Babylon and

Table 7: Babylon and New Jerusalem

Babylon	*New Jerusalem*
17:4; 18:16: adorned with gold	21:18: city made of pure gold 21:21: public square of the city made of pure gold
17:4; 18:16: precious stones	21:11: brilliance like a precious stone 21:18: city wall built of jasper 21:19–20: foundations of the wall adorned with twelve precious stones
17:4; 18:16: pearls	21:21: twelve gates made of twelve pearls
17:4: cup is full of detestable things and the uncleanness of her sexual immorality	21:27: nothing unclean allowed inside nor anyone who does anything detestable
18:16: dressed in fine linen, in purple and scarlet	19:8: dressed in fine linen, shining and clean

ongoing human commitment to her, but their purging and transfiguration. The working out of the divine plan happens precisely through a city, a centre of human civilisation, human culture and human community. Moreover, this city, though God-given, has not jettisoned the good things of God's creation: the precious stones of the mineral world; the wealth of the nations. However, in contrast to their manic accumulation by Babylon for the purpose of self-gratification, in this city they are gathered together for the benefit of all those who will enter by her open gates. Third, this city is also a garden, the restored Garden of Eden to be precise (cf. Genesis 2—3). Her life-giving water and tree evoke the heartfelt human longing for a restoration of what was intended to be in the beginning. What John now describes offers hope that God's purposes, so long frustrated by chaotic and rebellious powers allied to human rebellion, will come to fruition in paradise regained.

The Architecture of the New Jerusalem   (21:9–21)

(9) One of the seven angels who had the seven bowls full of the seven last plagues came and spoke with me: 'Come, I will reveal to you the bride, the wife of the Lamb.' (10) He carried me away in a spiritual trance to a huge, high mountain, and showed me the holy city Jerusalem descending out of heaven from God, (11) resplendent with God's glory. Her brilliance was like that of a precious stone, like a jasper stone, clear as crystal. (12) She had a huge, high wall with twelve gates, and

twelve angels stationed at the gates, on which names were inscribed, the names of the twelve tribes of the children of Israel. (13) On the east side there were three gates, on the north side three gates, on the south side three gates, and on the west side three gates. (14) The city's wall had twelve foundation stones, on which were inscribed the twelve names of the twelve apostles of the Lamb.

(15) The angel who was speaking to me had a gold measuring reed, with which to measure the city, her gates and her wall. (16) The city was a perfect square, as long as she was wide. The angel measured the city with the reed, and she was twelve thousand stadia, identical in length, breadth and height. (17) He also measured her wall, and it was one hundred and forty-four cubits thick by human measurement, which the angel was using. (18) Her wall was constructed of jasper, and the city herself was made of pure gold, like clear glass. (19) The foundation stones of the city's wall were decorated with every kind of precious stone: the first jasper, the second sapphire, the third chalcedony, the fourth emerald, (20) the fifth sardonyx, the sixth carnelian, the seventh chrysolite, the eighth beryl, the ninth topaz, the tenth chrysoprase, the eleventh jacinth, and the twelfth amethyst. (21) The twelve gates were twelve pearls, each of the gates made from a single pearl. The public square of the city was pure gold, like translucent glass.

9–11   John's *angelus interpres*, probably the same one of the seven angels who had the seven bowls who showed him Babylon the great, returns to reveal her antithesis: the bride, the wife of the Lamb. This bride was introduced briefly in an audition at 19:6–8, the heavenly symbol of God's faithful people, who have provided her with her wedding dress through their 'just deeds'. She has been manifested on earth whenever the holy ones have lived lives appropriate to this city rather than to Babylon. Now, however, she is about to make a permanent appearance, her rival having been removed from the face of the earth. It is perhaps appropriate that the angel who appeared to show John Babylon's downfall, one of those angels of the seven last plagues which prepared the ground for her collapse, now returns to reveal the renewed city that is to take her place.

As in the Babylon vision, John is carried away by the angel in a spiritual trance (cf. 17:3). Again, John is reliving the experience of the prophet Ezekiel, who was regularly carried away 'in spirit' (e.g. Ezek. 11:24; cf. 37:1, 9). Indeed, John's angelic guide will show him a city very similar to what Ezekiel saw before him (though with at least one significant difference: see verse 22), and will perform an action similar to that which Ezekiel's angel performed (21:15–21; cf. Ezek. 40:3—42:20). In contrast to the wilderness which provided the location for his Babylon vision, John is taken to a **huge, high mountain** (cf. Ezek. 40:2). This is almost certainly John's exalted vantage point, giving him proximity to the city as she descends **out of heaven from God** (see on 10:1 for descent from heaven in the Apocalypse). Nevertheless, given the parallel in Ezekiel, it is probably also the location to which the city will descend. Mountains serve throughout the Bible, as in other religious traditions, as places of encounter with God (e.g. Exod. 19:3–23; Deut. 34:1–4; Mt. 5:1; 28:16); moreover, in John's day the earthly Jerusalem was also a mountain city, built on Mount Zion and the connected Mount Moriah or Temple Mount. But this mountain is supernaturally exalted, expressing the superiority of this heavenly **holy city** of which the earthly was an imperfect copy (for Jewish expectation of a heavenly Jerusalem or Temple, prepared by God for the last days, see *1 En.* 90:28–36; *4 Ez.* 10:44–59; *2 Bar.* 4:2–6; *T. Ben.* 9:2; 11QT 29.8–10).

The magnificent appearance of the city is what strikes John first: **resplendent with God's glory**. The visual impact of this vision of new Jerusalem is in some ways more important than attempts to explain particular details: her splendour, radiance and brilliance – dazzling to the eye – are a powerful visual reflection of her origin in the God of glory. Because God is within her, the mediated divine presence of the earthly tabernacle and Temple have given way to immediate, unmediated access to the divine Presence, the **glory** or *kavod* of the Hebrew Bible (e.g. Exod. 16:7; 24:16; 1 Kgs 8:11; Isa. 60:1). Ezekiel's final visions describe Jerusalem and her Temple when the glory of the Lord finally returns after the Babylonian exile (Ezek. 43:1–5); John's Ezekielian vision describes that glory permeating every inch of the city. At a loss to give an exact description of what he sees, he lapses into a series of metaphors, which speak of an appearance which is both brilliant and translucent, thus refracting more powerfully the glory within: **like that of a precious stone, like a jasper stone, clear as crystal**. The ancient **jasper**, unlike its modern counterpart, was often transparent (Pliny, *N. H.* 37.115); it has characterized the one seated on the throne at 4:3, and will adorn one of the city's foundations at 21:19.

Ezekiel's interpreting angel showed him the various walls, gates and **12–14** courts of the Temple, and eventually of the surrounding city. John too is taken on a tour of the holy city, and describes what he sees. Mirroring the mountain on which she rests, the city has **a huge, high wall** (whose dimensions will be given when the angel measures it), **with twelve gates**. Walls were crucial to ensure the security of ancient cities, and like the divine measuring at 11:1–2 this wall ensures the divine protection of God's people. The number **twelve** not only recalls the twelve tribes of Israel, but through its earlier reinterpretation (7:1–17) highlights the completeness and inclusiveness of God's new people, no longer confined to the historic twelve tribes but coming from every people and nation (it is the multiple of the divine number three and the universe's number four). There may also be echoes of the twelve signs of the zodiac, particularly given the association of this woman-city with twelve stars at 12:1 (see e.g. Farrer 1949: 216–44); that connection is less explicit, however. There are **twelve angels ... at the gates** (cf. Isa. 62:6), presumably **stationed** there to protect the city and ensure that no-one unworthy enters her: parallels may be drawn with the cherubim who guard the entrance to the Garden of Eden (Gen. 3:24; Ezek. 28:14), and the angels on duty at the various levels of heaven (e.g. *Asc. Isa.* 9:1–4; *Ma'aseh Merkavah* 568). The gates also have names **inscribed** on them, **the names of the twelve tribes of the children of Israel** (cf. 7:4), perhaps to denote the gate by which the individual tribes should enter. These are perfectly divided around the four sides of the city wall, so that **three gates** are located on each side, looking outwards to **east, north, south** and **west**. Opening out to the four points of the compass, this city will invite the new enlarged Israel, not simply the dispersed tribes, to enter into her (21:24–26; cf. Ps. 107:3; Isa. 43:5–6; Mt. 8:11; Lk. 13:29).

Continuing this theme of the perfectly proportioned city, John learns how the wall has **twelve foundation stones**, together comprising the city's foundation (cf. the description of the foundation stones of Solomon's Temple: 1 Kgs 5:17). Balancing the names of the ancient tribes on the gates, the foundation stones bear **the twelve names of the twelve apostles of the Lamb**, reflecting the conviction that the Jerusalem which God has prepared cannot have been unmarked by the coming of Christ and the preaching of his gospel. Rather she is intimately related to the renewed community gathered in Christ's name. The description of the church of Christ's followers in architectural terms (whether as a house or a temple) is reflected elsewhere in the New Testament (e.g. Mt. 16:18; 1 Cor. 3:10–17; 1 Pet. 2:4–8). The most striking parallel, however, is to be found at Eph. 2:20, which speaks of the Church as having been built on the foundation(-stone) of the apostles and prophets, Christ Jesus being the cornerstone.

There is one major difference between Revelation and Ephesians, however: the number **twelve**. The Apocalypse's insistence that there are only **twelve apostles of the Lamb** betrays a significant debate in the early Church as to the role and extent of the apostolate. The word 'apostle' simply means 'one who is sent' (from ἀποστέλλω), and describes individuals sent in the name of Christ. Different New Testament texts provide different answers as to the precise relationship between 'the Twelve', the 'apostles' and the 'disciples' of Jesus (e.g. Mt. 10:1–2; Mk 14:16–17; Lk. 9:1; Acts 1:26; 14:14; 15:2; 1 Cor. 15:5–7; variant reading at Mk 3:14). Paul himself is quite clear that the apostles comprise a wider circle than the Twelve (e.g. Rom. 16:7; Gal. 1:19), and that he himself is among the former, though aware that not all would agree with him (1 Cor. 9:1–2; 15:9; Gal. 1:1). Later Christian tradition would often overlook Matthias, the replacement for Judas Iscariot in Acts 1:15–26, thus regarding Paul as the rightful twelfth apostle and blurring the early distinction between 'the Twelve' and 'apostles' in the Pauline sense.

Unlike Paul and the author of Ephesians (see Muddiman 2001: 141), John of Patmos seems to dissent from the view that Paul is to be numbered among the apostles. He has already alluded to the possibility of there being 'false apostles' among the congregation in Ephesus (2:2; though Paul himself is aware of the same possibility, 2 Cor. 11:13); the message to the congregation in Thyatira has castigated 'Jezebel' for a practice which arguably she might have derived from Paul's teaching (2:20; cf. 1 Corinthians 8—10; see Boxall 1998). Paul's name is not to be found inscribed on the **foundation stones** of the holy city, for these bear only **the twelve names**.

This similarity with Ephesians' appeal to a foundational generation of apostles and prophets has often been used in favour of the late dating of Revelation, and against apostolic authorship. Such a statement, it is claimed, could not have been uttered by one who is among the twelve apostles so inscribed. This would not be simply due to apostolic modesty, but to the sense that such a phrase looks backwards to an earlier foundational age, now in the past. Yet this objection is somewhat blunted if one takes seriously the nature of Revelation as a visionary text: visionaries and dreamers are able to witness themselves, in a somewhat detached manner, as active participants in what they see. Moreover, it is likely that already by the middle of the first century members of the Twelve came to regard themselves as 'pillars' in the new eschatological temple (Gal. 2:9); it is but a small step from this self-understanding to a claim to be foundation stones of a new temple-city.

Continuing his close relationship with Ezekiel, John now describes the measuring of the holy city by the angel, who had **a gold measuring reed** for the purpose (cf. Ezek. 40:3, 5ff.). The scene recalls 11:1–2, where John was commanded to measure the sanctuary of God with a measuring reed. Given the heavenly origin of this city, however, John cannot fulfil that function here: it requires a heavenly agent with an appropriate reed (hence it is made of gold). The angel's

15–18

measurements confirm and develop the impression already gained: that this city is beautifully ordered and perfectly proportioned. The contrast with the chaos and disorder of life in Babylon, or under the monster, could not be greater. The city is **a perfect square, as long as she was wide** (cf. Ezek. 45:2 LXX; 48:16). Yet this is not the end of the story: for when the angel has completed his task, she is revealed to be not simply a square but a perfect cube: **twelve thousand stadia, identical in length, breadth and height**. This begins the transformation of the bride-city into a temple, for the inner sanctuary of Solomon's Temple was a cube, covered in pure gold (1 Kgs 6:20). The new Jerusalem too is **made of pure gold, like clear glass**, another description of her dazzling appearance, which allows the glory of God to shine through. Such translucent metal, though difficult to visualise in literal terms, is a reminder that John is articulating that intense experience of brightness and light associated with the visionary realm.

Even in literal terms, the dimensions of the city are enormous: **twelve thousand stadia** is roughly the equivalent of 'fifteen hundred miles' (as translated by NRSV and NAB). This has led to attempts to reduce its size (and the vast difference between the measurements of city and wall), by treating **thousand** as an addition, or altering **stadia** here to 'cubits', as in verse 17 (e.g. Topham 1989b). But as elsewhere in Revelation, this number is to be read not literally but symbolically. As a multiple of twelve, it denotes completeness (it is the same number as those sealed from each of the twelve tribes at 7:1–7). The cubic city is complete and perfect in all her dimensions. Of course, the sheer enormity of those dimensions adds to the overall effect. That effect is lost once one begins to locate this visionary city on a terrestrial map.

The **wall** of the city, **constructed of jasper** to enable God's glory to shine through (see on 21:11), is also measured. Verse 17 has provoked considerable discussion, partly because of its ambiguity and partly on account of the discrepancy between the measurement it offers for the city's wall and that provided for the whole city in the previous verse. The measurement of the wall **was one hundred and forty-four cubits** (the cubit being measured from the elbow to the tip of the hand, roughly 18 inches or 45 centimetres). Again, to take this number literally (approximately 72 yards or 216 feet) is to risk missing its symbolic significance as a multiple of twelve, the number of completeness. The Greek does not make clear whether this measurement is the height (so NJB) or the breadth (so NIV). If it is the former, which presumably envisages an outer wall behind which the buildings of the city soar to a height of twelve thousand stadia, then the wall would be dramatically out of proportion to the city itself (ridiculously low, even allowing for the symbolic nature of both figures).

Some have offered a solution to this difficulty on the basis of the verse's second ambiguity: namely, the phrase explaining the cubit measurement, which literally translates 'the measure of a man, which is of an angel'. Caird, for example, takes this to imply that the cubit used here is the length of the angel's forearm, angels often being particularly large in stature (e.g. 10:1; Caird 1966: 273).

A simpler solution, however, is that the measurement is recording the width of the wall: **it was one hundred and forty-four cubits thick** (but presumably reaching, as has already been stated, to that overwhelming yet perfectly proportioned height of **twelve thousand stadia**). This would work even if the figure was according to **human measurement, which the angel was using**. Emphasis upon the thickness of the wall (a measurement of completeness) recalls the ancient concern to ensure that invaders did not easily break into the city and harm the citizens (Aune 1998b: 1162). An intriguing further suggestion about the number **one hundred and forty-four** here is that it is the numerical equivalent of the Hebrew *ben Elohim* (written in its longer form with a *waw*) or 'son of God'. This would then be the number or 'measurement' both 'of a man', the messianic restorer of Jerusalem, and 'of an angel' (e.g. Job 38:7; Dan. 3:25; Topham 1989a). While this is speculative, John's often complex fascination with numbers does not rule it out as a possibility.

John now describes in more detail **the foundation stones of the** 19–21 **city's wall**, those twelve foundation stones inscribed with the names of the twelve apostles. These are **decorated with every kind of precious stone**, which may mean that they have been faced with them, one precious stone for each of the foundations. The audience is thereby reminded that this city is none other than the bride of the Lamb, who is 'dressed' for her husband (21:2; cf. the description of Babylon at 17:4). The expectation that Jerusalem would be adorned with jewels is found at Isa. 54:11–12 and Tob. 13:16–17. Some have attempted to correlate these stones with the signs of the zodiac, suggesting that John has utilised an existing scheme but in reverse, as a hidden anti-zodiacal attack (e.g. Charles 1920: II, 165–68; against this, see Glasson 1975). But the primary echo here is of the breastplate of Israel's high priest, which was adorned with twelve precious stones representing each of the twelve tribes (e.g. Exod. 28:17–20; 39:10–13; Ezek. 28:13 LXX; Philo, *Leg. Alleg.* 1.81–82; Josephus, *B. J.* 5.5.7; *Ant.* 3.7.5). For this new Jerusalem is the city of the new priestly people, and of the Lamb who has already appeared to John in the guise of the heavenly high priest (1:13).

Of the twelve stones listed in Exodus (and copied in the LXX of

Ezek. 28:13, which describes the stones adorning the king of Tyre in Eden), John's list has eight (preferring **sardonyx** to the 'onyx' of Exodus LXX). He replaces Aaron's anthrax, ligury and agate with **chalcedony, chrysoprase** and **jacinth** (it is possible that the latter two were chosen because, together with **amethyst**, which they precede in the list, they evoke the colours of the high priestly vestments, gold, hyacinth and purple: Farrer 1949: 224). John's order also differs significantly from that given in Exodus (as do the lists in Josephus), although the Exodus passage does not attempt to correlate particular precious stones with specific patriarchs. In fact, the association with particular tribes is less important for Revelation, given that the foundation stones bear rather the names of the twelve apostles, while the gates are inscribed with the names of the tribes (Philo, *Leg. Alleg.* 1:81–82, correlates the first five stones of Exodus 28 with five of the patriarchs, following the order of the tribes found in Exodus 1).

More important is the fact that the holy city, which is also the cubic sanctuary, bears 'on her heart' the names of the enlarged people of God, rooted in Israel but attentive to the apostolic witness (cf. Exod. 28:29, where Aaron bears the names of the children of Israel in his heart when he goes into the holy place). That new Exodus people, which is represented in heaven by the angelic twenty-four elders, is in constant remembrance in the very fabric of the new Jerusalem, in the names of the twelve tribes and twelve apostles of the Lamb (the proposal that the first letters of the twelve stones contain hidden christological titles (Wojciechowski 1987) is ingenious, but seems arbitrary in places). In addition, the varying bright colours of the different stones, some of them translucent like the city's gold and jasper, contribute to the overall dazzling effect of this glorious heaven-sent city.

The **twelve gates** of the city, inscribed with the names of the tribes, are **twelve pearls**. The gates are not dressed with pearl as the foundation stones are with the precious stones; rather, each one is **made from a single pearl**. Though not commented on in the Hebrew Bible, pearls became highly sought after in the Hellenistic period, as objects 'of great value' (Mt. 13:46). Later rabbinic sources also speak of pearls and other jewels being set in the gateways of Jerusalem (*b. Sanh.* 100a; *b. Bat.* 75a; Harrington 1993: 214). Again there is a connection with the extravagant attire of Babylon (17:4), and the merchandise her population accumulated for themselves (18:12). Yet there is also a contrast, for the **pearls** of this woman-city are not for self-glorification, but are **gates** standing open to receive all those who choose to enter through them and enjoy the blessings which this city offers (see verse 25). Finally, John tells us that the πλατεῖα of the city is made of the same **pure gold, like**

translucent glass with which the city is constructed, adding to her dazzling effect (cf. Tob. 13:16, and the gold floor of Solomon's Temple at 1 Kgs 6:30). The word (literally 'wide') could describe the wide city streets, or as translated here **the public square** (which is an appropriate interpretation of where the bodies of the two witnesses were exhibited in the great city, 11:8).

The Interior of the New Jerusalem   (21:22—22:5)

(22) I saw no sanctuary in her, for the Lord God Almighty and the Lamb are her sanctuary. (23) The city had no need of the sun or the moon to give her light, for God's glory illuminated her, and her lamp was the Lamb. (24) The nations will walk by her light, and earth's kings will bring their glory into her. (25) By day (for there will be no night-time there) her gates will never be shut, (26) and the glory and honour of the nations will be brought into her. (27) But nothing defiled will come into her – no-one who does anything detestable or speaks lies – but only those whose names are inscribed in the Lamb's scroll of life.

(22:1) Then the angel showed me a river containing the water of life, clear as crystal, coming out from the throne of God and of the Lamb. (2) In the middle of the city's public square, on either side of the river, stood a tree of life which produced twelve kinds of fruit. It produced its fruit each month, and the leaves of the tree were meant for the healing of the nations. (3) There will not be anything cursed any more. But the throne of God and of the Lamb will be in the city, and his servants will worship him. (4) They shall look upon his face, and his name will be on their foreheads. (5) There will be no more night, so they will not need either lamplight or sunlight, for the Lord God will illuminate them. They will reign for ever and ever.

At this point Revelation departs significantly from its major 22–27
inspiration, Ezekiel, whose final visions were dominated by a detailed description of the restored Temple in the renewed city. Indeed, for the Jewish mind, Jerusalem without a temple would be well-nigh unthinkable, an attitude shared by every city in the ancient world. The seven cities of Asia too were dominated by their temples, sanctuaries and altars, the loss of which would have heralded the demise of those great urban centres. Yet John declares: **I saw no sanctuary in her**. We misunderstand this, however, if we take this statement as a rejection of the sanctuary per se. John's words suggest that he was looking for a temple *in* the city, as one building among

many, whereas it has already been revealed to him that the whole city is the sanctuary, built like Solomon's Holy of Holies as a perfect cube, and adorned with the precious stones of the high priest's breastplate. But Revelation goes further, claiming that **the Lord God Almighty** (for this title see on 1:8) **and the Lamb are her sanctuary.** The immediate presence of God now permeates the whole city, transforming her into one great sacred space. The close association of the Lamb with God is significant, for it points to the slaughtered one as the revelation of God (an exalted christology permeates this section of John's vision).

Trito-Isaiah's visions of a renewed Jerusalem, also inspirational for John at this point, had envisaged light and divine glory coming upon Jerusalem in the last days, which would witness an eschatological pilgrimage of the nations bringing their wealth to her (Isaiah 60). This provides the more universalistic focus to what John now describes, in contrast to Ezekiel's concentration on the tribes and land of Israel. The dazzling light of the new Jerusalem is **God's glory**, the illuminating divine Presence, which now renders unnecessary the two great lights of the first creation: **the city had no need of the sun or the moon** (cf. Gen. 1:16). The description of the Lamb as **her lamp** may suggest that the Lamb reflects the divine radiance emanating from the throne (cf. the description of John the Baptist as a burning and shining lamp at Jn 5:35). Whatever is implied, the glory of God renders unnecessary any alternative source of light (cf. Isa. 60:19–20).

Much of verses 24–26 are a paraphrase of Isa. 60:3, 5, 11. Trito-Isaiah had foreseen nations and kings coming to Jerusalem's light, reflected in Revelation's claim that **The nations will walk by her light, and earth's kings will bring their glory into her.** The reappearance of **earth's kings** is surprising, for on a literal reading of the Apocalypse these would already have been killed (19:21) and then presumably assigned to the lake of fire at the second resurrection for their participation in the monster's regime (20:15; 21:8). This is a warning against both an over-literal and an over-chronological reading of the book's visions. Though portraying the consequences for those who stubbornly cling to their attachment to the monster, these last visionary scenes are not driven by some fatalistic inevitability. Participation in the new Jerusalem remains a possibility even for earth's kings, who up to this point have been marked out by their hostility to the Lamb and its followers (6:15; 16:14; 17:2, 18; 18:3, 9; 19:19).

These kings **will bring their glory into her**: this phrase seems to parallel Isa. 60:5, which states that the 'wealth' or 'strength' of the nations will come to her. This wealth, understood by Isaiah in material terms to include such luxuries as gold and frankincense (Isa. 60:6; cf. Mt. 2:11), seems to have been reinterpreted by Revelation to refer to the kings' spiritual **glory** or 'splendour': '*themselves*, as those who offer to God at the end-time the worship of their renewed lives' (Smalley 2005: 558). In contrast to other cities, for which firm security from outsiders was paramount, in this city the presence of God and the Lamb are sufficient for protection. Hence, not only has the darkness of **night-time** been obliterated (a Johannine echo of the defeat of the evil powers: cf. 16:10; Jn 1:5; 3:19); **her gates will never be shut** (Isa. 60:11). There may be a suggestion here that, since there is no longer any distinction between day and night, the practice of closing city gates at evening no longer has a point. This permanent openness allows for **the glory and honour of the nations** to be **brought** into the new Jerusalem. **The nations**, for so long associated as were earth's kings with Babylon and the monster (11:2, 9, 18; 14:8; 16:19; 17:15; 18:3, 23; 19:15; 20:3, 8), have now broken free of the shackles of deception and enslavement, purged of their previous attachments and discovering their own glory and honour in the process. It is a glorious fulfilment of the Song of Moses and the Lamb at 15:4, which foretold that 'all the nations will come and worship before you'.

Despite the openness of the city's gates, however, not all may enter (at 21:12 John was shown an angel stationed at each gate). In order to preserve the purity and splendour of that city-sanctuary, and the glory and honour of those who come into her, the laws of purity apply: **nothing defiled will come into her**. The word **defiled** ('common' or 'unclean', κοινός) is sometimes used to describe those things to be excluded from the Temple or the sacrificial cult (e.g. 1 Macc. 1:47, 62; Acts 10:14; Heb. 10:29). There are those who exclude themselves from that intimate relationship with God which the new Jerusalem symbolises: the meaning of **nothing defiled** is explicated in a twofold manner. First, it excludes the person **who does anything detestable** (literally 'the one who does abominations'), a phrase associated with Babylon's idolatry at 17:4 and having that sense here. Second, it refers to the one who **speaks lies**, following the false prophet in perpetuating the lie that another apart from God is seated on the throne (e.g. 16:13). Entry into the city cannot be allowed to those unable to worship the God whose throne is located there. For **those whose names are inscribed in the Lamb's scroll of life**, see on 3:5 and 13:8.

If Revelation's new Jerusalem is a city and a sanctuary, it is also a **22:1–2** garden. Some strands in Jewish and early Christian tradition expected the end to mirror the beginning, or even to supersede it (e.g. *T. Dan* 5:9–13; *Ep. Barn.* 6:13), and John is shown Eden regained. The **river containing the water of life** reflects the river which flows out of Eden, where it divides into the four rivers of the

Pishon, Gihon, Tigris and Euphrates (Gen. 2:10–14). The first appearance of the **tree of life** was also in the garden of Eden (Gen. 2:9). But Genesis is not the only antecedent of this vision. Again, Ezekiel's influence continues to be present. Ezekiel's renewed Temple had a torrent of water flowing out from it towards the east, with a large number of trees on each bank. This life-giving water transformed the stagnant waters of the Dead Sea into a sea teeming with living fish (Ezek. 47:1–12; cf. Zech. 14:8).

There being no temple within the city, John's refreshing river, **clear as crystal** (cf. the sea of glass 'like crystal' before the heavenly throne at 4:6), emerges **from the throne of God and of the Lamb** (a contrast to the thunder, lightning and loud voices which previously emerged from the heavenly throne: e.g. 4:5; 8:5; 11:19). The word **throne** here is in the singular, hinting that God and the Lamb occupy the same throne and are therefore both worthy of worship (cf. 3:21). The heavenly throne is now to be located on the earth, in the midst of God's people (cf. 21:3). There is an interesting parallel to this river at Jn 19:34, where blood and water flow from the side of the crucified Christ, already identified as the true temple and tabernacle (cf. Jn 1:14; 2:21; 7:38; Jn 19:34 has baptismal allusions, and it is possible that the same holds here also). Mirroring Ezekiel's river, Revelation's river containing the water of life flows through the **middle of the city's public square** (or possibly 'the wide streets'). The sense of breadth and openness would have contrasted with the cramped conditions under which many, including Christians, would have lived in the great cities of the Roman Empire. This same sense has inspired interpreters in subsequent generations. The broad river flowing through the wide streets in William Blake's *The River of Life* (Tate Britain, London) contrasts powerfully with the narrow, constricted and overcrowded London of his day (Kovacs and Rowland 2004: 235).

The description of the **tree of life** is complicated by the issue of punctuation (whether there should be a full stop at the end of verse 1, as in this translation, or after 'in the middle of the city's public square'), and by the fact that John uses the singular 'tree of life' (no doubt to strengthen the link with Genesis), while stating that it is located **on either side of the river**. He may be exploiting the generic sense of 'tree' to apply to several examples of the same species, thus also evoking the many trees which Ezekiel saw on the riverbank as it flowed out of the city down to the Arabah (Ezek. 47:7). Ezekiel's various kinds of trees bore fruit every month, and their leaves, like the life-giving water which watered them, were for healing (Ezek. 47:12). John's combination of Ezekiel's many kinds of trees with Eden's one tree of life means that this one tree **produced twelve kinds of fruit**, presumably a different variety each month.

Moreover, he makes one significant addition to Ezekiel: **the leaves of the tree were meant for the healing of the nations** (again, Trito-Isaiah's more universalistic streak shines through). This presumes that humanity, including the nations from whom the Lamb has redeemed people for God (5:9), is able to eat the fruit from the tree of life. This is a dramatic reversal of Eden, where one of the reasons for Adam and Eve's expulsion was to ensure that they were unable to eat from this tree and thereby live for ever (Gen. 3:22–24). But it is a direct fulfilment of one of the promises made to the conqueror in the seven messages, allusions to which are scattered throughout this last great vision of salvation (see Table 8). This tree's healing properties, and its ability to reach out to all the nations, may suggest a further allusion to the life-giving cross of Christ. The cross is described elsewhere in the New Testament by the word ξύλον, used here (**tree** or 'wood': Acts 5:30; 10:39; 13:29; Gal. 3:13; 1 Pet. 2:24), so it is unlikely that the allusion would have been lost on early generations of Christians.

Again, the negative is ruled out of participation in this city: **there will not be anything cursed any more.** The immediate influence **3–5** here is Zech. 14:11, which states that Jerusalem of the last days will no longer be under a curse or destined for destruction (though Zechariah uses ἀνάθεμα rather than John's κατάθεμα, the latter a *hapax legomenon* in the Greek Bible). Yet some may recall that the serpent was cursed in Eden, thus serving as a further reminder that the ancient serpentine dragon has now been expelled, never to return and disrupt the tranquillity of paradise (Gen. 3:14; cf. Rev. 12:7–9; 20:10). Instead, the new Eden will be a place where humanity accept their creatureliness, and devote their lives to the worship of God. Because this remains a vision, and not yet an established reality, the future tense breaks in: **the throne of God and of the Lamb will be in the city, and his servants will worship him.** The liturgy of the heavenly throne-room, and the fragmentary acts of worship in which the earthly congregations currently engage, are destined to become as one. That the Lamb is associated with God as the object of worship is stressed again here, both by the singular **throne** and by the singular pronoun **him** to describe the two. **His servants** refer to the faithful people of God and followers of the Lamb (as at 1:1; 2:20; 6:11; 7:3; 19:2, 5; cf. 11:18). With the collapse of the distinction between heaven and earth, these are destined to join with the angels in exercising a priestly ministry in the holy city (cf. 1:6; 5:10).

This association with the angels is also reflected in the statement that **they shall look upon his face.** Not even Moses was privileged to look upon God's face (Exod. 33:20, 23). That privilege is sometimes reserved for angels (e.g. Mt. 18:10), although even angelic

Table 8: Fulfilment of Promises to the Conqueror

Promise	*Fulfilment*
Ephesus 2:7: eat from tree of life	22:2
Smyrna 2:11: unharmed by second death	20:6
Pergamum 2:17: receive hidden manna and a white stone	
Thyatira 2:26–28: given authority over the nations, and given the morning star	20:4–6; cf. 22:16
Sardis 3:5: clothed in white, name not blotted out of the scroll of life	19:14; 20:12
Philadelphia 3:12: become pillar in temple, bear name of new Jerusalem	21:9ff.
Laodicea 3:21: sit down on Christ's throne	20:4; 22:5

beings can shield their faces from the terrible Presence (e.g. Isa. 6:2). Nevertheless, seeing God's face – though not literally – was an expectation of pilgrims to Jerusalem (e.g. Ps. 17:15; 42:2), and a Christian tradition emerged of this privilege being granted to those who inherited the title of the angels, 'the holy ones', in the new age (e.g. 1 Jn 3:2; cf. Mt. 5:8; Heb. 12:14). As a mark of ownership, and perhaps reflecting the divine name worn on the forehead of the high priest (e.g. Exod. 28:36–38), **his name will be on their foreheads**: the **his** probably includes the Lamb, who now shares his Father's name (e.g. 3:2; 19:12; cf. 14:1). Illuminated by the light of the divine Presence (see on 21:23–25; cf. Isa. 60:19–20), **they will reign for ever and ever**. The promise made to the conqueror in the messages to Thyatira and Laodicea is now fulfilled: the priests will also share in the eternal royal rule (a deliberate contrast is drawn with the now defunct rule of the dragon and the monster, who suffer torment in the lake of fire for ever and ever: 20:10).

Conclusion to the Vision of the New Jerusalem   (22:6–11)

(6) Then the angel said to me, 'These words are trustworthy and true! The Lord God of the spirits of the prophets has sent his angel to show his servants what must soon come to pass.'

(7) 'Look! I am coming soon! Happy is the one who observes the words of the prophecy contained in this scroll.'

(8) I, John, am the one who hears and sees these things. When I had heard and seen them, I fell at the feet of the angel who revealed these things to me, to worship him. (9) But he said to me, 'Do not do that! I am only a fellow-servant with you and your brothers the prophets, and those who observe the words found in this scroll. Worship God!' (10) Then he said to me, 'Do not seal up the words of the prophecy contained in this scroll, for the crucial time is very close! (11) Meanwhile, let the one who acts unjustly continue to act unjustly, and the one who is impure continue to be impure; let the one who acts justly continue to act justly, and the one who is holy continue to be holy.'

Recalling words from the very beginning of this book (1:1–3), as well **6–7** as the recent words of the one seated on the throne (21:5), an authoritative speaker now confirms the reliability of **these words**: at the very least, this refers to the preceding vision of the new Jerusalem, though almost certainly it means the whole book, in which God has shown his servants **what must soon come to pass**. The speaker is not named, but simply introduced as 'he said'; given the context, however, the voice is probably still that of the bowl angel who has been speaking with John and explaining the vision since 21:9. God is referred to here by the unusual title **Lord God of the spirits of the prophets** (cf. 'the Lord of the spirits', a common title for God in *1 Enoch*). Its use is clearly related to the words of prophecy contained in the scroll of the Apocalypse, proclaiming that they have God as their source. Some would see in the phrase **spirits of the prophets** a reference to the Holy Spirit, who inspires prophetic utterance; alternatively, the plural could refer to the human spirits of individual prophets (Aune 1998b: 1182; cf. 1 Cor. 14:32), or even the seven angelic spirits of 1:4. **The prophets** probably include Old Testament prophets, who have been so important for John throughout the book, though they cannot be confined to these (see on 10:7; cf. 11:10; 16:6; 18:20, 24). God's **angel**, sent by him **to show his servants what must soon come to pass**, refers back to 1:1 (and is probably also to be identified with Jesus' angel who appears at 10:1; cf. 22:16). The immediate context, however, suggests that it is this angel who has reappeared as the bowl angel and interprets for John the new Jerusalem.

If it is the angel who is speaking in verse 6, the exalted Christ certainly interjects at verse 7, with the exclamation **Look! I am coming soon!** The coming here is primarily an urgent reference to Christ's final coming, though one should not rule out the intermediate 'comings' to the congregations gathered in worship (cf. 3:3, 20). Similar christological interjections have occurred at 13:9 and 16:15. The latter was combined with a beatitude, and another is found here (the sixth of Revelation's seven macarisms). Happiness is promised here for **the one who observes the words of the prophecy contained in this scroll**, that is the whole book. It has been described as prophecy before (1:3), and will be again (22:18–19): the dividing line between 'prophecy' and 'apocalyptic' is a fine one, for both claim to convey directly God's urgent message to his people. The acceptable response is not simply to hear it, but to act upon the challenge it extends.

8–11 This last of final visions concludes, as did the parallel vision of Babylon, with a frustrated attempt by John to worship the angel (see on 19:9–10). Prior to that, however, John names himself (the first time since 1:9), thus joining his authoritative witness to that of the angel, and of Christ himself: **I, John, am the one who hears and sees these things.** John has largely remained in the background throughout the book, although his audience has been dependent upon his particular communication of what he has seen. As the book prepares to return them from its visionary world to 'real time', it reminds them that John too is in real time on the island of Patmos.

The final angelic command to John is a negative one: **Do not seal up the words of the prophecy contained in this scroll.** This contrasts with the earlier command to seal up the seven thunders, with the result that their contents were not preserved for posterity (10:4). This negative command has a positive purpose, however. It ensures that the prophetic words are communicated immediately to the seven congregations. The author of the book of Daniel, working under the mantle of pseudonymity, used the motif of 'sealing' to explain how a revelation supposedly received in the sixth century BCE was not finally made public until four centuries later (Dan. 12:4, 9; cf. *4 Ez.* 14:46). John, writing at that urgent time when the monster has begun to stir and Babylon is yet again in the ascendant, has no need to resort to pseudonymity: **for the crucial time is very close** (cf. 1:3).

With this sense of urgency comes a series of parallel imperatives, probably still the words of the interpreting angel who has been speaking in verse 10 (Dan. 12:10 is in the background): **let the one** who acts unjustly continue to act unjustly, and the one who is impure continue to be impure. They can be read as excluding any further possibility of repentance (or apostasy), which jars somewhat with the openness of the city gates and the corresponding sense that repentance remains a possibility. It is indeed possible to read these words as ruling out repentance, now that the end is so close, or as expressing the inevitability of people persisting in their established habits. Alternatively, as part of Revelation's rhetorical strategy, these sayings (including the more positive parallel referring to the one who acts justly or who is holy) may be an appeal to audiences to consider where they stand: on the side of Babylon and the monster, ensnared in a pattern of existence marked by injustice and the impurity of idolatry, or on the side of the new Jerusalem, marked by the justice and holiness of citizens of the holy city.

EPILOGUE   (22:12–21)

(12) 'Look! I am coming soon, bringing my reward with me, to render to everyone in accordance with their deeds. (13) I am the Alpha and the O, the first and the last, the beginning and the end. (14) Happy are those who wash their robes clean, so as to have access to the tree of life, and to enter through the gates into the city. (15) But outside will be the dogs and the sorcerers, the sexually unfaithful and the murderers, the idolaters and everyone who loves or practises the lie. (16) I, Jesus, have sent my angel to bear witness to you about these things for the sake of the congregations. I am the root and the descendant of David, the bright Morning Star.'

(17) The Spirit and the bride say, 'Come!'
Let everyone who hears say, 'Come!'
Let everyone who is thirsty come,
and everyone who wishes receive the water of life without charge.

(18) I bear witness to everyone who hears the words of the prophecy contained in this scroll: if anyone adds to them, God will add to that person the plagues written about in this scroll. (19) If anyone removes any of the words of this prophetic scroll, God will remove that person's share in the tree of life and the holy city, which are written about in this scroll.

(20) The one who is bearing witness to these things says, 'Yes indeed! I am coming soon!' Amen! Come, Lord Jesus!

(21) The grace of the Lord Jesus be with all.

315

Commentators diverge considerably on the question of where the vision of the new Jerusalem ends and Revelation's epilogue begins. A decision on this question is hampered by the rather loose collection of sayings and differing voices preserved in Revelation 22. It is possible to locate the break after verse 5, given that the visionary description of the new Jerusalem ends there (e.g. Rowland 1998: 732), although structural parallels with the Babylon cycle strongly suggest that John's unavailing attempt to worship the angel at 22:8–9 ought also to be included. Alternatively, the epilogue might begin at verse 10, immediately after the command to 'Worship God' (e.g. Aune 1998b: 1201), or even at verse 18 (Smalley 2005: 581).

However, parallels with Revelation's prologue suggest a break after verse 11. This would mean that the epilogue opens with a heavenly utterance from **the Alpha and the O** that **I am coming soon,** matching the end of the prologue at 1:8 (a saying of 'the Alpha and the O', who is also described as the one 'who is coming'). Further parallels between prologue and epilogue include a beatitude (1:3; 22:14), the offer of divine **grace** (1:4; 22:21), the acclamation **Yes indeed!** or **Amen!** combined with a saying concerning Christ's coming (1:6b–7; 22:20b), the verb **bear witness** and related nouns (1:2, 5; 22:16, 18, 20), and a reference to the **angel** whom God or Jesus **sent** (1:1; 22:16). The prologue and epilogue together form a fitting *inclusio* to the whole, and serve to remind reader and hearers that this apocalypse is also a circular letter.

12–13 The epilogue begins with another interjection from the divine voice, repeating the words of the risen Christ at 22:7. If Christ is also the speaker here, as one might expect, then his exalted status is all the more explicit. He is coming as eschatological judge, a role accorded to him elsewhere in the New Testament (e.g. Mt. 25:31–33; Jn 5:22, 27; Acts 10:42; 2 Cor. 5:10; 2 Tim. 4:1): he is the one, as God's vicegerent, who has authority **to render to everyone in accordance with their deeds.** Moreover, he claims for himself the title hitherto ascribed to God, **the Alpha and the O** (1:8; 21:6, a title which became a popular symbol in early Christian wall-paintings). This should not surprise us, given that the Lamb has already shared God's throne, and that the two can be spoken of together using a singular pronoun (see on 22:3). Each successive occurrence of this divine title has expanded upon it to explicate its meaning; this third and final occurrence adds **the first and the last** (1:17; 2:8; cf. Isa. 41:4; 44:6; 48:12; the second instance at 21:6 had already added the phrase **the beginning and the end**). Christ is present as both the pre-existent agent of creation (see 3:14) and the one who is coming in judgement and salvation at its climax. Parallels in the magical papyri show how variants of ΑΩ were used by suppliants as an incantation in an attempt to control the deity. By using this formula himself, Christ shows that he is in supreme control and cannot be manipulated (Aune 1987).

The seventh and last of Revelation's beatitudes is now uttered. As 14–15 Christ has been speaking in the previous two verses, it is appropriate to regard this beatitude also as coming from his mouth (cf. the same combination of interjection and beatitude from the exalted Christ at 22:7). This macarism has a significant textual variant. The widely adopted reading, following both Sinaiticus and Alexandrinus, is **those who wash their robes clean** (οἱ πλύνοντες τὰς στολὰς αὐτῶν); the similar-sounding 'those who do his commandments' (οἱ ποιοῦντες τὰς ἐντολὰς αὐτοῦ, found in the Textus Receptus and therefore adopted by the AV), is attributable to scribal error, or even scribal correction on the basis of 12:17 or 14:12. **Those who wash their robes clean** refers back to 7:14, where the great multitude are described as those who have washed their robes and made them white in the blood of the Lamb. This beatitude offers eschatological happiness to those who have benefited from the redeeming death of the slaughtered Lamb, and who have patterned their lives on the Lamb's faithful witness (cf. 3:4). These are able to participate in the gift of eternal life in God's presence, symbolised as having **access to the tree of life** and of being able **to enter through the gates into the city**.

Revisiting the warnings already reiterated at 21:8, 27 and 22:3, 11, verse 15 reminds Revelation's hearers that it is possible to be excluded, by the fundamental orientation of one's heart, from the holy city. A list of those consigned to the **outside** is added to the series of vice lists throughout the book (e.g. 9:21; 21:8, 27). Most of the groups mentioned in this particular list occurred in the list at 21:8, where they were linked to the activities and characteristics of the monster and Babylon. The one new category is that of **the dogs**. Dogs are not highly regarded in the Hebrew Bible and later Jewish tradition, and the word often serves as a term of abuse, referring to despised groups, including evildoers and occasionally Gentiles (e.g. Ps. 22:16; 1 Sam. 24:14; Mt. 7:6; 15:26; Phil. 3:2; 2 Pet. 2:22). This list functions rhetorically to warn the contemporary generation of how easy it is to forfeit one's inclusion on the Lamb's scroll of life, and therefore citizenship in the new Jerusalem.

The voice of the exalted Christ, by implication speaking since the 16–17 beginning of verse 12, is now explicitly mentioned, as the speaker returns to the first person: **I, Jesus, have sent my angel to bear witness to you about these things for the sake of the congregations**. At 22:6 John was told that it was God who had sent his

317

angel to reveal 'what must soon come to pass'; here Jesus, so closely associated with God as the one who acts on his behalf, claims the same prerogative in sending **my angel** (see on 10:1). Here we are reminded of that chain of revelation set out in 1:1–3: the revelation is given by God to Jesus, who makes it known through his angel to his servant John; John is then to make it known, through the public reader of his scroll, to the members of **the congregations**. **These things** must refer not simply to the words spoken by Christ in the preceding verses, but to the whole visionary section of the book, addressed to the seven congregations to unveil to them the reality of their situation and the prophetic invitation extended to them.

Jesus' words are accompanied and validated by two messianic titles, which appeared much earlier in the Apocalypse. These are introduced in the form of a Johannine **I am** saying, the final one of five scattered throughout the book (1:8, 17; 2:23; 21:6). The first, **the root and the descendant of David**, presents Christ as the shoot or root of Jesse, the messianic Branch (Isa. 11:1, 10; Sir. 47:22), one of the titles which heralded the appearance of the Lamb at 5:5–6. The second is **the bright Morning Star**, a star which was cryptically promised to the conqueror in the message to Thyatira (2:28; cf. 2 Pet. 1:19). Originally a reference to Venus, in a Christian context this probably alludes to Balaam's prophecy of a star which would arise out of Jacob (Num. 24:17, a prophecy interpreted messianically by Jews and early Christians: e.g. *T. Levi* 18:3; *T. Jud.* 24:1; CD 7:18–21; 4QTest 9—13; Mt. 2:1–2).

The words of Jesus now give way to a dialogue in which a number of voices participate, including **the Spirit**, **the bride** of the Lamb, and probably also John himself. The combined voice of **the Spirit and the bride** utters a fervent prayer or invitation: **Come!** While some have suggested that their word is addressed to outsiders to come to Christ, paralleling the second half of the verse, the singular ἔρχου is certainly addressed here to Christ himself, a prayer for his eschatological Parousia. It is not problematic for the Holy Spirit to utter a prayer together with the Church in its guise as the bride: although the Spirit has appeared elsewhere in the book as the pro-phetic vehicle of Christ's message to the congregations, the Holy Spirit has a function elsewhere of inspiring and articulating Christian prayer (cf. Rom. 8:26–27; 1 Cor. 12:3; Gal. 4:6). The prayer uttered here is the *maranatha* prayer, an Aramaic prayer transliterated into Greek (e.g. 1 Cor. 16:22; *Did.* 10:6) which could be read as either *marana tha* ('Our Lord, come!') or *maran atha* ('Our Lord has come'): the earliest New Testament manuscripts lacked spaces between words. Revelation's Greek translation here and at verse 20 suggests that the former is the original.

This *maranatha* prayer is a reminder that Revelation was intended to be read publicly, probably in a liturgical context. As the book and its visions draw to a close, that liturgical setting becomes all the more important for preserving the Apocalypse's alternative worldview. The prayer of the Spirit-led Church merges into three invitations to believers and would-be believers to **Come!** The invitation to the thirsty to **receive the water of life without charge** has already been made at 21:6. It recalls the invitation to come to the water at Isa. 55:1 (a passage which has influenced another text of the Johannine corpus, Jn 7:37–38). It stands in stark contrast to the invitation from the monster and its associate, which requires buying and selling, and the exchange of coinage bearing the monster's image (13:17).

Before the book concludes it utters a solemn warning, probably via **18–19** the voice of John, to those who hear its prophetic words. Using Deuteronomy as a model (Deut. 4:2), Revelation threatens dire consequences to the one who **adds to** or **removes any of the words of this prophetic scroll.** Those who **add** to them are threatened with **the plagues written about in this scroll** (those described in the seals, trumpets and bowls cycles): in other words, they will be treated as those associated with the monster or with Babylon, 'those who make their home on the earth'. **Anyone** who **removes any of the words** will lose their **share in the tree of life and the holy city.** Both amount to the same thing. These are stern words, particularly threatening for scribes forced to copy manuscripts of the Apocalypse prior to the advent of printing, or for compilers of ecclesiastical lectionaries in any age. Perhaps most striking, however, is the self-understanding that such a statement presupposes. Revelation's author is consciously placing it on a par with Deuteronomy, and therefore with the core of the authoritative Jewish scriptures (similar claims are made for the Pentateuch in its Septuagintal version in *Ep. Arist.* 310–11). Perhaps the warning also betrays a fear on the part of John of scribal tampering with his text (on this, see Aune 1998b: 1232).

The prologue to the book contained a liturgical dialogue, in which the **20–21** congregation may have been expected to respond with the liturgical refrains **Yes indeed!** and **Amen!** (1:4–8). Similar vocabulary, and similar echoes of a liturgical dialogue, now bring the apocalypse-letter to its conclusion. Given the parallels with the openings of the seven messages, **the one who is bearing witness to these things** is Jesus, whose final words repeat those with which he opened this prologue: **Yes indeed! I am coming soon!** This is in fact the third time in the space of fourteen verses that Christ has uttered such a promise, heightening the sense of expectancy that his coming is near (also 22:7, 12). As the final section of the book is read out publicly, and visionary time prepares to give way to liturgical time, this urgent emphasis upon the Lord's return links his final coming to that coming which is about to take place in the eucharistic assembly (*Did.* 10:6 locates the *maranatha* prayer within a eucharistic context). In the dialogue formula, the response not only of John but of the listening congregation is the traditional one: **Amen! Come, Lord Jesus!**

The very last verse is a reminder of the epistolary form of this visionary book, composed as a circular letter to be delivered to the seven congregations of Asia. After an initial superscription (1:1–3), the Apocalypse follows the conventional form of an epistolary opening, albeit with some distinctive features (1:4–8). The epistolary greeting is one of 'grace and well-being', adopting a Christian form of words well known from the Pauline letters. John's apocalypse-letter concludes in a similar manner to other New Testament letters, particularly those in the Pauline tradition: **The grace of the Lord Jesus be with all** (e.g. 1 Cor. 16:23, the closest parallel; Gal. 6:18; Phil. 4:23; 1 Thess. 5:28; Heb. 13:25). The **grace** or unmerited favour of God is offered to all through **Jesus** Christ, the slaughtered Lamb who is now acclaimed as **Lord** (cf. 11:8; 14:13; 17:14; 19:16; 22:20). The preferred reading here is the shorter reading (**with all**), attested by Alexandrinus. The variant 'with the holy ones' is also worthy of consideration. There is a range of other readings (on these see Metzger 1971: 768–69), some of which are not well attested, or which can be accounted for as harmonisations with the conclusions of Pauline letters (e.g. 2 Cor. 13:13; 2 Thess. 3:18). The conclusion 'Amen', found in the Textus Receptus but missing from some significant witnesses, may have been added for liturgical usage.

BIBLIOGRAPHY

Ashanin, C. B., 1990. 'The Orthodox Liturgy and the Apocalypse', *PBR* 9: 31–40.

Ashton, J., 2000. *The Religion of Paul the Apostle*. New Haven and London: Yale University Press.

Aune, D. E., 1983. 'The Influence of Roman Imperial Court Ceremonial on the Apocalypse of John', *BR* 28: 5–26.

—— 1987. 'The Apocalypse of John and Graeco-Roman Revelatory Magic', *NTS* 33: 481–501.

—— 1990. 'The Form and Function of the Proclamations to the Seven Churches (Revelation 2—3)', *NTS* 36: 182–204.

—— 1997. *Revelation 1–5*. WBC 52a; Dallas, Tex.: Word.

—— 1998a. *Revelation 6–16*. WBC 52b; Nashville: Thomas Nelson.

—— 1998b. *Revelation 17–22*. WBC 52c; Nashville: Thomas Nelson.

Barker, M., 2000. *The Revelation of Jesus Christ*. Edinburgh: T&T Clark.

Barnett, P., 1989: 'Polemical Parallelism: Some Further Reflections on the Apocalypse', *JSNT* 35: 111–20.

Barr, D. L., 1984. 'The Apocalypse as a Symbolic Transformation of the World: A Literary Analysis', *Int* Jan.: 39–50.

—— 1986. 'The Apocalypse of John and Oral Enactment', *Int* July: 243–56.

—— 1998. *Tales of the End: A Narrative Commentary on the Book of Revelation*. Santa Rosa, Calif.: Polebridge Press.

Bauckham, R., 1991. 'The List of the Tribes in Revelation 7 Again', *JSNT* 42: 99–115.

—— 1992. 'Hades, Hell', in D. N. Freedman (ed.), *The Anchor Bible Dictionary*, 3: 14–15. New York: Doubleday.

—— 1993a. *The Climax of Prophecy: Studies on the Book of Revelation*. Edinburgh: T&T Clark.

—— 1993b. *The Theology of the Book of Revelation*. NTT; Cambridge: Cambridge University Press.

Beale, G. K., 1985. 'The Origin of the Title "King of Kings and Lord of Lords" in Revelation 17.14', *NTS* 31: 618–20.

—— 1999. *The Book of Revelation*. NIGTC; Grand Rapids: Eerdmans and Cambridge/Carlisle: Paternoster Press.

321

Beasley-Murray, G. R., 1974. *The Book of Revelation*. NCB; Grand Rapids: Eerdmans and London: Marshall, Morgan & Scott.

Bell, A. A., 1978/79. 'The Date of John's Apocalypse: The Evidence of Some Roman Historians Reconsidered', *NTS* 25: 93–102.

Ben-Daniel, J., and Ben-Daniel, G., 2003. *The Apocalypse in the Light of the Temple: A New Approach to the Book of Revelation*. Jerusalem: Beit Yochanan.

Bent, J. T., 1888. 'What St John Saw on Patmos', *Nineteenth Century* 24: 813–21.

Bøe, S., 2001. *Gog and Magog: Ezekiel 38–39 as Pre-text for Revelation 19,17–21 and 20,7–10*. WUNT 2/135; Tübingen: Mohr Siebeck.

Boesak, A. A., 1987. *Comfort and Protest*. Edinburgh: St Andrew Press.

Boismard, M. É., 1950. *L'Apocalypse*. LSB; Paris: Éditions du Cerf.

—— 1952. 'Notes sur l'apocalypse,' *RB* 59: 161–72.

Bonhoeffer, D., 1965. *No Rusty Swords: Letters, Lectures and Notes 1928–1936*. London: Collins.

Boring, M. E., 1989. *Revelation*. Interpretation; Louisville: John Knox Press.

Bovon, F., 2000. 'John's Self-Presentation in Revelation 1:9–10', *CBA* 62: 693–700.

Boxall, I., 1998. ' "For Paul" or "For Cephas"? The Book of Revelation and Early Asian Christianity', in C. Rowland and C. H. T. Fletcher-Louis (eds), *Understanding, Studying and Reading: New Testament Essays in Honour of John Ashton*, 198–218. JSNTS 153; Sheffield: Sheffield Academic Press.

—— 1999. 'Who is the Woman Clothed with the Sun?', in M. Warner (ed.), *Say Yes to God: Mary and the Revealing of the Word Made Flesh*, 142–58. London: Tufton Books.

—— 2001. 'The Many Faces of Babylon the Great: *Wirkungsgeschichte* and the Interpretation of Revelation 17', in S. Moyise (ed.), *Studies in the Book of Revelation*, 51–68. Edinburgh and New York: T&T Clark.

—— 2002. *Revelation: Vision and Insight*. London: SPCK.

—— 2004. ' "Jezebel" of Thyatira to John of Patmos', in P. R. Davies (ed.), *Yours Faithfully: Virtual Letters from the Bible*, 147–51. London: Equinox.

Bratcher, R. G., and Hatton, H. A., 1993. *A Handbook on the Revelation to John*. UBS Handbook Series; New York: UBS.

Brown, S., 1966. ' "The Hour of Trial" (Rev 3 10)', *JBL* 85: 308–14.

Caird, G. B., 1966. *The Revelation of St John the Divine*. BNTC; London: A. & C. Black.

Carey, G., 1999. *Elusive Apocalypse: Reading Authority in the Revelation to John*. SABH 15; Macon, Ga.: Mercer University Press.

Carrell, P. R., 1997. *Jesus and the Angels: Angelology and the Christology of the Apocalypse of John.* SNTSMS 95; Cambridge: Cambridge University Press.

Case, S. J., 1919. *The Revelation of John: A Historical Interpretation.* Chicago: University of Chicago Press.

Casey, J., 1988. 'The Exodus Theme in the Book of Revelation Against the Background of the New Testament', *Concilium* 189: 34–43.

Charles, R. H., 1913. *Studies in the Apocalypse.* Edinburgh: T&T Clark.

—— 1920. *A Critical and Exegetical Commentary on the Revelation of St John.* 2 vols. ICC; Edinburgh: T&T Clark.

Charlesworth, J. H. (ed.), 1983. *The Old Testament Pseudepigrapha. Volume 1: Apocalyptic Literature and Testaments.* London: Darton, Longman & Todd.

Collins, A. Y., 1976. *The Combat Myth in the Book of Revelation.* Missoula, Mont.: Scholars Press.

—— 1977. 'The Political Perspective of the Revelation to John', *JBL* 96: 241–56.

—— 1980. 'Revelation 18: Taunt-Song or Dirge?', in J. Lambrecht (ed.), *L'Apocalypse johannique et l'Apocalyptique dans le Nouveau Testament*, 185–204. BETL LIII; Gembloux: Éditions J. Duculot and Leuven: Leuven University Press.

—— 1984. *Crisis and Catharsis: The Power of the Apocalypse.* Philadelphia: Westminster Press.

—— 1996. *Cosmology and Eschatology in Jewish and Christian Apocalyptic.* JSJS 50; Leiden: E. J. Brill.

—— 1998. 'Pergamon in Early Christian Literature', in H. Koester (ed.), *Pergamon: Citadel of the Gods*, 163–84. HTS; Harrisburg, Pa.: Trinity Press International.

Collins, J. J. (ed.), 1979. *Apocalypse: The Morphology of a Genre.* Semeia 14. SBL; Missoula, Mont.: Scholars Press.

—— 1995. *The Sceptre and the Star: The Messiahs of the Dead Sea Scrolls and Other Ancient Literature.* ABRL; New York: Doubleday.

Corsini, E., 1983. *The Apocalypse: The Perennial Revelation of Jesus Christ.* GNS 5; Wilmington, Del.: Michael Glazier.

Court, J. M., 1979. *Myth and History in the Book of Revelation.* London: SPCK.

—— 1994. *Revelation.* NTG; Sheffield: JSOT Press.

—— 2000. *The Book of Revelation and the Johannine Apocalyptic Tradition.* JSNTS 190; Sheffield: Sheffield Academic Press.

Davidson, G., 1967. *A Dictionary of Angels, Including the Fallen Angels.* New York: Free Press.

Day, J., 1992. 'Leviathan', in D. N. Freedman (ed.), *The Anchor Bible Dictionary*, 4: 295–96. New York: Doubleday.

—— 1994. 'The Origin of Armageddon: Revelation 16:16 as an Interpretation of Zechariah 12:11', in S. E. Porter, P. M. Joyce and D. E. Orton (eds), *Crossing the Boundaries: Essays in Biblical Interpretation in Honour of Michael D. Goulder*, 315–26. Leiden: Brill.

Desrosiers, G., 2000. *An Introduction to Revelation*. Continuum Biblical Studies Series; London and New York: Continuum.

Draper, J. A., 1983. 'The Heavenly Feast of Tabernacles: Revelation 7.1–17', *JSNT* 19: 133–47.

Duff, P. B., 2001. *Who Rides the Beast? Prophetic Rivalry and the Rhetoric of Crisis in the Churches of the Apocalypse*. Oxford and New York: Oxford University Press.

Dulaey, A., 1997. *Victorin de Poetovio, Sur l'Apocalypse suivi du Fragment Chronologique et de la Construction du Monde: Introduction, Texte Critique, Traduction, Commentaire et Index*. SC 423; Paris: Éditions du Cerf.

Dunkerley, R., 1961. 'The Five Johns', *LQHR* 186: 292–98.

Ellul, J., 1977. *Apocalypse: The Book of Revelation*. New York: Seabury.

Farrer, A., 1949. *A Rebirth of Images: The Making of John's Apocalypse*. Westminster: Dacre Press.

—— 1964. *The Revelation of St John the Divine*. Oxford: Clarendon Press.

Fekkes, J., 1990. ' "His Bride Has Prepared Herself": Revelation 19—21 and Isaian Nuptial Imagery', *JBL* 109: 269–87.

Feuillet, A., 1965. *The Apocalypse*. Staten Island, NY: Alba House.

Fiorenza, E. S., 1980. 'Apokalypsis and Propheteia: The Book of Revelation in the Context of Early Christian Prophecy', in J. Lambrecht (ed.), *L'Apocalypse johannique et l'Apocalyptique dans le Nouveau Testament*, 105–28. BETL LIII; Gembloux: Éditions J. Duculot and Leuven: Leuven University Press.

—— 1985. *The Book of Revelation: Justice and Judgment*. Philadelphia: Fortress Press.

—— 1986. 'The Followers of the Lamb: Visionary Rhetoric and Social-Political Situation', *Semeia* 36: 123–46.

—— 1991. *Revelation: Vision of a Just World*. PC; Minneapolis: Fortress Press.

Flegg, C. G., 1999. *An Introduction to Reading the Apocalypse*. Crestwood, NY: St Vladimir's Seminary Press.

Ford, J. M., 1965–66. 'The Meaning of Virgin', *NTS* 12: 293–99.

—— 1975. *Revelation*. AB 38; New York: Doubleday.

Friesen, S. J., 2001. *Imperial Cults and the Apocalypse of John: Reading Revelation in the Ruins*. Oxford: Oxford University Press.

Frilingos, C. A., 2004. *Spectacles of Empire: Monsters, Martyrs and the Book of Revelation*. Philadelphia: University of Pennsylvania Press.

Gamble, H. Y. 1995. *Books and Readers in the Early Church*. New Haven and London: Yale University Press.

Garrow, A. J. P., 1997. *Revelation*. New Testament Readings; London and New York: Routledge.

Geoffrey of Auxerre, 2000. *On the Apocalypse*. Trans. J. Gibbons. CFS 42; Kalamazoo, Mich.: Cistercian Publications.

Geyser, A., 1982. 'The Twelve Tribes in Revelation: Judean and Judeo-Christian Apocalypticism', *NTS* 28:388–99.

Giblin, C. H., 1974. 'Structural and Thematic Correlations in the Theology of Revelation 16—22', *Bib* 554: 487–504.

—— 1984. 'Revelation 11.1–13: Its Form, Function, and Contextual Integration', *NTS* 30: 433–59.

—— 1994. 'Recapitulation and the Literary Coherence of John's Apocalypse', *CBQ* 56: 81–95.

—— 1998. 'From and Before the Throne: Revelation 4:5–6a Integrating the Imagery of Revelation 4—16', *CBQ* 60: 500–13.

Glasson, T. F., 1975. 'The Order of Jewels in Revelation xxi.19–20: A Theory Eliminated', *JTS* 26: 95–100.

Goulder, M. D., 1981. 'The Apocalypse as an Annual Cycle of Prophecies', *NTS* 27: 342–67.

Grubb, N., 1997. *Revelations: Art of the Apocalypse*. New York, London and Paris: Abbeville Press.

Gruenwald, I., 1980. *Apocalyptic and Merkavah Mysticism*. Leiden: E. J. Brill.

Gundry, R. H., 1994. 'Angelomorphic Christology in the Book of Revelation', in E. H. Lovering (ed.), *Society of Biblical Literature 1994 Seminar Papers*, 662–78. Atlanta, Ga.: Scholars Press.

Hall, R. G., 1990. 'Living Creatures in the Midst of the Throne: Another Look at Revelation 4.6', *NTS* 36: 609–13.

Harrington, W. J., 1993. *Revelation*. SP 16; Collegeville, Minn.: Michael Glazier.

Haussoullier, B., 1902. 'Les îles milésiennes: Léros, Lepsia, Patmos, les Korsiae', *RP* 26: 124–43.

Helmbold, A., 1961. 'A Note on the Authorship of the Apocalypse', *NTS* 8: 77–79.

Hemer, C. J., 1972. 'The Sardis Letter and the Croesus Tradition', *NTS* 19: 94–97.

—— 1986. *The Letters to the Seven Churches of Asia in Their Local Setting*. JSNTS 11; Sheffield: Sheffield Academic Press.

Hill, C. E., 2001. *Regnum Caelorum: Patterns of Millennial Thought in Early Christianity*, 2nd edn., Grand Rapids and Cambridge: Eerdmans.

Hill, D., 1972. 'Prophecy and Prophets in the Revelation of St. John', *NTS* 18: 401–18.

Howard-Brook, W., and Gwyther, A., 1999. *Unveiling Empire: Reading Revelation Then and Now*. Maryknoll, NY: Orbis.

Hurtado, L. W., 1985. 'Revelation 4—5 in the Light of Jewish Apocalyptic Analogies', *JSNT* 25: 105–24.

—— 2003. *Lord Jesus Christ: Devotion to Jesus in Earliest Christianity*. Grand Rapids and Cambridge: Eerdmans.

James, M. R., 1931. *The Apocalypse in Art*. SLBA; London: Oxford University Press for the British Academy.

Janzen, E., 1994. 'The Jesus of the Apocalypse Wears the Emperor's Clothes', in E. H. Lovering (ed.), *Society of Biblical Literature 1994 Seminar Papers*, 637–61. Atlanta, Ga.: Scholars Press.

Jung, C. G., 1984. *Answer to Job*. Trans. R. F. C. Hull. London: Routledge & Kegan Paul.

Kerkeslager, A., 1993. 'Apollo, Greco-Roman Prophecy, and the Rider on the White Horse in Rev. 6.2', *JBL* 112: 116–21.

Kiddle, M., 1940. *The Revelation of St John*. MNTC; London: Hodder & Stoughton.

Klauck, H.-J., 2001. 'Do They Never Come Back? *Nero Redivivus* and the Apocalypse of John', *CBQ* 63: 683–98.

Knight, J., 1999. *Revelation*. Readings; Sheffield: Sheffield Academic Press.

Koester, C. R., 2001. *Revelation and the End of All Things*. Grand Rapids and Cambridge: Eerdmans.

Koester, H. (ed.), 1998. *Pergamon: Citadel of the Gods*. HTS; Harrisburg, Pa.: Trinity Press International.

Kovacs, J., and Rowland, C., 2004. *Revelation*. Blackwell Bible Commentaries; Malden, Mass. and Oxford: Blackwell.

Kraybill, J. N., 1996. *Imperial Cult and Commerce in John's Apocalypse*. JSNTS 132; Sheffield: Sheffield Academic Press.

Kreitzer, L., 1996. *Striking New Images*. JSNTS 134; Sheffield: Sheffield Academic Press.

Krodel, G. A., 1989. *Revelation*. ACNT; Minneapolis: Augsburg.

Lawrence, D. H., 1931. *Apocalypse*. Florence: G. Orioli.

Le Frois, B., 1954. *The Woman Clothed with the Sun (Ap. 12): Individual or Collective?* Rome: Orbis Catholicus.

Le Moignan, C., 2000. *Following the Lamb: A Reading of Revelation for the New Millennium*. Peterborough: Epworth.

Longenecker, B. W., 2003. *The Lost Letters of Pergamum*. Grand Rapids: Baker Academic.

Maier, H. O., 2002. *Apocalypse Recalled: The Book of Revelation After Christendom*. Minneapolis: Fortress Press.

Malina, B. J., 1995. *On the Genre and Message of Revelation: Star Visions and Sky Journeys*. Peabody, Mass.: Hendrickson.

Malina, B. J., 2000. *The New Jerusalem in the Revelation of John.* Collegeville, Minn.: Liturgical Press.

Malina, B. J., and Pilch, J. J., 2000. *Social-Science Commentary on the Book of Revelation.* Minneapolis: Fortress Press.

Mathewson, D., 2003. *A New Heaven and a New Earth: The Meaning and Function of the Old Testament in Revelation 21.1—22.5.* JSNTS 238; Sheffield: Sheffield Academic Press.

Mazzaferri, F. D., 1989. *The Genre of the Book of Revelation from a Source-Critical Perspective.* Berlin: Walter de Gruyter.

McCabe, D. F., and Plunkett, M. A., 1985. *Patmos Inscriptions: Texts and List.* Princeton: Institute for Advanced Study.

McKelvey, R. J., 1999. *The Millennium and the Book of Revelation.* Cambridge: Lutterworth Press.

Mealy, J. W., 1992. *After the Thousand Years: Resurrection and Judgement in Revelation 20.* JSNTS 70; Sheffield: Sheffield Academic Press.

Metzger, B. M., 1971. *A Textual Commentary on the Greek New Testament.* London and New York: United Bible Societies.

Michaels, J. R., 1997. *Revelation.* IVP New Testament Commentary Series; Downers Grove, Ill. and Leicester: Inter-Varsity Press.

Minear, P., 1953. 'The Wounded Beast', *JBL* 72: 93–102.

Mounce, R. H., 1977. *The Book of Revelation.* NICNT; Grand Rapids: Eerdmans.

Moyise, S., 1995. *The Old Testament in the Book of Revelation.* JSNTS 115; Sheffield: Sheffield Academic Press.

—— 2001. 'Does the Lion Lie Down with the Lamb?', in S. Moyise (ed.), *Studies in the Book of Revelation*, 181–94. Edinburgh and New York: T&T Clark.

Muddiman, J., 2001. *The Epistle to the Ephesians.* BNTC; London and New York: Continuum.

Murphy, F. J., 1998. *Fallen is Babylon: The Revelation to John.* NTIC; Harrisburg, PA: Trinity Press International.

Newport, K. G. C., 2000. *Apocalypse and Millennium: Studies in Biblical Eisegesis.* Cambridge: Cambridge University Press.

Niditch, S., 1980. 'The Visionary', in G. W. E. Nickelsburg and J. J. Collins (eds), *Ideal Figures in Ancient Judaism*, 153–79. Chico, CA: Scholars Press.

Osborne, G. R., 2002. *Revelation.* BECNT; Grand Rapids: Baker.

Oster, R. E., 1992. 'Ephesus,' in D. N. Freedman (ed.), *The Anchor Bible Dictionary*, 2: 542–49. New York: Doubleday.

Paley, M. D., 1986. *The Apocalyptic Sublime.* New Haven and London: Yale University Press.

Paul, I., 2003. *How to Read the Book of Revelation.* GBS B28; Cambridge: Grove Books.

Peterson, E. H., 1988. *Reversed Thunder: The Revelation of John and the Praying Imagination*. San Francisco: HarperCollins.

Pippin, T., 1992. *Death and Desire: The Rhetoric of Gender in the Apocalypse of John*. Louisville: Westminster/John Knox Press.

—— 1994. 'The Revelation to John', in E. S. Fiorenza (ed.), *Searching the Scriptures. Volume Two: A Feminist Commentary*, 109–30. London: SCM Press.

—— 1999. *Apocalyptic Bodies: The Biblical End of the World in Text and Image*. London and New York: Routledge.

Potter, D. S., 1992. 'Smyrna', in D. N. Freedman (ed.), *The Anchor Bible Dictionary*, 6: 73–75. New York: Doubleday.

Prévost, J.-P., 1995. *L'Apocalypse: Commentaire pastoral*. Paris: Bayard Éditions.

Prigent, P., 1959. *Apocalypse 12: Histoire de l'exégèse*. BGBE 2; Tübingen: J. C. B. Mohr (Paul Siebeck).

—— 1964. *Apocalypse et Liturgie*. CT 52; Neuchâtel and Paris: Delachaux et Niestlé.

Ramsay, W. M., 1904. *The Letters to the Seven Churches of Asia*. London: Hodder & Stoughton.

Reddish, M. G., 1988. 'Martyr Christology in the Apocalypse', *JSNT* 33: 85–95.

—— 2001. *Revelation*. SMBC; Macon, Ga.: Smyth & Helwys.

Rhoads, D. (ed.), 2005. *From Every People and Nation: The Book of Revelation in Intercultural Perspective*. Minneapolis: Fortress Press.

Richard, P., 1995. *Apocalypse: A People's Commentary on the Book of Revelation*. BLS; Maryknoll, NY: Orbis.

Robinson, J. A. T., 1976. *Redating the New Testament*. London: SCM Press.

Roloff, J., 1993. *The Revelation of John: A Continental Commentary*. Minneapolis: Fortress Press.

Rossing, B., 2004. *The Rapture Exposed: The Message of Hope in the Book of Revelation*. Boulder, Colo. and Oxford: Westview Press.

Rowland, C., 1980. 'The Vision of the Risen Christ in Rev. i. 13 ff.: The Debt of an Early Christology to an Aspect of Jewish Angelology', *JTS* 31: 1–11.

—— 1982. *The Open Heaven*. London: SPCK.

—— 1985. 'A Man Clothed with Linen: Daniel 10.6ff. and Jewish Angelology', *JSNT* 24: 99–110.

—— 1993. *Revelation*. EC; London: Epworth Press.

—— 1998. 'The Book of Revelation', in *New Interpreter's Bible*, 12: 503–743. Ed. L. E. Keck. Nashville: Abingdon.

—— 2002. 'The Apocalypse in History: The Place of the Book of Revelation in Christian Theology and Life', in C. Rowland and J. Barton (eds), *Apocalyptic in History and Tradition*, 151–71. London and New York: Sheffield Academic Press.

Royalty, R. M., 1998. *The Streets of Heaven: The Ideology of Wealth in the Apocalypse of John*. Macon, Ga.: Mercer University Press.

Royse, J. R., 1980. '"Their Fifteen Enemies": The Text of Rev. xi. 12 in P^{47} and 1611', *JTS* 31: 78–80.

Ruiz, J. P., 1989. *Ezekiel in the Apocalypse: The Transformation of Prophetic Language in Revelation 16,17—19,10*. EUS 23/376; Frankfurt am Main: Peter Lang.

—— 1994. 'Hearing and Seeing But Not Saying: A Look at Revelation 10:4 and 2 Corinthians 12:4', in E. H. Lovering (ed.), *Society of Biblical Literature 1994 Seminar Papers*, 182–202. Atlanta, Ga.: Scholars Press.

Saffrey, H. D., 1975. 'Relire l'Apocalypse à Patmos', *RB* 82: 385–417.

Sanders, E. P., 1977. *Paul and Palestinian Judaism*. London: SCM Press.

—— 1992. *Judaism: Practice and Belief 63 BCE–66 CE*. London: SCM Press.

Scherrer, S. J., 1984. 'Signs and Wonders in the Imperial Cult: A New Look at a Roman Religious Institution in the Light of Rev 13:13–15', *JBL* 103: 599–610.

Scribner, R. W., 1981. *For the Sake of Simple Folk: Popular Propaganda for the German Reformation*. Cambridge: Cambridge University Press.

Sizer, S., 2004. *Christian Zionism*. Leicester: Inter-Varsity Press.

Smalley, S. S., 1994. *Thunder and Love: John's Revelation and John's Community*. Milton Keynes: Nelson Word.

—— 2005. *The Revelation to John: A Commentary on the Greek Text of the Apocalypse*. London: SPCK.

Smith, C. R., 1990. 'The Portrayal of the Church as the New Israel in the Names and Order of the Tribes in Revelation 7.5–8', *JSNT* 39:111–18.

Smith, R. H., 2000. *Apocalypse: A Commentary on Revelation in Words and Images*. Collegeville, Minn.: Liturgical Press.

Stanton, G. N., 2004. *Jesus and Gospel*. Cambridge: Cambridge University Press.

Stone, M. E., 1976. 'Lists of Revealed Things in the Apocalyptic Literature', in F. M. Cross, W. E. Lemke and P. D. Miller (eds), *Magnalia Dei: The Mighty Acts of God*, 414–52. Garden City, NY: Doubleday.

Strand, K. A., 1981. 'The Two Witnesses of Rev 11:3–12', *AUSS* 19: 127–35.

Sweet, J., 1979. *Revelation*. SCM Pelican Commentaries; London: SCM Press.

—— 1981. 'Maintaining the Testimony of Jesus: The Suffering of Christians in the Revelation of John', in W. Horbury and B.

McNeil (eds), *Suffering and Martyrdom in the New Testament*, 101–17. Cambridge: Cambridge University Press.

Swete, H. B., 1906. *The Apocalypse of St John*. London: Macmillan and Co.

Taushev, A., and Rose, S., 1995. *The Apocalypse in the Teachings of Ancient Christianity*, 2nd edn. Platina, CA: St Herman of Alaska Brotherhood.

Thimmes, P., 2003. 'Women Reading Women in the Apocalypse: Reading Scenario 1, the Letter to Thyatira (Rev. 2.18–29)', *CBR* 2: 128–44.

Thompson, L. L., 1990. *The Book of Revelation: Apocalypse and Empire*. Oxford: Oxford University Press.

—— 2000. 'Lamentation for Christ as a Hero: Revelation 1:7', *JBL* 119: 683–703.

Topham, M., 1989a. 'A Human Being's Measurement, which is an Angel's', *ExpTim* 100: 217–18.

—— 1989b. 'The Dimensions of the New Jerusalem', *ExpTim* 100: 417–19.

Turner, S., 2004. 'Revelation 11:1–13: History of Interpretation'. Unpubl. D. Phil. thesis, University of Oxford.

van der Meer, F., 1978. *Apocalypse: Visions from the Book of Revelation in Western Art*. London: Thames & Hudson.

van Henten, J. W., 1994. 'Dragon Myth and Imperial Ideology in Revelation 12–13', in E. H. Lovering (ed.), *Society of Biblical Literature 1994 Seminar Papers*, 496–515. Atlanta, GA: Scholars Press.

Vanhoye, A., 1962. 'L'utilisation du Livre d'Ezéchiel dans l'Apocalypse', *Bib* 43, 436–76.

Vanni, U., 1991. 'Liturgical Dialogue as a Literary Form in the Book of Revelation', *NTS* 37: 348–72.

Vassiliadis, P., 1985. 'The Translation of Martyria Iesou in Revelation', *The Bible Translator* 36: 129–34.

Vermes, G., 1997. *The Complete Dead Sea Scrolls in English*. London: Penguin.

Wainwright, A. W., 1993. *Mysterious Apocalypse: Interpreting the Book of Revelation*. Nashville: Abingdon Press.

Walsh, W., 1899. *The Secret History of the Oxford Movement*, 6th edn. London: C. J. Thynne.

Watch Tower, 1988. *Revelation: Its Grand Climax at Hand!* Brooklyn, NY: Watchtower Bible and Tract Society.

Wick, P., 1998. 'There was Silence in Heaven (Revelation 8:1): An Annotation to Israel Knohl's "Between Voice and Silence"', *JBL* 117: 512–14.

Wilson, S. G., 1992. 'Gentile Judaizers', *NTS* 38: 605–16.

Witherington, B., 2003. *Revelation*. NCBC; Cambridge: Cambridge University Press.

Wojciechowski, M., 1987. 'Apocalypse 21.19–20: Des titres christologiques cachés dans la liste des pierres précieuses', *NTS* 33: 153–54.

Worth, R. H., 1999. *The Seven Cities of the Apocalypse and Roman Culture*. New York and Mahwah, NJ: Paulist Press.

Yamauchi, E. M., 1980. *New Testament Cities in Western Asia Minor*. Grand Rapids: Baker.

INDEX OF SCRIPTURAL REFERENCES

INDEX OF MODERN AUTHORS

SUBJECT INDEX

CPSIA information can be obtained
at www.ICGtesting.com
Printed in the USA
LVHW021547060922
727660LV00009B/331